The Wired Homestead

The MIT Press Sourcebooks

The Digital Divide: Facing a Crisis or Creating a Myth?
edited by Benjamin M. Compaine, 2001

Communication Researchers and Policy-making: An MIT Press Sourcebook
edited by Sandra Braman, 2003

The Wired Homestead: An MIT Press Sourcebook on the Internet and the Family
edited by Joseph Turow and Andrea L. Kavanaugh, 2003

The Wired Homestead

An MIT Press Sourcebook on the Internet and the Family

Edited by
Joseph Turow and Andrea L. Kavanaugh

The MIT Press
Cambridge, Massachusetts
London, England

This book was set in Sabon on 3B2 by Asco Typesetters, Hong Kong.
Printed and bound in the United States of America.

Library of Congress Cataloging-in-Publication Data

The wired homestead : an MIT Press sourcebook on the internet and the family / edited by Joseph Turow and Andrea L. Kavanaugh.
   p. cm.
  Includes bibliographical references and index.
  ISBN 0-262-70094-8 (pbk. : alk. paper)
  1. Computers and family. 2. Internet—Social aspects. I. Turow, Joseph. II. Kavanaugh, Andrea L.
  QA76.9.F35 W57   2003
  303.48′34—dc21   2002040794

10 9 8 7 6 5 4 3 2 1

This book is dedicated to our families,
who make our homesteads worthwhile.

Contents

Introduction

The adoption of the internet—especially of the World Wide Web and e-mail—by families in the home marks a development that rivals the advent of television and the cellular phone. The web is already a taken-for-granted part of life among the majority of U.S. families. To ask whether children or their parents really need to have the web may be irrelevant; the computer-linked internet is quickly becoming an integral part of the audiovisual and physical environment. In a few years, there may be little real distinction between *television* and *the internet*. At the same time, the internet era brings with it crucial features of interactivity, personalization, and information abundance that raise profound new issues for parents and children.

Scholars and students are looking for models and theories that can help them evaluate the social impact of the internet on families. Most start from the proposition that the family is the central force for preparing children to live in society and that the home is the dominant location in which socialization takes place. Yet while research on children's cognitive development with respect to the web and other new-media developments has accelerated in recent years, written work analyzing the implications of the internet on the family unit and its members' interrelated social lives is still at a very early stage and scattered in disparate publications. Assembling the best of existing literature into a volume issued by a major press might point to a critical mass of rich ideas that will provoke important streams of writing and research across a variety of disciplines.

That is the aim of *The Wired Homestead*. In four parts, we present provocative works that encourage readers to see the worlds of the internet and the family in new ways. The book consists of material written for this book as well as previously published pieces that we culled through a wide-ranging search or that were nominated by major figures in the field as having enduring quality. We hope that all the pieces chosen will contribute to the ways that academics, policymakers, and interested parents talk about the web for years to come.

Our selections were not guided by data about web diffusion or the specific quantifications of use because that kind of information becomes so quickly out of date. We also did not have fully fixed meanings for *web*, *family*, or *home*. Rather, we cared mostly for the quality of the writers' ideas and their potential for (1) helping us to think about the interrelation of web, family, and home in creative ways; and (2) challenging us to ask other innovative questions about the wired homestead.

Our purpose in this introduction is to set the stage for exploring this book. First, we present a brief overview of the historical, technical, industrial, and regulatory context of the internet's relation to the family and home. We emphasize that the internet (and its graphical interface, the World Wide Web) is part of an evolution in technology that raises new issues (or resurrects old ones) regarding the relationship of the home and the outside world. We then present an overview of the book with an eye toward the ways our authors consider these developments.

The Internet and the Transformation of Media

To begin understanding the relationship of the internet to the family, it is important to see that relationship as an active feature in the major transformation of media technology from analog to digital that took place with increasing speed in industrially advanced nations beginning the second half of the twentieth century. As many scholars have pointed out, technologies do not just appear ready to be used. Rather, their application, and the social problems and solutions they raise, are constructed through social practice. Investigations of the early reception of, for example, the telephone, radio, and television in the United States and elsewhere suggest that although they have distinctive technological features, the social meanings and controversies around these features developed over time through elaborate interactions among various constituencies, value systems, and regulatory regimes (Marvin 1998; Rakow 1992; Silverstone and Hirsch 1992).

To truly understand the development of the web in the context of the family, then, one must look historically at the ways families in different societies have invested internet and web technologies with meaning, shaped them in their interactions at home and elsewhere, and influenced the various companies and governments guiding the technologies to shape them. Basic research to create this sort of roadmap does not yet exist for the United States or other societies, however, and drawing it is beyond the scope of this essay. What follows is a necessarily limited overview of key developments in digital technology and their integration into the domestic lives of parents and their children.

Analog to Digital

The roots of the contemporary digital transformation can be traced as far back as the seventeenth century, when German mathematician Gottfried Leibnitz set out important theoretical principles for the use of binary digits, the zero-one system that is the core of digital technology. The move to digital began in earnest with the electronic computer for the military in the mid-1940s.

A simple way to understand the distinction between digital and analog is to think about what distinguishes an old-fashioned vinyl record from a CD or MP3 music file. If you look at a record, you will see grooves. When the phonograph needle moves through the grooves, it picks up vibrations that were made when the singer recorded the song. The sound coming from the singer's vocal cords went through the air and caused instruments in the recording studio to oscillate. The CD, by contrast, does not contain a physical reproduction of the sound. Instead, during the recording process, computers transform the singer's voice patterns into a string of binary digits, or *bits* (0s and 1s).

When it comes to recordings, a clear advantage of digital over analog signals is that although grooves inevitably wear down, leading to distortion of the sound, bits that are read by a laser beam suffer no such attrition. Cared for properly, CDs will produce the same sound years after they are purchased. Extended life, though, is not the primary impetus behind the growth of digital engineering. Digital has taken off because it allows for *convergence* of media technologies. Convergence means that seemingly different media can end up doing the same things because they all accept digital information. So, for example, a laptop computer can take on the functions of a DVD player, a CD player, a typewriter, and a magazine.

Just as important, the application of computer codes to mass media materials opens the door to the possibility that audience members can manipulate the materials to suit their interests. Blending digitized music, photos, videos, and text, family members and friends can collaborate via the internet to produce a common record of their experience together (summer vacation, camping trip, visits with friends). We are leaving the analog age and entering the age of interactive digital media.

As this example suggests, in the decades that followed the first electronic computer, large segments of business recognized that profits from developing digital technologies would come not just from the military or business but from the household. Pushing the process along was the invention of the transistor and microprocessor. They made miniaturization possible, allowing engineers to design new electronic products to fit the traditional architecture of the home.

The microprocessor led to the creation of the personal computer (PC), one that could fit on a desk. Here too the home became a key domain. The first people to use PCs were home hobbyists who built PCs from kits. In the 1970s Apple developed an operating system for its Macintosh computer that was based on graphical user interfaces (GUIs, such as icons and menus) and manipulation by the click of a mouse; these advances made it much easier for non-experts to use a computer. By the early 1980s, Apple, Tandy, Osborne, Kaypro, and IBM were building fully assembled PCs for domestic as well as business use. A software industry arose to develop word processing, spreadsheet, presentation, and game programs that inexorably led the computer to replace the typewriter as the central homework and home-office technology in middle- and upper-middle-class homes. The software corporation Microsoft, following Macintosh's example, developed a graphical user interface (that also used a mouse) called Windows in 1983 for personal computers. This simpler interface, developed through the 1980s and popularized in the 1990s, made it possible for children who could not yet read to use computers and sparked an "edutainment" software industry aimed at the preschool and elementary school markets. Parents, too, found the Windows interface an easier way to use word processing and finance software. By the turn of the twenty-first century, over 70% of U.S. households with children under age 18 owned a computer.

The Rise of the Web

The typical 1980s-vintage computer that sat in a home office consisted of a video display, keyboard, central processing unit, and storage device (a replaceable, or floppy disk drive,[1] and, increasingly, a permanent, or hard drive). What the early home-based computers did not have was a way to send messages to computers elsewhere in the world. Before too long, however, computers did come equipped with the ability to go online—to receive digital information from anywhere by telephone. The hardware that makes online activity possible is the MOdulator/DEModulator (modem), a device attached to the computer that performs a digital-to-analog conversion of data and then transmits the data to another modem. That modem reverses the process, performing an analog-to-digital conversion that permits the computer to which it is attached to use the data.

Beginning in the mid-1980s, an industry began to develop around household use of the modem. Commercial online networks such as Prodigy, CompuServe, and Delphi aggressively offered consumers the ability to play games with people across the nation, to get help with homework through online encyclopedias, and chat with people about common interests. All these activities were text-based; their software did not allow for the transfer of graphics over the phone lines. Also text-based was interactive shopping, an early initiative of the commercial online world. Just before Christmas 1993, Prodigy proclaimed that twenty merchants in its electronic mall were offering last-minute delivery for last minute shoppers who wanted to purchase their goods from home online.[2] At the time, Prodigy and CompuServe each boasted about a million subscribers, and the fast-growing America Online had about half as many. The *San Francisco Examiner* pegged total online users at about 4 million people, their typical fee being a flat $10 to $20 per month.[3]

The *Examiner* article didn't mention the internet. In the next couple of years, though, online information firms such as Prodigy, CompuServe, and AOL came into competition with the internet to such an extent that they had to drastically change their business models or risk being shoved aside. The internet was hardly new in the 1990s, however. It had been conceived by the Advanced Research Projects Agency (ARPA) of the Department of Defense in 1969 and was first known as ARPANET. Although the network was initially supposed to be for scientific use, nonscientists within universities and executives from companies outside universities saw linking their computers to this network as a speedy way to send documents to others around the world.

Initially, though, the documents could not be shared in real time—that is, as they were being created—and they had to be transmitted in text form. Sending graphical images was possible, but the images had to be encoded as letters and numbers before they were sent and then were decoded by the receiver. Scientists confronted both obstacles in the early 1990s. The "real time" problem was solved by Tim Berners-Lee. A British citizen working as a research fellow at the European CERN physics laboratory in Geneva, he created a system of protocols (HTTP and HTML) for what he called a *World Wide Web* that allowed for immediate sharing of scientific data between different computer operating systems. The graphics difficulty was overcome when the University of Illinois created NSCA Mosaic, a breakthrough web browser. Mosaic allowed its users' computers to decode graphical hypertext documents. Now, using the right software, any web user could easily view complex drawings or photographs created virtually anywhere on the vast internet.

Any web user increasingly included children and parents with no particular skills with computers. For the first time, the internet could be sold as a tool and entertainment medium for all family members, not just for dedicated hobbyists. The pictorial nature of the web and its ease of use encouraged the rise of internet service providers—ISPs—that offered connection to the internet to the general public at home and work via telephone lines. CompuServe and America Online switched to a modified ISP model, whereby subscribers would first connect to the firms' proprietary areas and then, if they wanted, move to the web.

Much of the activity in cyberspace (that is, in the online world of computer networks) involved individuals interacting with others through e-mails or web sites. As the number of people going online grew, however, commercial activities sprang up on the web. The new online companies (*.com*, known as dot-coms) ranged from selling products and services (Amazon.com and Expedia.com, for example), to auctioning goods and services (eBay.com), to presenting content, often with advertising (Yahoo.com, MSNBC.com, and Slate.com). The growth of the U.S. commercial sector of the internet beginning the mid-1990s was startling compared to the growth of the already established university (*.edu*), government (*.gov*), and military (*.mil*) domains. Figure 1 depicts this growth for just a six-month period in 1998.

An entire industry accompanied this commercialization of the web, with site producers, content syndicators, ad agencies, firms that deliver ads to web sites, market research companies, and ratings firms vying furiously for business. The business environment of the period was marked by the rise of media conglomerates and a blurring of boundaries between different media. Companies such as AOL Time Warner, NTT DoCoMo, and Vivendi Universal had an interest in moving people across a variety of interconnected digital systems, only part of which matched the historically specific meanings of *Internet* and *Web* (connection to one global network with a specific, TCP IP, protocol). By the turn of the century, the technical "proper noun" meaning of the specific internet had evaporated from popular parlance. It was replaced by a general sense of an interconnected system for anything from traditional multi-user

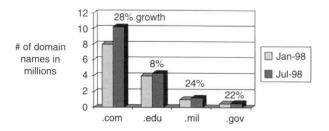

Figure 1
Growth of domain names, January 1998–July 1998.
Source: Internet Standard, 9/7/98, p. 46.

domains (MUDS), Telnet and usenet groups, to web pages, e-mail, phone text messaging, and AOL-based shopping malls. Because this generic, all-encompassing meaning of the internet and web appears to have taken hold among most users—and certainly in the domestic arena—we have decided typically not to capitalize the terms in the new material in this volume.

Accessing the Internet at Home

The mounting number of homes with online connections in the mid-1990s both encouraged and was encouraged by the web's increasing commercialization and ease of use. Whereas in 1993 just a few million U.S. homes were online, by 1996 various estimates put the number of online households at between 23% and 34% of the country's approximately 100 million households.[4] Households were not, of course, the only place where people accessed the internet. Schools, especially colleges, were popular locations. Moreover, evidence suggested that people who had home links still used the web a lot at work because of high-speed connections at those locations. The Media Metrix internet rating firm, in fact, argued to marketers as late as 2002 that "daytime is prime time" when it came to the web.[5]

Still, the home was increasingly a place for going online for children and parents in the late 1990s. The trend was underscored in a report in 2002 by the Pew Internet & American Life Project, a major source of reliable survey data about online Americans at the turn of the century. "When the internet population was growing rapidly in the late 1990s and 2000," the report noted, "the growth in home access was the driver." Pew estimated that by January 2002, 103 million Americans over age 18 had access at home, while around 55 million Americans said they went online from work. Of those, 49% said they went online only at home, 39% mentioned work and home, 8% said they went online only at work, and the remaining 4% of "online" Americans mentioned another place—presumably schools or libraries—was their point of contact with cyberspace.[6]

A large number of the adults who used the internet at home shared it with kids. A study of 2000 census data revealed that single-person households were least likely to have a PC or internet access. By contrast, in that year two-thirds of households with a school-age child had a PC and 53% had internet access. The census also found what many other studies were finding—that online connections were also linked to household income. Almost 90% of households with annual incomes above $75,000 had a PC at home and 80% had internet access. By contrast, less than 30% of households with incomes below $25,000 had a PC and about 20% had internet access.[7]

As connections to the web were growing unevenly in U.S. homes, a similar pattern seemed to be taking place around the world. On the global level, "users" often took the place of "households" when presenting data about the internet's spread. Despite this easier approach, the whole exercise of believing it is possible to get an accurate fix on the web's global footprint might well be considered close to foolhardy. As Nua.org, an authoritative aggregator of internet data noted, "the art of estimating how many are online throughout the world is an inexact one at best. Surveys abound, using all sorts of measurement parameters."[8]

In February 2002, Nua estimated that the number of online users worldwide was 544.2 million.[9] As table 1 shows, Africa and the Middle East had the fewest people online. The Asia/Pacific region's numbers were close to (and by many accounts growing more quickly than) those of Europe. The table also indicates that one third of those online in late 2001 were situated in the United States and Canada. It was a large per-

Table 1
Estimated Number of People Online February 2002

World Total	
544.2 million	
Africa	
4.15 million	
Asia/Pacific	
157.49 million	
Europe	
171.35 million	
Middle East	
4.65 million	

centage but still quite a bit smaller than the over 50% of approximately 150 million internet users in late 1998.[10] Moreover, in April 2002, the ACNielsen research company announced it had determined that households online in China had grown to second in the world, behind only the United States and barely surpassing that of Japan. China's number—57 million—represented just 5.5 percent of its household population.[11] Its quick growth—as well as the growth of internet households in other areas of Asia—suggests that the accepted notion that most families online live in U.S. and European middle- and upper-middle-class homes will soon have to be fundamentally rethought.

Discourse on the Web's Meaning for the Family

These and a general flood of numbers about the web's growth in the United States and around the world beg a key question: What does it mean for families today? In the United States mixed views about the internet and the family cascaded rather early and vigorously into the public arena. Under the direction of one of the present editors (Turow), researchers at the Annenberg Public Policy Center conducted a systematic content analysis on all the articles that dealt with the internet and the family in twelve major U.S. newspapers early in the web's diffusion—from October 15, 1997, to October 15, 1998. In locating articles for the analysis, they decided that for their purpose a "family" was at least one parent with at least one school-age child. Using the Nexis database, they examined every article in those newspapers that (1) mentioned the internet, AOL, web, or used the term online and (2) included the words family, families, child, children, parent, parents, youth, or teens.

The researchers found that when articles mentioned the internet and the family, the overwhelming majority—97%—did so in terms of the problems and/or benefits of the web. About two-thirds of the pieces described problems and about half the web's benefits. When it came to benefits, discussions of the web's "psychological" or "mental" utility for children were most common—for example, that the web could encourage a child to read or improve a child's ability to find out about the world. Social advantages for children and the family—using e-mail to keep in touch with relatives, for example—were also mentioned frequently. When it came to concerns regarding the web, the papers centered on a small number of specific dangers—mostly sex crimes (sexual predators and child pornographers), children's ability to access pornography, and privacy invasion. Only 5% of all articles during that period mentioned other issues such as parents' management of children's internet time, the web and parents' careers, hate groups on the web, and income divisions between web haves and have-nots.

Just as striking, the discussions of benefits and problems of the web were quite separate. Only 16% of the articles discussed both. The researchers concluded that the press presented the internet as a Jekyll-and-Hyde phenomenon. They saw the overall message as "Your children need the internet. But if they do go online, be terrified."[12]

This portrayal of the internet was particularly significant because it directly reflected the results of a national survey that the Annenberg Public Policy Center conducted in late 1998. Telephone interviews by Roper Starch with 1,102 parents of 8- to 17-year-olds in households with at least one working computer found that the rush to connect to the web was happening despite parents' substantial insecurities about it. Parents said they felt that a web connection was necessary, but they also feared its influence on their children. For example, over 75% of those parents voiced concern that their children might give out personal information and view sexually explicit images on the internet.[13]

Other surveys replicated these findings. Whether the press reflected or created these concerns—or did both—the articles were paralleled by angry drumbeats from a panoply of U.S. advocacy groups that zeroed in on them, often with the goal of legislative action. Broadly speaking, the issues fell into two bailiwicks. One had to do with the material that could come into the home as a result of the web; the other had to do the information that web sites could take away. Concerns about incoming material centered on sex and violence, especially sex. Worried adults pointed out that the web was filled with sexually explicit images that were just a click away. (The click, they argued, could even result from an inadvertent spelling: Whitehouse.gov led to the U.S. president's site, while Whitehouse.com led to naked women.)

A legislative consequence of the uproar was the creation of two children's online "protection" acts that attempted to impose restrictions on web sites that could allegedly harm youngsters' minds. After U.S. courts invalidated those attempts as unconstitutional infringements on the press, the focus of advocates' attention turned to encouraging parents to use filters at home. Filters are computer programs that parents can use to stop certain words or web sites (or both) from being accessed by children. Monitors are computer programs that parents can install on computers to track (secretly or openly) where their children go on the web and what they do when they get there. Safe haven sites are child-friendly domains on the web that provide parents with software to ensure that children go online only within those domains. Television, radio, and print media discussions raged about the pros and cons of all three, particularly as they related to public spaces like the library. Everyone realized that many adolescents could find ways to get around the limits placed on them, such as going to homes of friends without such restrictions.

Concerns by parents that web sites could *take away information* from their children tended to center on exploitable personal information that marketers could gather from children about themselves and their family. The growing ability of web sites to solicit information electronically from people without their knowledge drew enormous general concern. What was odd about the web privacy debate was that it overshadowed the fact that in the late 1990s marketers gleaned far more information about people from offline activities (such as credit card purchases) than from online moves. The press, however, emphasized the great potential for retrieving and organizing people's personal information in the digital environment. There was, in particular, great consternation about the revelation that web sites for children were eliciting information from them about parents' incomes and lifestyles.

Responding to these worries, the U.S. Congress in 1998 passed the Children's Online Privacy Protection Act (COPPA). It directed the Federal Trade Commission (FTC) to regulate data collection by commercial web sites that target kids under age 13. The FTC decreed that sites wanting information from them must get consent from parents. The required nature of the consent varied depending on the site's intended use of the information.[14]

Beyond Immediate Consternation

The consternation (some might call it a moral panic) about sex, violence, and information privacy have continued to grab the greatest attention regarding children, parents, and the web in the U.S. popular press. Seen through an academic lens, the problems addressed in public discourse suggest research into the extent to which, and the way in which, the two-way access marketers and governments now have to the home is changing the power equation between families and the "outside world." Other academic lenses can be brought to bear on the internet as well. They relate to its implications for

• notions of home and community;

• ideas about time in the home and outside it;

• conventional distinctions of public and private, work, and leisure; and

• traditional social distinctions regarding gender, ethnicity, age, and income.

A glance back in time makes clear that this is certainly not the first time that important academic and social questions have arisen regarding the implications of new media for all the categories noted above. Researchers and journalists have been parsing controversies about television's impact on the family since even before its widespread introduction in the mid-twentieth century. Before TV, the arrival of radio (and before that, the movies) ignited scholarly explorations and public debates about the extent to which and the way in which they would change various aspects of society.

What makes the internet particularly interesting, however, is that its technology has the capacity to encourage interactions that are impossible with traditional media. Mass media, from books to newspapers to broadcast TV, are unidirectional—from one entity (usually a media organization) to many (the individuals who make up the audience) but not the other way around. By contrast, one-to-one media such as the telegraph and the telephone allow two-way interactions but without the audience size and audiovisual versatility of the mass media. As Joseph Turow suggests in chapter 1, the web has three features that, taken together, combine both mass media and one-to-one media. The web's digital nature means that users can send, retrieve, transform, and store the material that moves across it. The web's two-way, interactive nature means that senders and receivers can respond to one another in an ongoing fashion. The web's ability to function through sophisticated computer software and hardware means users activities can be tracked, sorted, and predicted through increasingly intelligent agents.

From the standpoint of the family, these interactive capabilities raise a number of historically important issues about the relationship between the home and the world outside. This distinction—between the domestic, private sphere and the non-domestic, public realm—took hold among the middle class in Western societies during the nineteenth century. Tough work environments along with the crowded and dangerous urban landscapes encouraged people to see the home as a "haven in a heartless world" for its family members.[15]

In the United States, especially, this idea that people should "shut out what is inimical to us" (as *Godey's Ladies Book* put it in 1894[16]) discouraged intellectuals who believed that true democracy could flourish only by bringing large numbers of people together for discussion of social issues. Optimists, however, pointed to the new mass media—large-circulation newspapers and magazines—as potentially substituting for the public commons and the town hall when it came to learning about issues. Even the optimists, however, worried that the new one-way mass media encouraged people to be mere spectators who were not directly active in shaping events.

This worry that "the new public was defined increasingly by its vulnerable condition of isolation and spectatorship"[17] became a long-term concern of academics worried about the civic life. In 1948, sociologists Paul Lazarsfeld and Robert Merton coined the term "narcotizing dysfunction" to refer to a phenomenon whereby citizens' immersion in media stories about politics short-circuited their desire to get personally involved in issues.[18] Fifty years later, in an article and book titled *Bowling Alone*, political scientist Robert Putnam marshaled evidence for the notion. He contended that increased viewing of television in the United States discouraged people from going out into their communities and contributing to social life.

Some civic optimists of the twenty-first century point to the internet as a way to reverse this alleged decline in social participation. They contend that the new digital technology combines an ability to learn about a huge range of topics with a facility to get actively involved in that topic by immediately writing or talking back to the posters of the material. In that way, they argue, a true area for social—even civic—involvement is created. Pessimists reply that public engagement through the web takes place for small segments of the public. Most people, they say, spend virtually all of their web time in the commercialized area of the web which is merely a more targeted version of traditional mass media—with added information privacy concerns.

The historical context as well as the contemporary social activities and angst around the internet suggest a broad realm for research. Three questions can serve as starting points:

· What are the most fruitful conceptual frameworks through which to think about these topics?
· What can past experiences with other media teach us about what to fear, and not fear, regarding the internet and related technologies?
· Can the experiences of other societies with the web offer useful insights?

The following pages address the topics and questions raised above in thought-provoking ways. They discuss "the family" variously from the standpoint of children, parents, the home, and the group as a whole. The book is divided into four parts: "The New World in Context," "On Parents and Kids," "The Wired Homestead and Online Life," and "The Wired Homestead and Civic Life."

The essays in the first section explore conceptual frameworks and comparative historical perspectives on the internet and the family and what we should study about it. In the tradition of media scholarship, the pieces draw on work from a variety of disciplines. In chapter 1 Joseph Turow borrows from sociology, family studies, and communication to present an "information boundaries" perspective that lays out a model for viewing the family in relation to the web. Elihu Katz (chapter 2) borrows the concept of "disintermediation" from business writings in considering the way in which media and marketers have historically tried to get around parents and speak directly to their kids. In chapter 3 Ellen Wartella and Byron Reeves survey a number of academic fields and note that many of the same questions about violence, sex, stereotyping, and other issues were asked with respect to books, movies, radio, comics, and TV. Daniel Anderson and Marie Evans show the utility of using cognitive psychological research on the impact of TV as a measuring stick to assess the internet's implications for children in chapter 4. And Ellen Seiter (chapter 5) brings a critical sociology to bear on the similarities that she finds between the family dynamics that surround television and those that seem to be evolving around the internet.

"On Parents and Kids," the second part, shifts the book to more specific web issues that concern parents and kids. Maria Papadakis's review of current literature in chapter 6 underscores how little we know about the internet and the family. The other works fill in parts of the picture. In chapter 7 Amy Jordan points out ways that the home environment provides certain meanings to space and time in relation to media. Joseph Turow and Lilach Nir (chapter 8) present results of a national survey in 2000 of parents and youngsters and paint a complex and potentially controversial picture of the attitudes parents and youngsters hold toward the various aspects of the web. In chapter 9 Sonia Livingstone presents a comparison of "young people's changing media environment in Europe," highlighting important differences as well as similarities between countries in the conceptualization and use of the technology. The Livingstone chapter, as well as those by Gitte Stald (chapter 10) of Denmark and Mark Griffith of the United Kingdom (chapter 11), provides windows on attitudes and activities that may or may not reflect the U.S. situation.

Part III shifts from family members' attitudes toward the web and its consequences to studies of the web's implications for family members' lives together. In chapter 12 Steven Izenour broaches a crucial question about the extent to which the web is or will be changing the actual architecture of the home. In chapter 13 David Frohlich, Susan Dray, and Amy Silverman ask whether in the future family life will center on internet-linked PCs or on so-called internet appliances that spread different aspects of the web experience around the house. In chapter 16

Robert Kraut, Sara Kiesler, Bonka Boneva, Jonathon Cummings, Vicki Helgeson, and Anne Crawford explore whether the internet reduces social involvement and psychological well being. Catherine Burke (chapter 14) and Lisa-Jane McGerty (chapter 15) discuss the implications of web use for the domestic lives of women and men. And in chapter 17 Sherry Turkle looks at the way in which some people use the internet in search of interpersonal connections outside the home—in virtual worlds that she describes as "neighborhoods in cyberspace."

Turkle notes that people reach out to cyberspace from the home to find personal satisfaction, but do they also do it with an awareness of the relationship of their home and family to the world around them? Part IV, "The Wired Homestead and Civic Life," addresses this question. It starts with Jorge Schement's chapter on the relationship between "households and media in the creation of twenty-first-century communities" (chapter 18). It then presents three case studies to illustrate the interaction between the web, the homestead, and its surroundings. Andrea Kavanaugh (chapter 19) explores the extent to which a "networked" community can encourage people to reach out to one another in various ways. Lodis Rhodes (chapter 20) presents a case study of a "literary festival" in a Black and Hispanic neighborhood to illustrate how the interplay of families and community-based organizations led to the incorporation of internet technologies into a neighborhood's daily activities. And in the final chapter Keith Hampton and Barry Wellman find evidence that no cost, high-speed internet connections in a suburban Toronto development can encourage neighborhood socialization, awareness of local issues, and political mobilization.

Future Research on the Internet and the Family

Hampton and Wellman underscore the provisional nature of their analysis and add that "the extent to which the use of no-cost, very high-speed access to the internet influenced the personal networks of [the suburb's] residents remains to be explored in more detail." A similar notice proclaiming the tentative nature of conclusions and the need to learn much more can undoubtedly be tacked on to every chapter in this volume. That is the state of our knowledge about the internet and the family, and in this rapidly changing social-technological environment, it may be the state of affairs for quite a while. The aim here is not so much to present definitive data but to present provocative ideas on topics of importance.

Clearly, there is much to learn about the family's relation to the internet and the panoply of technologies that stream from and around it. The research project has just begun. We hope that this book will spur people to ask good questions and come up with answers that, in turn, lead people to ask more good questions.

Joseph Turow
Andrea L. Kavanaugh

Notes

1. The early $5\frac{1}{4}$ replaceable plastic disks were so thin that they did, in fact, flop back and forth—hence the name.

2. Jennifer Lowe, "Dial G for Gift," *Orange County Register* (December 20, 1993): E-01.

3. Tom Abate, "Apple Plans New On-line Service; Information Network Akin to Prodigy, CompuServe," *San Francisco Examiner* (December 16, 1993): E1.

4. ⟨http://www.nua.com/surveys/analysis/graphs_charts/1996graphs/uspopulation.html⟩.

5. Comments made during a Jupiter Media Metrix forum, "Will People Pay for Content?" March 18, 2002.

6. John Horrigan and Lee Rainie, "Getting Serious Online," Pew Internet & American Life Project, March 3, 2002. See ⟨http://www.pewinternet.org⟩.

7. U.S. Department of Commerce, "Children Have Computer Access; Internet Use Pervasive, Census Bureau Reports," press release, U.S. Dept of Commerce, Sept 6, 2001.

8. ⟨http://www.nua.ie/surveys/how_many_online/methodology.html⟩.

9. According to NUA, these figures represent both adults and children who have accessed the internet at least once during the three months prior to being surveyed:

Where these figures are not available, we use figures for users who have gone online in the past 6 months, past year, or ever. An Internet User represents a person with access to the Internet and is not specific to Internet Account holders. When the figure for Internet Account holders is the only information available, this figure is multiplied by a factor of 3 to give the number of Internet users. The figure for "Asia/Pacific" includes Australia and New Zealand. When more than one survey is available on a country's demographics, NUA will take the mean of the two surveys or, in the case where NUA feels one study may be more comprehensive/reliable than the other, NUA will quote this figure over the other. See ⟨http://www.nua.ie/surveys/how_many_online/methodology.html⟩.

10. See Computer Industry Almanac, "Over 300 Million Internet Users in Year 2000," press release, September 28, 1998. ⟨http://www.c-i-a.com/pr0998.htm⟩.

11. "China number two in home net usage," Reuters, April 22, 2002. Found on ⟨http://www.nua.com/surveys/index.cgi?f=VS&art_id=905357873&rel=true⟩.

12. Joseph Turow, John Bracken, and Lilach Nir, "The Internet and the Family: The View From the Press." In Joseph Turow (ed.), *The Internet and the Family: The View from Parents, the View from the Press* (Philadelphia: Annenberg Public Policy Center, May 1999), p. 34.

13. Joseph Turow, "The Internet and the Family: The View from Parents." In Joseph Turow (ed.), *The Internet and the Family: The View from Parents, the View from the Press* (Philadelphia: Annenberg Public Policy Center, May 1999), p. 34.

14. See Joseph Turow, "Privacy Policies on Children's Websites: Do They Play By the Rules?" (Philadelphia: Annenberg Public Policy Center, March, 2001).

15. See Christopher Lasch, *Haven in a Heartless World* (New York: Basic Books, 1977).

16. Florence Hull, "The Home," *Godey's Ladies Book* (February 1894): 173–175.

17. Stuart Ewen, *PR! A Social History of Spin* (New York: Basic Books, 1996).

18. Paul Lazarsfeld and Robert Merton, "Mass Communication, Popular Taste and Organized Social Action." In Lyman Bryson (ed.), *The Communication of Ideas* (New York: Institute for Religious and Social Studies, 1948).

References

Marvin, C. 1998. *When Old Technologies Were New*. New York: Oxford University Press.

Rakow, L. 1992. *Gender on the Line*. Urbana: University of Illinois Press.

Silverstone, R., and E. Hirsch. 1992. *Consuming Technologies*. London: Routledge.

I

The New World in Context

One way to try to understand the role that a new medium is beginning to play in social life is to search for conceptual frameworks that can help make sense of it. Another way is to look for historical precedents that can help assess how really new the medium is. The essays in this section use one or both of these approaches on the way to presenting provocative ideas about why we should care about the internet and the family and what we should study about it. In the tradition of media scholarship, the pieces draw on work from sociology, communication studies, psychology, cognitive development, family studies, and social history to develop their positions.

Joseph Turow borrows from sociology, family studies, and communication to present "information boundaries" perspective that lays out a model for viewing the family in relation to the web. Turow argues that one way to understand this new phenomenon is to see it as bumping up against long-standing family concerns about what is "private" and what is "public." He uses the model to explore two very different notions about the web's family role. One sees the rapid commercialization of the internet as helping to reinforce divisive tensions that researchers say are typical of U.S. families today. The other hails e-mail and related activities as countering this dysfunctional development by strengthening family relationships and reducing stress. Because of the far-reaching power of marketers, Turow sees the divisive influences of the web on family life unfortunately trumping those that help to counter family stress, but he points out that much research is needed to really understand what is going on and whether social and family policies ought to be changed.

As Turow notes, home-based Internet connectivity allows commercial interests to contact various family members directly, thereby by passing a spouse or a parent. Taking a historical view informed by an economic metaphor, Elihu Katz explains that this is not the first time that parents have been by-passed—or, "disintermediated"—by the media. Parents have traditionally tried to act as intermediaries or gatekeepers with regard to most aspects of their children's lives, seeking to steer them toward what they consider positive influences and to deflect what they consider negative ones. This intermediating role effects with whom their children associate, to which experiences they are exposed, and which books and television programs they consume. It has not always worked, because clearly every book, magazine, video, or TV program a child sees is within the parent's knowledge or control. What seems to make the home-based internet connection different from books or TV selections is that the range and diversity of content is vastly greater, easier to access, and more difficult to monitor.

Despite these differences between the internet and previous media, a look at the past suggests that every new mass medium evokes similar worries and objections when it comes to children. In their review of research trends on children and media from 1900 to 1960, Ellen Wartella and Byron Reeves note that many of the same questions about violence, sex, stereotyping, and other issues were asked with respect to books, movies, radio, comics, and TV. Indeed, we can find nervousness about children's inability to distinguish between fact and fiction as far back as Plato's *Republic*. We should not, then, be surprised that such issues have become central to many of the discussions of children, parents, and the web. As Wartella and Reeves write (in a statement as relevant today as when it first appeared in 1985), "as we stand at the threshold of research about new technologies, a look back at public controversy and concern about older media is useful both to point out where we have been and to determine how we might proceed in the future."

The researchers who responded to the cyclical concerns Wartella and Reeves discuss developed a wealth of insights about children and media. These might prove valuable in assessing the internet's implications. Using research on television as a guideline, Daniel R. Anderson and Marie

Evans show the utility of that approach. Because their disciplinary background is developmental psychology, Anderson and Evans focus on TV's effects on children as they relate to cognitive and emotional processes such as attention, comprehension, memory, emotion, and social attribution. Although much of what they say most directly translates to considerations about the internet's impact on the individual child, their discussion of media and personal development inevitably brings up issues of social maturity. That, in turn, raises topics of interactive communication in the home that very much carry over into dynamics regarding parents and siblings around TV—and, by extension, around the internet.

Ellen Seiter is much more direct about her interest in making links between the family dynamics that surround television and those that are evolving around the internet. Coming at the subject from the standpoint of critical sociology, Seiter argues that "we need to view the Internet from the perspective of its many parallels with broadcast media, maintaining a healthy skepticism about its novel qualities as a communication medium." She adds that "as personal computers proliferate in middle-class homes, the boundaries between leisure and work time, public and private space, promise to become increasingly blurred. As the Internet develops from a research-oriented tool of elites to a commercial mass medium, resemblances between Web sites and television will increase."

What does this combination of work and play technology mean for family life—and especially for women's roles in the home? Seiter offers no direct answers, but she performs an important service by placing the new technology solidly in the context of previously home-based media. She also charts a fascinating array of questions for studying the internet and the family through qualitative, ethnographic research.

1

Family Boundaries, Commercialism, and the Internet: A Framework for Research

Joseph Turow

1.1 Introduction

During the past few years, the Internet—especially its World Wide Web graphics interface—has become a fixture in a rapidly growing number of U.S. homes. Although electronic mail and chat rooms are popular, the fastest growing use of the Internet seems to be in its commercial domain. Marketers of all stripes have found the Web a great place to target parents and youngsters with ad messages and products while getting information out of them that can be used for further marketing. These activities have raised controversy and alarm—and even led to new government regulations.

The growing social debate and the rapidly rising presence of commercialized Web sites in U.S. households have so far not led to a stream of published studies that attempt to understand its impact on the family. Many writings do exist on the implications of traditional mass media, such as television. That literature, however, barely begins to address a raft of new questions about commercial intrusion and family privacy that the Web raises.

This paper presents an *information-boundaries* perspective on the family and the Internet with the aim of helping to set the context for child development in the new media environment. Drawing from family studies, sociology, and communication, it lays out a model for viewing the family in relation to the Web. It uses the model to elucidate two views of the Web. One sees the new and enduring commercial dynamics

Reprinted from *Applied Developmental Psychology* 22 (2001): 73–86, Copyright © 2001, with permission from Elsevier Science.

as helping to reinforce divisive tensions that researchers say are features of families throughout society. The other view hails e-mail and related activities as countering this dysfunctional development by strengthening family relationships and reducing stress in households.

To what extent is one tendency triumphing over the other, and how might that change over time? To suggest ways to answer this question, the paper first lays out the family information-boundaries approach and relates it to the emerging domestic, media, and regulatory environment. The paper then draws research ideas out of the framework that center on four areas: family communication patterns; filters and monitors; information disclosure practices; and the Internet in the larger media context. Because the Web is a harbinger of an even broader digital interactive media environment, the issues raised about the context of child development through the information-boundaries prism will increase in importance as the new media world takes hold.

1.2   The Family and the Private/Public Realms

For the purpose of this paper, a family will be defined as one or more adults and at least one child or teenager who live together on an ongoing basis. A dominant theme of scholarly discussions of the family centers on the functions of "public" and "private" realms of interaction in society, with the family traditionally dubbed "the private." Thinking of the family as private as opposed to public may seem natural, but the separation is not a very old one (see Zaretsky, 1986). Although writers have traditionally discussed public and private realms as though they were objective, externally observable phenomena, recent scholars have argued that the distinctions are socially constructed and negotiated (Fahey, 1995). The terms *private* and *public* may therefore hold different meanings for different family members in different family environments. Some scholars even argue that the boundary between home and work is a false one, for these boundaries are malleable and easily penetrated by the welfare state or even by mass media (see, e.g., Habermas, 1989; Lasch, 1977).

Nevertheless, distinctions between private and public are still extremely important to society's view of the family because people act as if the differences mean something (Fahey, 1995). The epigram that "your home is your castle" continues to survive as a reflection of the adamant social belief that strong boundaries between the two domains should be the norm even if they are not always the reality. Researchers insist that this belief has crucial consequences. Hess and Handel (1985) argue that strong family relationships evolve through an awareness of boundaries between family members and the rest of the world. In their lives together, parents and children negotiate ideas about how and why they are similar to and different from each other and various other people.

Bronfenbrenner (1975) extends this notion directly to argue that dysfunctional social institutions can, through impact on the family, adversely affect child development. Berger and Kellner (1964/1985) suggest that "the plausibility and stability of the world, as socially defined, is dependent upon the strength and continuity of significant relationships in which conversation about this world can be continually carried on" (p. 13). As a kind of corollary to these ideas, the Carnegie Council on Adolescent Development (1995) argues that a strong and caring family relationship can be a potent force to help children, adolescents and parents cope with the fast-changing learning and working conditions in which Americans find themselves at the turn of the twenty-first century. However, dual careers, single parenting tensions, poverty, and a host of other factors have converged to make strong family units difficult to achieve at a time when they are sorely needed.

The Council also points its finger at the mass media. It asserts that in recent times, they have been helping to short circuit the potential for supportive family relationships to an unprecedented extent. Electronic media have permeated the lives of American youth. Through television, radio, records, films, and videos a "heavily materialistic youth culture has emerged, weakening and challenging parental authority and stable, supportive bonding with a caring adult" (1995, p. 36). One obvious solution—more time with parents—is increasingly unrealistic because youngsters' increased media use is accompanied by less family time. "Although there has been less research than the problem deserves, the time that American children spend with their parents has decreased significantly in the past few decades" (1995, p. 36).

Elkind (1994) extends this theme about the way commercial media are implicated in the "splintering" of the U.S. family. He points out that "the entertainment, information, and communication industries have fueled a new and heightened consumerism by targeting and catering to the diverse interests of the buying public" (p. 24). He suggests that the marketing-driven media environment increasingly urges parents and children, men and women, and people of varied ages to consider their differences rather than their similarities. He argues that this target-oriented media world encourages individual interests over family togetherness. It privileges child decision making over parental authority, and it pushes outside marketing influences over parents' influences and, perhaps, values. With the increasing role in children's world views being shaped by marketers, children's sense of family identity (and through that kids' sense of social stability) may erode.

Elkind and other writers are important for calling attention to the role that commercial media may play in reinforcing and extending crucial family problems. Ironically, though, the media world that family analysts critique is quickly being eclipsed, and they have not turned their attention to the implications of that change. Taking the place of the traditional electronic environment of radio, videos, audio CDs and one-way television is a digital interactive world symbolized by the Internet and interactive television. Neglect of these developments is unfortunate because the new technologies that are moving rapidly into U.S. homes raise a raft of new questions about the relationship between family boundaries, commercialism and information that few family theorists have systematically considered together.

One view of the new technologies leads to the conclusion that their commercially driven dynamics may reinforce the dysfunctional family dynamics that Elkind and the Carnegie Council have bemoaned. It might, for example, cause tension between teens and parents regarding the disclosure of information to Web sites that offer free products for valuable information. Other aspects of the Web—e-mail is one—have been hailed as activities that strengthen family relationships and reduce stress in households. To what extent is one tendency already triumphing over the other, and how might that change over time? Virtually no research has spoken to this topic. The first step in addressing it is to pull back and look at the emerging environment.

1.3   The Internet and Family Boundaries

Although the Internet itself dates back to its creation by scientists in the 1950s, its graphical interface, the World Wide Web is much more recent, dating to 1993. The number of U.S. households going online has grown so rapidly that any numbers presented as current are sure to become obsolete quite soon afterwards. In the middle of 1999, Dataquest found that 36% of American households were "online" (Wired, 1999). By the middle of 2000, a variety of sources pegged online households at 44% (Elkin, 2000).

The Web is paradigmatic of the kind of digital interactive technology that will permeate the home during the twenty-first century. It has three features that, taken together, distinguish it from all past media that bring the outside into the home. First, its digital nature means that parents, children, and outsiders can send, retrieve, transform, and store the material that moves across it. (A 13-year-old can carry on a discussion in a chat room, and the firm that operates it can store the text for future analysis.) Second, the Web's two-way, interactive nature means that family members and outsiders can respond to one another in an ongoing fashion. (The chat room operator can send ads for products that reflect the interests that the teen reveals through the ongoing chat.) Third, its ability to function through sophisticated computer software and hardware means that family members' activities can be tracked, sorted and predicted through increasingly intelligent agents. (The company hosting the chat room can analyze the discussions and sell the results—and even the opportunity to reach the discussants—to market researchers.)

The Web is becoming a major communication vehicle for much of American society—so much so that trade magazines now refer to an *Internet economy*.[1] Consulting firm estimates in 1998 were that the Internet economy generated U.S.$301 billion in revenue and employed 1.2 million Americans. Much of that use is to engage in electronic mail, chat room conversation, and personal Web sites. As the Web has matured, however, a larger and larger portion of it—and a larger portion of its use—has related to commercial purposes. The Web's commercial (.com) sector has skyrocketed, outpacing by far the growth rate of nonprofit (.org), educational (.edu), and government (.gov) sites. Electronic commerce is also growing by leaps and bounds. Marketers of all stripes, from soap manufacturers to porn purveyors have found the Web a great place to deliver their ad messages quickly and efficiently.

Americans are going online in large numbers. A study in early 1999 by Nielsen Media Research and CommerceNet found that 92 million people over the age of 16 in the U.S. and Canada used the Internet at work or home (Bridis, 1999). Although affluent, highly educated white males dominated the Web in its first few years, figures near the turn of the century find almost as many women as men online. Moreover, the numbers of African Americans and Hispanic Americans who have online connections have been rising steadily. Although the Web population is still skewed toward the upper–middle class, it is becoming less so as the months past.

A national survey of parents released in March 2000 found that 28% of all U.S. children access the Internet from home. Parents in 49% of U.S. households reported that their children access the Internet from some location, at home or elsewhere (National School Boards Association, 2000). Around the same time, other studies noted that about 45% of U.S. households had online connections. Marketers saw the Web becoming a hub of activities. "Nearly half of North America uses the Internet," exulted a CommerceNet executive in 1999. "We use it to communicate, to learn, to shop and to buy. It is as integral a part of our lives as the telephone" (Bridis, 1999, p. D7).

The analogy to the telephone is important beyond its recognition of the Web's centrality. As Marvin (1988) points out, in the telephone's early years, many Americans were thrilled with the possibilities of the technology at the same time that they worried about the intrusions it would bring to the home and the private information it might take out. The Internet has also evoked a combination of fear and hope. A national survey of U.S. parents of 8- to 17-year-olds in late 1998 and at the start of 2000 (Turow, 1999a; Turow & Nir, 2000) found most American parents deeply conflicted about the Web. Across the nation, parents and the press have heralded the Web as a way to help the family by connecting them to relatives, schools, and informative Web sites for homework. Fully 81% of parents with online connections at home said that the

Internet is a place for children to discover "fascinating, useful things" and nearly 68% said that children who do not have the Internet are disadvantaged compared to their peers who do. At the same time, over 77% of parents worried that their children might give out personal information and view sexually explicit images on the Internet. Fifty percent agreed that "families who spend a lot of time online talk to each other less than they otherwise would" (Turow & Nir, 2000, p. 12). In a 1998 survey (Turow, 1999a), 79% said that it bothered them when advertisers invite children to Web sites to tell them about products.

Many of these tensions and hopes reflect a desire to properly calibrate the permeable boundaries between the family and the world outside it—particularly when it comes to the protection and socialization of children. Concern about the Web as a conduit for advertisements, "fascinating, useful things" and "sexual images" underscores that familiar program genres make up a key part of the online experience. That, in turn, raises the concerns that Elkind (1994) and the Carnegie Council on Adolescent Development (1995) have expressed regarding commercialized mass media materials coming into the home. Public worries about children giving out "personal information," by contrast, underscores that digital interactive media challenge family boundaries with respect to another information flow—one *going out* of the home. This challenge to the "private" nature of the family recalls similar fears about the telephone. A close look at marketers' work in the developing digital interactive environment suggests, however, that what is developing is not simply a combination of traditional mass media and the telephone. It is a new commercial domain, with new features and possibly new implications for the family.

1.3.1   The Internet and Information Flows into the Home

Since video, music, and direct mail are easily available online, it is tempting to see Web materials coming into the home as merely an amalgamation of all of these and other mass media. From the standpoint of parental boundary setting, however, three features of the Web make auditing the flow and enforcing rules about it much more difficult than with previous media. One feature is the Web's virtually unlimited nature; individuals can access literally millions of sites at any time, on subjects from pandas to pornography. A second aspect is the presence of a huge number of commercial sites targeted to virtually any demographic, psychographic, and lifestyle interest one can imagine—including many that aim at children and teens. The third feature of the Web that makes parental auditing more difficult than before is the complexity of the technology. Not only do many adults have trouble with it many of their own youngsters are more savvy and confident about the digital world than they are.[2]

The emphasis on commercial targeting is so great on the Web that concerns about family splintering that Elkind and the Carnegie Council raised regarding traditional media would seem to apply here to a much greater extent. Web technology increasingly allows visitors to sites to "personalize" the material sent to them by specifying what they want. Marketers see today's teenagers as the replacement consumers for their parents, the aging baby-boom generation that so captivated business for 50 years. To the commercial realm, these "echoboomers" are prime targets for the development of brand loyalties at a particularly sensitive time in their lives. By cordoning off entertainment and advertising areas of the Web with personalized materials that are just for them, and then creating separate consumption arenas for their parents and younger siblings, marketers may well reinforce family splintering in ways that go beyond traditional media.

The potential implications of the Internet as a target marketer's dream have not made it into public discourse about the Web and the family. Instead, the great percentage of concerns centers on the wide availability of sex, violence, and commercialism on the Web (see Turow, 1999a). Web versions of sex, violence, and advertisements, however, are often exactly the same as those on a video game cartridges or magazines that an adolescent can surreptitiously bring home through nonelectronic means. What is different is the torrent of objectionable material easily available to the home and the consequent difficulty that parents feel they have in controlling what their kids access.

So far, three solutions to concerns about objectionable material have emerged. They involve filters, monitors, and safe haven sites. Filters are computer programs that parents can use to stop certain words or Web sites (or both) from entering the home. Monitors are computer programs that parents can install on computers to track (secretly or openly) where their children go on the Web and what they do when they get there. Safe haven sites are child-friendly sites on the Web that provide parents with software that ensure children go to them and nowhere else.

Filters are certainly the most controversial of the three boundary-protecting mechanisms. Critics argue that the programs are often severely flawed. Parents who block sites with the word "sex," for example, may find that all educational biology sites are off limits. Moreover, say the critics, many of the firms that create filters do not make clear the ideological biases of their software programs. So that competitors will not steal the data that makes them unique, they are often reluctant to release the names of the sites they block or the filtering terms they use (Hunter, 1999).

The biggest drawback of monitors and safe haven sites—and a big drawback of filters as well—is that parents with only basic computer and Web skills may not feel comfortable using them. Almost as big a drawback is that adolescents can find ways to circumvent or disable many of these attempts to place limits on them. One nontechnological way they do that is simply by accessing the Web from places—friends' homes, libraries—where such barriers do not exist.

1.3.2   The Internet and Information Flows out of the Home

If the Internet creates new control challenges for parents with respect to the commercialized information it brings into the home, these challenges pale next to the ones the Web is creating with respect to commercially useful information about the family that commercial interests *take out* of the home. Until rather recently, the information that marketers could retrieve from children and teenagers at home was limited by the need to go through a parent or school to speak to the youngsters or track their habits. The Internet has changed all that, with implications that family research have hardly begun to consider.

At the center of this activity is consumer profiling for the purpose of direct and relationship marketing. Profiling involves gathering specific demographic, psychographic, and lifestyle intelligence about individuals and families from a variety of public and private databases (Business Wire, 1998). Digital technologies enter the home with features that revolutionize the data marketers can get from people. Quite widespread are Web sites that offer free information, paraphernalia, phone calls, even cash if the user will enter personal information into a registration window and then visit the Web site.

Even when it does not appear that Web sites are collecting a lot of information about their visitors, it is likely that they are quite busy doing that. A close reading of Web "privacy policies" will reveal that virtually all the activities that individuals perform on Web sites can be tracked and catalogued. To make Web sites particularly attractive to advertisers and visitors, companies are using increasingly sophisticated "cookies" and intelligent agents that determine the interests and habits of the visitors. The sites aim to offer them personalized ad and editorial environments based on an analysis of previous purchases, clickstream interests, and the personal characteristics noted during site registration.

Marketers hope that sophisticated data gathering and database management will converge in digital media to allow them to actually speak to segments, even individuals, in ways that reflect what they know about them (Turow, 1997). The growing ability to solicit information electronically from people without their full knowledge about its use has, however, drawn enormous concern from parents (Turow & Nir, 2000), as well as a gamut of advocacy groups. Advocates see the issue as one of information privacy, "the claim of individuals, groups or institutions to determine for themselves when, how, and to what extent information about them is communicated to others" (see Westin, 1967, p. 3). Of particular concern have been attempts by children's Web sites to elicit information about parents' incomes and lifestyles. Responding in part, the U.S. Congress in 1998 passed the Children's Online Privacy Protection Act (COPPA), which directed the Federal Trade Commission (FTC) to regulate data collection by commercial Web sites that target kids under age 13. The FTC decreed that Web sites wanting information from children under 13 years old must get consent from parents. The required nature of the consent varies depending on the site's intended use of the information (Clausing, 1999).

1.3.3 The Family Challenge of Two-way Commercialism

Although marketers generally support COPPA, they insist that Web users 13 years and older are savvy enough to be able to handle information about themselves. Increasingly, Web executives say, society must move away from the notion that consumers hold that the absolute secrecy of certain types of information about themselves is their fundamental human right. Rather, they argue consumers will give up all sorts of sensitive information to companies if they trust the firms to use it properly and get commensurate benefits in return. They argue further that, with the rise of digital interactive media, information is and ought to be an important coin of exchange for the individual in the twenty-first century. As evidence, marketers point to the large numbers of Web users who freely give information about themselves to get information and material goods.

Advocates and academics have weighed in with a variety of opinions about the possible social impact of this "exchange" approach to information privacy. Despite the uproar over children's naive release of information to Web sites, few writers have explored the general implications of an individual's barter of information for the family unit. Most see information disclosure on the Web as an issue of individual rather than group information inflow and outflow. Coming at the topic from the standpoint of family information boundaries points to the importance of the latter view. Take the example of a 14-year-old who reveals his parents' favorite Web sites to a Web site for a "free" gift, not realizing that his parents consider such data sensitive. It turns out that his mother has a health problem that is reflected in the list of sites and that might, if revealed publicly, lead to employment discrimination or have implications for health insurance.

Writings on family information privacy suggest that concerns about this and other types of information leakage across their private/public boundaries may have profound impact on the family group, as well as on its individual members' psychological well being. Summarizing a stream of work on the topic, Berardo (1998) posits that society requires some monitoring of individuals and groups in order to enforce social norms. Domestic violence by men against women and children is an example of the dark side of information that families sometimes keep within their boundaries and should not. Yet, argues Berardo, there must be a balance between surveillance and privacy for effective functioning of a social structure. "Full surveillance of activities in a group would become psychologically overwhelming and, as a consequence, dysfunctional for the maintenance and stability of the group as a whole" (p. 8). "Information privacy," he adds, "allows ... sufficient autonomy from disruptive extra-familial scrutiny to foster a feeling of group cohesiveness, thereby enhancing solidarity" (p. 10).

The possibility that a loss of control over information about the family that goes out of the home—or even the fear—can weaken family bonds places a new light on Web privacy. Concern about the integrity of family information boundaries may be heightened when one considers that digital interactive technology provides, for the first time, a media environment where information surveillance and targeting marketing can work together in real time. Web information and, eventually, television programming, can be personalized to a family member based on volunteered, collected, and purchased data. In turn, creators of that programming collect information about the individual and his or her clickstream while the viewing is taking place. Parents may be concerned both about what information leaves the home as a result of the youngster's clickstream, and about the kinds of materials that he or she is bringing into his computer (or Web-TV) as a result of this personalization.

What we have, then, is an unprecedented, continual example of what Shapiro (1997) terms the "leakage of particular facets of one's life across the home boundaries and of the intrusion of undesired aspects of the world back across those boundaries" (p. 275). If what Berardo, Elkind, the Carnegie Council and others say is correct, what may be happening over time is a weakening of the family in a spiraling manner. In a general social environment of embattled families, tensions over information leakage may help erode family cohesiveness. That, in turn, may make it easier for target marketing messages to reinforce separatism within the family—which, in turn, may allow for more information leakage and greater family tensions. And so on, in an increasing spiral of family tension and fractionalization created by information leakage.

1.4   Internet Research and Family Boundaries

Evidence to support or refute this scenario about the family in the new media environment is almost totally absent. A recent national random telephone survey of 1001 parents of children aged 8–17 and 304 children aged 10–17 (Turow & Nir, 2000) attempted to break ground in this area. About half of the youngsters were linked to the parents, and half were not. The authors concluded that in many families the Web is becoming an arena for discord around the release of sensitive information. Their survey found that 45% of U.S. 10–17-year-olds are much more likely than parents to say it is OK to give sensitive personal and family information to commercial Web sites in exchange for a free gift. Examples of such information include their allowance, the names of their parents' favorite stores, and what their parents do on weekends.

The study also noted that 41% of U.S. parents and 36% of youngsters recall tensions at home over kids' release of information to the Web. Curiously, 69% of the parents say they have had discussions with their children about what kinds of information to give up to Web sites, and 66% of the kids say they have had these discussions with their parents. However, when interviewers specifically focused on the 150 pairs of parents and kids in the same family, they found that most did not agree on whether these sorts of discussions had ever taken place. The authors infer that parent–child conversations about Web-privacy issues are fleeting at best, perhaps in the form of "don't give out your name" or "don't talk to strangers" that parents have traditionally urged upon their children. They suggest that it is wrong to think that such simple discussions between parents and kids about what information to give to the Web can easily resolve family tensions over information privacy.

Clearly, there is much more work to do in this area. Existing data that can be brought to bear on the issue is scattered across a variety of studies. The family-boundaries framework presented above can help point research in useful directions. It suggests that questions and hypotheses will usefully center around four general areas: the Internet and family communication; filters, monitors, and the family; information disclosure practices and the family; and the Internet in the general media environment. The following pages will briefly sketch a few key issues in each domain and suggest how they intersect.

1.4.1 The Internet and Family Communication

The proposition that private/public boundaries will likely be constructed differently in different families can serve as a good departure point. A basic hypothesis is that families vary in the extent to which and the way in which they care about what information comes in and what goes out of the house via the Web. This seemingly straightforward statement, however, opens a variety of issues.

A key set of questions centers on what it really means to say that "families vary" in "setting boundaries" regarding the Web information that comes in and goes out of their homes. Who in the family sets the boundaries? Do family members challenge them and force changes? If so, who, when, why, and how?

A major problem is whether it is, in fact, realistic to assume the existence of one private/public information boundary that individuals within a family perceive in the same way. The very idea of social construction makes it likely that what writers call a *boundary* is really a melange of contested statements, actions, and accommodations regarding the Web by family members that not only change over time but that might be described quite differently by various individuals involved. Researchers should describe the dynamic nature of such private/public boundary making within families. Studies may well find that families differ substantially in the nature of their contested, continually changing statements, actions, and accommodations regarding what can come in and go out of the home via the Web.

This basic understanding of these family dynamics will allow for the exploration of the central issue suggested by the family-boundaries perspective: the extent to which the Web's commercialization is reinforcing differentiation between family members, tensions about incoming materials some family members find objectionable, and worries about family information privacy. Another key is whether and how Web benefits such as e-mail, chat rooms, interesting information, and homework help yield a counterbalancing force that supports family unity. Operationalizing words such as *differentiation, tensions, objectionable, worries,* and *counterbalance* will be a challenge and incite debate. Moreover, the work must take place with a textured understanding of the social and historical contexts in which families live.

1.4.2 Filters, Monitors, and the Family

One way in which a growing number of parents have been trying to control family boundaries when it comes to their children bringing objectionable Web materials into the home is by using filters and monitors. Despite vigorous debate about the use of filters in libraries, no research has actually explored the use and implications of Internet filters in homes. Basic questions need to be addressed, with an eye on whether filters really do mitigate the anxieties of the parents involved about the permeability of their families' boundaries. Of special interest is whether parents decide to use filters more out of fears of the Web that they pick up from the press than from bad experiences within their families or the families of people they know. One project (Turow, 1999a) found that the opinions of a national sample of parents about the Web mapped quite closely onto the way a national sample of newspapers discussed the family and the Internet. A long tradition of *media agenda-setting* research, as well as a newer stream of *framing* studies, can help to shape work on this important question.

Almost lost in the discussion of filtering is a straightforward alternative that retains adult oversight but does not lock out the Web. It is the use of monitoring software to observe children's behavior, either with or without their knowing it. Someone opposing monitoring might argue that it invades a youngster's privacy. Someone supporting it might reply that use of monitor software is akin to a parent looking over the youngster's shoulder, especially if the child knows that the monitor exists. Careful study of the use of such monitors may stir or calm this controversy.

1.4.3 Information Disclosure Practices and the Family

While research surrounding Web filters and monitors speaks to family boundary negotiations in the face of nervousness about material coming into the home, the topic of information disclosure practices relates to data that marketers and others try to take out of the house. Here lie great opportunities for exploration of the relationship between family information boundaries and changing social environments. It seems logical to assume that families hold norms about information disclosure. Adults may have their own implicit and explicit rules about what to say about family affairs to "outsiders." Parents may tell children not to tell strangers their names, not to talk to telephone marketers, not to talk about certain sensitive family practices. They may elaborate definitions of "outsiders" for the kids. Children, in turn, may develop their own rules about disclosing certain kinds of information about themselves, their siblings, or their parents to friends, relatives, teachers, and other outsiders.

Are parents articulating norms about the release of information to the Web—and, if so, how? How sophisticated are different types of families and specific family members when making sure that only the information they want released will go out? The possibility that in some families the greatest knowledge about the Web may lie with the children rather than the parents may make it difficult for some parents to articulate and police certain Web disclosure norms. Wartella (personal communication, 1999) notes that this sort of knowledge asymmetry recalls the predicament of U.S. immigrants, who often find themselves feeling much less savvy than their quickly Americanizing and English-speaking children. The intriguing comparison deserves elaboration with an eye to its implications for younger and older family members' negotiation of, and adherence to, family information boundaries.

1.4.4   The Internet in the General Media Environment

Adults and youngsters constantly monitor their environment. Implicitly or explicitly, they make decisions about what can go in and go out, fight about those decisions, circumvent them, forget them, ignore them. Researchers' awareness of this process can guide many questions about the Internet and the family.

However, researchers also need to recognize that the Internet does not exist on its own. It is part of a much larger web of media and nonmedia activities that relate to the home and the family. This development particularly affects the direction of commercial media. The marketing mandate of the twenty-first century is to follow target audiences wherever they go, on any medium that they use (see Turow, 1999b, chapters 18–19). To truly understand the implications of the Web for the family, researchers must stay on top of media and marketing trends that might affect the family and its members.

How do advertisers understand the family? How and why do advertisers try to target family members in certain ways? How do media firms respond to advertiser interests in their attempts to reach the targets? What do the changing media tactics mean for the commercial blandishments that different family members receive? What do changing marketing tactics mean for information that marketers want to bring in and take out of the home? In what way and to what extent do these tactics affect family boundary making with respect to the Web and other media?

Addressing these questions will place the Internet, commercialism, and the family into a broad societal context. Doing that will require a close understanding of the media and marketing industries. Studies that explore the historical and cultural roles of media and commercialism in American family life are critical for a proper understanding of the Web's impact. Similarly, assessments of contemporary industry strategies are key to understanding contemporary business strategies toward family information boundaries, the social discourse about it, and the possible large-scale implications of that.

1.5   A Look Ahead

There is certainly much to study. Moreover, the Web is changing quickly. Every month, the Web gets bigger, more commercialized, and more quickly accessible to many Americans. The notion of a discrete "Web" in the home is also likely to blur as interactive digital television, radio, and print materials become common via broadband technologies. Along with these new developments will come a wide array of target-marketing activities aimed at youngsters, as well as parents and entire families.

To get a good grasp on the nature and implications of these developments, research methods to explore them should vary. Some studies will involve interviewing family members in depth; others may take place through paper-and-pencil surveys; and still others through ethnographic or experimental approaches. Because the United States is only at early stages in adopting the Web, many of the family dynamics may still be too new or too subtle to observe. Longitudinal research on families is therefore warranted, as is research comparing otherwise similar families who have had the Web at home for different lengths of time.

The Web we have now, though, represents the beginning of this new digital realm. It, or versions of it, is here to stay. So is the family, the cradle of child development. How the two relate to one another is a subject that is likely to occupy researchers in the coming century. Looking at these developments through the prism of family information boundaries would seem to be a good way to start.

Notes

1. The Industry Standard, a popular magazine that focuses on Web business, is subtitled "The Newsmagazine of the Internet Economy."

2. This circumstance may change when the current generation, comfortable with the Internet, gets older and has children. Then again youth's supremacy over the Web may not change because the technology involved in the newer media will, being updated, be updated for purposes, and in ways, that seem to attract agile young minds.

References

Berardo, F. (1998). Family privacy: Issues and concepts. *Journal of Family Issues*, 19, 4–19.

Berger, P., & Kellner, H. (1985). Marriage and the construction of reality: An exercise in the microsociology of knowledge. In: G. Handel (Ed.), *The psychosocial interior of the family* (3rd ed.). New York: Aldine. (Original work published 1964)

Bridis, T. (1999). Net users hit 92 million in U.S., Canada. *Austin American-Statesman*, D7 (June 18).

Bronfenbrenner, U. (1975). The origins of alienation. In: U. Brenfenbrenner & M. A. Mahoney (Eds.), *Influences on human development* (2nd ed., pp. 485–501). Hinsdale, IL: Dryden Press.

Business Wire (1998). Businesses radically rethinking how they view customers, according to Andersen Consulting/Economist Intelligence Unit study (October 13).

Carnegie Council on Adolescent Development. (1995). *Great transitions: Preparing adolescents for a new century*. New York: Carnegie Corporation of New York.

Clausing, J. (1999). New privacy rules for children's web sites. *New York Times*, G11 (October 22).

Elkin, T. (2000). How MSN connects to the world of free ISPs. *Advertising Age* (March 27), p. 46.

Elkind, D. (1994). *Ties that stress: The new family imbalance*. Cambridge, MA: Harvard Univ. Press.

Fahey, T. (1995). Privacy and the family: Conceptual and empirical reflections. *Sociology*, 29, 687–703.

Habermas, J. (1989). *The structural transformation of the public sphere.* Cambridge, MA: MIT Press.

Hess, R., & Handel, G. (1985). The family as a psychosocial organization. In: G. Handel (Ed.), *The psychosocial interior of the family* (3rd ed.). New York: Aldine (Original work published 1959).

Hunter, C. (1999). *Filtering the future: Software filters, porn, pics, and the Internet content conundrum.* Philadelphia, PA: Annenberg School For Communication, Master's Thesis.

Lasch, C. (1977). *Haven in a heartless world.* New York: Basic Books.

Marvin, C. (1988). *When old technologies were new: Thinking about communications in the late nineteenth century.* New York: Oxford Univ. Press.

National School Boards Association. (2000). *Safe and smart: Research and guidelines for children's use of the Internet.* Alexanderia, VA: National School Boards Association.

Shapiro, S. (1997). Places and spaces: The historical interaction of technology, home and privacy. *The Information Society,* 14, 275–284.

Turow, J. (1997). *Breaking up America: Advertisers and the new media world.* Chicago: University of Chicago Press.

Turow, J. (1999a). *The family and the Internet: The view from parents/the view from the press.* Philadelphia, PA: Annenberg Public Policy Center of the University of Pennsylvania (Report No. 27).

Turow, J. (1999b). *Media today: An introduction to mass communication.* Boston: Houghton Mifflin.

Turow, J., & Nir, L. (2000). *The Internet and the family 2000: The view from parents/the view from kids.* Philadelphia, PA: Annenberg Public Policy Center of the University of Pennsylvania (Report No. 33) ⟨http://www.appcpenn.org/finalrepor_fam.pdf⟩.

Westin, A. (1967). *Privacy and freedom.* New York: Athaneum.

Wired (1999). Net hookups double in Europe. Net Hookups Double in Europe. Wired (on the Web) (June 7).

Zaretsky, E. (1986). *Capitalism, the family, and personal life* (2nd ed.). New York: Perennial Library.

2

Disintermediating the Parents: What Else Is New?

Elihu Katz

Disintermediation is a word borrowed from finance, but it applies equally well to communication. The idea is that communicators are continually trying to reach over the heads of intermediaries in order to establish direct relations with some target audience. This holds both for interpersonal relations as well as for mass communication. When talking about the family, the intermediaries are the parents. That statement may startle at first, but a moment's thought will reveal how familiar we are with institutional efforts to circumvent parental gatekeeping in order to reach children; consider education and the church, for example. The same thing holds for the media. For decades, the media have been talking to children over the heads of their parents; the web is only more of the same. To say that this is not new, however, is to offer another question: in view of this long history of disintermediation, what is left of the parents' traditional role?

The idea of disintermediation by the media is inspired by technological theorists of communication such as McLuhan, Innis, Eisenstein, and Meyrowitz (Katz 1988). A good example comes from Beniger (1981), who asks us to recall the corner grocers who decided which breakfast cereals to offer their customers. The grocer made rational choices about what to stock and served as a kind of consultant to the customers. Then, around the turn of the century, national advertising happened, whereby a cereal manufacturer could place an ad for a brand of granola or crisped rice in all the Sunday supplements nationwide. According to Beniger, the grocers panicked. The shelves were cleared of all other brands in anticipation of the rush for the advertised brand. In this sense, national advertising disintermediated the grocer. The grocer's role as consultant was undermined by the assumption that people were influenced by the advertising campaign.[1]

Take another case: in medieval Europe, the Church spoke God's language and the priest served as intermediary between the deity and the worshippers. Then came Guttenberg and the printing press, and soon the bible was mechanically reproduced, translated into spoken languages, and widely distributed. Thus, the book disintermediated the priest and paved the way for Protestantism (Eisenstein 1979).

Or, take the case of Franklin Roosevelt. The Congress was not happy about Roosevelt's New Deal when Roosevelt took to the radio and began his fireside chats. He disintermediated the Congress, talking to the people over the heads of their representatives. He created a direct relationship between leaders and followers.

Or, consider e-medicine. The patient searches the internet for information about her condition. By the time she arrives for a doctor's appointment she has essentially gone over the doctor's head, presenting herself as a very different kind of client.

In each of these cases, the new medium—advertising, the radio, the internet—diminishes or changes the status of the intermediary, while ostensibly liberating, or empowering, the audience—the customer, the citizen, the patient—to act on their own. At the same time, these examples suggest that disintermediation also substitutes a remote affiliation for the kind of proximate community that their clients had with the grocer, the priest, or the doctor. As we know, this kind of liberation has its costs; it is the kind of thing that led Durkheim (1951) to the idea that the rate of suicide among Protestants would be higher than among Catholics; it led Erich Fromm (1941) to worry about the authoritarian movements that assemble those who have "escaped from freedom," and Putnam (2000) to worry about "bowling alone." In other words, disintermediation gives us three things to worry about: (1) the loss of an informed and reliable intermediary who is close by; (2) the community of others who gather around him or her; (3) the loss of the countervailing power that is implicit in this kind of informal organization. If enfranchisement is the reward of disintermediation, its "punishment" is becoming newly dependent on direct relations with Kellogg's, God, or the medical encyclopedia, or worse, on the media that deliver their messages.

From a more deterministic point of view, one might argue that disintermediation not only invites dependence on the new medium, but also subjects us to its dictates. Following McLuhan (1964), one might say that when print disintermediated the priest, it constrained our minds to think linearly and to organize our society in assembly lines and railroad lines. He thought that electric media would bring people together—although the togetherness of film, radio, television, and the internet imply different forms of togetherness.

It's important to note that disintermediation does not so much destroy the intermediary; more often, it changes his role. The doctor now has to play a different kind of role than before. The Protestant minister leads her congregation in a sectarian interpretation of the shared text. And so on.

And one more thing. The more sophisticated the communicator, the more he might try to enlist the intermediary in the service of his message. Lazarsfeld and Merton (1948) called this "supplementation," after they realized that mass persuasion addressed to whom it may concern is rarely effective. Research findings about the intermediacy of opinion leaders in fashion, for example, or in politics, led certain communicators —*Time* magazine, for example—to try to harness opinion leaders. The drug companies use "detail men" for such supplementation (Coleman, Katz, and Menzel 1966).

Parents as Intermediaries

Now consider parents as intermediaries. As heads of the family, they used to be the agents for training children to take their place both in the family and in the larger society. The traditional (extended) family used to be an educational organization, a unit of production and consumption, a religious and political clan. One by one, these functions have been transferred from the family to other institutions, leaving the family to serve functions of consumption, caregiving, and socialization. But even these functions are in dispute as the consumer economy, the church, and, most notably, the schools, reach over the heads of the parents. Nowadays, even the institutional go-betweens are being overtaken by such media as distance learning, religious television, internet advertising, and retailing.

What's left to the family, then, is the role of generalized socializing agent—that is, bringing up children who are fit to understand and affiliate with organizations and institutions outside the family, whether educational, political, religious, or economic. An important question today is how parents manage this kind of mediation and cope with the constant battering by media that are trying to disintermediate them even in this role.

Note that the family is a particularly vulnerable institution because it is an organization designed to self-destruct! Parents are supposed to redirect the loyalty of their children to the "outside"—to a mate, to a job, to values that compete with those of the family. Freud notes that just as the child is cozying up to his mother, feeling that all is going well, the father intervenes from the world and makes clear to the child and mother that he is in charge: "You cannot have her, and you can't fight me, because I am stronger than you. And if you want to be like me, internalize my superego, but get your id to search outside for another woman." As the bible says, "therefore shall a man abandon his father and mother and shall cleave to his wife, and they shall be one flesh." I won't even begin to enumerate the many ways in which this urge to find someone to cleave to disintermediates the parents.

Talcott Parsons (1955) theorized that the family socializes children according to the values of particularism. A child learns from her parents that she is the second daughter in a particular family, not in some other family, and that her status is ascribed, not achieved. But the child, says Parsons, needs to be socialized to the values of universalism and achievement which predominate outside the family—and therefore, he reasons, the family can socialize only up to a certain point. Following Parsons, Eisenstadt (1956) argues that this is where peer groups come in to disintermediate the family. The peer group is particularistic in the sense that it welcomes, say, all twelve-year-olds in the neighborhood, but status in the group must be achieved. In this case, peer groups disintermediate the parents because the parents cannot perform this function. Eisenstadt points out that peer groups in immigrant communities are much stronger and probably appear earlier than peer groups in established communities because immigrant parents can do less to socialize a child in an environment that is new to them as well. So, here is another example of the self-limiting role of family and another glimpse into the disintermediation of parents.

In research in Israel, we find that peers pull their members toward self-fulfillment, toward individualism, where parents pull their children toward collectivity, toward obligation and responsibility. This points to a paradox whereby parents support the army more than friends, even though the parents have everything to lose by putting their children at risk. And yet, parents more than friends are active in encouraging the fulfillment of military obligation (Katz, Troper, and Haas, 1984).

New Media and Disintermediation

We have already alluded to how the media enter into this process, when children can learn things that their parents will not (or cannot) teach them or things that they do not wish to learn from their parents. In *The Lonely Crowd* and other writings, David Riesman (1950) talks about the child browsing in his parents' library and suddenly realizing that he can reach into the big world over the heads of his parents. This is the moment that some parents have waited for, but others will be concerned over having been disintermediated.

An analogous and interesting example comes from Orthodox Judaism. Joseph Dov Soloveitchik (1992) argues that in spite of all the books and other writings, the rituals of Orthodox Judaism tended to be transmitted through the family. Family lore guided the definition of what was kosher or what preparations to make for the several holidays. Suddenly, however, a high-church mood has invaded Orthodox Judaism, whereby teachers in religious schools and rabbinical seminaries are telling their students not to mind what their parents are saying and offering the real thing from primary sources, to the consternation and diminution of parents and family. This development parallels the Riesman idea of empowering the child by giving her access to the book. Of course, it also opens the possibility that it is the rabbi—not the book—that is disintermediating the parents.

What is true of the book holds true, a fortiori, for television. The most radical statement comes from Beverly Houston (1984) who proposes that the infant child has to compete with television for his mother's attention and thus that the TV set may be displacing the father as an oedipal object! Further touting television's ability to disintermediate the parents, Meyrowitz (1985) argues that in the era of the book, it took a long time for children to acquire the skills needed to match their parents'. Even when children learned to read, parents and children had different literatures. Television, says Meyrowitz, requires only minimal literacy, giving access to the world even to illiterate children. The heart of Meyrowitz's argument is that there are no secrets in the television era: children know as much about parents as parents do about children, once again undermining the authority of the parents and their roles as intermediaries.

Along the same lines, Joseph Turow (1997; 1981) points out that television, for decades, has been selling toys to children over the heads of their parents. The difference, in this case, is that children nevertheless "need" to appeal to parents to serve as intermediaries in the transaction. In her *Playing with Power*, Kinder (1991) discusses toys in a different way, as media that themselves have a disintermediating influence. In looking at the role that handheld electronic toys play in children's lives, she argues that they invite children to simulate the status that their parents haven't yet given them. Having been persuaded to buy the new electronic toy, the parents find that they have given the child a new sense of his own power (as in Lacan's "mirror moment"), but that the child has also acquired knowledge in the electronic world to which the parents aspire—and may never achieve. Thus, the internet presents a much more acute example of disintermediation in this double sense: giving the child direct access to information that the parents cannot filter and giving the child expertise overshadowing that of his parents.

One would imagine that such developments would breed resistance, and they certainly do. Some grocers were not happy when manufacturers co-opted their customers, to which the growth of boutiques is a kind of response. We also know that parents get angry at the materialistic, and sometimes violence-filled, relationships that mass media try to cultivate in children, to which the V-chip and other technologies have been developed in response.

Yet, many parents seem to accept such disintermediation readily. Television is used as a baby sitter, even when the parents are educated enough to know—from the Sesame Street studies, for example—that joint viewing with their children makes for substantial increments in learning from the medium. Many proudly disqualify themselves in the face of the children's surfing prowess.

It is an open question when and how and whether parental authority can work in the face of media such as the internet, where the parents actively collaborate in their own disintermediation. Indeed, technological determinism might even suggest that a new egalitarianism and a new culture of sharing may emerge. Clearly, we must encourage research that tries to track and understand these cross-currents (for example, Livingstone and Bovill 2001) even while worrying that the new media technologies may be disintermediating parents from their historically closest relationships.

Note

1. There is no reason for us to assume a powerful effect. We really don't know whether or not the customers were influenced. It is enough that the grocer thought they were.

References

Beniger, James. 1981. *The Control Revolution.* Cambridge: Harvard University Press.

Coleman, James, Elihu Katz, and Herbert Menzel. 1966. *Medical Innovation.* Indianapolis: Bobbs-Merrill.

Eisenstadt, S. N. 1956. *From Generation to Generation.* New York: Free Press.

Eisenstein, Elizabeth. 1979. *The Printing Press as an Agent of Change.* Cambridge: Cambridge University Press.

Durkheim, Emile. 1951/1897. *Suicide.* New York: Free Press.

Fromm, Erich. 1941. *Escape from Freedom.* New York: Rinehart.

Houston, Beverly. 1984. "Viewing Television: The Meta-Psychology of Endless Consumption," *Quarterly Review of Film Studies* 9: 184–205.

Katz, Elihu. 1988. "Disintermediation," *InterMedia*, 16: 30–32.

Katz, Elihu, Yaacov Troper, and Hadassah Haas. 1984. "Primary Groups, Mass Communication, and Integration in Armed Forces and Nation." In Eric Cohen, Moshe Lissak, and Uri Almagor (eds.), *Tradition and Modernity: Essays in Honor of S. N. Eisenstadt.* Boulder, Colo.: Westview Press.

Kinder, Marsha. 1991. *Playing with Power in Movies, Television, and Video Games*. Berkeley: University of California Press.

Lazarsfeld, Paul F., and Robert K. Merton. 1948. "Mass Communication, Popular Taste, and Organized Social Action." In L. Bryson (ed.), *Communication of Ideas*. New York: Harper and Row.

Livingstone, Sonia, and Moira Bovill, eds. 2001. *Children and Their Changing Media Environment: A European Comparative Study*. Mahwah, N.J.: Erlbaum.

McLuhan, Marshall. 1964. *Understanding Media: Extensions of Man*. New York: McGraw-Hill.

Meyrowitz, Joshua. 1985. *No Sense of Place: The Impact of Electronic Media on Social Behavior*. New York: Oxford University Press.

Parsons, Talcott. 1955. "Family Structure and the Socialization of the Child." In Talcott Parsons and Robert F. Bales (eds.), *Family, Socialization and Interaction Process*. New York: Free Press.

Putnam, Robert. 2000. *Bowling Alone*. New York: Simon and Schuster.

Radway, Janice. 1986. *Reading the Romance: Reading, Patriarchy, and Popular Literature*. London: Verso.

Riesman, David, Reuel Denny, and Nathan Glazer. 1950. *The Lonely Crowd*. New Haven, Conn.: Yale University Press.

Soloveitchik, Joseph DOV. 1992. *The Lonely Man of Faith*. New York: Doubleday.

Turow, Joseph. 1997. *Breaking Up America*. Chicago: University of Chicago Press.

Turow, Joseph. 1981. *Entertainment, Education, and the Hard Sell: Three Decades of Network Children's Television*. New York: Praeger.

3

Historical Trends in Research on Children and the Media: 1900–1960

Ellen Wartella and Byron Reeves

For the past several years, scholars of mass communication have reflected on the history of American media research and found it lacking. Gerbner, for instance (26), has noted that the "received history" of mass communication research "should not be taken literally." Rowland (64) has argued for a revision of early American media research history and a recovery of the cultural studies traditions that predate the era of Paul Lazarsfeld and the Columbia school. And Chaffee and Hochheimer (8) were critical of the dogma that followed from the political communication studies of the 1940s.

This article is an attempt to address questions about the history of mass communication research in the United States by examining a particular research domain, that of media effects on children. Our study is part of a larger ongoing analysis of the history of public controversy about media effects on children and youth.

A major thesis of our project is that the traditional history of media effects research is biased toward considerations of public opinion, propaganda, public affairs, and voting. As embodied in basic textbooks, this history can be outlined as follows. Earliest concerns about the mass media at the turn of the century and through the 1920s and early 1930s took the form of the direct effect or "hypodermic needle" model of media impact. The latter term, coined by political scientist Harold Lasswell during his analysis of World War I propaganda techniques, reflects an assumption that messages have a direct and undifferentiated impact on individuals. In the 1940s, Lasswell's ideas were challenged by studies

Reprinted from *Journal of Communication* 35 (Spring 1985): 118–133, by permission of Oxford University Press.

that questioned the ability of media to influence directly important political decisions. What little influence was found was thought to operate through opinion leaders who in turn influenced others. This idea about indirect effects was crystallized in the "two-step flow" theory and was applied to other areas of media content, most notably fashion, product choices, and movie attendance (38). The research characterized a trend toward practical and applied communication research that looked at immediate short-term effects of messages for the benefit of communication administrators in advertising, public relations, and government information campaigns (39).

There are many contexts in which this history has been recounted (6), although most discussions preface current research in all media effects areas (e.g., 39). Moreover, even scholars who are critical of the mainstream of media effects research, such as Gitlin (27) and Rowland (63), recite essentially the same history, although for the purposes of uncovering the roots of administrative emphasis. Consequently, it is important to examine the accuracy of this received view.

With the development of each modern means of storytelling—books, newspapers, movies, radio, comics, and television—social debates regarding their effects have recurred. A prominent theme in all these debates has been a concern with media's impact on youth, a concern which in fact predates the modern era. Plato's *Republic* (58) warned about storytellers:

Children cannot distinguish between what is allegory and what isn't, and opinions formed at that age are usually difficult to eradicate or change; it is therefore of the utmost importance that the first stories they hear shall aim at producing the right moral effect.

Davis (16) noted the prominence of issues surrounding the impact of media on children's morality in an analysis of popular arguments about the introduction of film, radio, and television into American society:

A major attack on movies, radio and television involved the influence of the media on morality. Both sides (opponents and proponents) agreed that the media exerted a moral influence. The disagreements centered on the direction of that influence. Attackers argued that the media undermined conventional systems of morality, caused children to engage in illicit sexual adventure and were a primary influence in stimulating criminal lessons and might be used to substitute for real life in learning ethical principles. (p. 142)

Although much of the literature has been lost to contemporary students of television effects, the earlier part of the twentieth century was a time of active and substantial research on children and youth. In this article we review this early research and examine how well it fits the received history of mass communication research.

We have three major points. First, the traditional history of American mass communication research, whatever its faults and biases, does not describe scholarship about children and media. The study of media effects on youth has developed independently of the broader media effects tradition. Second, the origin of research about children lies in concern expressed by the public about each medium as it was introduced. Public debate helped shape research agendas—at least with respect to topics— rather than research shaping public concerns or policy. Third, arguments about twentieth-century media have recurred throughout the century. Although the expression of concern highlights novel attributes of each medium, the bases of objections and promises have been similar.

Although the period from 1900 to 1940 has been labeled the "direct effects era," one in which media were thought to have a direct and undifferentiated impact on all audience members, this is not the case for research on children and media. Some histories suggest that the "direct effects" model derives from learning theory and simple stimulus-response models in behavioristic psychology (39, 40). Yet the best-known research from this era contradicts a direct effects conclusion. The 1933 Payne Fund studies—twelve volumes of research conducted by the most prominent psychologists, sociologists, and educators of the time—represent a detailed look at the effects of film on such diverse topics as sleep patterns, knowledge about foreign cultures, attitudes about violence, and delinquent behavior. These studies have not often been cited in the last 25 years, despite the fact that they represent a research enterprise comparable to the 1972 Surgeon General's Committee on Television and Violence. But at the time the Payne studies generated significant press attention, academic review, and critical comment, and were the basis of recommendations for government action on what the authors believed were significant social problems.

A major conclusion of the report was that the same film would affect children differently depending on each child's age, sex, predispositions, perceptions, social environment, past experiences, and parental influence. In this sense, the report was similar to the most current summaries of research about children and television. Further, the effects were said to be conditional on whether the criterion concerns were behaviors, attitudes, emotions, or knowledge about people and events. For example, Blumer's study of *Movies, Delinquency and Crime* (5) concluded that the effects of film on criminal behavior may be diametrically opposed, depending on the diversity of themes presented and the social milieu, attitudes, and interests of the observer.

Although Blumer's contingencies were largely sociological, the conclusions of several other researchers involved affective and psychological differences. Dysinger and Ruckmick (19) studied emotional reactions and concluded, based on a physiologic measure, that children varied widely in emotional stimulation. They suggested that age differences in response were caused by varied abilities to comprehend information on the screen. For example, young children tended not to understand the romantic scenes to which adolescents responded enthusiastically.

Cognitive variables received similar attention elsewhere in the Payne Fund volumes. In a study about learning from film, Holoday and Stoddard (33) focused on information retention as a function of grade in school. Not only did they look at individual differences in relation to long- and short-term effects, but they examined retention in relation to specific message content, thereby foreshadowing research to come a half-century later. The authors concluded that action was remembered best when it was about sports, action, and crime, when the information had an emotional component, and when the action occurred in a familiar background such as home or school. Such attention to age differences can be found in research on film attendance conducted prior to the Payne Fund studies, such as a 1917 survey of children's leisure activities (49) and Mitchell's (50) 1929 survey of Chicago children's attendance and reactions to films.

Nor is it true that the logic of this research depended on stimulus-response models. There are several different meanings for the phrase "stimulus-response," each with different theoretical assumptions, but none applies to the research about children. One definition links stimulus-response with a strict behavioristic notion of reinforcement and a scientific philosophy that ignores what cannot be objectively observed—namely, mental concepts. As Katz and Lazarsfeld (38) commented about the scheme with which media research began, this idea was "that of the omnipotent media, on the one hand, sending forth the message, and the atomized masses, on the other hand, waiting to receive it—and nothing in-between" (p. 20). Even though this conception was not explicitly pro-behaviorist, it still implied that intervening mental processes were irrelevant. Such a conclusion is clearly not applicable to the Payne Fund studies or to writing earlier in the century. In fact, the Blumer studies of movies and criminal behavior were the only research in the Payne series to measure behavior; the remainder of the research dealt with mental concepts assumed to intervene between exposure and effect. The psychologists and educators on the Payne committee studied ideas and factual learning (34), social attitudes (56), emotions (19), sleep patterns (60), and moral development (12).

A cognitive orientation was not new even in 1933, however. An important book by Hugo Munsterberg (52), published in 1916, had also focused on mental processes. The author was one of the first laboratory psychologists and a student of Wilhelm Wundt, the acknowledged father of experimental psychology and an avowed introspectionist. Munsterberg devoted the first half of his book to comments on mental attention, memory, imagination, and emotions.

Nor is it true that the Payne Fund studies were anomalous in the 1930s. Other research of that era similarly was concerned with how children use and are affected by the media. Eisenberg (20), for instance, conducted the first major study of radio's effects on child audiences, surveying over 3,000 New York children and their parents. In addition to examining the frequency of radio listening and children's preferences for radio programs, he assessed the impact of radio on children's factual learning about the world, attitudes, imitation of radio characters' language and behavior, and requests for advertised products.

In short, the pre-1940 period included study of cognitive concepts, attention to developmental differences in children's use of media, and a focus on children's knowledge of the world, their attitudes and values, and their own moral conduct. Although the commentators felt that media effects could be powerful, they also recognized that other factors, such as the child's developmental level or social class, could modify the media's impact. It is difficult to find evidence of the "hypodermic needle" model of media effects in pre-1940 studies of children and media.

Nor, as is commonly assumed, did theorizing about media effects on children in the period 1940–1960 follow an "indirect effects" model. For example, Herzog's 1941 review of research on children's radio listening habits has a developmental emphasis in demonstrating age differences in children's attraction to and preference for radio programming (31). She also notes evidence of children's direct learning of information and standards of conduct from radio. Later radio studies in the 1940s examined a wide range of "effects," such as the influence of radio drama in producing differential emotional reactions in children (17, 18), psychological differences in children's abilities to distinguish between reality and fantasy (35), and the influence of radio on children's school performance (31). The commercial nature of radio was noticed as well. Surveys of mothers documented the appeal of radio ads to children (31) and the effects of premium advertising on children's responses to advertising and product requests (29).

The few studies on children and media related to the Columbia Bureau of Applied Social Research did not use an indirect effects model of media impact on youth. For example, studies by Meine (47) and Wolf and Fisk (72) are noteworthy both for what they include—psychological explanations of media effects—and what they do not—the model of "indirect media effects" most identified with the Columbia school that predicts different effects based on sociological ideas about "opinion leadership" or "multiple steps in information dissemination." Meine (47) found a direct relationship between children's consumption of newspaper and radio news and their knowledge of current affairs, even after controlling for age, sex, and intelligence. Similarly, Wolf and Fisk (72) conducted an extensive study of children and comics that previewed many concepts that would be discussed as new ideas in later television research. Children were thought to progress through three qualitatively different stages of sophistication in their ability to read and understand comics. Parental mediation of media experiences was advocated by almost all mothers, yet few actually prohibited their children from reading the comics.

Attention to questions about use and preference for television programs predominated in the literature of the 1950s, when the "indirect effects" model is said to have become "reified" (28, 63) and when the earliest studies of television influence on children were being conducted. Not only were notions of indirect effects not articulated, however; they were not even implied by the authors. A far more common theme in the 1950s, illustrated by Shayon's 1952 book (67), is a concern with gauging the impact of television, widely thought to have enormous influence on children and labeled by Shayon the new "Pied Piper."

If studies about media and children do not follow the received history of media effects research, then how can the research history be described? It is our contention that emphasis on research topics was influenced by public debate about changing media technologies. That is, as public concerns about film gave way to concern about radio and then television, academic research made corresponding shifts.

Has the quantity of research on a medium changed as popular attention shifted? Evidence about the relationship between media research and media popularity comes from two sources: (a) a bibliography, compiled by us, of academic studies published between 1900 and 1960 about the effects of media on youth, and (b) statistics about the growth of film, radio, and television as popular entertainment. In the bibliography of published studies we included articles and books that meet three criteria. The reference must have addressed the issue of media effects on children and youth, been written for an academic or professional audience, and been published in the United States. Technical reports and research papers were excluded. The bibliography was compiled from printed and on-line bibliographies and published references on media effects (e.g., 3, 53). The final bibliography contains 242 entries from the period between 1900 and 1960—a time frame corresponding to the introduction of film, radio, and television into American life.

Each study was classified by the type of medium addressed: film, radio, television, print (newspapers, comics, magazines, and reading in general), or cross-media issues (any combination of media effects, such as comparison of radio and print or TV and movies). Five studies of print media and 21 cross-media studies were found. The remaining 216 studies were about electronic media.

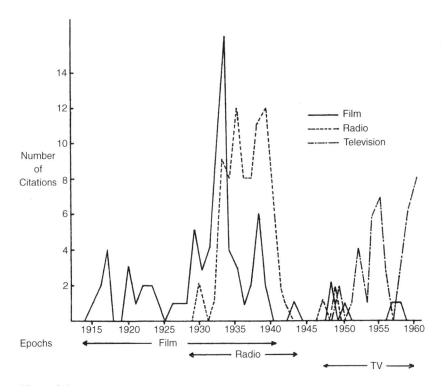

Figure 3.1
Number of citations about children and film, radio, and television, 1900–1960.

Figure 3.1 shows the number of citations to studies about children between 1900 and 1960. There are three identifiable epochs of research, one associated with each electronic medium. The film epoch begins in 1904, ends in 1939, and reaches a peak in 1932 during the Payne Fund investigations (9). The radio epoch begins in 1930 and ends just before World War II. There is some overlap in the beginning of the period with the decline of film research. The television epoch, the period most separated from other research, begins in 1949 and builds through 1960, with a one-year lapse in 1957.

Our major emphasis is on variance in research activity *within* each epoch; however, features of the entire distribution are both apparent and counterintuitive. First, the *cumulative* number of studies did not increase monotonically prior to 1960. Most research activity occurred during the 1930s. In fact, two-thirds of the research on children prior to 1960 was completed by 1939. Second, it is clear that the 1940s, a time of active research on politics and persuasion, lacked such activity in the area of children and media.

The three epochs obviously correspond to the introduction and dissemination of the three technologies. The clearest relationship is for television, a medium that came on the market at an identifiable time (about 1948) and diffused rapidly. By 1954, a mere seven years after its introduction, 55 percent of American households had a television set (68). The number of television receivers in use by year is correlated at .82 (n = 13, p < .05) with the number of studies on television and children published each year. The same relationship for the diffusion of radio receivers and radio research is also positive, but smaller (r = .55, n = 15, p < .05). The smallest correlation is between studies of film effects on children and annual film audience data (r = .20, n = 23, n.s.).

Figure 3.2 shows two time series for each medium—one for the number of research citations and one for the rate of diffusion (number of TV sets, number of radio receivers, and average weekly film audience). Cross-correlations between these two series indicate that the relationship between research activity and media popularity is not simultaneous. For the film epoch, the highest correlation between film audience data and film research is .25, with a positive three-year lag. The lag for television is also three years, when the correlation reaches its highest level of .80. On the other hand, the highest lagged correlation between radio receivers in use and research on radio and children (.63) is reached with a negative six-year lag, suggesting that research on children and radio anticipated the rise in radio's growth.

Unlike the television epoch, the film and radio epochs show a decline in research activity, although audience use of the medium continues. In the case of radio, the number of receivers in use actually grows during the late 1940s and 1950s. All of these lagged correlations, however, are positive and they do not show substantial increases over the correlations matched in time. Although the rise in research interest corresponds to the growth of audiences for film, radio, and television, abatement of the research has no counterpart in diminishing audiences for these media. Rather, the quantity of research shifted as a result of the *growth* of each new medium.

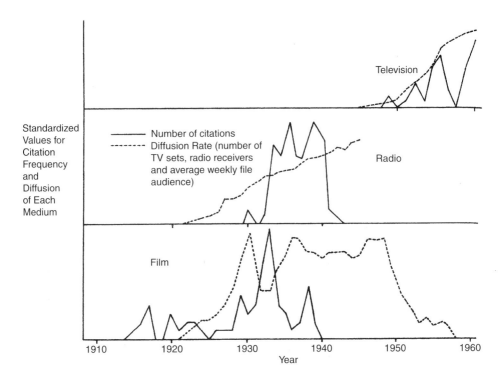

Figure 3.2
Number of citations about media and youth by diffusion rate for film, radio, and television, 1910–1960.

Note: This scale represents the association between citations and diffusion rates. The absolute values cannot be compared because each function represents a different metric, as follows: The number of citations per year ranges from 0 to 16 in 1933 for film, from 0 to 12 in 1935 and 1939 for radio, and from 0 to 8 for television in 1960. The diffusion rate scales for each medium are taken from Sterling and Haight (68). Film audience attendance data begin in 1922, when the average weekly attendance is 40,000 people; it peaks in 1930 and 1946 through 1948, with average weekly attendance at 90,000 people (68, p. 352). Households with radio receivers range from 60,000 in 1922 to a high of 35.9 million in 1947 (68, p. 367). There were 8,000 television sets in use in American homes in 1946; in 1960, 45.7 million homes had TV sets (68, p. 372).

Have researchers addressed the same kinds of questions about the effects of film, radio, and television? Our review found a progression from early attention to studies of media use to increasing emphasis on issues of physical and emotional harm, and changes in children's knowledge, attitudes, and behaviors. In addition, studies about violence, sex, and advertising recur.

Media use studies are not published exclusively in the earliest part of an epoch, but they are most likely in the years right after a medium's introduction. In the case of film, only a few of the pre-1930 studies in the bibliography (e.g., 25) deal with effects of movies. Most studies are either discussions of the need for children to see wholesome family-oriented programs (e.g., 22, 36, 49, 54, 62, 73) or, beginning in the late 1920s, reports about audience attendance and the type of movies that appeal to children (e.g., 11, 37, 50, 70, 74). Mitchell's (50) examination of children's attendance at Chicago theaters is the best-known early study of children's film use.

Similarly, the earliest studies of radio effects are examinations of children's listening habits and preferences (e.g., 10, 15, 28, 32). Here, too, many of the early studies are catalogues of available radio programs and/or extended discussions (without evidence) of their likely impact on listeners (e.g, 2, 40, 43, 71). A landmark study of children's radio listening and preferences by Eisenberg (20), for which over 3,000 children were surveyed, received the same attention in the subsequent radio literature as the early study of film audiences by Mitchell (50) received in the film literature.

The television literature, too, began with studies of children's use of the medium and preference for different types of programming. The earliest study of television effects in our bibliography (42) is about teenage viewing preferences and is similar to most of the television studies in the early 1950s (e.g., 44, 45, 61, 66). Although what is frequently referenced as the landmark study of the impact of television on children, Schramm, Lyle, and Parker's *Television in the Lives of Our Children* (65), did not appear until 1960, considerable research on TV's impact on knowledge, attitudes, and behavior preceded this study (e.g., 1, 23, 30, 46, 51, 57).

In reviewing these pre-1960 studies, two observations are particularly pertinent. First, there is a surprisingly large scientific literature on children and media, and we continue to discover more, particularly that which precedes the television era. Second, and more important, we are impressed by the overwhelming similarity in the research studies from epoch to epoch, with a new technology substituted as the object of concern. How can we account for these similarities?

One obvious explanation for similarities in research is that earlier studies may have set the agenda for later research. There is limited evidence that later scientists either attempted to replicate research from an earlier epoch or were at least enough aware of past efforts to cite them in their own work. For instance, radio and film studies may have influenced each other. DeBoer's work on children's emotional responses to radio (17, 18) made frequent reference to the Dysinger and Ruckmick (19) research on film. Herzog (31), in her review of radio research on children, also cited a number of earlier film studies. The extent to which television research was influenced by the earlier studies of film and radio is far less clear, however. The first studies on television made infrequent reference to earlier media studies on children and youth, and then chiefly to the Payne Fund studies (see, e.g., 65, 66).

There is also evidence from cross-media studies that direct comparison between radio and movie effects on children was a popular topic only in the 1940s (24, 34, 41, 48, 59, 69, 75). Moreover, we found only four people who conducted research that spanned at least two decades and that addressed different media. Rather, the bibliography suggests that *different* scholars conducted the research about each medium and that these people came from diverse disciplines: psychology, sociology, education, communications, and social work.

It may be, however, that earlier research, particularly the Payne Fund studies, set future agendas even though they were not cited. In particular, the strategies for studying media as a social problem that surrounded the Payne Fund may have had an influence on the later efforts of both organized commissions and individual researchers. In order to understand such an influence, we need to locate the Payne Fund studies within their social and cultural milieu and ask why the academics who conducted these studies defined media's influences as they did. As Rowland (63) has pointed out, the Payne Fund researchers chose to study film impact in terms of film content, film use, film's short-term effects, and approaches to teaching children how to use film more selectively. Charters's overview of the studies (9) acknowledges that they ignored questions about the structure of the film industry and the larger institutional arrangements that gave rise to the film culture of the United States in the 1920s. This is not to imply, however, that the Payne Fund researchers were uninterested in changing the film industry. As Charters concludes:

Certainly the problem of the movies and children is so important and critical that parents, producers, and the public must willingly and intelligently cooperate to reach some happy solution. The producers occupy the key position. The public at present must take, within the limits of the censorship of the states, whatever pictures are made.... The simple obligation rests upon the producers who love children to find a way of making the motion picture a beautiful, fascinating, and kindly servant of childhood. (9, p. 63)

Throughout the 1930s, Charters championed the development of films directed to and intended for the juvenile market (see 14) and addressing the particular needs of youth.

What influenced the Payne Fund approach to studying film effects as a social problem? One possibility is the University of Chicago's program on communication. As Pecora (55) has noted, seven of the twelve Payne Fund volumes were written by University of Chicago faculty or former students (4, 5, 9, 12, 13, 14, 55). In addition, authors of two other earlier influential studies, Mitchell (50) and DeBoer (17, 18), received Ph.D.s from the same university. Chicago's commitment to scientific research about visible social problems may have encouraged attention to questions of media's impact on youth.

Precisely how and why the studies were conceptualized as they were, however, is not readily explained. Although the University of Chicago approach to communications studies is frequently identified with symbolic interactionism (63), as represented by Blumer's (4) approach to studying film's influence through the use of life histories, the Chicago school had broader definitions of appropriate research methods and definitions of effects. For instance, Peterson and Thurstone's experimental studies of children's attitudes toward ethnic groups (56) employed some of the earliest interval measures of attitude change. The highly quantitative content analysis of film themes and portrayals by Dale (14), and the survey research of Mitchell (50) and Dale (13), also represent methods identified with the University of Chicago.

In locating effects studies at an individual rather than cultural level and in connecting film portrayals to short-term changes, the Payne Fund studies utilized a definition of "effect" that runs throughout U.S. media research. Some critics have mistakenly suggested that such a definition came from Lazarsfeld's administrative research on radio in the 1940s (see 27, esp. p. 79). That such a definition of media effects both predates Lazarsfeld and appears in a literature widely separate from the "received history" of media effects research suggests that we need to look elsewhere to account for its presence. It is far more likely that such definitions of "effects" were responsive to deeper roots in American social science.

Another likely influence of the whole body of research on media and youth is the social reform movement early in the century. Rowland (63) locates the roots of media violence research in the progressive era of social reform before World War I. Indeed, throughout the literature on children and media, there is a recurring self-professed interest in addressing what scientists perceive to be public concerns. In the early studies within each epoch, scholars introduced their research with self-conscious acknowledgments of widespread public concern about the influence of media on children (see, e.g., 9, 20, 40, 42, 66). For instance, Eisenberg (20) comments:

The popularity of this new pastime [radio] among children has increased rapidly. This new invader of the privacy of the home has brought many a disturbing influence in its wake. Parents have become aware of a puzzling change in the behavior of their children. They are bewildered by a host of new problems, and find themselves unprepared, frightened, resentful, helpless. (pp. 17–18)

It may be that such public concerns were only one part of a group of middle-class progressive reforms. However, an argument can be made that researchers more specifically directed their inquiries to questions posed by an anxious public composed of worried parents. Theorizing about "effects" at the individual level—how children acquire discrete knowledge and perform discrete behaviors—can be seen as responsive to the questions of parents and teachers about media's impact on "their children."

The roots of this paradigm for media research are not as clear as critics of U.S. media effects research would imply. There are a few glaring exceptions of studies that directly try to examine children's media use for market exploitation (e.g., 7, 29), but it is difficult to see how the research is necessarily tied to the administrative interests of media industries.

In sum, we observe a history much different from the received history of U.S. media effects research, one that is characterized by trends in research epochs that focus on different media and recurring topics. The roots of these trends are not easily characterized and probably reside in an understanding of the nature of public controversy about the adoption of new media technology into American life.

We are not the first to note recurrences in the literature. This is more apparent now that we are at the threshold of yet another set of new communication technologies such as cable and computers. Over thirty years ago Mary Seagoe observed:

Television is the newest addition to the illustrious family of our mass entertainment enthusiasms. We have had dime novels, movies, radio, comics—and now television. Each time we seem to go through the same stages. We remember the alarm raised soon after the advent of the talking picture, which in time gave rise to the Payne Fund studies, which in turn showed that the same movies might either help or hinder growth, reinforce social standards, or teach the techniques of crime, depending upon the person who saw them and the attitudes he took to the seeing. For a while films seemed designed more for children than adults: then when we had examined the matter and learned how to use movies, the alarm died away. The same thing happened with the widespread use of radio, leading to the studies of Eisenberg and others. The same thing went on in relation to the comics. Now we are starting that cycle with television. Whenever there is a new social invention, there is a feeling of strangeness and a distrust of the new until it becomes familiar. (66, p. 143)

As we stand at the threshold of research about new technologies, a look back at public controversy and concern about older media is useful both to point out where we have been and to determine how we might proceed in the future. The recurring nature of public concern for and scientific study of media influence on youth thus speaks to our field's responsiveness to the wider social and cultural context of American media.

References

1. Banning, E. L. "Social Influences on Children and Youth." *Review of Educational Research* 25, 1955, pp. 36–47.

2. Beuick, M. D. "The Limited Social Effect of Radio Broadcasting." *American Journal of Sociology* 32, January 1927, pp. 615–622.

3. Blum, E. *Basic Books in the Mass Media.* Urbana: University of Illinois Press, 1972.

4. Blumer, H. *Movies and Conduct.* New York: Macmillan, 1933.

5. Blumer, H. and P. M. Hauser. *Movies, Delinquency and Crime.* New York: Macmillan, 1933.

6. Brown, R. "Approaches to Historical Development of Mass Media Studies." In J. Tunstall (Ed.) *Media Sociology: A Reader.* Urbana: University of Illinois Press, 1970, pp. 41–57.

7. Brumbaugh, F. N. "What Effect Does TV Advertising Have on Children?" *Educational Digest* 19, 1954, pp. 32–33.

8. Chaffee, S. and J. L. Hochheimer. "Mass Communication and American Politics: A New Look at the Early Studies." Paper presented to the conference of the International Communication Association, Dallas, Texas, May 1983.

9. Charters, W. W. *Motion Pictures and Youth.* New York: Macmillan, 1933.

10. Child Study Association. "Radio for Children: Parents Listen In." *Child Studies* 10, April 1933, pp. 44–48.

11. Cressey, G. "The Motion Picture as Informal Education." *Journal of Educational Sociology* 7, April 1934, pp. 504–515.

12. Cressey, P. G. and F. M. Thrasher. *Boys, Movies and City Streets.* New York: Macmillan, 1934.

13. Dale, E. *Children's Attendance at Motion Pictures.* New York: Macmillan, 1935.

14. Dale, E. *Content of Motion Pictures.* New York: Macmillan, 1935.

15. Darrow, B. H. "The Child and the Radio." *Parental Education* 4, April 1934, pp. 84–95.

16. Davis, R. "Response to Innovation: A Study of Popular Arguments About New Mass Media." Unpublished Ph.D. dissertation, University of Iowa, 1965.

17. DeBoer, J. J. "Determination of Children's Interests in Radio Drama." *Journal of Applied Psychology* 21, 1937, pp. 456–463.

18. DeBoer, J. J. "Radio and Children's Emotions." *School and Society* 50, 1939, pp. 290–295.

19. Dysinger, W. S. and C. A. Ruckmick. *The Emotional Responses of Children to the Motion Picture Situation.* New York: Macmillan, 1933.

20. Eisenberg, A. L. *Children and Radio Programs.* New York: Columbia University Press, 1936.

21. Ervy, H. "TV Murder Causes Bad Dreams." *Film World* 8, 1952, p. 247.

22. Ferguson, I. M. "Movies for Children." *Minnesotan*, August 1917, pp. 30–31.

23. Feshbach, S. "The Catharsis Hypothesis and Some Consequences of Interaction with Aggressive and Neutral Play Objects." *Journal of Personality* 24, 1956, pp. 449–462.

24. Frank, J. *Comics, Radio and Movies and Children.* New York: Public Affairs Office, 1949.

25. Geiger, J. R. "Effects of Motion Pictures on the Mind and Morals of the Young." *International Journal of Ethics* 34, October 1923, pp. 69–83.

26. Gerbner, G. "The Importance of Being Critical—In One's Own Fashion." *Journal of Communication* 33(3), Summer 1983, pp. 355–362.

27. Gitlin, T. "Media Sociology: Dominant Paradigm." *Theory and Society* 6, 1978, pp. 205–253.

28. Gruenberg, S. M. "Radio and the Child." *Annals of the American Academy of Political and Social Science*, June 1935, pp. 123–130.

29. Grumbine, E. E. *Reaching Juvenile Markets.* New York: McGraw-Hill, 1938.

30. Haines, W. H. "Juvenile Delinquency and Television." *Journal of Social Theory* 1, 1955, pp. 192–198.

31. Herzog, H. *Children and Their Leisure Time Listening to the Radio.* New York: Radio Council on Children's Programs, 1941.

32. Hewes, R. K. "A Study of 1,000 High School Listeners." *Education on the Air: Fourth Yearbook.* Columbus: Ohio State University, 1933, pp. 326–329.

33. Holaday, P. W. and G. D. Stoddard. *Getting Ideas from the Movies.* New York: Macmillan, 1933.

34. Jersild, A. T. "Radio and Motion Pictures." *Thirty-Eighth Yearbook for the Study of Education.* Bloomington, Ill.: Public School Publishing Co., 1939.

35. Jersild, A. T. *Child Psychology.* New York: Prentice-Hall, 1940.

36. Johnson, J. S. "Children and Their Movies." *Social Service Review* 6, September 1917, pp. 11–12.

37. Jones, H. E. "Attendance at Movie Pictures as Related to Intelligence and Scholarship." *Parent-Teacher*, March 1928.

38. Katz, E. and P. Lazarsfeld. *Personal Influence.* New York: Free Press, 1955.

39. Klapper, J. *The Effects of Mass Communication.* Glencoe, Ill.: Free Press, 1960.

40. Langworthy, B. F. "More About Children's Programs." *Education by Radio* 3, 1936, p. 26.

41. Lazarsfeld, P. F. "Motion Pictures, Radio Programs, and Youth." In F. Henne, A. Brooks, and E. R. Ersted (Eds.) *Youth, Communication and Libraries.* Chicago: American Library Association, 1949.

42. Lewis, P. "TV and Teenagers." *Educational Screen* 28, 1949, pp. 159–161.

43. Longstaff, P. H. "Effectiveness of Children's Radio Programs." *Journal of Applied Psychology* 20, June 1936, pp. 264–279.

44. Lyness, P. "The Place of the Mass Media in the Lives of Boys and Girls." *Journalism Quarterly* 29, 1952, pp. 43–54.

45. Maccoby, E. E. "Why Do Children Watch Television?" *Public Opinion Quarterly* 18, 1954, pp. 239–244.

46. Meerlo, J. A. "Television Addiction and Reactive Empathy." *Journal of Nervous and Mental Diseases*, 1954, pp. 290–291.

47. Meine, F. J. "Radio and the Press Among Young People." In P. Lazarsfeld and F. Stanton (Eds.) *Radio Research*. New York: Duell, Sloan and Pearce, 1941.

48. Merry, F. K. and R. V. Merry. "Children's Interest in the Radio and Movies." *From Infancy to Adolescence*. New York: Harper Brothers, 1940, pp. 236–256.

49. Michael, R. "Better Films." *Child Welfare Magazine* 12, November 1917, pp. 41–42.

50. Mitchell, A. M. *Children and Movies*. Chicago: University of Chicago Press, 1929.

51. Munn, M. "The Effect on Parental Buying Habits of Children Exposed to Children's Television Programs." *Journal of Broadcasting* 2, 1958, pp. 253–258.

52. Munsterberg, H. *The Photoplay*. New York: Appleman, 1916.

53. Murray, J. P. *Television and Youth: 25 Years of Research and Controversy*. Boys Town, Neb.: Boys Town Center, 1980.

54. Nutting, D. B. "Motion Pictures for Children." *The Woman Citizen* 5, November 1920, pp. 659–660.

55. Pecora, N. "Children, Mass Media and the University of Chicago." Paper presented to the Conference on Culture and Communication, Temple University, Philadelphia, 1983.

56. Peterson, R. C. and L. K. Thurstone. *Motion Pictures and the Social Attitudes of Children*. New York: Macmillan, 1933.

57. Pittman, D. "Mass Media and Juvenile Delinquency." In R. J. Roucek (Ed.) *Juvenile Delinquency*. New York: Philosophical Library, 1958, pp. 230–247.

58. *Plato's Republic*. Cambridge: Cambridge University Press, 1966.

59. Preston, M. "Children's Reactions to Movie Horrors and Radio Crime." *Journal of Pediatrics* 19, 1941, pp. 147–168.

60. Renshaw, S., V. L. Miller, and D. P. Marquis. *Children's Sleep*. New York: Macmillan, 1933.

61. Riley, J. W., F. V. Cantwell, and K. F. Muttiger. "Some Observations on the Social Effects of Television." *Public Opinion Quarterly* 13, 1949, pp. 223–234.

62. Rogers, A. and C. Rowland. "Can the Movies Teach?" *Transactions*, 1922, pp. 125–135.

63. Rowland, W. *Politics of TV Violence*. Beverly Hills, Cal.: Sage, 1982.

64. Rowland, W. "Recreating the Past: Problems in Rewriting the Early History of American Communication Research." Paper presented to the conference of the International Association for Mass Communication Research, Prague, September 1984.

65. Schramm, W., J. Lyle, and E. B. Parker. *Television in the Lives of Our Children*. Stanford, Cal.: Stanford University Press, 1960.

66. Seagoe, M. V. "Children's Television Habits and Preferences." *Quarterly of Film, Radio and Television* 6, 1952, pp. 143–152.

67. Shayon, R. L. *Television and Our Children*. New York: Longman, 1952.

68. Sterling, C. H. and T. R. Haight. *The Mass Media: Aspen Institute Guide to Communication Industry Trends*. New York: Praeger, 1978.

69. Sterner, A. P. *Radio, Motion Pictures and Reading Interests: A Study of High School Pupils*. New York: Bureau of Publications, Columbia University, 1947.

70. Sullenger, T. E. "Modern Youth and the Movies." *School and Society*, October 1930, pp. 459–461.

71. Thomas, C. "A Comparison of Interests of Delinquent and Non-Delinquent Boys." *Journal of Juvenile Research* 16, 1932, pp. 310–318.

72. Wolf, K. M. and M. Fisk. "The Children Talk About Comics." In P. Lazarsfeld and F. Stanton (Eds.) *Communications Research 1948–1949*. New York: Harper, 1949.

73. Woodard, A. P. "Motion Pictures for Children." *Social Service Review* 6, September 1917, pp. 10–11.

74. Woodbury, R. F. "Children and Movies." *Survey* 62, May 1929, pp. 253–254.

75. Witty, P., S. Garfield, and W. Brink. "Interests of High School Students in Motion Pictures and the Radio." *Journal of Educational Psychology* 32, 1941, pp. 176–184.

4

The Impact of the Internet on Children: Lessons from Television

Daniel R. Anderson and Marie K. Evans

Over the last two centuries, multiple forms of new communication media have been made available to children. Books, records, movies, radio, comic books, television, and computers have entertained generations of young people. As each new medium appeared, the public, seeing its educational potential, reacted with enthusiasm. However, as children were increasingly exposed to the new medium, adults became concerned about its possible harms. This historical pattern (Wartella and Jennings 2000; Wartella and Reeves 1985) is being repeated with the internet. Although the public initially responded to it enthusiastically, as exemplified by the Clinton administration's promise to provide internet access to all children (Telecommunications Act of 1996), calls arose for limiting children's Internet access and regulating its content (Chandrasekaran and Schwartz 1997; Kelly 2000). Some groups have even argued that young children should not be exposed to computers and the internet, much as groups such as TV Free America have argued for reducing or eliminating children's exposure to television (Kelly 2000). Parents, having heard positive claims of the internet's educational potential, as well as negative claims about its harmful potential, have become decidedly ambivalent about this new medium (Turow 1999).

Because the internet is rapidly evolving, and almost no research has addressed its effects on children (Wartella, O'Keefe, and Scantlin 2000), its present and ultimate impact is open to speculation. Keeping the historical pattern in mind, we consider here the potential impact of the internet on children. To guide our consideration, we examine a medium, television, about which we know much more. Recalling concerns about the impact of television, we briefly summarize what we know from research about its effects. For each area of concern, we consider similarities and differences between the internet and television, and we speculate on ways in which the internet may ultimately affect children. Our goal is to provide researchers, research funders, and policymakers with some ways to approach thinking about the impact of the internet on children.

Reflecting our disciplinary background, we approach the problem as developmental psychologists. We emphasize how researchers in our field have thought about the impact of television. Developmental psychologists generally focus on how media affect individuals (as opposed, for example, to families and family dynamics, or to mass audiences). We are sensitive to issues of cognitive and social maturity in relation to considerations of their impact. Theories of media impact tend to focus on intervening psychological processes including cognitive and emotional processes related to attention, comprehension, memory, arousal, emotion, and social attributions.

Comparing Television and the Internet

Television
In the more than fifty years since it became a mass medium, the technology and content of television have greatly evolved. In television's early years, it presented grainy black and white images on a very small screen with monaural audio. Its content was essentially live stage productions, unedited except for camera movements and cuts between cameras. Only a few broadcast channels were available. In 2002, a typical television provides color images with moderately good resolution, accompanied by high-quality stereo sound. A wide variety of digital-imaging and sound-processing techniques provide the television producer with numerous possibilities for presenting content, and hundreds of channels may be available to viewers. Despite this evolution, television remains essentially a one-way medium. While viewers can mute the audio, change channels, watch two or more channels simultaneously, and shift TV-watching time by using video recorders, they typically cannot functionally interact with TV content.

Television does not require active participation or even active visual attention from its viewers. Consequently, viewers may look away from the screen and engage in other activities such as playing, doing homework, and interacting with others, while periodically returning attention to the ongoing TV program (Anderson and Field 1991). Leaving the room, especially during commercials, is a frequent occurrence (Collins 1993). At other times, viewers may be engrossed with the program for many consecutive minutes, breaking attention only occasionally (e.g., Anderson and Field 1991; Bechtel, Achelpohl, and Akers 1972).

Importantly, a child does not need to be literate in order to watch and enjoy television. To the best of our knowledge, consistent attention to television begins at about 18 months of age, and TV viewing is firmly established by about 30 months (Anderson, Alwitt, Lorch, and Levin 1979; Richards and Cronise 2000). Although comprehension of television content depends on children's cognitive maturity, even very young children can enjoy and at least partially understand a substantial amount of TV. Once television viewing is firmly established, American children spend between 2 and 3 hours a day watching television, although there is great individual variability (Rideout, Foehr, Roberts, and Brodie 1999).

The Internet

At its present level of development, the internet is analogous to television in its early broadcast period. Consequently, any discussion of the impact of the internet on children has to distinguish between the present internet and the internet of the future.

In its present form, the internet is primarily a hypertext medium. The user enters a World Wide Web page, scans its contents, and selects a highlighted entry. After a variable delay, the user enters another web page, originating from the same or a different site, and the process continues. Although highlighted items may include animated icons (accompanied by brief and repetitive audio), or streaming video, text items are most common. Thus, in its most typical form, the internet experience can be described as a nonlinear progression through illustrated pages of text. Compared to any prior medium, however, the internet provides the user with relatively rapid access to a vast, international array of information and entertainment. Hence, a child user can be exposed to almost any human inspiration, idea, fact, or perversion.

The internet also offers a wide variety of interactive possibilities. These typically involve sending and receiving text and static visual images. With the help of downloaded or separately purchased software, however, the user can participate in sophisticated multiplayer audiovisual games and simulations. Users can also download streaming video and audio, allowing an experience much like television or radio.

Use of the present-day internet requires two forms of literacy. First, because so much of the information is in text form, being able to read (and write) is essential. Second, the user must be able to comprehend browser functions in order to navigate the web. These requirements are generally beyond the capabilities of preschool and younger children. While popular web sites for preschoolers exist, it is generally assumed that young children use them with the help of a parent or older sibling. Independent use of the internet begins at about 6 years and, with the help of school instruction, steadily increases with age. Unlike television, then, the impact of the present-day internet is mostly on older, school-age children.

Moreover, use of the internet requires focal attention and overt participation. Consequently, the internet is not likely to be time-shared with other activities to the same extent as television, albeit there is some evidence that adults time-share computer use with TV viewing (Media Metrix 1999). Because the internet requires greater attention, knowledge, and participation, we believe that users are less likely to employ the internet to relax and relieve stress, as we know television is used (e.g., Anderson, Collins, Schmitt, and Jacobvitz 1996). For all these reasons, including literacy requirements, the necessity of active attention and overt participation, and the typical lack of high-quality moving images and sound, the present-day internet continues to be substantially less popular with children than television (Rideout, Foehr, Roberts, and Brodie 1999). For example, as of September 1999, more children were exposed to Pokémon in the first five minutes of the Pokémon television program than in a full month of visits to the Pokémon web site (analysis of commercial ratings data by Horst Stipp of NBC, personal communication, November 19, 1999). This same situation likely holds in 2002, as this chapter is being written.

All this is changing as internet technology and content evolve. The most obvious forthcoming change is medium convergence. Radio is already widely available on the internet, and eventually television will be, too. As display technologies improve, television becomes a digital medium, and the bandwidth of transmission to the home increases, television will be delivered to the home as part of the internet. When television becomes a subset of internet content, what we know about the impact of television on children will be directly relevant to understanding the impact of the internet as a whole. In addition, as user interfaces become easier, incorporating speech recognition and movement capture, increasing numbers of preschoolers and toddlers will use the internet.

In the remainder of this chapter, we discuss some major areas of concern about television's impact on children, briefly review what we know about TV's actual effects, and speculate how the internet may differ from television. We will consider social behavior, time displacement, cognitive development and educational achievement, and health-related behaviors.

Social Behavior

Aggressive Behavior

One of the most common concerns expressed about mass media is that portrayals of violence induce aggressive behavior. This concern has been, at various times, voiced about dime novels, crime magazines, comic books, radio, movies, and television. In fact, the impact of violent content is the most heavily researched topic on the effects of television on children. This research has produced a near consensus in the academic community—that television violence plays at least a small causal role in aggressive behavior (for reviews see Bushman and Huesmann 2001; Comstock 1991; Huston and Wright 1997).

Violent television has this effect through several different mechanisms. For example, children tend to emulate attractive figures, including television heroes, as they engage in violent behavior. Children also construct enduring mental schemas, based on television viewing, about how to interpret and respond to situations where aggression is one possible behavior. Additionally, through repetition, children become both pleasurably aroused by and desensitized to violence.

There is little doubt that television violence, conveyed through rapidly paced editing and exciting music, is both attractive and arousing to children. It is not clear, however, that violence, per se, is the source of the attraction, or whether the attraction comes from the fact that violence is ordinarily conveyed as rapidly paced action sequences (see Huston and Wright 1989). In our research, we found that production features associated with action sequences are generally associated with increased attention to television at all ages (Schmitt, Anderson, and Collins 1999).

Taken together, the research indicates that television violence is exciting and arousing to children and adults. Consequently, broadcasters provide violent programming because it often attracts and holds large audiences. Numerous content analyses indicate that violence does, in fact, inhabit a substantial amount of television programming watched by children (e.g., National Television Violence Study 1997).

To our knowledge, no research has established the frequency with which child internet users are exposed to violent content. As we see it, violence on the internet comes in two main forms. One form is audiovisual games with violent themes. The second is text-based discussion groups and web sites that may directly or indirectly encourage violent behavior. Understanding the impact of these two forms will likely require substantially different research approaches.

Many children and adults use internet gaming sites to play violent games online. Some of these sites allow players to establish online connections with each other to play commercially purchased computer games. Others allow players to download software necessary for playing games. These games share many of the graphic audiovisual components of violent television content, so there is no reason to suppose that these games would have less impact on young players than violent television does.

Some games make the player a virtual perpetrator of violent acts. This "first-person shooter" perspective provides a substantially different experience from television violence, where the viewer usually watches the action from an external, or third-person, perspective. The available research suggests that violent audiovisual games have behavioral consequences consistent with those of violent television and that first-person shooter games are especially arousing and may have a greater impact than television (see Calvert 1999 for a review). As first-person shooter games become increasingly realistic with improved graphics, sound, tactual feedback, and a sense of virtual reality, the possibility exists that murdering a game character will experientially become much like real murder. The consequences for desensitization toward real violence are obvious.

In our view, text-based web sites and discussion groups that are focused on violence have no other media parallel (magazines such as *Soldier of Fortune* come closest). However, they have the greatest potential for producing real-world violent behavior in the short term. We speculate that socially alienated teenage boys, who are already predisposed to appreciating violent messages, are the children most likely to frequent such sites. Furthermore, these discussion groups and web sites, as opposed to those obviously associated with fantasy play, are more likely to involve real-world issues and potential real-world targets of violence. Most dangerously, they may glorify violent acts and foster hate for particular groups. What makes such text-based sites most compelling, we believe, is that they allow lonely and alienated teenagers to believe that they are part of an extended social group. Consequently, they may believe that they have social support for real-world violent behavior. Additionally, such groups can directly or indirectly (by identifying other relevant sites) provide instruction for obtaining and using weapons, constructing bombs, and identifying targets. We consider research on such sites and the impact of these sites on the children who frequent them to be of the highest priority.

Prosocial Content

Although much of the historical focus on television has concerned its negative impact, there is clear evidence that television content can have a positive effect as well. One kind of positive impact is due to prosocial content. This is content that, while not necessarily explicitly educational, models developmentally appropriate social behavior and teaches useful and moral social lessons. Such lessons can include positive exposure to a wide variety of ethnic groups, alternatives to aggression as a response to conflict, positive ways to deal with issues like dating, and many others. Research on the impact of prosocial content has generally shown that children absorb prosocial lessons and that prosocial content positively influences behavior (for reviews, see Comstock 1991; Huston and Wright 1997). Such effects are potentially of long duration. For example, we found that teens were less likely to endorse aggressive solutions to situations involving stress and conflict if they had been regular preschool viewers of programs with prosocial content such as *Mister Rogers' Neighborhood* and *Sesame Street* (Anderson et al. 2001).

As with violence, we are not aware of any research that documents children's exposure to prosocial content on the internet. While there may be audiovisual games that feature prosocial lessons, they do not appear to be as widely available or used compared to those with predominantly violent content. It is more likely that text-based discussion groups and web sites provide the greatest opportunity for exposure to prosocial content. Such content, especially if moderated by adults with appropriate education and experience, can in principle have a beneficial effect on children.

Sexual Content

Due to the sensitivities involved in research with children, there has been relatively little research on the impact of televised sexual portrayals (for a review, see Malmuth and Impett 2001). It is commonly supposed, however, that as a result of such portrayals, children become more interested in sexual content and perhaps are more likely to engage in sexual activity. Content analyses indicate that sexual innuendo on television is common, while explicit portrayals of sex acts are relatively rare. Whether the sex act is portrayed or implied, however, there is rarely any discussion of the potential for pregnancy or sexually transmitted diseases (Kunkel et al. 1999).

Even the casual internet user can be accidentally exposed to pornography. A child's innocent search entry such as "girls" or "boys" can lead straight to explicit pornographic sites. The currently widespread practice of "page-jacking" and other technical tricks can redirect the user to sites, including pornography sites, far removed from those desired. Erasing click histories can prevent the user from backing out of the site. At this point it is not known how frequently child internet users accidentally or deliberately gain access to such sites or how these sites affect them.

The internet presents the possibility of providing discussion groups and educational resources with respect to children's concerns about sex. We are not aware of any research evaluation concerning the impact, positive or negative, of such resources. However, the Internet could potentially provide valuable advice and information concerning sex, social pressures with respect to sexual activity, and health issues including depression, substance abuse, and others.

Cognitive Development and Education

Discussions about the impact of television on cognitive development and education have centered on time displacement, television's formal structure, or television's content.

Time Displacement

It is commonly assumed that if children weren't watching television, they would be doing something more valuable such as reading. Although considerable research has addressed this issue, remarkably little evidence supports this assumption. The arrival of television primarily displaced time spent watching movies, listening to radio drama, and reading comic books (see Comstock 1991). These functionally similar activities have not, by and large, been considered more valuable than watching TV. Furthermore, there is no consistent evidence that television has displaced activities such as doing homework or reading, in part because these activities can be time-shared with television viewing. As Robert Hornik (1981) noted, "there was not much reading before television and there is not much now" (p. 202).

It is not yet clear what activities are being displaced by time on the internet. Because the internet is functionally most like reading, talking on the telephone, and playing non-internet computer games, these are the areas most likely to be immediately affected. Additionally, some time is likely taken from television viewing. At this point, time displacement does not seem to us to be a major problem for the impact of the internet on children.

Form

A consistent concern about television is that its rapid visual changes may have deleterious effects on children, for example, shortening their attention span (e.g., Singer 1980; Winn 1977). In contrast, some have argued that television's formal features may actually improve aspects of attention and cognition (e.g., Salomon 1979). A detailed review of the research literature provides no consistent support for the proposition that television's forms or pace shortens children's ability to deploy or sustain attention (Anderson and Collins 1988). In fact, there is some evidence that TV can be used to explicitly teach attentional skills (Salomon 1979). Neisser (1997), furthermore, has suggested that the generational increase in IQ scores (known as the Flynn effect) is primarily due to increases in spatial skills. He suggests that children's use of electronic media (primarily television) may have contributed to this trend. This has not yet been verified by systematic research.

There has not yet been an extensive analysis of the predominant forms of the internet (analogous to cuts, visual movement, zooms, and the like). On a typical web page there may be local repetitive animation and perhaps sound effects. Otherwise, the forms tend to be those of illustrated text. Over time, however, the internet user navigates the web using hyperlinks. These hyperlink transitions are probably the most unique and internet-typical form. It is very likely that extensive use of hypermedia by children may influence their cognition, but just how is not clear. The degree to which hyperlinks are followed according to a preset goal may enhance thinking skills in much the same way that extensive use of an encyclopedia or major library has in the past. Pursuing nonlinear paths through the web, as a user becomes distracted by unexpected and interesting web pages as well as nonfunctioning links, may provide a somewhat different and less enhancing experience. Whether extensive experience with such nonlinear information will affect thinking skills or creativity is completely unknown and not easily predictable from research on television.

With respect to computer games, there is somewhat more evidence that certain visual-motor and spatial skills may be enhanced by extensive experience playing these games (e.g., Greenfield, Brannon, and Lohr 1994). This is supported by brain-imaging research showing activation of brain areas involved in spatial cognition when playing games such as *Tetris* (Haier et al. 1992). Insofar as such games are part of children's internet experience, a long-term enhancement of spatial cognition may result.

Content

Curriculum-based television programs are, in fact, educational. Consider the program *Sesame Street*, which has an ambitious preschool curriculum and is one of the longest-running children's programs. While the original assessments of *Sesame Street* indicated that children learned the intended content (Ball and Bogatz 1970; Bogatz and Ball 1971), there was some controversy as to how general these effects were and to what extent they were mediated by parental involvement during viewing (Cook et al. 1975). Research has found, however, that the program substantially improves children's vocabulary (Rice, Huston, Truglio, and Wright 1990; Rice and Woodsmall 1988) and readiness for school (Zill, Davies, and Daly 1994). In the long term, preschool viewing of *Sesame Street* is positively related to high school grades in English, math, and science, amount of leisure book reading in high school, and participation in extra-curricular academic and leadership activities. These effects are found even after statistically adjusting for a variety of demographic factors such as parent education (Anderson et al. 2001). While other educational programs have not received the same amount of research attention, numerous evaluations indicate a substantial positive impact. A two-year longitudinal study of preschool viewers of *Blue's Clues*, for example, showed increases in a variety of cognitive skills compared to children who were not exposed to the program (Anderson et al. 2000).

On the negative side, several investigations suggest that violent TV content may have a deleterious impact on children's education. A variety of studies have found that violence viewing by children is associated with greater impulsivity, problems sustaining attention, and poorer evaluations by teachers (for reviews, see Anderson and Collins 1988; Huston and Wright 1997). In a study following children from age 5 years through high school, preschool violence viewing was associated with poorer high school grades and less participation in extracurricular activities (Anderson et al. 2001).

Although television content has had a demonstrable impact on education, internet content will probably have an even greater impact. First, television is not easily used as a research tool directed at a particular topic. In contrast, the internet is rapidly becoming a research tool *par excellence*. Companies such as Sesame Workshop, Scholastica, and

TERC have developed commercial educational sites, and thousands of educational sites have been developed by universities, museums, government agencies, health groups, school systems, and other nonprofit agencies. A child interested in insects or space exploration, for example, can find many informative web sites. Currently, American children are being taught to use the internet in school, so that they have early exposure to sites with educational value. Eventually, using the internet as an educational tool will be at least as common among Americans as using the dictionary or encyclopedia. In fact, teenagers aged 13 to 17 report that their most frequent activity online is schoolwork (Turow 1999). Because the information will be in audiovisual as well as textual forms, the potential impact is likely to be even greater than tools such as encyclopedias in book form. In addition, the internet will increasingly provide interactive educational simulations that will enable or enhance children's understanding of dynamic systems such as hydrodynamics, physiology, or economics that are otherwise difficult to convey.

Like television, of course, the vast amount of content on the internet is not primarily educational. As commercial sites provide the most attractive and entertaining content, many children predictably gravitate to those sites rather than to educational sites. If the non-educational sites are violent, negative consequences are predictable. In addition, because the internet is distributed in nature, with no central vetting authority, there is nothing to prevent web sites from providing misleading, wrong, and inappropriate information. Examples are sites that present religious creation myths as "science" and sites that claim the Holocaust of World War II never happened. The potential for miseducation of children by the internet is great.

Future Research

It is apparent that the internet may have a large impact on education, both positive and negative. As television converges with the internet, moreover, all the impact of television on education will become a part of the overall impact of the internet. Unlike television, however, there is almost no research on the impact of the internet on cognitive and educational development. All of the hypotheses applicable to television, including time displacement, form effects, and content effects are or will be applicable to the internet. However, the internet has potential effects having to do with hypertext, interactivity, and two- or *n*-way communication that are fundamentally different from television.

Health

There is substantial evidence that time spent with television is positively related to obesity. Causal factors include snack advertising and the sedentary nature of TV viewing (e.g., Dietz and Gortmaker 1993). Time with the internet may produce this same result, insofar as the time is sedentary and there may be heavy doses of snack advertising on children's sites.

Researching the Impact of the Internet

After about forty years of television research, we have a substantial understanding of the medium, its use, and its effects. That research has informed public policy and has helped in the creation of programs designed to benefit children. Research on the internet's use and impact is as yet minimal and will require a wide variety of approaches similar to those used in television research. These approaches may include content analysis, experimental laboratory investigations, field studies, and longitudinal research. The substantive areas of investigation will also be analogous to those of television, including patterns of internet use, violence, attention and cognitive engagement, cognitive development and education, and health behaviors, among others. The substantive and methodological problems in doing such research, however, will be somewhat different.

Consider the formidable problems presented for content analysis. Because there are so many web sites (and sometimes widely varying web pages within sites), serious methodological work has to be done just to figure out how to appropriately sample internet content. It is not obvious, for example, how one would go about determining what proportion of web content likely to be seen by children is violent, sexual, prosocial, or educational in nature. In contrast, content analyses of television, as a result of television's relatively limited and centralized nature, have given us fairly good ideas of such proportions. Additionally, the web presents a huge amount of content that does not easily fit into the kinds of categories used in television studies. The many personal web sites (featuring family histories, children's drawings, and links to other favorite web sites) are just one example.

Experimental laboratory- or school-based investigations are clearly manageable for gaining an initial understanding of internet use and impact. Web pages are easier to create for experimental purposes than is credible television programming, and we expect that early progress in understanding internet impact will come from controlled experiments using relatively small samples of children. Experiments can examine in detail what aspects of web sites children of various ages find most interesting and understandable, and they can determine why children are attracted to some sites and not others. Controlled experiments can also examine short-term consequences of web use of various kinds, for example, the impact of violent content on behavior immediately following an internet session.

Necessary field research includes children's time use studies in order to determine what activities are being displaced by time spent on the internet. Additionally, detailed analyses of actual internet use and content analyses of sites visited by children are essential. As the medium develops, it is important to know how much time children of various ages are spending in e-mail correspondence, chat groups, news groups, entertainment sites, educational sites, and so on. Studies of children at risk for influence by hate groups (socially alienated teens, for example) are of considerable importance.

Paralleling some of the most important television research, prospective longitudinal studies of internet use and long-term outcome will be essential. One of the problems with such studies, however, is the rapidly changing nature of the internet as an information and entertainment medium for children. Taking into account the secular changes in the medium and the way it is used may require complicated overlapping panel designs so that the effects of changes in the internet itself can be considered in terms of child outcome. Such studies are expensive.

As with research on children and television, there is no certain source of funding for research on children and the internet. While the National

Institutes of Health (especially the National Institute of Mental Health) and the National Science Foundation have over the years provided sporadic funding for research on children and television, there have never been regular review panels devoted to children and media. As a consequence, grant reviewers usually have no background in children and media, and relatively few media-focused proposals have been funded. Consequently, it has been difficult for researchers to develop substantial and consistent programs of research on children and media.

Nevertheless, with funding from a wide variety of sources including foundations, government grants, and industry, the media research community has, over about forty years, made real progress in understanding children's use of television and its impact. The research has also been a significant factor in developing and improving such groundbreaking and successful educational television programs as *Sesame Street* and *Blue's Clues* (Anderson 1998; Fisch and Truglio 2001). We can hope that in the future funding for consistent and long-term programs of research will be available for understanding the impact of the internet. It would be a shame if forty years have to elapse before we can understand what we are doing to our children.

Conclusions

Using research on television as a guideline, we have speculated about the impact of the internet on children. At this time, unlike television, we see little impact of any kind on children under six years of age. On the other hand, this is likely to change as television merges with the internet and as user interfaces become easier for children to use.

We see plausible reasons for concern about the internet's negative impact on aggressive and violent behavior. We also see a huge potential for the internet in providing prosocial content, educational content, and health information. It is an open question as to whether children's experience with nonlinear aspects of internet hypertext, topic searches, and navigation will affect fundamental aspects of cognitive development and modes of thought.

Finally, it is not clear to us how the internet may affect social behavior and social cognition (how children come to understand the nature of other people's motivations and inner life). While television can be an isolating experience for children, it is often used as an occasion for family and peer social interactions (Alexander, Ryan, and Munoz 1984). Because more focused attention is required, internet uses as compared to watching television, is a more solitary experience and may therefore be more isolating (perhaps somewhat like book reading). Initial research on family use of the internet was interpreted along these lines (Kraut et al. 1998). On the other hand, internet use can be a highly social (if primarily textual) experience when used for interactive communication and e-mail, and later research suggests that the initial research may have overstated the isolating aspect (Subrahmanyam, Kraut, Greenfield, and Gross 2000). There are surely significant consequences for social development, but just what those consequences are also awaits future research.

On the whole, we believe that as we gain knowledge through research, society will find ways to enhance the positive and minimize the negative impact of the internet on children as is beginning to happen with television. Educational programs based on research have been commercially successful (e.g., *Blue's Clues*; see Anderson 1998), and appropriate regulation (e.g., Children's Television Act of 1990; Federal Communications Commission 1991; 1996) has begun to reduce the amount of harmful programming in favor of programming designed to be beneficial (Schmitt 1999). Eventually, we expect the same societal wisdom will be applied to the internet. But the form that wisdom will eventually take will, we hope, be informed by a research-based understanding.

References

Alexander, A., M. Ryan, and P. Munoz. 1984. "Creating a Learning Context: Investigations on the Interactions of Siblings during Television Viewing." *Critical Studies in Mass Communication* 1: 345–364.

Anderson, D. R. 1998. "Educational Television Is Not an Oxymoron." *Annals of Public Policy Research* 557: 24–38.

Anderson, D. R., L. F. Alwitt, E. P. Lorch, and S. R. Levin. 1979. "Watching Children Watch Television." In G. Hale and M. Lewis (eds.), *Attention and Cognitive Development*. New York: Plenum.

Anderson, D. R., J. Bryant, A. Wilder, A. Santomero, M. Williams, and A. M. Crawley. 2000. "Researching *Blue's Clues*: Viewing Behavior and Impact." *Media Psychology* 2(2): 179–194.

Anderson, D. R., and P. A. Collins. 1988. *The Influence on Children's Education: The Effects of Television on Cognitive Development*. Washington, D.C.: U.S. Department of Education.

Anderson, D. R., P. A. Collins, K. L. Schmitt, and R. S. Jacobvitz. 1996. "Stressful Life Events and Television Viewing." *Communication Research* 23: 243–260.

Anderson, D. R., and D. E. Field. 1991. "Online and Offline Assessment of the Television Audience." In D. Zillman and J. Bryant (eds.), *Responding to the Screen: Perception and Reaction Processes* (pp. 199–216). Hillsdale, N.J.: Erlbaum.

Anderson, D. R., A. C. Huston, K. L. Schmitt, D. L. Linebarger, and J. C. Wright. 2001. "Early Childhood Television Viewing and Adolescent Behavior." *Monographs of the Society for Research in Child Development* 66, no. 1.

Ball, S., and G. A. Bogatz. 1970. *The First Year of* Sesame Street: *An Evaluation*. Princeton, N.J.: Educational Testing Service.

Bechtel, R., C. Achelpohl, and R. Akers. 1972. "Correlates between Observed Behavior and Questionnaire Responses on Television Viewing." In E. A. Rubinstein, G. A. Comstock, and J. P. Murray (eds.), *Television and Social Behavior (Vol. 4): Television in Day-to-Day Life: Patterns of Use* (pp. 274–344). Washington, D.C.: U.S. Government Printing Office.

Bogatz, G. A., and S. Ball. 1971. *The Second Year of* Sesame Street: *A Continuing Evaluation*. Princeton, N.J.: Educational Testing Service.

Bushman, B. L., and L. R. Huesmann. 2001. "Effects of Television on Aggression." In D. G. Singer and J. L. Singer (eds.), *Handbook of Children and the Media*. Thousand Oaks, Calif.: Sage.

Calvert, S. 1999. *Children's Journeys through the Information Age*. Boston: McGraw-Hill.

Chandrasekaran, R., and J. Schwartz. 1997. "White House Opposes Censorship of Internet; But Support of '96 Decency Act is Unchanged. *Washington Post* (June 17): D01.

Collins, P. A. 1993. The Development of Children's Attention to Television at Home: The Role of Commercial Content Boundaries. Ph.D. diss., University of Massachusetts, Amherst.

Comstock, G. (with H. Paik). 1991. *Television and the American Child*. San Diego, Calif.: Academic Press.

Cook, T. D., H. Appleton, R. F. Conner, A. Shaffer, G. Tamkin, and S. J. Weber. 1975. *Sesame Street Revisited*. New York: Russell Sage.

Dietz, W. H., and S. L. Gortmaker. 1993. "TV or Not TV: Fat Is the Question." *Pediatrics* 75: 807–812.

Federal Communications Commission. 1991. "Policies and Rules Concerning Children's Television Programming." *Federal Communications Commission Record* 6: 2111–2127.

Federal Communications Commission. 1996. "Policies and Rules Concerning Children's Television Programming: Revision of Programming Policies for Television Broadcast Stations." MM Docket No. 93–48.

Fisch, S., and R. T. Truglio. 2001. *G Is for Growing: Thirty Years of Research on* Sesame Street. Mahwah, N.J.: Erlbaum.

Greenfield, P. M., C. Brannon, and D. Lohr. 1994. Two-Dimensional Representation of Movement through Three-Dimensional Space: The Role of Video Game Experience." *Journal of Applied Developmental Psychology* 15: 87–103.

Haier, R. J., B. V. Jr. Siegal, A. MacLachan, E. Soderling, S. Lotenberg, and M. S. Buchsbaum. 1992. "Regional Glucose Metabolic Changes after Learning a Complex Visuospatial/Motor Task: A Positron Emission Tomographic Study." *Brain Research*, 570(1–2): 134–143.

Hornik, R. 1981. "Out-of-School Television and Schooling: Hypotheses and Methods." *Review of Educational Research* 51: 193–214.

Huston, A. C., and J. C. Wright. 1989. "The Forms of Television and the Child Viewer." In G. Comstock (ed.), *Public Communication and Behavior* (Vol. 2, pp. 103–159). Orlando, Fla.: Academic Press.

Huston, A. C., and J. C. Wright. 1997. "Mass Media and Children's Development." In W. Damon, I. Sigel, and K. A. Reminger (eds.), *Handbook of Child Psychology, Vol. 4: Child Psychology in Practice* (5th ed.). New York: Wiley.

Kelly, K. 2000. "False Promise." *U.S. News & World Report* (September 25): 48–55.

Kraut, R., M. Patterson, V. Lundmark, S. Kiesler, T. Mukhopadhyay, and W. Scherlis. 1998. "Internet Paradox: A Social Technology That Reduces Involvement and Psychological Well-being? *American Psychologist* 53: 1017–1031.

Kunkel, D., K. M. Cope, W. M. Farinola, E. Biely, E. Rollin, and E. Donnerstein. 1999. "Sex on TV: Content and Context." A biennial report to the Henry J. Kaiser Family Foundation. Menlo Park, Calif.: Henry J. Kaiser Family Foundation.

Malmuth, N. M., and E. A. Impett. 2001. In D. G. Singer & J. L. Singer (eds.), *Handbook of Children and the Media*. Thousand Oaks, Calif.: Sage.

Media Metrix. 1999. Simultaneous Use of PC and Television Growing Rapidly. (Press release, July 12). New York: Media Metrix.

Neisser, U. 1997. "Rising Scores on Intelligence Tests." *American Scientist* 85: 440–447.

National Television Violence Study, vol. 1. 1997. Beverly Hills, Calif.: Sage.

Rice, M. L., A. C. Huston, R. Truglio, and J. C. Wright. 1990. "Words from *Sesame Street*: Learning Vocabulary While Viewing." *Developmental Psychology* 26: 421–428.

Rice, M. L., and L. Woodsmall. 1988. "Lessons from Television: Children's Word Learning when Viewing." *Child Development* 59: 420–429.

Richards, J. E., and K. Cronise. 2000. "Extended Visual Fixation in the Early Preschool Years: Look Duration, Heart Rate Changes, and Attentional Inertia." *Child Development* 71(3): 602–620.

Rideout, V. J., U. G. Foehr, D. F. Roberts, and M. Brodie. 1999. "Kids and Media @ the New Millenium: A Comprehensive National Analysis of Children's Media Use." Menlo Park: The Henry J. Kaiser Family Foundation.

Salomon, G. 1979. *Interaction of Media, Cognition, and Learning.* San Francisco: Jossey-Bass.

Schmitt, K. L. 1999. *The Three-Hour Rule: Is It Living Up to Expectations?* Report No. 30. Philadelphia: University of Pennsylvania, Annenberg Public Policy Center.

Schmitt, K. L., D. R. Anderson, and P. A. Collins. 1999. "Form and Content: Looking at Visual Features of Television." *Developmental Psychology* 35: 1156–1167.

Singer, J. 1980. "The Power and Limitations of Television: A Cognitive Affective Analysis." In P. H. Tannenbaum and R. Abeles (eds.), *The Entertainment Functions of Television* (pp. 31–65). Hillsdale, N.J.: Erlbaum.

Strasburger, V. C. 1995. *Adolescents and the Media: Medical and Psychological Impact.* Thousand Oaks, Calif.: Sage.

Subrahmanyam, K. D., R. E. Kraut, P. M. Greenfield, and E. F. Gross. "The Impact of Home Computer Use on Children's Activities and Development." *Children and Technology: The Future of Children* 10(2): 123–144.

Telecommunications Act of 1996, Publ. No. 104-104, 110, STAT. 56, 1996.

Turow, J. 1999. *The Internet and the Family: The View from Parents. The View from the Press* (Report Series No. 27). Philadelphia: The Annenberg Public Policy Center.

Wartella, E., and N. Jennings. 2000. "Children and Computers: New Technology—Old Concerns." *The Future of Children: Children and Computer Technology* 10(2): 31–43.

Wartella, E., B. O'Keefe, and R. Scantlin. 2000. *Children and Interactive Media: A Compendium of Current Research and Directions for the Future.* New York: The Markle Foundation.

Wartella, E., and B. Reeves. 1985. "Historical Trends in Research on Children and the Media: 1900–1960." *Journal of Communication* 35: 118–133.

Winn, M. 1977. *The Plug-In Drug.* New York: Viking Press.

Zill, N., E. Davies, and M. Daly. 1994. *Viewing of Sesame Street by Preschool Children in the United States and Its Relationship to School Readiness.* Rockville, Md.: Westat.

5

Television and the Internet

Ellen Seiter

Claims that the Internet will revolutionize communications (as well as education, work life, and domestic leisure) are now commonplace. Yet there is a danger that computer communications—and by this I mean their uses, the discourses surrounding computers and the Internet, and research about them—will substantially buttress hierarchies of class, race, and gender. One healthy corrective is to recognize the many parallels between television and the Internet, and incorporate the insights of television audience research into the uses of technologies in the domestic sphere, the articulation of gender identities through popular genres, the complexity of individuals' motivations to seek out media and the variety of possible interpretations of media technologies and media forms. Ethnography can offer a rich context of understanding the motivations and disincentives to using computers: an important research topic in a world in which non-users are likely to be labeled recalcitrants, technophobes, or slackers.

I will argue that it is what John Corner has called the "particularly ambitious form of interdisciplinarity" of media studies—its attempted, if not always successful, merging of criticism and sociology—that holds a unique promise as a model for studying new media and new technologies (Corner 1995). Most academic research on digital technologies is currently being produced by departments of library and information science, schools of business and management, education schools, and computer science departments. This research tends to emphasize information seeking and statistical patterns of usage, while ignoring perceptions about computers, the cultural contexts in which they are used, and the images, sounds, and words to be found on computer screens. We need a means of touching upon the form and content of the Internet as well as the practices and motivations of computer users. We need to view the Internet from the perspective of its many parallels with broadcast media, maintaining a healthy skepticism about its novel qualities as a communication medium. We need to be alert to the ways that stereotyped notions of the audience are constructing a discourse around the Internet that privileges white, middle-class males.

In this chapter I begin by reviewing the ways that familiar forms of television are migrating to computer screens, while television, for its part, is busily promoting the use of the Internet by television viewers. These connections between television and computers are taking place at the level of (1) corporations, as Microsoft attempts to enter the mass-market entertainment business by investing in media firms; (2) technology, as computers with television tuners and video stream capabilities become more commonplace; and (3) at the level of form and content, as familiar forms and genres from television, radio and newspapers are tried out on the Internet, many of them sponsored by such giants of television advertising as Procter & Gamble and Nabisco. In the second section, I survey qualitative research on the use of computers in domestic settings among families and trace the similarities between these findings and research on television watching in the home. I argue that television audience research is well positioned to help us understand the heavily gendered use of computers in domestic space. At the same time, research on computer use may help to push television audience research to a more thorough investigation of the connections between domestic and public uses of media and to think more about television viewers as workers—not only as family members or individual consumers. In the third section, I look at the various work issues related to computer use, especially the increase of "telecommuting" and its implications for the study of communication technologies in the domestic sphere.

5.1   Television on Computers

Television sets and computer terminals will certainly merge, cohabit, and coexist in the next century. In 1996, computers with built-in television tuners became available as well as set top boxes to allow Internet access via television sets. Because of the proliferation of television sets throughout many homes, television sets and computers are increasingly likely to share space in the same room. Many people (most of my students, it seems) have become adept at watching television while using the computer. As personal computers proliferate in middle-class homes, the boundaries between leisure and work time, public and private space, promise to become increasingly blurred (Kling 1996). As the Internet develops from a research-oriented tool of elites to a commercial mass medium, resemblances between Web sites and television programming will increase.

While the Internet can be used to organize users around political matters in ways unimaginable through broadcast television or small format video, it seems increasingly likely that commercialization of the Web will discourage activism in favor of consumerism and the duplication of familiar forms of popular mass media, such as magazines, newspapers, and television programs (Morris and Ogan 1996). The World Wide Web reproduces some popular genres from television (and radio) broadcasting: sports, science fiction, home shopping clubs, news magazines, and even cyber-soap operas with daily postings of the serialized lives of its characters. In fact, the most popular Web sites—science fiction, soap operas, and "talk" shows—represent the same genres that form the topics of some of the best television audience research (see, for example, Gillespie [1995], Jenkins [1992], Press [1991], Shattuc [1997]). The much-publicized presence of pornography on the Internet also parallels the spectacular success of that genre on home video.

The prevalence of television material on the Web confirms the insight provided by media ethnographies of the importance of conversation about television in everyday life and suggests that television plays a central role as common currency, a lingua franca. Television fans are a formidable presence on the Internet: in chatrooms where fans can discuss their favorite programs or television stars; on Web sites where fan fiction can be posted; as the presumed market for sales of television tie-in merchandise. The dissemination of knowledge of the programming language for the creation of Web sites (or home pages) unleashed thousands of die-hard television fans eager to display their television knowledge—and provide free publicity for television producers. Hundreds of painstakingly crafted home pages have been devoted to old television shows; for example, one site devoted to the 1970s Hanna-Barbera cartoon *Johnny Quest* provides plot summaries and still frames of every *Johnny Quest* episode ever made. In fact the Web is a jamboree of television material, with thousands of official and unofficial sites constituting television publicity, histories (with plots summaries of every episode ever made), cable and broadcast schedules, and promotional contests. Search engines turn up roughly three times as many references to television as they do for topics such as architecture, chemistry, or feminism. Apparently television was one of the first topics people turned to when trying to think of something to interest a large and anonymous group of potential readers—other Net users.

It would be a mistake, however, to see the rise of television material on the Internet exclusively from a fan or amateur perspective, because the connections between television and computer firms are proliferating. The association between television and the Internet has been heavily promoted at the corporate level by access providers eager to lure as sponsors companies that invest heavily in television advertising, and by others seeking sources and inspiration for the new Internet "programming" (Schiller 1997). The software giant Microsoft has acquired stakes in media entertainment companies, developed an interactive television network, and looked to television and film for the basis for entertainment "software" with a more "universal"—i.e., mass market—appeal. Microsoft's partnership with NBC to form the 24-hour news cable channel and online news and information service, MSNBC, is the most obvious example. Microsoft also has joint ventures with the cable channel Black Entertainment Television (BET) and Spielberg's company DreamWorks SKG, and Paramount Television Group, leading to speculation that Microsoft is "morphing into a media company for the new millennium" (Caruso 1996). Disney, now the owner of the television network ABC, is also one of the biggest interactive media producers in the world. America Online, the commercial internet and e-mail access provider, has followed a vigorous commercial strategy, which includes extensive coverage of television in all its familiar publicity aspects as well as encouragement of fan activity, to build a broad base of subscribers and to court advertisers. The ACNielsen company, the television industry leader in audience ratings, has begun producing reports on Internet Users.

In 1996, Microsoft made the association to broadcast media explicit when it launched a revised version of its online service whose browser interface sends users straight to an "On Stage" section with six different channels, each hosting "shows" (Helm 1996). The goal was to give users a better idea of what to expect from each program by standardizing its offerings, a strategy strikingly familiar to the history of early radio and television (Boddy 1990; McChesney 1996). Video-streaming, already commonplace on the World Wide Web, has been implemented on Web sites such as CNN's to replay the "News Story of the Week." Advertising industry analysts predict that animated advertisements on the Web will dominate in the years ahead.

Hardware and software manufacturers are scrambling to secure the market for sales to noncomputer owners of devices that will convert the plain old television set to an Internet browser, or win the battle between the high-definition TV sets favored by the electronics industry or the digital television/monitors favored by the computer industry. The computer position is that "consumers would rather have a cheaper box that would be either a computer monitor or a TV than have the less complicated, high-definition-TV set that the consumer-electronics industry favors" (Auletta 1997, 77). Microsoft is exerting considerable muscle in political lobbying and industry influence over issues of digital television (Bank and Takahashi 1997). Gates's decision to purchase WebTV for 425 million dollars and to announce this decision at the annual convention of the National Association of Broadcasters is a significant example of this.

The relatively high penetration rates of home computers among the professional classes (including writers about computer issues) often give the false impression that everyone has a computer. The majority of homes do not have a PC, but they do have a television. Therefore, the computer industry continues to eye television greedily as a future market. Microsoft has entered the cable television business, exploring set-top boxes and television programming; while Sega has developed Net Link for use with its video game system as a Browser. Sony and Phillips Consumer Electronics have formed a partnership to sell set-top boxes with a wireless keyboard and a printer adapter that can be plugged in to existing television sets and a telephone line for Internet access via the WebTV network. Mitsubishi also plans to sell a set top box for use on the "DiamondWeb television" system. Sanyo and Samsung are also building Internet access into their TVs for the Japanese market. Sanyo's 28-inch model features a double window that allows viewers to watch television and use the Internet at the same time. Samsung's product features a television remote control that can take over some of the data entry features of the computer keyboard (Loeb 1996).

The extent to which Microsoft is explicitly using television and its mass appeal as a model for future endeavors was made explicit in a recent article by Ken Auletta about Nathan Myhrvold of Microsoft. Microsoft realizes that "the skills that made Microsoft successful in software—technical proficiency, rapid response—are not transferable to what the company calls the content business, which relies more on a bottom-up rather than a top-down model" (Auletta 1997, p. 76). The fact that personal computers are stuck at a penetration rate of about 36% has led computer industry people to eye television jealously and to try to develop ways to link perceptions about computers to entertainment. At Interval Research Corporation, the think tank started by Microsoft's co-founder Paul Allen, the Explorers market research group has adopted the strategy of using television—a universally accepted domestic technology—as a model for the development of future communication technologies (Ireland and Johnson 1995).

For its part, television plays a crucial role as publicizer of the Web and computer use. Television programs are already filled with references to computers and the Internet that dramatize the importance of the new technologies and attempt to play a major role in educating the public about new media. Television's appetite for novelty, as well as its fears about losing viewers to computer screens, make computers one of its predictable obsessions. Silverstone and Hirsch are on the right track to point to the dual nature of communication technologies such as television sets and computers: "as quintessentially novel objects, and therefore as the embodiment of our desires for the new" which simultaneously act as "transmitters of all the images and information that fuel those desires" (1992, p. 3).

Computer references have gone far beyond the television character staring into the computer screen—although this long-standing movie cliché has been solidly established as a convention of television drama. Television commercials refer viewers to Web sites; call-in programs now ask that e-mail be submitted, as do television shows from *Meet the Press* to Nickelodeon's children's line up. MTV runs a daily program, *Yak Live*, where e-mails (reflecting the striking banality of much chatroom conversation) scroll across the screen below the music videos, Television news shows, especially docudramas and news magazines, have become so enamored of reproducing e-mail and Internet communications (which are both easy to capture on camera and lend a feeling of novelty and a sense of connection to the real world of viewers), that the practice has become a copyright/privacy concern among computer specialists (Lesch 1994).

Online communications have been used both to support and to attack television shows and their sponsors. Television networks are exploiting e-mail and Internet communications with audiences to gain feedback on script or character changes, to compile mailing lists for licensed products relating to shows, and to publicize tie-in merchandise. The creation of an Internet home page for the *X-Files* was credited with saving the show from cancellation after its first season. The *X-files* producers recognized the perfect synergy of its high demographic fans and the Internet and targeted its audience through the World Wide Web, a move that helped to both prove its audience share to executives contemplating axing the show and generate more publicity for the program. Protests against television animate the online communications as well: Christian Right Organizations such as the American Family Association use the Internet to organize protests against television sponsors of objectionable material (a list it calls "The Dirty Dozen") and "filth" (*NYPD Blue*).

Computer and Internet research can benefit greatly from television research on television flow and the use of remote controls, the installment of the television as a domestic object, and conversation around television. For example, the Internet poses problems similar to that of television "flow" (Williams 1975), as Web "programmers" (especially those with commercial sponsors) attempt to guide the user through a pre-planned sequence of screens and links. While nearly every branch of the advertising industry is making moves to work on the Internet, anxieties are already rife about ways to measure consumers. At first, the number of "hits" a Web site received were enough. Surveys revealed that half of all visitors to a Web site did not even read the "banner" advertisements, and of those that did, less than half clicked on the ad. Even when they do click, "Most Web tracking software can't tell whether someone clicked on an ad but then changed his mind and stopped the transfer" (Williamson 1996). Thus talk of hits has given way to a preference for "impressions"—a word more likely to carry weight with sponsors, with its desirable associations with lasting mental influence. Cybergold has launched a market research service (of dubious merit) whereby subjects are paid fifty cents or a dollar to click through and "read" ads. This concern for the meaningfulness of exposure to Web advertising closely parallels the anxieties of television advertisers about the attention span of television viewers and their proclivity for "zapping" commercials by switching channels or "zipping" past commercials on videotapes of prerecorded programs. From the advertiser's perspective, Web surfers can be just as fickle as television watchers, it seems.

In *Desperately Seeking the Audience*, Ien Ang (1991) carefully deconstructed the fantasies of control over television viewers and the necessity of such fantasies to the television industries daily functioning. In the trade publication *Advertising Age*, these fantasies and the battle over competing claims for accurate measurement of Web surfers are now a major preoccupation. On the one hand, the Internet is projected as a much better vehicle than television, because the Web user is presumably more attentive, more goal-directed—and wealthier. Yet anxieties about measuring and controlling Web users are escalating, and energies are focusing around the development of measurement devices adequate to convince sponsors.

For its target market of the professional upper-middle class, the computer is being installed as a domestic object in a process similar to the guidelines for installing the television set in the home in the 1950s, as studied by Lynn Spigel (1992). Computers are advertised on utopian claims to enrich family life, enhance communications, strengthen friendship and kin networks, and, perhaps most important, make children smarter and give them a competitive advantage in the educational sphere. In advertising, in news broadcasts, in education journals, the computer is often defined against, and pitched as an improvement on, the television set: where television viewing is passive, computer use is interactive; where television programs are entertaining in a stale, commercialized, violent way, computer software and the Internet are educational, virtuous, new.

In research on television audiences, I have stressed the ways that negative feelings about television viewing (shame or defensiveness) affect what people are willing to say about television. Comparisons between television viewing and use of the World Wide Web are inevitable. Both television programming and computer software, Web sites, etc., serve as topics of conversation and chat (the former being more legitimate among the educated middle classes). Among middle-class professionals, the group best positioned to parlay computer use into improved earning power, discussing a new Web site holds more cachet than talking over last night's sitcom. The negative associations of being a computer nerd, as in a hacker, have abated considerably in the last decade (Turkle 1995), while computer magazines such as *Wired* have promoted fashionable "postmodern" associations with computer use. While some sanctions are associated with being a nerd, the computer stereotype has a higher gender, class, and intellectual standing than the couch potato. On the other hand, those with less disposable income and less familiarity with computers may reject computers for the values they represent (such as dehumanization), their emphasis on written rather than oral culture, their associations with white male culture (hackers and hobbyists), and their solitary, anti-social nature. The operations of "distinction" will be especially important to bear in mind when doing empirical work on the social contexts of computer use.

5.2   Gendered Uses of Computers at Home

Television sets and computers introduce highly similar issues in terms of placement in domestic space, conflicts among family members over usage and control, value in the household budget, and we can expect these to be articulated with gender roles in the family. Some research on gendered conflicts over computers (Giacquinta, Bauer, and Levin 1993; Haddon

1992; Murdock 1992) reproduces themes of family-based studies about control of the television set. Already researchers have noted a strong tendency for men and boys to have more access to computers in the home. Television studies such as Ann Gray's, David Morley's, and my own work suggest that women in nuclear families have difficulty watching a favorite television show (because of competition for control of the set from other family members and because of shouldering the majority of child care, housework and cooking). If male family members gravitate towards the computer as hobbyists, the load of chores relegated to female family members will only increase, and make it more difficult for female members to get time on the home computer. Computers require hours of trial and error experimentation, a kind of extended play demanding excess leisure time. Fully exploring the Internet needs time for lengthy downloading and patience with connections that are busy, so much so that some have dubbed the World Wide Web-the World Wide Wait.

In the family, computers can create anxiety, too: Young children must be kept away from the keyboard because of potential damage to the machine. Mothers, who have traditionally been charged with securing the academic success of their children, would have a strong incentive to relinquish computer time to older children, who are thought to benefit greatly from all contact with the technology. When anxieties increase and moral panics are publicized about children's encounters with pornography through the computer, or the unhealthy effects of prolonged computer use, the brunt of responsibility for enforcing restrictions on computer use will fall to mothers and teachers.

Some qualitative research has already explored these areas, and some of the most valuable work has been informed by British cultural studies work. Silverstone, Hirsch, and Morley (1990) have offered a fascinating case study of a well-to-do London family whose home included a wide array of new technologies and whose explicit ideology was one of encouraging children to use them. Yet the mother remained at a weary distance from the computer. She responded with irritation to researcher's questions about her feelings toward the communication technologies, claiming not to have feelings about technologies at all. (1990; p. 35) Both parents desired that their children gain computer experience and preferred this to television watching, but expressed irritation with the boy's domination of their home computer. Measures were taken to try to secure computer time for the daughters in the home but with mixed success. The mother/wife felt alienated from the developing "father and son" culture around the computer and suffered arguments about the selection of computer games, but her frustration led her to take a course on computing. Tensions among highly motivated well-educated females over computer technology deserve much more investigation.

Similarly, Giacquinta, Bauer, and Levin, in their qualitative study of white middle-class New York families found that marked differences existed between males and females, both adults and children, including less use by females, and "mothers were particularly estranged from the machines" (1993, p. 80). The study, conducted in 1984–1987, included 69 mothers, two-thirds of whom were employed full time outside the home. Mothers tended to use computers for word processing and "did not engage in programming, tinkering, pirating, or game playing" (1993, p. 81). Mothers found the violence in computer games objectionable. In general, they lacked "the interest, the need and the time" to develop computing skills (1993, p. 89). Daughters were more likely than mothers to use the computer and had more resources to support them such as classroom teaching, but they were not a focus of the girls' leisure time activities.

Friendships, kin networks, and work relationships are crucial to the successful adoption of new technologies such as computers (Douglas 1988) Computer use often involves borrowing software, troubleshooting problems, trying out new programs, boasting or discussing successes, cross-checking machines. Advice and encouragement are important components of this. The Giacquinta, Bauer, and Levin study found women rarely spoke with other women about their computers or assisted each other in learning. If women and girls tend not to talk about computers, they are at a sizable disadvantage over boys and men, especially those with considerable practice at hobby talk. In another study of home computing in the English Midlands, Murdock (1992) found, in their sample of one thousand households, that males outnumbered females as the primary computer user by a ratio of seven to one. They also found that those who did not talk to others about computers or borrow programs from friends or relatives were most likely to have stopped using their computers (p. 150).

Jane Wheelock (1992) found, in a British study of thirty nine families in "a peripheral region of the national economy" that there were three times as many sons interested in the home computer as interested daughters. Wheelock's study focuses on the ways that the household, operating as a complementary economy to the formal one, reproduces and produces labor power as related to computer use (pp. 98–99). Daughters were more likely to be interested in computers if such interest was facilitated by parental and teacher encouragement, or if there were no sons in the family—or after the machine had been abandoned by the sons in the family (p. 110).

Boys were much more likely than girls to use computers as a part of their social networks, something that, Wheelock notes, "increases boys' socializing, and shifts its locus towards the home; traditionally both are features of girls' experience" (p. 111). Lesley Haddon's (1992) observations based on time spent in a computer club similarly suggest that girls may not use computers as a topic for school conversation even when they do use computers at home, being more likely to discuss rented videos (p. 91). The girls in Haddon's study were also unlikely to play computers in public places, stores, arcades, or school clubs but used them at home.

Most of these studies are somewhat dated and do not provide any information about the use of electronic mail and the World Wide Web. These two uses of the computers, in their facilitation of personal communications, most closely resemble the telephone, a communications technology particularly valued by women (Livingstone 1992; Rakow 1988; Spender 1995). Reliable information about Web users is hard to come by, and most research relies upon self-selection of its sample, i.e., people responding to various postings asking for Net users to fill out a survey form. Some of this recent survey information suggests that the Internet may be attracting women, especially younger, white, middle-class women under thirty-five, at surprising rates. In 1995, the Georgia Tech World Wide Web Users Survey (1995) reports 29% of their respondents are female—a number that has increased significantly over the last three years. There has been a substantial increase in female Web users between the ages of sixteen and twenty years of age and an increase in female users in who teach kindergarten through twelfth grade—there was a 10% increase in female users in this category observed in one year, 1994–1995. The importance of access through public education institutions for women is significant: 39% of women responding gained Internet access that way compared to 28% of men. Yet there are clear signs that women are less likely to use computers intensively in their free time. On the weekends—an indication of hobbyist users, the gap widens to 75% male and only 25% female: thus three times as many men are weekend users of computers compared to women. Women users were less likely than men to spend time doing "fun computing" or to use a computer for more than 31 hours a week. Although the Web is attracting men over 46 in increasing numbers—many of them as a retirement hobby, the relative numbers of women over 46 years of age who use the Internet are declining.

Much has been written about the ways that the Internet can be used to explore personality and identity (for example, Star 1995; Turkle 1995). But women and the poor are going to be less advantageously positioned to engage in such activities for a complex set of reasons (Star 1995). As Roger Silverstone (1991) has explained:

the ability to use information and communication technology as a kind of extension of the personality in time and space ... is also a matter of resources. The number of rooms in a household relative to the number of people, the amount of money that an individual can claim for his or her own personal use, the amount of control of his or her own time in the often intense atmosphere of family life, all these things are obviously of great relevance. (p. 12)

5.3   Computerized Work

Are women more likely to use the Internet if they use computers on the job? Working on a computer can mean very different things: if we are to understand the differential desire to use computers during leisure time, it is essential to make distinctions between kinds of computerized work. For example, huge numbers of female employees occupy clerical jobs that use computers for processing payroll, word-processing, conducting inventory, sales, and airline reservations—over 16 million women held such positions in the United States in 1993 (Kling 1996). Less than half a million women work as computer programmers or systems analysts. Women overwhelmingly outnumber men in the kinds of jobs where telephones and computers are used simultaneously: airline reservations, catalog sales, telephone operators.

The type of employment using a computer that is likely to be familiar to the largest numbers of women, then, is a kind of work where key-strokes might be counted, where supervisors may listen in on phone calls uninterrupted, where productivity is scrutinized on a daily and hourly basis, where conversation with coworkers is forbidden (Clement 1996; Iacono and Kling 1996). The stressful and unpleasant circumstances under which this kind of work is performed might explain women's alienation from computer technology and tendency to stay away from it during their leisure time.

Some parallels exist between clerical work and teaching—one of the sole white collar professions dominated by women. As Steven Hodas (1996) points out in his discussion of what he calls "technology refusal" in schools, most teachers are women; most educational technologists are men who target their efforts at introducing computer technologies toward classroom teachers, not male administrators. The need for class-room computers is usually expressed in ways that derogate the work of teachers: in these discussions of educational technologists, "the terms used to describe the insufficiency of the classroom and to condescend to the folk-craft of teaching are the same terms used by an androgenized society to derogate women's values and women's work generally" (p. 206). When technologies fail in the classroom the reaction is to "blame the stubborn backwardness of teachers or the inflexibility and insularity of the school culture" (206). Hodas usefully reminds us that present-day arguments about the need for computers in schools mirror the same redemption through technology arguments that accompanied other media, most notably for our purposes, educational video:

The violence that technologists have done to our only public children's space by reducing it to an "instructional delivery vehicle" is enormous, and teachers know that. To abstract a narrow and impoverished concept of human sentience from the industrial laboratory and then inflict it on children for the sake of "efficiency" is a gratuitous, stunning stupidity and teachers know that, too. Many simply prefer not to collaborate with a process they experience as fundamentally disre-spectful to kids and teachers alike. (Hodas 1996, p. 213)

Telecommuting, working from the home through a modem or Internet access to the office, is a different category of computerized work that is supposed to hold special appeal to women. Telecommuting is now officially sanctioned by the U.S. government, according to Rob Kling (1996):

A recent report developed under the auspices of the Clinton administration included a key section, "Promoting Telecommuting," that lists numerous advantages for telecommuting. These include major improvements in air quality from reduced travel; increased organizational productivity when people can be more alert during working hours faster commercial transit times when few cars are on the roads; and improvements in quality or worklife. The benefits identified in this report seem so overwhelming that it may appear remarkable that most organizations have not already allowed all of their workers the options to work at home.

While there are growing numbers of women doing pink-collar jobs such as clerical and sales work at home, i.e., using their home computers, at jobs such as credit card verification and telephone solicitations, this form of telecommuting is also largely invisible in the mass media. Instead we see images of female professionals using computers to work from home, perhaps while their one and only child conveniently naps in the next room. Computer publications suggest "a hybrid site of home and work, where it is possible to make tele-deals while sitting in your kitchen." As Lynn Spigel has noted in her discussion of a *Mac Home* magazine cover: "The computer and Net offer women a way to do two jobs at once—reproduce and produce, be a mother and hold down a high-powered job. Even while the home work model of domestic space finds a place for women, it does not real y break down the traditional distinctions between male and female" (Spigel 2001). As more workers struggle to get their work done from home without benefit of an office, questions about the use of communication technologies become especially interesting and well-suited to ethnographic approaches.

Another interesting issue for audience research is the entertainment uses of computers in offices, as office workers have access to more entertainment and play functions through their computers. Sherry Turkle's book, *Life on the Screen* (1995), examines a group comprised mainly of students or white-collar computer programmers who work on computers throughout the day. Turkle is especially interested in participation in

MUDs: online fantasy games that can have dozens of players. As Turkle describes this balance of play and work:

> I have noted that committed players often work with computers all day at their regular jobs. As they play on MUDs, they periodically put their characters to sleep, remaining logged on to the game, but pursuing other activities. The MUD keeps running in a buried window. From time to time, they return to the game space. In this way, they break up their day and come to experience their lives as cycling through the real world and a series of virtual ones. (1995, p. 189)

While Turkle is primarily interested in the psychological dynamics of play with a variety of virtual selves, she rarely foregrounds the very specific class fraction who has the privilege to play on the job. In this world, white-collar, upper-middle-class employers are finding that after a period of vigorous encouragement, if not requirement, of nearly constant computer and Internet use in many occupations, employees are spending large parts of the day playing computer games, writing personal e-mails, and cruising the Internet, and that it is increasingly difficult to confine white-collar employees to work-related rather than entertainment uses of these technologies—or in some cases to distinguish between the two. As one expert wryly put it in a discussion of the impact of digital video discs, "The big application for DVD later this year will be desktop video playback, which will eliminate any remaining worker productivity that hasn't already been destroyed by Web surfing" (Hood 1997).

Turkle gives many examples of women immersed in the play with identity and the capacity for writing one's own dramatic narratives that MUDs offer, and she is especially interested in the phenomenon of players impersonating the opposite sex in their virtual personae. Turkle's study fails to interrogate the particular class background of the MIT students and computer programmers she interviewed for her study, or to ask how particular class positions may predispose women to be attracted to the kind of play with virtual selves that she describes as postmodern. The luxury of such computer play is unimaginable in the context of most clerical computer work and unlikely in the home work station when women race to get their work done before children come home from school or hurry to turn their attention from the computer to housecleaning, shopping, or food preparation.

For writers such as Turkle, the Internet offers an arena for exploring—and deconstructing—traditional gender roles that can be quite liberating.

Such an analysis contrasts sharply with the concerns of Cheris Kramarae, who in her analysis of the genres and kinds of information available on the World Wide Web, has noted the rapid proliferation of genres such as pornography, and modes of discourse, such as flaming, which may act as a deterrent to women going online. Similarly, linguist Susan Herring (1996) has cast doubt on utopian claims for online communications in the workplace that have suggested these technologies may be advantageous for women getting ahead in professions. This work suggests that even among white-collar professionals, computers may be more fun for men than for women. For example, in a study of academics using electronic discussion groups, Herring found that:

[M]ale and [F]emale academic professionals do not participate equally in academic CMC [computer-mediated communication]. Rather, a small male minority dominates the discourse both in terms of amount of talk, and rhetorically, through self-promotional and adversarial strategies. Moreover, when women do attempt to participate on a more equal basis, they risk being actively censored by the reactions of men who either ignore them or attempt to delegitimize their contributions.

Herring concluded that there was nothing inherently wrong with the technology of computer bulletin boards, rather the problem stemmed from the ways that old, familiar forms of gender discrimination—from the academic workplace and from society—dictated the ways that participants would communicate. Laura Miller has dismissed this type of complaint about the Internet, warning that we need to be wary of the media's attempt to cast women as victims on the Internet, as in discussions of flaming or the prevalence of pornography:

The idea that women merit special protections in a environment as incorporeal as the Net is intimately bound up with the idea that women's minds are weak, fragile, and unsuited to the rough and tumble of public discourse. It's an argument that women should recognize with profound mistrust and resist, especially when we are used as rhetorical pawns in a battle to regulate a rare (if elite) space of gender ambiguity. (1995, p. 58)

What is needed in this discussion between two different camps of feminists—those who see the Internet as rife with sexism (a group Miller unhelpfully calls the "schoolmarms") and those who see such behaviors as incidental problems, easily overcome by assertive behaviors—is research that links women's reaction and attraction to the Internet to other

aspects of their lived experience, including education, class, sexual orientation, religion, and workplace culture, including how frequently they
experience and how they deal with sexual harassment in their workplace.

As Cynthia Cockburn (1992) reminds us, "Gender is a social achievement. Technology too" (p. 39). The trick for media researchers will be
to avoid a kind of static gender essentialism, where women, the elderly,
and the poor are eternally, innately deficient vis-à-vis new technologies,
while all men benefit from inborn technical know-how, an affinity to
toying with machines, and an enthusiastic embrace of time-intensive
forms of hobbyism. Ethnographic studies can help to provide materialist
explanations for women's reluctance to immerse themselves in computer
use and online communications as well as explicating the circumstances
under which women are attracted to and excel at computer skills.

The role of feminist researchers will include tempering enthusiasm for
these new technologies, as Kramarae and Kramer (1995) argue:

The so-called popular media treat the new electronic systems as sexy, but the
media fail to deal seriously with most of the gender-related issues. As those who
are working closely with its developments know, the Internet will not, contrary
to what the media tout, rid the world of hostility, ignorance, racism, sexism,
greed and undemocratic governments. The Internet has the potential for creating
a cooperative collective international web; but, as with all technologies, the
Internet system will be shaped by prevailing communication behaviors, economic
policy, and legal decisions. (p. 15)

One of the most important functions of ethnography then may be as an
antidote to the hype about computers. Ethnography can describe, for
example, the full context in which barriers to entrance on to the information highway exist—especially among people still worrying about
keeping a car running on the real highway, much less having the extra
time and money to maintain a computer at home.

Studying the use of computers may force communication scholars to
examine the links between public and private, work and home more
closely and encourage audience researchers to take stock of the role of
television outside the home. While domestic studies of television audiences often report rather depressing views of traditional divisions of
labor—and the early studies of computer use in the home seem to follow
along similar lines, this picture may become more complicated and more
nuanced if we examine the ways that women use computers in the

workplace and how employment uses affect the likelihood that they will become computer enthusiasts (Haddon 1992, p. 86). We need to engage both in domestic studies of computers and the study of public uses of television while examining the connections between office and home use. Both technologies—computers and televisions—need to be studied in both contexts: the domestic and the workplace.

5.4   Conclusion

We need to be explicit about the stakes involved in our representations of media audiences and computer users and present our research in forms that are accessible to journalists and policymakers. The digital revolution is creating huge numbers of "information have-nots." With about $\frac{1}{3}$ of U.S. homes yet to receive cable television, the penetration of home computers is unlikely to reach anything like that of television sets. Researching only those who are already working with computers or have computers in the home will skew our understanding. As Dan Schiller usefully reminds us:

> It is only among the better-off—households with $75,000 or more in annual income—that PCs had become routine, with a 60–65% penetration rate.... Even the experience of the most favorably endowed ones in the global political economy shows, therefore, that the level and character of access remained a function of entrenched income inequality. (1997, p. 5)

Robert McChesney cautions about the catastrophic impact of the Internet on the widening class divide: "In a class-stratified, commercially oriented society like the United States, cannot the information highway have the effect of simply making it possible for the well-to-do to bypass any contact with the balance of society altogether?" (1996, p. 117).

The massive investment in a technology so heavily skewed toward benefiting the white middle class must be viewed with skepticism, and convincing arguments for the importance of sustaining funding for television and video production need to be mounted. John Caldwell has noted the logical leap made by many advocates of "telecomputers" and the information superhighway "to a vision of the world in which infinite individual needs are met through interactivity and technological responsiveness" (1995, p. 348). As Caldwell reminds us: "Most audiences have yet to clamor for the headaches of menus, interactive branching, and nonlinearity. They want Schwarzenegger and production value, and they want it now. Many audiences do not want Nintendo and e-mail either, they want narrative and character" (p. 348). Television scholars must be prepared to protest the drastic cuts in funding for public television and for independent productions—television sets and VCRs are to be found in nearly every home (and many classrooms), television and video will continue to be vastly more accessible than computer communications for a very long time—and probably a better investment for a democratic society. It will be important to do field work close to home, especially with aggrieved communities whose second-rate access to media technologies and whose representational exclusion from the mass media have long and relatively unchanging histories, and for whom the push towards computerization threatens to exacerbate economic hardship and a widening class divide.

University administrators now pressure academics to form "partnerships" with business (Soley 1995). All of us would do well to make sure that there are clear-cut differences between our research questions and those of market researchers. Bringing to bear on our analysis a full understanding of economic and historical determinants of the situations we study is an important strategy. Maintaining a high degree of consciousness about the markets currently targeted by business, as well as the spread of marketing techniques globally, is another important strategy. I feel uneasy recalling that during the years when audience researchers were focusing on close readings of the text, the structure of media corporations underwent massive deregulation, conglomeration, and shifts in power. As we move to study the confluence of television and other technologies, we should strive to incorporate into this work a greater awareness of accompanying shifts in the political economic structure of the media industries.

The challenges for future research on media audiences and computer users are to broaden our scope, through a stronger theoretical engagement with political economy, and a widening of focus beyond television to include new computer technologies. When turning to the Internet it will be especially important to treat computer communications as deeply cultural, as employing fiction and fantasy as well as information, and as open to variable interpretations based on gender, race, and ethnicity. As the Internet is championed as the ultimate in "interactive" media use, it will be extremely important for media researchers to put forward appropriate skepticism about the laudatory uses of the term "active" in discussions of media use and to problematize the complex factors involved in attracting both television watchers and computer users to particular contents and genres.

Ethnography can offer an appreciation of some of television's advantages over computers (such as its accessibility by more than one person at a time, and its visual and aural modes of communication) and guard against the unnecessary pathologization of television viewing, which almost always acts to stigmatize the already socially powerless. It will be important to look at the reasons why and the contexts in which television might be more appealing than the Internet. We know that television—for all of its failings—has been cheap, easy to watch at home, enjoyable to talk about with others, and reasonably successful as an educational tool. It will be important to understand the ways that such social features of broadcast technologies are missing or modified in new technologies. Finally, scholars should work to change the media and the structures of access to communication technologies, while politicizing the public discussion of media in ways that make explicit the gains and the losses at stake in promoting different representations of the audiences and computer users.

References

Ang, I. *Desperately Seeking the Audience*. London: Routledge, 1991.

Auletta, K., "The Microsoft Provocateur," *The New Yorker* (May 12, 1997): 66–77.

Bank, D., and D. Takahashi, "Microsoft Plans Big Digital TV Push, Stressing Hardware and Programming," *Wall Street Journal* (April 16, 1997): B6.

Boddy, W. *Fifties Television: The Industry and Its Critics*. Urbana: University of Illinois Press, 1990.

Caldwell, J. *Televisuality: Style, Crisis, and Authority in American Television*. New Brunswick, N.J.: Rutgers University Press, 1995.

Caruso, D. "Microsoft Morphs into a Media Company," *Wired* 4, no. 6 (June 1996): 126–129.

Clement, A. "Computing at Work: Empowering Action by 'Low-level users,'" *Communications of the ACM* 37, no. 1 (January 1994): 52–65, reprinted in Kling 1996.

Cockburn, C. "The Circuit of Technology: Gender, Identity and Power," in Silverstone and Hirsch 1992.

Corner, J. "Media Studies and the Knowledge Problem," *Screen* 36, no. 2 (1995): 147–159.

Douglas, M. "Goods as a system of Communication," in Mary Douglas, *In the Active Voice*. London: Routledge and Kegan Paul, 1988.

Georgia Tech Research Corporation, Graphics, Visualization and Usability Center (GVU's WWW Surveying Team) world wide web users survey. (www-survey@cc.gatech.edu), 1995.

Giacquinta, J. B., J. A. Bauer, and J. E. Levin, *Beyond Technology's Promise: An Examination of Children's Educational Computing at Home*. Cambridge: Cambridge University Press, 1993.

Gillespie, M. *Television, Ethnicity and Cultural Change*. London: Routledge, 1995.

Gray, A. "Behind Closed Doors: Video Recorders in the Home," in H. Baehr and G. Dyer (eds.), *Boxed In: Women and Television*. New York: Pandora, 1987.

Gray, A. *Video Playtime: The Gendering of a Leisure Technology*. London: Routledge, 1992.

Haddon, L. "Explaining ICT consumption: the case of the home computer," in Silverstone and Hirsch 1992.

Helm, L. "Microsoft Unveils Revamped Online Service," *Los Angeles Times* (October 11, 1996): D2.

Herring, S. C. "Gender and Democracy in Computer-mediated Communication," *Electronic Journal of Communication* 3(2). Reprinted in Herring, *Computer-mediated Communication: Linguistic and Cultural Perspectives*. Amsterdam: J. Benjamins, 1996.

Hochschild, A., *The Second Shift*. New York: Avon Books, 1989.

Hodas, S., "Technology Refusal and the Organizational Culture of Schools," *Education Policy Analysis Archives*, 1, no. 10 (September 1993) reprinted in Kling 1996.

Hood, P., "The Wizard of Silicon Valley," *NewMedia* 6 (January 1997): 14.

Iacono, S., and R. Kling, "Computerization Movements and Tales of Technological Utopianism," in Kling 1996.

Ireland, C., and B. Johnson, "Exploring the Future in the Present," *Design Management Journal* 6, no. 2 (1995): 57–64.

Jenkins, H. *Textual Poachers: Television Fans and Participatory Culture*. London: Routledge, 1992.

Kling, R., *Computerization and Controversy: Value Conflicts and Social Choices* (2nd ed.). San Diego: Academic Press, 1996.

Kramerae, C., ed., *Technology and Women's Voices: Keeping in Touch.* New York: Routledge and Kegan Paul, 1988.

Kramerae, C., and J. Kramer, "Legal Snarls for Women in Cyberspace," *Internet Research: Electronic Networking Applications and Policy*, 5 (1995): 14–24.

Livingstone, S., "The Meaning of Domestic Technologies: A Personal Construct Analysis of Familial Gender Relations," in Silverstone and Hirsch 1992.

Lesch, S. G., "Your Work on Television? A View from the USA," *Computer-Mediated Communication Magazine* 1, no. 4 (August 1994): 5.

McChesney, R. W., "The Internet and U.S. Communication Policy-Making in Historical and Critical Perspective," *Journal of Communication* 46, no. 1 (1996): 98–124.

McChesney, R. W., "Corporate Media and the Threat to Democracy," *Open Media Pamphlet Series*. New York: Seven Stories Press, 1997.

Miller, L., "Women and Children First: Gender and the Settling of the Electronic Frontier," in *Resisting the Virtual Life*, James Brook and Iain A. Boal (eds.). San Francisco: City Lights, 1995.

Morley, D. *Family Television*. London: Comedia/Routledge, 1986.

Morley, D. *Television, Audiences and Cultural Studies*. London: Routledge, 1992.

Morris, M., and C. Ogan, "The Internet as a Mass Medium," *Journal of Communication* 46, no. 1 (Winter 1996): 39–50.

Murdock, G. "Contextualizing Home Computing: Resources and Practices," in *Consuming Technologies*, G. Murdock, P. Hartmann, and P. Gray (eds.). London: Routledge, 1992.

Newhagen, J., and S. Rafaeli, "Why Communication Researchers Should Study the Internet: A Dialogue," *Journal of Communication* 46, no. 1 (Winter 1996): 4–14.

Press, A., *Women Watching Television*. Philadelphia: University of Pennsylvania Press, 1991.

Rakow, L., "Women and the Telephone: The Gendering of a Communications Technology," in Kramerae 1988.

Schiller, D., "Cornering the Market in Cyberspace," *Le Monde Diplomatique* (March 1997).

Seiter, E., "Making Distinctions in Audience Research," *Cultural Studies* 4, no. 1 (1991): 61–84.

Seiter, E., H. Borchers, G. Kreutzner, and E. Warth, *Remote Control: Television, Audiences and Cultural Power*. London: Routledge, 1989.

Shattuc, J., *The Talking Cure: TV Talk Shows and Women*. New York: Routledge, 1997.

Silverstone, R., "Beneath the Bottom Line: Households and Information and Communication Technologies in an Age of the Consumer," Policy Research Papers no. 17. London: PICT, 1991.

Silverstone, R. and E. Hirsch, eds., *Consuming Technologies: Media and Information in Domestic Spaces*. London: Routledge, 1992.

Silverstone, R., E. Hirsch, and D. Morley, "Listening to a Long Conversation: An Ethnographic Approach to the Study of Information and Communication Technologies in the Home," discussion paper for the Centre for Research in Innovation, Culture and Technology, Brunel University, 1990. Reprinted in *Cultural Studies*, 5, no. 2 (1991).

Silverstone, R., E. Hirsch, and D. Morley, "Information and Communication Technologies and the Moral Economy of the Household," discussion paper for the Centre for Research in Innovation, Culture and Technology, Brunel University, 1990. Reprinted in Silverstone and Hirsch 1992.

Soley, L., *Leasing the Ivory Tower: The Corporate Takeover of Academia*. Boston: South End Press, 1995.

Spender, D., *Nattering on the Net: Women, Power and Cyberspace*. North Melbourne: Spinifex Press, 1995.

Spigel, L., *Make Room for TV: Television and the Family Ideal in Postwar America*. Chicago: University of Chicago Press, 1992.

Spigel, L. 2001. *Welcome to the Dreamhouse: Popular Media and Postwar Suburbs*. Durham, NC: Duke University Press.

Star, S. L., "Introduction," *The Cultures of Computing*. Oxford: Blackwell, 1995.

Turkle, S., *Life on the Screen*. New York: Simon & Schuster, 1995.

Wheelock, J., "Personal Computers, Gender and an Institutional Model of the Household," in Silverstone and Hirsch 1992.

Williams, R. 1975. *Television: Technology and Cultural Form*. New York: Schocken Books.

Williamson, D. A. 1996. "Web Ads Mark Second Birthday with Decisive Issues Ahead," *Advertising Age* (October 21): 1.

II

On Parents and Kids

Part I took a broad historical perspective on the Internet and the family. Part II zooms in a bit to focus on contemporary parents, their kids, and the web. Maria Papadakis's review of current literature reveals that most of what we know about family internet use centers on general demographics and usage patterns—that is, on who uses the internet, for how long, and for what purposes. Not only is there little research to date on the impact of the home connection on families, but the findings on use are themselves sometimes conflicting. One area of agreement, however, is that the households with children are more likely to have a computer and network connection than households without children. Moreover, a majority of adult internet users in multiple studies indicate that the internet (particularly e-mail) has strengthened ties with friends and family; a sizeable proportion of children report the same. A majority of household members also report that they do not feel neglected because another family member is using the internet. Reliable evidence of negative effects (e.g., isolation, asocial behavior) appears to pertain to a small minority of households.

What about parental guidance and involvement in children's media use? Amy Jordan's essay notes that family use of media not only reflects but also shapes the overall norms and beliefs of the home environment. Developing ideas from family system theory, she notes that the home environment provides certain meanings to space and time in relationship to media. Certain spaces—sofas in TV rooms, for example—can be shared, while others—computers with one chair in front of them—may not be. Similarly, rules about time in front of the TV, the computer and the web teach children about the nature and value of time. Jordan suggests that these rules about time and space encourage online choices and habits that may reflect and shape the social dimension of the family system.

Jordan reports that when it comes to TV parents are more concerned about what their children watch than about how much they watch, despite admitting that their efforts to control television consumption are only moderately successful. The difficulty they report in exercising authority over television consumption by their children is likely to carry over to their internet use. The "what they watch" concern is especially heightened with the internet, since there is such a greater range and diversity of content online than on the television. Moreover, the power of children to let commercial organizations "watch the household" (self-disclosure over the Internet of personal household information) is largely unique to this medium.

This point raises the issue of information privacy, a big one when it comes to families and the web. It is one of the many issues raised by Joseph Turow and Lilach Nir in *The Internet and the Family*, which reports on a national survey of parents and children. Overall, the study charts a complex picture of the attitudes parents and youngsters hold toward the web. Large percentages of U.S. parents reported that the online world holds strong educational possibilities, while high percentages also feel that the web can powerfully harm young minds because of its sometimes sexual, violent, and predatory content. The survey also found that American parents and children aged 12–17 have conflicting attitudes about privacy and disclosure, with the kids being much more cavalier about commercial interests than their parents.

Many U.S. policy analysts and critics are chagrined at these findings. They contend that lax U.S. laws along with the convergence of databases and easy retrieval, storage and customizing of information by service providers, makes the willingness of youngsters to give up family information to marketers in exchange for a free gift an important policy issue. They argue that disclosure of sensitive personal information can have serious ramifications if it is used to track people—and especially to determine access to social services, insurance, health care, or employment opportunities.

U.S. policy analysts also note that rules for internet privacy are much more stringent in Europe, diminishing the chances that youngsters' data would be used in untoward ways. The difference between Europe and the United States over the web raises the larger topic of differences and similarities in the way families relate to the web in different parts of the globe. So far, very little research speaks to this subject. Sonia Livingstone's comparison of "young people's changing media environment in Europe" is an exception that points to an enormously important area for investigation. The phrase "the World Wide Web" and press discussions about the dissemination of the internet around the world suggest that the web is indeed a global medium, the same everywhere. Livingstone and her colleagues found, however, important differences as well as similarities between countries in the conceptualization and use of the technology. In general, she suggests that "the situation in any one country can be usefully understood in terms of the convergence of differentiation of national (or regional) cultures as part of ... broader processes—particularly globalization, privatization, individuation, and consumerism."

The Livingstone essay, as well as those by Gitte Stald and Mark Griffith, provides windows on attitudes and activities that may or may not reflect the U.S. situation. Livingstone notes that British children are more likely than European children to own personalized media (such as a TV in their bedroom)—a finding that she attributes to privatization and individualism. Stald finds that in Denmark, adolescents use of the internet affects their identity as Danes and as citizens of the world and facilitates cultural transformation. Furthermore, the web facilitates the transfer of English language skills and knowledge and reinforces the language study begun in the early years of school. While greater proficiency in English may well be a benefit of the global computer network, Griffiths sees a negative consequence. He argues that the proliferation of sexual content on the internet is a worrisome development for parents that requires a global policymaking response.

How common are such worries—as well as worries about web violence, sex, and information privacy? Are conceptions of web benefits shared among internet users around the world? To what extent do parent and child concerns and enthusiasms about the web change the dynamics of work and play in the home—and with what consequences? These are questions that the chapters in part II raise. Clearly, they invite much discussion and increased research, in the United States and elsewhere.

6

Data on Family and the Internet: What Do We Know and How Do We Know It?

Maria Papadakis

Introduction

The internet is so pervasive it is easy to forget that it has been present in U.S. households for fewer than 10 years—commercial access to the internet became a service widely available to U.S. households only around 1994. Since that time, the number of homes with internet linkages has increased from 2 percent to 42 percent, a figure that masks the significant presence of this technology for American families. By August 2000, nearly three-quarters of all couples with children had the internet at home, as did almost one-half of single-parent households headed by men (National Telecommunications and Information Administration 2000). These adoption rates are so strikingly above the national average that we can safely assume families are somehow more highly motivated to use the internet than other homes; indeed, studies consistently show that the most important reason parents give for purchasing their computer and gaining access to the internet is to provide educational advantages to their children,[1] and that parents' decisions to go online is affected by discussions with their kids (Lindlof 1992; Orleans and Laney 2000; Roper Starch Worldwide 1999a, 1999b).

Yet what exactly do we know about the widespread presence of this technology in the home and its implications for family values, the nature and frequency of family interactions, and the role of the home for the individuals in it? The answer is not terribly much, and the problem lies primarily with the nature of the data that we have and the extraordinary difficulty and cost of implementing research programs that would let us get at many of these concerns. Most of what we do know that broadly characterizes U.S. patterns of family internet use relate to what is called *internet demographics and usage patterns*—who uses the internet, for how long, and why. We have very little understanding about how the internet might systematically affect family relations and the quality of home life, and can only speculate about these issues at best, a difficulty that is echoed in the chapter by Anderson and Evans (see chapter 4) as well.

The purpose of this chapter is to review what we know empirically about family and the internet, how we know it, and what the obstacles are to knowing more. It is organized into three main sections that discuss (1) the availability of data, (2) general patterns of family internet use, and (3) the problem of conflicting research findings. This latter topic in particular illustrates the difficulty in making general conclusions about family and the internet, not only because we are working with a limited body of research, but also because the potential to misunderstand and misrepresent findings on the internet and the family is considerable.

Data on Families and the Internet: How We Know

Publicly accessible data that potentially explain systematic patterns of family internet access and use originate from three main sources: the U.S. Bureau of the Census, research institutions affiliated with the Pew Charitable Trusts, and commercial market research firms. Three survey programs have provided continuous coverage of internet demographics since the mid-1990s; these are the computer and internet supplements to the Census Current Population Survey,[2] the CommerceNet Nielsen Internet Demographic Survey,[3] and Cyber Dialogue's CyberCitizen Program Surveys (formerly the American Internet User Survey).[4] Several organizations used to conduct demographic surveys on a regular basis but no longer do so.[5]

While dozens of "research findings" on household use of the internet are reported in the press each year, these reports typically reflect periodic studies conducted by such national market research organizations as Forrester Research, PC Meter, Media Metrix, ActivMedia, Zona, the Yankee Group, International Data Corporation, Gartner

Group Interactive, Jupiter Communications, NFO Interactive, and many others. In addition, two web-based meta sites—NUA Internet Surveys and CyberAtlas—issue a daily stream of summaries regarding internet market research studies, many of which relate to family and household behavior online.

What we know about the internet, families, and the home is constrained by the scope of all these national studies. Most surveys focus particularly on the demographics of users and their primary activities on the web; age, gender, income, ethnicity, and rural/urban locations are compared and contrasted with respect to (for example) use of e-mail, chat rooms, types of web sites visited, and online shopping habits. While these data shed light on family access to and use of the internet, they tell us very little about the *consequences* of that use for the family, family interactions, or quality of home life. Because the market research studies are conducted for a commercial clientele, their focus is particularly centered on consumer behavior and characteristics rather than on intimate relations, roles, and the dynamics of family life. Reports are also costly and therefore not readily accessible to the public or the scholarly research community—the price of individual market reports is often several hundred dollars, and full access to CommerceNet's internet demographics database, for example, costs $10,000 per year.

Insights into the impacts of the internet on the family consequently derive from more specialized studies that concentrate on these issues. The Pew Internet & American Life Project (funded fully by the Pew Charitable Trusts) regularly conducts nationally representative surveys on family and internet issues. Findings from this project include, for example, an analysis of how women use the internet to sustain their family relationships in comparison to men (Pew Internet & American Life Project 2000). Another example is the HomeNet study based at Carnegie Mellon University, a longitudinal research program of approximately 100 families and their internet use. Although HomeNet is not a nationally representative sample and can't be generalized to the American public, results of this research are nonetheless suggestive about the internet and family behaviors. HomeNet findings about the psychological and social impacts of the Internet (Kraut et al. 1998) have been particularly prominent in the scholarly literature and popular press. Other family-focused internet studies include Turow's (1999) analysis of parental perceptions and concerns about the internet, and the America Online/Roper Starch "cyberstudies" that examine the influence of the internet on family relationships, among other issues (Roper Starch Worldwide 1999a, 1999b).

With the exception of the U.S. Census data[6] and the HomeNet study, these national internet surveys typically obtain their data from random digit dial telephone samples. These methodologies, when done properly, yield national probability samples that allow us to make some basic generalizations about the internet, the family, and the home in the United States.

Families and the Internet: What We Know

American families are wired to the internet at much higher levels than American households without children. U.S. Census data for August 2000 show that 42 percent of all U.S. households had internet connectivity, while nearly 75 percent of all married couples with children had the internet at home, as did almost one-half of single-parent households headed by men (homes headed by single mothers were connected at the national average). Although the level of family income clearly has a strong contributing role in these patterns of household connectivity (see Organisation for Economic Co-operation and Development 1998), the basic fact remains that households with children are connected at higher rates than households without. Market research projections indicate that the internet gap between households with and without kids will narrow over the next several years, but will not disappear entirely (see fig. 6.1).

Families with children are clearly eager internet adopters and are motivated by a variety of factors—particularly that of providing educational advantages to their children. Interestingly, Turow (1999) found that the most important predictor of whether or not a household with a computer also had an internet connection was parental experience with the web outside of the home. Parents who had used the internet at work or elsewhere were significantly more likely to also have internet services in their homes. What this suggests is that, among other factors, prior

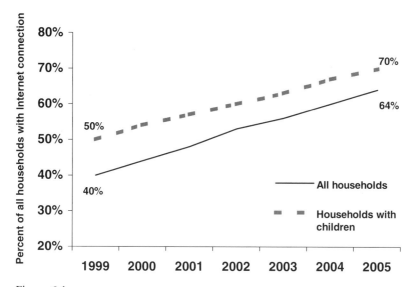

Figure 6.1
Percent of U.S. households with internet connectivity.
Source: Fulcrum Analytics; data are projected.

knowledge of the internet affects the interests and willingness of family households to go online.

Family Use of the Internet

The abundance of internet demographics and user studies allows us to make some stylized generalizations about the internet and its use by family members. E-mail and information gathering are overwhelmingly the "killer applications" for adults. Market research and other surveys typically show that more than 80 percent of individuals use the internet to search for information, and that more than 80 percent use it to communicate with friends, family, and colleagues (National Telecommunications and Information Administration 2000; Roper Starch Worldwide 1999a; UCLA Center for Communication Policy 2000). For children, 59 percent use the internet to write letters, and 52 percent use it for instant messaging; these communications applications are slightly more popular than game playing for kids.

Large numbers of adults report that communicating with friends and family is a highly important feature of their online activities *at home* (Roper Starch Worldwide 1999a). More than half of the women and men surveyed in one study reported that e-mail improved their connections to family members and significant friends, and that they now communicate with friends and family more often (Pew Internet & American Life Project 2000). Women in particular use and rely on e-mail more than men do to build and maintain family connections, and e-mail is much more central to women's communication patterns than to men's (Pew Internet & American Life Project 2000).

The importance of e-mail to creating, maintaining, and strengthening kinship and friendship ties for children and adults is repeatedly demonstrated in multiple public opinion surveys (Pew Internet & American Life Project 2000; Roper Starch Worldwide 1999a, 1999b; UCLA Center for Communication Policy 2000). While e-mail is clearly a central function of the internet for American families, it would appear that many family members regard it as a supplement to other primary forms of communication, and not a substitute. For example, the Roper Starch surveys (1999a; 1999b) found that even though e-mail was an important medium of communication for all respondents, nearly two-thirds of adults and children still preferred the telephone over e-mail for communicating with family members, and half or more preferred the telephone for communicating with friends.

In addition to e-mail, information gathering is the dominant activity for most internet users, and not surprisingly, children and adults have a distinctive mix of activities in terms of entertainment and content interests (Clemente 1998; Dibeehi and Miller 2000; Roper Starch Worldwide 1999a, 1999b; UCLA Center for Communication Policy 2000). For adults, top information needs involve (in rough rank order) news, health and medicine, travel and recreation, weather, and local area content. For kids, getting information about rock stars or music groups, sports, news or current events, and TV shows top the list (Roper Starch Worldwide 1999b). About the same proportion of adults and children—just under half—go online to play games, Educational activities are also comparable for adults and children: 29 percent of kids use the internet for homework, and 26 percent of adults used it for adult education and professional training (Dibeehi and Miller 2000; Roper Starch Worldwide 1999b).

Children and the Internet

A case study by Orleans and Laney (2000) suggests that the majority of children's time (60–70 percent) on a computer is spent on the internet, and survey research indicates that the amount of time that kids spend online varies by age. There is also a sizeable group of children who are daily internet users.

The *America Online/Roper Starch Youth Cyberstudy* (Roper Starch Worldwide 1999b) found that 20 percent of youths aged 9–17 went online everyday, although the mean number of days online for this age group was just about four days a week. In a typical day's use, eight out of ten kids spent an hour online, whereas teenagers (ages 12–17) spent two hours on the internet. The amount of time their kids spend online doesn't seem to trouble parents; in the UCLA internet study, nearly 90 percent of parents thought that their children spent just the right amount of time *or too little time* on the internet (UCLA Center for Communication Policy 2000).

Parents are clearly concerned, however, about the potential risks and dangers their children are exposed to online (Orleans and Laney 2000; Turow 1999; UCLA Center for Communication Policy 2000). In this respect they are not complacent, and actively set rules for their children's internet use. About one-third of parents use software filters to screen content their children may view online (Turow 1999; UCLA Center for Communication Policy 2000), and many more restrict the sites their kids can go to, limit their time online, and require them to check with an adult first (Roper Starch Worldwide 1999a).

What is perhaps not too surprising is that children do not perceive the presence of internet rules in quite the same way as their parents. Table 6.1 compares data from Roper Starch Internet surveys administered in 1999 to both adults and children. These two surveys asked identical questions about parental rules of internet use, and this table shows that children systematically *underreport* the presence of specific rules relative to their parents. The differences often exceed the margins of error for the

Table 6.1
Comparison of Parents' and Children's Perceptions of Parental Rules about Internet Use

Survey Item	Percent of Parents Responding Affirmatively	Percent of Children Responding Affirmatively
Parents set rules on children's internet use	77%	63%
Parents restrict areas that can be visited online	90	80
Parents limit amount of time children can spend online	82	51
Children must check with an adult first before going online	71	50
Children can go online only after homework is done	70	67
An adult must be present while children are online	42	14

Sources: Roper Starch Worldwide 1999a, 1999b. The combined margin of error for these two surveys is ±9 percentage points.

surveys, which combined for these questions are ±9 percentage points. While there could be issues related to responder bias and false reporting in these surveys,[7] the wide disparities in some answers also suggests that there may be a gap in understanding the boundaries of proper internet use within the home (and may also reflect a lack of "enforcement" on the part of parents).

Boys and girls also use their internet and computing time a little differently, although the net effect in both instances may be socialization with their peers. The Roper Starch survey found that more girls used the Internet for writing letters, instant messaging, and meeting new people with similar interests than boys; more boys, on the other hand, used the internet for playing games and getting sports information. Girls' applications of the internet clearly involve more communication and social interactivity *online*; however, case study research by Orleans and Laney (2000) suggests that boys may instead socialize face-to-face about their computing skills. Gender-based differences in computing and socialization are complex among children.

Conflicting Findings: Internet Impacts on the Family

Unfortunately, research on the actual impacts of the internet on the home and family, as opposed to descriptive insights into how it is used, is extremely limited in scale and scope. Findings on whether the internet does or does not displace other family activities (such as spending time together or watching TV) is contradictory and inconclusive; we also know little about the impact of telecommuting, a social development that has the potential to re-structure family life in significant ways. For example, Habib and Cornford (1996) identified several key areas of concern about the influence of telecommuting arrangements on rules, norms, and roles in the household; the blurring of spatial boundaries between home and office; and the disruption of time patterns in family routines. Too few studies shed light on these issues, and often with vastly different findings.

For example, Gurstein's (1991) research on 45 home teleworkers indicates that these individuals experienced guilt over neglecting their families, discomfort with the loss of their home as a "refuge" from work, and a sense of isolation while also worrying about being devalued by their office colleagues. Gurstein concludes that home-based telework "results in role conflicts, inadequate workspaces, the blurring of the work/leisure time division, and the tendency for 'overwork' to occur" (p. 177), a sharp contrast to the work of Riley and McCloskey (1996) who find that limited use of distributed work arrangements may have positive home impacts. Reporting on a pilot program in which GTE Corporation allowed managerial employees to work at home one day a week for six months, the authors find that "of the 120 participants in the telecommuting pilot study, 75 percent reported increased feelings of satisfaction with their home life [and] 44 percent reported having more quality time with the family" (p. 87).

Several studies from the past few years have also received considerable media attention regarding the harmful social and psychological effects of the internet. Prominent among these are the HomeNet finding that increased use of the internet is statistically associated with social isolation from one's family and depression (Kraut et al. 1998), and the Stanford study, which reported that "the more hours people use the Internet, the less time they spend with real human beings" (Nie and Erbring 2000). Although the potential harms of internet use should not be diminished, the HomeNet and Stanford studies reflect subtleties that are not typically reported in discussions about their results. A larger body of surveys and research suggests—on balance—that internet use may enhance socialization, friendship formation, and an individual's sense of connectedness to family and community.

Is the Internet Harmful to Families?

Kraut et al. (1998) found evidence that greater use of the internet was associated with (1) "small but statistically significant declines" in social integration as reflected by family communication and the size of the individual's social network, (2) self-reported loneliness, and (3) increased depression. These correlations held even after controlling for initial states of loneliness, social involvement, internet use, depression, stress, and so forth.

Several subtleties about these findings are not typically acknowledged in media and scholarly discussions of the results. First is the authors' own observations that the decline in social integration was *small*. Second, while the authors argue that their methods and findings indicate a causal relationship between increased internet usage and worsening psychological states, the study does not account for the possibility that an external condition—such as loss of a job or marital conflict—might have triggered social withdrawal and depression during the period of study. Because of this, greater internet use could be the *consequence* of depression, loneliness, and social withdrawal caused by events that occurred during the course of the study, a dynamic that was not explicitly considered by the authors. In addition, because HomeNet analyzes data from a volunteer group of families in Pittsburgh, the study is not representative of the larger population, so it is also possible that there were factors at work unique to this location (such as economic cycles or seasonal affective disorder).

Findings from the Stanford study reflect similar nuances. Although the study claims to be a representative sample of the U.S. population, it reports figures that are highly inconsistent with U.S. Bureau of the Census data, which are widely considered to be the most nationally valid statistics. For example, the Stanford study reports that in December 1999, 65 percent of American households had at least one computer, whereas the August 2000, the U.S. Census computer survey found that only 51 percent of American households had a PC (National Telecommunications and Information Administration 2000), a 14 percentage point difference that substantially exceeds the margin of error for both surveys.

In addition, while much was made in the Stanford study of the fact that increased internet activity reflected a loss of contact with an individual's "social environment," the context and details of that finding were missing. Only 15 percent of the study's respondents spent more than ten hours per week on line; of these individuals, 13 percent reported spending less time attending events outside of the home, and 15 percent reported spending less time with family and friends. The vast majority of internet users in this study (two-thirds) logged on five hours or less each week, and fewer than 10 percent of these said they spent less time outside of the home or with family and friends. Reduced social interaction as a consequence of internet use reflected, in context, a relatively small proportion of the individuals in this study. Fewer than 7 out of every 100 respondents reported spending less time outside of the home or with family and friends as the amount of time they spent online increased.

The Stanford study and the language used to describe it (the lack of contact with "real human beings" or one's "social environment") are troublesome in terms of their portrayal of internet activities as somehow not real and not social. As seen in many valid statistical research surveys (National Telecommunications and Information Administration 2000; Pew Internet & American Life Project 2000; Roper Starch Worldwide 1999a, 1999b; UCLA Center for Communication Policy) adults and children in families spend a good deal of their time online using e-mail and instant messaging to socialize with friends and family members. Perhaps most importantly, their perceptions are that being online has in fact *strengthened* those ties and social relationships.

For example, two-thirds of adults in one study indicated that e-mail has improved their connections with significant friends, and more than half reported that their e-mail activity has improved relations to family members (Pew Internet & American Life Project 2000). Thirty-nine percent of children believe that the internet has made their friendships better, and only 1 percent thought that the internet had a negative effect on their friendships (Roper Starch Worldwide 1999b). The *UCLA Internet Report* (UCLA Center for Communication Policy 2000) also identified several positive and neutral aspects of family use of the internet:

• Nearly half of internet users reported spending "at least some time each week using the Internet with other household members."

• Three-quarters of respondents said they *never* felt ignored because a household member spent too much time online, in contrast to the 6 percent who often felt ignored.

• Internet users and non-users spent the same amount of time socializing with friends, and only nominal differences existed in the amount of time they spent socializing with family.

• Only nominal differences existed in the amount of life dissatisfaction, interaction anxiety, powerlessness, and loneliness that people who did and did not use the internet felt. Overall, people who *did not* use the internet had slightly higher levels of social discomfort that those who did.

Case study and survey research also strongly suggests that time online can mirror face-to-face community building and affiliation. Katz and Aspden (1997) found that long-term internet users belonged to more community organizations than any other group in their study (those not online or former internet users, for example). Kavanaugh and Patterson (2001) report that citizens' participation in the Blacksburg Electronic Village reflected broader patterns of community involvement and did not diminish local community-building efforts. Parks and Floyd (1996) and Parks and Roberts (1998) consistently found that a sizeable proportion of individuals developed real and meaningful friendships online that then migrated to face-to-face contact. Baym (1999), Jones (1995; 1998), Rheingold (1993) and Turkle (1996) all reported that a real, human sense of community can develop online.

Perhaps the most significant contrast to the "negative" internet studies is the research that reports reduced isolation and a greater sense of social connection through online interactions. Although not pertaining to family activities online per se, these studies do indicate that people are finding social support and affiliation online, and that it is not safe to assume that time spent online is less social or somehow not "real" compared to face-to-face interactions. For example, Dunham et al. (1998) found that single teenage moms were active users of a bulletin board community set up for them. The more socially isolated these mothers were in their real lives—without support from family, friends, or the baby's father—the more likely they were to go online for help and social relations. These authors found that there were statistically significant differences in the levels of stress these mothers felt and the amount of time they interacted online; teen single mothers who spent more time online were less stressed than mothers who didn't.

Mickelson's (1997) comparative study of face-to-face and online support groups for parents with children who had mental retardation, autism, or developmental delays was also revealing: the more parents perceived their child's condition as a social stigma, the more likely they were to go online for support. Online parents in this study also regarded their social networks as much less supportive than parents in the face-to-face support groups, and the more stress they perceived with respect to their child's needs, the more likely they were to go online.

These findings parallel that of research conducted by Davison and Pennebaker (1997) and McKenna and Bargh (1998). Davison and Pennebaker found in an extensive survey of online and face-to-face support groups that people with stigmatized or potentially embarrassing conditions sought out online support more so than people with more socially acceptable conditions. Thus people with AIDS, alcoholism, and prostate cancer were more likely to go online for social support than people with illnesses such as heart disease, who tended to join face-to-face support groups. In a complex set of three studies on socially marginalized conditions (including those that are visible, such as obesity, and those that are not, such as sexual orientation), McKenna and Bargh found that participation in online newsgroups consistently contributed to "the transformation of an individual's social identity" (p. 691). For many participants in these newsgroups, conversing online helped them feel more socially acceptable and less marginalized, and enhanced a more positive sense of their self-identity.

In short, what people do online matters. The amount of time spent online by itself does not indicate whether real socialization with real human beings is compromised. Adults and children use e-mail to communicate with friends and family, and many people are able to find online communities that provide emotional support and affiliation. Indeed, in instances when our face-to-face families and communities may not be particularly supportive, as in the case of illness or socially stigmatizing conditions, individuals may find solace from online friendships. For family members and individuals who are suffering in "real life," being online may very simply help them feel better.

Two avenues of research do highlight ways in which internet use may be damaging to families, although the findings are at best suggestive and not conclusive. First, internet addiction may affect about 10 percent of internet users (Egger and Rauterberg 1996; Young 1998), and for this segment of the population, individual and family social life may truly suffer. Similarly, gambling online may compromise the financial well-being of a number of families; estimates are that about 5 percent of the adult population goes online to gamble and play games of chance (Dibeehi and Miller 2000).

Second, research on video game playing by children may have implications for game playing on the web. This body of research is mixed, however, and evidence is found for both positive and negative behaviors associated with the use of video games. There is also evidence of neutral outcomes: these games do not necessarily have any observable effect on children. For example, video game playing does not necessarily make children less sociable (Wiegman and van Schie 1998), but it may encourage them to spend less time on homework, may be addictive for a number of children (just under 10 percent), and may lead them be more aggressive toward others (Phillips et al. 1995; Wiegman and van Schie 1998).

Video games appear to be more intellectually challenging and stimulating than television, and even though playing video games alone increases with age, children are more engaged with their families and friends when they do play with others (Kubey and Larson 1990). Of greater cause for concern is the strong preference of boys for more aggressive video games, and for these preferences to be associated with more aggressive behavior and reduced sociability (Funk 1993; Wiegman and van Schie 1998). Since game playing on the web covers everything from solitaire to the intense role-playing environments of multi-user domains (MUDs), we may speculate that a similar breadth of findings will apply to children's use of games online—positive, neutral, and negative outcomes. However, given the amount and character of time children currently spend online—in 2000, most spent about one hour online about four days a week, with e-mail and instant messaging accounting for much of that use—it is likely that television and video games will have a much more significant impact on kids' prosocial and antisocial behavior than the internet.

Conclusions

Research on the implications of the internet for the family must be approached with a critical eye. In spite of some sensationalized reports, the current evidence does not suggest that family use of the internet encourages antisocial behavior, results in psychological harm, or increases social isolation. In contrast, the majority of adult internet users in multiple surveys indicate that the internet—particularly its e-mail functions—has resulted in strengthened ties with friends and family, and a sizeable proportion of children report likewise. A preponderant majority of household members do not feel neglected because of another family member's internet use, and internet users are likely to feel slightly less social discomfort than those who don't use the internet. Case studies and surveys also indicate that when their face-to-face families and communities fail them, individuals may find support, affiliation, and enhanced self-esteem online. While there may be clearly damaging effects of internet use on American families, the evidence suggests that this outcome may be experienced by a small minority of households.

The general lack of impacts research and the contradictory nature of findings that do exist suggest a strong *caveat lector*—led the reader beware—for consumers of internet research. It is altogether too easy to over generalize from findings that may be situation-specific, and frequently the findings are either misstated or misrepresented in the media. Research on the implications of the internet for the family must therefore be approached with a critical eye. As a first concern, if the methodology doesn't reflect a valid, nationally representative sample, the findings must be regarded as suggestive at best, no matter how intriguing the results. As a second issue, press releases and media sound bites are likely to misrepresent the findings through sins of omission: details that might qualify the results or put the magnitude of the findings in perspective are often too complicated to include in simple public announcements. The burden is therefore put on the reader to put the reports in perspective and dig deeper into the studies.

What we do not know about impacts is substantial. Much of the research findings reflect the dominant demographic and socioeconomic character of household internet users—relatively affluent white families. Studies that examine variations in the role of the internet for different American minorities and ethnic groups are few, and preliminary evidence suggests that, for example, African Americans use the internet differently than white Americans (Spooner and Rainie 2000).

In addition, how do families and individuals use information gained from the web and with what consequences? Can disadvantaged families use the internet to offset their information poverty (Childers 1975)? Are families with the internet any better off or happier than families without? How does the presence of the internet and home computing affect family dynamics and relationships? Are there pathologies associated with extensive internet use? How does telework at home affect the nature of home and the roles of family members? These questions and others immediately come to mind when reflecting on "the wired homestead."

While it is cliché to call for more surveys, more data collection, and more research, it is also clear that the data needed to answer fundamental questions about the impact of the internet on the family are lacking. We simply do not know whether the presence of this technology in the home "makes a difference," how, and whether it is worth the costs. These knowledge and inquiry gaps will be hard to fill. Impact research, when properly conducted, is labor intensive, expensive, and time consuming.

Notes

This research was supported as part of a special program on Social and Economic Implications of Information Technologies (see ⟨http://srsweb.nsf.gov/it_site/it/infotech.htm⟩) sponsored by the National Science Foundation through contracts to the Science and Technology Policy Program of SRI Inc. I would like to thank Eileen Collins at the National Science Foundation and Robert Carr at SRI Inc. for their insights on earlier versions of this work.

1. Because household income is the factor that correlates most strongly and most consistently with household purchases of computers/Internet (Organisation for Economic Co-Operation and Development 1998), it is undoubtedly a strong determinant here. Two-parent households and male single-parent households generally fall into higher income categories; female-headed single parent homes have rates of internet adoption (43 percent) comparable to that of the nation as a whole.

2. See U.S. Bureau of the Census, Current Population Survey, Computer Ownership Supplements, ⟨http://www.bls.census.gov/cps/computer/computer.htm⟩. Accessed December 11, 2000.

3. See CommerceNet, Gateway to Internet Demographics Online, ⟨http://www.commerce.net/research/gideon/start.html⟩. Accessed December 11, 2000.

4. Fulcrum Analytics was previously known as Cyber Dialogue. See ⟨www.fulcrumanalytics.com⟩. Accessed June 11, 2002.

5. For example, the WWW User Survey sponsored by the Graphics, Visualization, and Usability Center at Georgia Tech occurred twice a year from 1994 to 1998 but has since been discontinued until a more statistically valid survey methodology can be developed.

6. Internet data obtained through supplements to the Current Population Survey of the U.S. Bureau of the Census are based on a sampling of actual households as physically verified by the ten-year census. In contrast, national random digit dial telephone surveys are based on a sampling of residences as listed in telephone directories. Both forms of sampling are generalizable to the U.S. population.

7. There is also the possibility that older children answered the survey, creating the disparity is responses. Parents generally had stricter rules for younger children under age 11.

References

Baym, Nancy K. 1999. *Tune In, Log On: Soaps, Fandom, and On-Line Community*. Thousand Oaks, Calif.: Sage.

Childers, Thomas. 1975. *The Information-Poor in America*. Metuchen, N.J.: Scarecrow Press.

Clemente, Peter. 1998. *State of the Net*. New York: McGraw-Hill.

Davison, Kathryn P., and James W. Pennebaker. 1997. "Virtual Narratives: Illness Representations in Online Support Groups." In Keith Petrie and John A. Weinman (eds.), *Perceptions of Health and Illness: Current Research and Applications* (pp. 463–486). Singapore: Harwood Academic Publishers.

Dibeehi, Qaalfa, and Tom Miller. 2000. "The Virtual Future: Five-Year Internet Forecast," Cyber Dialogue, Inc. Industry Brief, *The Internet Consumer*, Year 2000, No. 2 (New York, NY). [Report available from Fulcrum Analytics, ⟨www.fulcrumanalytics.com⟩ accessed June 11, 2002.]

Dunham, Phillip J., Alan Hurshman, Elaine Litwin, Joanne Gusella, Christine Ellsworth, and Peter W. D. Dodd. 1998. "Computer-Mediated Social Support: Single Young Mothers as a Model System," *American Journal of Community Psychology* 26(2): 284–306.

Egger, Oliver, and Matthias Rauterberg. 1996. "Internet Behaviour and Addiction." Web page accessed April 12, 1999. ⟨http://www.ifap.bepr.ethz.ch/~egger/ibq/res.htm⟩.

Finn, Jerry. 1999. "An Exploration of Helping Processes in an Online Self-Help Group Focusing on Issues of Disability." *Health and Social Work* 24(3): 220–231.

Funk, J. B. 1993. "Reevaluating the Impact of Video Games." *Clinical Pediatrics* 32(2): 86–90.

Gurstein, Penny. 1991. "Working at Home and Living at Home: Emerging Scenarios." *Journal of Architectural and Planning Research* 8(2): 164–180.

Habib, Laurence, and Tony Cornford. 1996. "The Virtual Office and Family Life." In *SIGCPR/SIGMIS '96; Proceedings of the 1996 Annual Meetings of the Association for Computing Machinery Special Interest Group on Computer Personnel Research/Special Interest Group on Management Information Systems* (pp. 296–304). Denver: Association for Computing Machinery.

Jones, Steven G., ed. 1995. *CyberSociety: Computer-Mediated Communication and Community*. Thousand Oaks, Calif.: Sage.

Jones, Steven G., ed. 1998. *CyberSociety 2.0: Revisiting Computer-Mediated Communication and Community*. Thousand Oaks, Calif.: Sage.

Katz, James E., and Phillip Aspden. 1997. "A Nation of Strangers?" *Communications of the ACM* 40(12): 81–86.

Kavanaugh, Andrea, and Scott Patterson. 2001. "The Impact of Community Computer Networks on Social Capital and Community Involvement." *American Behavioral Scientist* 45(3): 496–509.

Kraut, Robert, Vicki Lundmark, Michael Patterson, Sara Kiesler, Tridas Mukhopadhyay, and William Scherlis. 1998. "Internet Paradox: A Social Technology That Reduces Social Involvement and Psychological Well-Being?" *American Psychologist* 53(9): 1017–1031.

Kraut, Robert, William Scherlis, Tridas Mukhopadhyay, Jane Manning, and Sara Kiesler. 1996. "The HomeNet Field Trial of Residential Internet Services." *Communications of the ACM* 39(12): 55–63.

Kubey, Robert, and Reed Larson. 1990. "The Use and Experience of the New Video Media among Children and Young Adolescents." *Communication Research* 17(1): 107–130.

Lindlof, Thomas R. 1992. "Computing Tales: Parents' Discourse about Technology and Family." *Social Science Computer Review* 10(3): 291–309.

McKenna, Katelyn Y. A., and John A. Bargh. 1998. "Coming Out in the Age of the Internet: Identity 'Demarginalization' through Virtual Group Participation." *Journal of Personality and Social Psychology* 75(3): 681–694.

Mickelson, Kristin. 1997. "Seeking Social Support: Parents in Electronic Support Groups." In Sara Kiesler (ed.), *Culture of the Internet* (pp. 157–178). Mahwah, N.J.: Erlbaum.

National Telecommunications and Information Administration. 2000. *Falling through the Net: Toward Digital Inclusion.* Washington, D.C.: U.S. Department of Commerce. ⟨http://www.ntia.doc.gov/ntiahome/fttn00/contents00.html⟩ accessed November 15, 2000.

Nie, Norman, and Lutz Erbring. 2000. *Internet and Society: A Preliminary Report*, Stanford Institute for the Quantitative Study of Society, Stanford University. [www.stanford.edu/group/siqss/]. Accessed June 28, 2000.

Organisation for Economic Co-operation and Development. 1998. *Information Technology Outlook 1997.* Paris: Organisation for Economic Co-operation and Development.

Orleans, Myron, and Margaret C. Laney. 2000. "Children's Computer Use in the Home: Isolation or Sociation?" *Social Science Computer Review* 18(1): 56–72.

Parks, Malcolm R., and Kory Floyd. 1996. "Making Friends in Cyberspace." *Journal of Communication* 46(1): 80–97.

Parks, Malcolm R., and Lynne D. Roberts. 1998. "'Making MOOsic': The Development of Personal Relationships On-Line and a Comparison to Their Off-Line Counterparts." *Journal of Social and Personal Relationships* 15, no. 4 (August): 517–537.

Pew Internet and American Life Project. 2000. Tracking Online Life: How Women Use the Internet to Cultivate Relationships With Family and Friends. ⟨http://www.pewinternet.org/reports/index.asp⟩ Accessed December 11, 2000.

Phillips, Carol A., Susan Rolls, Andrew Rouse, and Mark D. Griffiths. 1995. "Home Video Game Playing in Schoolchildren: A Study of Incidence and Patterns of Play." *Journal of Adolescence* 18: 687–691.

Rheingold, Howard. 1993. *The Virtual Community: Homesteading on the Electronic Frontier.* Reading, Mass.: Addison-Wesley.

Riley, Francine, and Donna W. McCloskey. 1996. "GTE's Experience with Telecommuting: Helping People Balance Work and Family." In *SIGCPR/ SIGMIS '96; Proceedings of the 1996 Annual Meetings of the Association for Computing Machinery Special Interest Group on Computer Personnel Research/ Special Interest Group on Management Information Systems* (pp. 85–93). Denver: Association for Computing Machinery.

Roper Starch Worldwide. 1999a. The America Online/Roper Starch Cyberstudy, Roper Report Number CNT-154. [http://corp.aol.com/press/roper.html] accessed December 11, 2000.

Roper Starch Worldwide. 1999b. The America Online/Roper Starch Youth Cyberstudy, Roper Report Number CNT-154. ⟨http://corp.aol.com/press/roper. html⟩ accessed December 11, 2000.

Sharf, Barbara F. 1997. "Communicating Breast Cancer On-Line: Support and Empowerment on the Internet." *Women and Health* 26(1): 65–84.

Spooner, Tom, and Lee Rainie. 2000. African Americans and the Internet. Pew Internet & American Life Project ⟨http://www.pewinternet.org⟩ accessed December 11, 2000.

Turkle, Sherry. 1996. "Virtuality and Its Discontents." *The American Prospect* 24 (Winter): 50–57.

Turow, Joseph. 1999. *The Internet and the Family: The View from Parents, The View From the* Press, The Annenberg Public Policy Center Report Series No. 27, University of Pennsylvania. ⟨http://www.appcpenn.org/pubs.htm⟩ accessed December 11, 2000.

UCLA Center for Communication Policy. 2000. *The UCLA Internet Report: Surveying the Digital Future.* ⟨http:www.ccp.ucla.edu⟩ accessed January 9, 2001.

Wiegman, O., and E. G. van Schie. 1998. "Video Game Playing and Its Relations With Aggressive and Prosocial Behavior." *British Journal of Social Psychology* 37: 367–378.

Weinberg, Nancy, Janet S. Uken, John Schmale, and Margaret Adamek. 1995. "Therapeutic Factors: Their Presence in a Computer-Mediated Support Group." *Social Work with Groups* 18(4): 57–69.

Young, Kimberly S. 1998. *Caught in the Net.* New York: Wiley.

7

A Family Systems Approach to Examining the Role of the Internet in the Home

Amy B. Jordan

Children today live in environments that are highly saturated with media. Virtually every American home has at least one television set and over half of all children have a TV in their bedroom (Stanger & Gridina 1999). In the last two decades, television has been joined by several new media technologies that extend the capabilities of the medium. Nearly every family (97.8 percent) has a videocassette recorder, and more than three-quarters (77.4 percent) have cable or satellite television. In addition to the ubiquity of television, there are more household media available to children in their homes than ever before, including videogame equipment (67 percent) and home computers (68.2 percent). Into this media mix comes the Internet—an extension of the television screen or home computer that brings a new dimension of the outside world into the inner sanctum of the home.

Families make available certain kinds of media within the home but also provide notions about *how* and *when* to use media (e.g., the Internet is for socializing and television is for entertainment) and how to interpret media content (e.g., newspaper stories are real, TV sitcoms are pretend). Much of this socialization does not occur though the explicit directives of parents. Instead, the interactions of family members subtly create patterned ways of thinking about and using the media. These patterns become habits, and these habits become the stuff of everyday experience. As Berger and Luckman have argued: "The reality of everyday life maintains itself by being embodied in routines" (1966, p. 137). In today's family, the media have become part and parcel of the routine of family life.

One might take any one of a number of approaches to integrate ideas about the family into media research. Some family researchers emphasize the *roles* the individual members assume in their families (Morley 1980). Others examine the way families construct a common social reality by building meaning through repeated, patterned *interactions* (Berger and Luckman 1966; Pollner and McDonald-Wilker 1985). Still others think about the family through its individual and collective *life cycles*, tracing the changes in structure and function over time (Aldous 1978).

Each of these approaches is helpful for understanding how families assimilate, adapt and accommodate to new media. Yet as a research framework, the family systems theory approach incorporates elements from each of these perspectives and provides researchers with terms and tools for exploring Internet usage within the totality of the family's experience.

Family Systems Theory: A Brief History

Family systems theory grew out of the broader general systems theory, which adheres to the basic premise that one must study "wholes" rather than "parts" in order to understand how the system functions (Bavelas & Segal 1982; Vetere & Gale 1987). Early research in the area of systems theory was conducted by von Bertalanffy, a biologist interested in how organisms maintained and adapted to their changing environments. A decade later, general systems theory was applied to military technology and organizational behavior (Vetere & Gale 1987). It wasn't until the 1950s, however, that clinicians in psychology began to apply systems theory concepts. Most notable were Bateson and his colleagues, who extended the theory to schizophrenic symptoms (Bateson et al. 1956). With the systems approach, a schizophrenic's behavior came to be viewed as an adaptive response to dysfunctional family environment (Bavelas & Segal 1982).

During the next twenty years, general systems theory became a strong component when thinking about "normal" families (Bochner & Eisenberg 1987). Individuals were conceptualized as members of an ecological system. Family members are seen as sharing physical and emotional closeness and as mutually influential. Moreover, the emerging cadre of family systems theorists recognized the importance of identifying how the distinct members and dimensions of the family work to establish and regulate the functioning of the whole, despite internal and external pressures to change. As Bochner and Eisenberg state:

[This] represented an epistemological turn away from thinking of "forces" or "causes" and toward thinking of "relationships" and "contexts"; away from emphasizing what "goes on under the skin" or "inside the head" and toward a focus on the communicative behavior that takes place between people; away from linear models and toward recursive or circular descriptions. (1987, p. 4)

Systems theory has come to span the physical, biological, cognitive and social worlds (Rosenblatt 1994). Its application to family life encourages the study of whole families and focuses on the process by which family life emerges as patterned and meaningful to its members. Family systems theory provided the researcher interested in family and media with a new way to think about relationships within the home. It attempts to account for all family members and their reciprocal influences on one another, as well as the monitoring and negotiation of how the external world should be rejected, assimilated, or accommodated. Finally, it emphasizes the importance of family communication and family relationships in defining media use rather than focusing on the technology itself as driving patterns of behavior.

The family systems framework examines how the family creates patterns of media use that "fit" with the norms, values, and beliefs that define the family system. It draws out components of the family system that provide important contexts for behavior—for example, family boundaries and members' roles. From this perspective, researchers consider mass media within a larger structure of patterned behaviors and relationships. It posits that in order to truly understand media in children's lives—and for the purposes of this chapter, children's use of the Internet—one must understand the medium's role in family life and the variety of contexts that will determine its meaning.

Strictly speaking, family systems theory is more a conceptual framework than a theory. As Rosenblatt (1994) has pointed out, the systems approach—particularly as it is applied to the family—does not offer integrated or comprehensive propositions, nor does it offer much in the way of predictive value. One might argue that it does, however, offer explanations for retrospectively observed patterns of phenomena. Like Rosenblatt, I will use the terms "conceptual framework" and "theory" interchangably.

Structural and Social Dimensions of the Family System

The numerous components of family life can be considered for the ways in which they shape and reflect the "whole" of the family system. As a heuristic device, this section divides the home into two domains of family life: The "structural dimension" (how space and time are organized) and the "social dimension" (the family member's acquisition of identity, roles, rules, and interactions).

Time and Space within the Home

The structural domain of family life contains those aspects of the home which provide the family with notions about where and when day-to-day living should be carried out. The importance of space to human interaction and functioning has been recognized by social scientists, most notably Edward Hall who argued that there are both norms for the distances people keep between one another and the implications of the spatial construction of any given social environment for human behavior (Hall 1966).

The idea that space within the home is meaningful and consciously constructed has implications for the role media will play in family life (Ashcraft & Scheflin 1976; Lull 1980). In their ethnographic study of television and VCR use in the home, Lindlof and his colleagues revealed that rooms are arranged around television sets while allowing for other, simultaneous activities, such as eating or ironing (Lindlof, Shatzer & Wilkinson 1988). Television, for example, occupies a central position in many family gathering areas, leading one scholar to dub it the "electronic hearth" (Tichi 1991). Furniture is arranged not for ease in conversation or interaction but for ease in viewing (Leichter et al. 1985).

Others have argued that the visibility of a medium in a room is related to the importance of the role it plays in a family. Studies from the early

1980s, for example, found that the accessibility of the TV set was related to the amount of viewing done by families. Bryce and Leichter (1983) write that "television sets that were visually and aurally accessible from the centers of social interaction were on more often ... were viewed more often and were more available for family mediation than were sets in socially isolated locations" (p. 132).

Later researchers have found that the rise of multi-television households has altered the ability of families to centrally locate themselves around the TV (Lawrence & Wozniak 1989; Wartella & Mazzarella 1990) and the means by which parents oversee their children's TV consumption (Huston et al. 1992). Research also indicates that children with bedroom sets are less likely to have rules about the medium and are more likely to watch programs their parents would not approve of (Holz 1998). This relationship may be the result of tacit approval of the medium (i.e., parents who think television to be a harmless or positive force are more likely to approve bedroom TVs) or the consequence of spatial arrangements (since bedroom TV viewing is outside of the purview of the parents). These trends with television may provide insight into the role of the Internet in the family system's spatial structure.

Studies also show that computers are often located in children's bedrooms. According to a recent study by the Kaiser Family Foundation (1999), approximately 16 percent of American children have computers in their bedroom and 7 percent have online access in there. Though bedroom computers are not as common as bedroom TVs, many "experts" recommend that Internet-linked computers be kept in a central location in order to aid parental oversight of the medium (Carlson 1999; Stroh 1999). They argue that without such monitoring, children may accidentally or purposefully access sexually explicit sites that are disturbing to children or participate in chat rooms that are inappropriate or potentially compromising their safety.

In addition to the potential relationship between the spatial location of the online computer and parents' monitoring capability, the systems approach calls for a consideration of the arrangements of the room that encourage or discourage children's use of space and time in particular ways. At a recent Annenberg Public Policy Center conference, industry insiders discussed the increasing tendency of children to use multiple media simultaneously. One television executive argued that since many online computers are located in rooms equipped with television sets, children should be encouraged to provide instantaneous online feedback to the producers of television programs they are watching (Woolf & Allen 2001).

Family members' notions about time—its importance and its ideal use—can vary within and between homes. Time can be seen as a scarce resource which must not be wasted or as an abundant commodity that needs to be filled. Time can even be both scarce and abundant, depending on the situation (e.g., work vs. vacation) or the family members' responsibilities (parent vs. child). Notions of time may lead to varying temporal structures within and across family systems. In his cross-cultural studies, Hall (1959) uncovered a dichotomy of temporal orientation: "monochronic" cultures—which emphasized segmentation of activities, focus, and promptness; and "polychronic" cultures—which reflected multiple and simultaneous tasking and emphasized the importance of completing transactions. One can see a variety of temporal orientations within the culture of the family as well.

In an ethnographic study of the role of media in family life, I have found that the temporal ideologies of families varied according to their socioeconomic status (Jordan 1991). Parents' orientations toward time (polychronic vs. monochronic) were reflected in the ways they socialized their children to use media, particularly television viewing. Children from more affluent and well-educated homes tended to be socialized to view time as a precious resource, one that should not be "wasted" with excessive amounts of viewing. Though children from less affluent homes also had some restrictions on time spent viewing television, their parents' rules were more likely to be centered around content (what they could watch). This difference could be traced to parents' own valuation of time and experiences with managing time within the workforce (Jordan 1991). Parents with occupations that offer autonomy but demand self-motivation (e.g., professors, lawyers, writers) are more likely to try to instill in their children notions of managing and scheduling time than parents whose jobs were externally controlled (e.g., factory workers, secretaries, and firefighters). Others have demonstrated the relationships between education and workplace experiences and childrearing practices as well, most notably in the domain of discipline (Kohn & Schooler 1983).

Parents' conceptions of time (how it should be valued, how it should be used) are likely to be reflected in their views of their children's use of the Internet. For those who see the World Wide Web as a potentially enriching resource of information and/or a valuable educational tool, Internet use may be encouraged as a productive leisure time activity. Parents' views of the Internet's educational promise, however, may be driven by their own experiences with it. Turow (1999), for example, found that parents who use the Web for work are much more "gung ho" about it (and more likely to bring it into the home) than parents whose jobs do not involve the Internet. In addition, it is possible that, in general, parents are more likely to use the Internet for work while children use it for entertainment. This may impact conceptions of online time use. Unlike television, which is more likely to be seen as a monolithic medium (with little variation in use and content), the Internet provides a variety of experiences for children—from chat rooms to encyclopedias to pornography. Thus, it is critical to examine how the form and content of the medium intersect with parents' judgments of its value. In addition, it is important to explore how parents' judgments of the Internet's value shape the ways children perceive it and ultimately use it.

Research thus far seems to indicate that the majority of children do not spend much time online. A 1999 Kaiser Family Foundation survey of children's media use indicates that only 3 percent of children ages 2 to 16 spend more than one hour a day online while 64 percent spend more than one hour per day with television. In fact, on average, children spend only about 8 minutes per day on the Internet. As the more and more families get online, and more and more children become comfortable surfing the Web, the amount of time children spend on the Web may increase dramatically. In addition, it is difficult to get an accurate measure of online time through self-report. It is also difficult to get up-to-date statistics on children's time with the Internet, given the exponential growth of availability both in and out of the home. With these caveats, it should be noted that the majority of parents with children online say that they restrict when their children can access the Internet and how much time they can spend online (Turow 1999).

The technological capacity of the Internet itself may begin to shape how children use the medium. It is possible to engage in multiple activities simultaneously online. For example, children researching a term paper for social studies can minimize several sites and bring them up on demand, while, at the same time, engage in instant messaging (IM) with their friends without ever closing out of a window.

The Social Dimensions of the Home

The uses of media within the social domain of the home have historically been of interest to media researchers, in part because of concerns over the impact of media on family relationships (Liebert, Sprafkin & Davidson 1982; Maccoby 1954; Morley 1986). In the following section, family's patterns of interaction, the development of gendered roles and individual identities, and the mediation practices of parents are separated for discussion here in order to consider the Internet in the social dimension of the family system. It is recognized, however, that the structural and the social dimensions of family life are tightly intertwined.

Interaction One of the most frequently expressed concerns about children's use of the Internet in both the press and in national surveys is the fear that children's connections to a "machine" and the development of relationships that are disconnected in physical space will create a generation of children who have no social skills (Turow 1999). Indeed, much of the early commentary on television's ill effects centered around fears of creating children who were isolated and "drugged" into a zombie-like stupor (Winn 1977). There were also fears that television created a home environment in which children no longer talked with one another or their parents (Schramm, Lyle & Parker 1961). Over the years, researchers have found that while family interaction decreases to some degree as a result of TV viewing, physical closeness (Medrich et al. 1982) and common conversational agendas (Lull 1980) are often retained when TV viewing is a shared activity.

Interestingly, many of the same fears about the isolating effect of television have reemerged with the Internet. In 1998, Kraut and his colleagues released research that indicated that the use of the Internet was associated with a decline in communication with family members in the household. Another study found that nearly half of online parents agree with the statement that "Families who spend a lot of time online talk to each other less than they otherwise would" (Turow 1999). Yet as with television, the relationship between Internet use and social avoidance has become less clear. Kraut has recently reported that the same online users, three years later, show no signs of the negative effects of Internet use that were initially present when Internet use was novel to them (Guernsey 2001).

Lull's research (1980) on the social uses of television by the family illustrates that, in fact, families may be assimilating the Internet into the family system in ways that are not easily measured through survey and interview questions. His observations of families illustrated that television content often found its way into conversations between family members at times outside of the viewing context. Similarly, Messaris (1983) argues that "mediation" in the form of "interaction" may be difficult to pick up since so much of it is unconscious behavior. Nevertheless, the Internet is less likely than television to be a shared medium. Unlike television, Internet content tends to cater to the specialized interests of family members—for example, Web sites for trading baseball cards or for researching a term paper on Henry Hudson. And unlike television, the Internet allows its users to "chat" in telephone-like situations (dyads) or party-like situations (groups of like-minded chatters). For these reasons, one is unlikely to see parallel use by members of the same family the way one might observe the patterns around TV. Rather, the Internet may provide a literal and figurative space in which family members are isolated and private. As Livingstone (1992) writes: "If television once brought the family together around the hearth, now domestic technologies permit the dispersal of family members to different rooms or different activities within the same space" (p. 128).

One interesting facet of Internet use is that it takes on unique social forms depending on the person within the family system who uses it. As others have written (see Subramanyam et al. 2002), the Internet has become a socially useful tool for adolescents who have appropriated it as a post-modern telephone. Adolescents have found ways to connect with one another in real time though the Internet (e.g., instant messaging), although perhaps at the expense of time that might be spent in face-to-face communication with one another and with other family members. This has yet to be examined carefully and is an important direction for future research.

Different family members may feel differing senses of efficacy with the Internet. The prevailing belief is that, in these early days of Internet use, children may often feel more comfortable with the technology than parents (Connolly & Schwartz 1999; Schmitt 2000; Stroh, 1999). Children may therefore be using computers (and by extension, the Internet) in isolation and may be living in homes where parents, who are less familiar with the medium, do not know how to use or even talk about the medium with them (Murdock et al. 1992).

Gender Roles In family systems theory, each member of the family contributes in unique ways to the family system and, as such, maintains "roles" that may be patterned by age, gender or other characteristics of the individuals (Rosenblatt 1994). One must recognize the reciprocal nature of the roles, and the functionality of them for the developing child and the organization of the family.

Researchers in media studies have long recognized that there are gender-related patterns surrounding the technologies, particularly in the domestic setting. Seiter (1999), for example, has written of men's tendency to dominate decision-making around the television set by dominating the remote control. Similarly, Gray (1992) found that the acquisition and use of the videocassette recorder by families in England was gendered; specifically, males typically decided upon the necessity of the machine, researched the options available, and set up the device within the home. The time-shifting function of the VCR is rarely used, in part because mothers never mastered the ability to program the device (Gray 1992; Lin 2001).

Computers have also been associated with gender-related behaviors. Turkle (1995) writes of the "computerphobia" and the interest and expertise men show relative to women vis-à-vis the technology. Gershuny's (1992) index reveals that the more "high tech" the device is, the more likely it is to be male-dominated in its use. Although the adoption and early use of new innovations may be gendered, there is also a tendency for discomfort to be transitional, particularly in the case of entertainment media which are eventually used by all family members (Gershuny 1992; Gray 1992; Turkle 1995).

When a new technology such as the Internet is brought into the domestic sphere, it is important to consider not only which family members adopt or use the new technologies, but which family members set up the guidelines about how, when and where it is used. In the case of television, research indicates that mothers typically set up the rules and restrictions with respect to children's TV viewing (Jordan 1990; Schmitt 2000), perhaps because she plays a greater role in the everyday supervision of children's activities (Hochschild 1989). Fathers, in turn, frequently "un-do" these guidelines (Jordan 1990; Schmitt 2000). Similarly, fathers typically make decisions about computer purchases and online access, and, presumably, fathers feel they know the technology best. Yet it is mothers who historically socialize children's media use. Will mothers feel less comfortable supervising online than television activities? Will they have a sense of how to construct guidelines and the capacity to enforce them, particularly if mothers don't know how to use the Internet well?

Adolescent Identity Development   According to many developmental psychologists, most American children go through a period during which they "separate" from adults. We call it adolescence. Media remain important to children in adolescence, though television use declines substantially and lower emotional involvement takes place when they watch TV (Comstock 1991). Studies suggest that during adolescence, television viewing becomes associated with the family. In his research on adolescent media use, Larson (1995) writes that "TV viewing reflects, or may be deliberately used, to maintain close emotional bonds to the family" (p. 542).

Generations of adolescents have used their bedrooms as sites of refuge and spaces in which they can express and explore their identities. These sites of identity formation are filled with cultural products and pathways to the world outside the home. Not surprisingly, children's bedrooms are increasingly becoming media centers (Kaiser Family Foundation 1999; Livingstone 1999; Stanger & Gridina 1999). The increasing diversity of media targeted specifically to adolescents allows young audiences greater specificity in choosing media that suit their moods and their passing interests, often in isolation from other family members (Arnett 1995). For adolescents seeking to "find themselves," television viewing becomes a more solitary activity (Larson 1995); music listening becomes associated with the process of disengagement from the family (Larson 1995; Roe 1987); magazines provide teenage girls with exemplars of beauty (Steel & Brown 1995); and telephones (or online chat rooms) offer social connection to peers (Steel & Brown 1995). Introducing the Internet into the plethora of choices for adolescents allows for an even greater ability to specifically address teens' issues, concerns, and interests. But it also provides an opportunity to connect with virtual social worlds outside of the family system. (See Calvert [2002] for a more in-depth discussion of the Internet and identity formation.)

Parental Mediation Strategies Andreasen (2001) has observed that television use is predicted by family rules rather than television rules—an observation that underscores the importance of recognizing the family as a system in which patterns are interwoven with media practices. Television scholars now have strong evidence that parents' mediation strategies vis-à-vis their children's television viewing are linked to larger norms; values and beliefs both reflect and shape what happens with the medium in the home.

Many researchers have considered "co-viewing" (parents and children watching together) to be a mediation strategy that would allow parents to monitor their children's choices and provide opportunity for discussion about TV-related content (Dorr, Kovaric & Doubleday 1989; Messaris 1983). But what leads parents to sit down and watch television with their children? Research has uncovered some interesting trends. First, it turns out that when parents and children watch television together, they are much more likely to watch adult than children's programming (Huston et al. 1992; Lin & Atkin 1989). Second, parents who co-view with their children tend to have a greater affinity toward the medium; that is, they like watching television (Austin et al. 1999). Thus, it appears that co-viewing as a mediation strategy may say more about parents' habits with television than any conscious strategy they have devised to "protect" or "inform" their children.

Experts have argued that it is important for parents and children to "co-view" the Internet (Connolly & Schwartz 1999; Stroh 1999)—that is, spend time together exploring and discussing Internet content and activities. While this may be a natural and comfortable process with television, the Internet may present more of a challenge. One obstacle is that parents who are not comfortable online may be less likely to use the medium as a way to share leisure time with children. Moreover, research on television co-viewing illustrates that parents watch TV with their children because they enjoy the content. Since Internet Web sites are created with highly specific audiences in mind (e.g., 4th graders who love Harry Potter, soccer moms who don't have time to shop), it is less likely that there would be content that is of mutual interest to both parents and children. In many ways, the Internet is designed to provide an individualistic rather than a shared experience (Montgomery 2000).

This pattern may be age-dependent. By necessity, very young children have to go online with their parents. Nick Jr., for instance, has a site with content directed at preschool children and their parents. Mothers and fathers do many of the activities on the child site with their own child (e.g., reading online stories). In addition, there is a parent section of the site where Nickelodeon provides information for parents, such as activities to do with their child. By adolescence, children and parents' interest in going online together will predictably wane, as adolescents increasingly assert their independence from parental control.

Another mediation strategy that has been explored by researchers is parents' practice of prohibiting and recommending programs for their children. Many of the restrictions parents have for children's television viewing involve children's exposure to violent (Cantor 1999) or scary (Valkenburg et al. 1999) content. However, research also indicates that there can sometimes be a discrepancy between what parents say they "protect" their children from and what children sometimes watch. Holz's (1998) focus group discussions with children reveal that though restrictions are in place, they are not consistently enforced—a finding which may partially explain the consistently high viewer ratings of violent programs such as *WWF Wrestling*, *Cops*, and *Walker, Texas Ranger* among children ages 2 to 12 (A. C. Nielsen 1999).

Issues with the Internet arise when parents worry that their children may visit age-inappropriate sites or unwittingly have their names added to e-mail lists. "Spam" (which is similar to "junk mail" in the non-virtual world) is a phenomenon that has been perceived as dangerous and annoying as robots harvest names from chat rooms and then spam all e-mail addresses. In this way, unwanted sexually explicit material and links can come to children anonymously through their own e-mail accounts (Calvert 2000).

In addition to forbidding or discouraging content that they don't want their children to see, parents may also positively direct children's media use; for example, they make specific recommendations for television programs their children should watch. In one study, nearly 42 percent of 10- to 17-year-old children said there are specific programs their parents encourage them to watch. Interestingly, the programs they listed were not targeted to children but were programs for a general audience—for example, the news, *Touched by an Angel*—or specific channels—for example, PBS or the Discovery Channel (Stanger 1997). It is possible for parents to provide the same sort of direction with the Internet as well; for example, parents can use the bookmark function on Internet service providers to direct children to desirable sites.

Research on parental mediation of television, however, indicates that in order for parents to be effective in shaping the media habits of their children, they must be familiar with the way the technology works and the kind of content that is available. Many parents of school age children, however, do not even seem to know enough about what is on television to be able to recommend specific program recommendations. In several recent studies, parents were virtually unaware of any of the educational programs being offered by the major networks to satisfy their public interest obligations to children (Holz 1998; Stanger & Gridina 1999).

Obstacles to active mediation of the Internet are even higher when one considers the range of content available through this medium. Though parents may be able to use filtering devices to screen children from potentially harmful content, recent studies indicate that the majority of parents do not employ them (Turow 1999). Moreover, there appears to be little consistently available information about the quality and content of Web sites appropriate for children (such as the information one might get from *TV Guide*). Turow suggests that parents track children's online visits in order to monitor and discuss the appropriate use of the Internet (and provide reminders to children that their parents care about where they go and what they do on the Web). This, he argues, may offer a mechanism for inculcating the norms and values of the family system into children's online habits (see Turow, this volume).

Such recommendations, however, may not fit with existing systems of family norms that value, for example, privacy. In addition, children entering adolescence need to develop a measure of autonomy, which may be expressed through choices of media that are counter to what parents would choose for their children or choose for themselves (Larson 1995).

Conclusion

Family systems theory holds that family norms, values and patterns of the system will both reflect and shape the general approach children take to media and the particular role the Internet will have in the individual and collective lives of family members. The home environment provides structural dimensions of space and time—domains of family life that reflect larger social values and orientations to media. Space within the home is a constructed element of the system that—consciously or not— provides family members with a sense of that which is shared (e.g., living room sofas arranged around the electronic hearth [Tichi 1991]) and that which is personal (computers with only one chair in front of them). Within this domain, children learn to think about the nature of time and the value of time. Such learning is subtly woven into the patterns of the family's day but also explicitly expressed through statements about the best ways to spend time and manage time. Children are socialized to beliefs about how much time to devote to online activities and whether "going online" is a productive way to spend time within this larger system.

Children's online choices and habits may also reflect and shape the social dimension of the family system. Mass media use in general may alter patterns of interactions between family members; and Internet use may give rise to unique issues—including the extent to which family members can share space, time and content in ways that promote family functioning and individual expression. New media such as the Internet are also assimilated into family members' ongoing need to define their role within the system (often in gender patterned ways) and develop a personal identity (a process that is particularly salient for adolescent family members). Finally, the mediation strategies parents use in the new multi-media environment of the home may not only reflect the kinds of mediation strategies they employ with television and other media, but also reflect their ongoing interest in socializing children to the larger norms and values of the family system.

Missing from this discussion of children's use of the Internet is the fact that children's knowledge of and expectations about the medium may be *external* to the family. Many children are now being exposed to computers for the first time in schools and, because of the e-rate which provides Internet service to schools at a discount, children may be introduced to the Web through peers and teachers—systems that are outside of the context of the home. One recent study conducted in Belgium found that quite often it is the children who initiate the demand for Internet access in the home and serve as the family experts on navigating the Web (Struys, Roe and van Rompaey 2001). Such dynamics in the family system—the openness of the family to external agents of change, the fluidity of roles vis-à-vis the Internet—likely have important implications for how the Internet shapes and is shaped by the home context. Ultimately, the family system is nested within larger social and cultural systems that have role (reword) in the experience of childhood and the Internet's role in the familial setting.

References

ACNielsen. 1999. Nielsen Television Index Top 100 Demographics for the Period 02/11–08/22/98. Special Report for Annenberg Public Policy Center of the University of Pennsylvania.

Aldous, J. 1978. *Family Careers: Developmental Change in Families.* New York: Wiley.

Andreasen, M. 2001. "Evolution in the Family's Use of Television: An Overview." In J. Bryant and A. Bryant (eds.), *Television and the American Family.* Mahwah N.J.: Erlbaum.

Arnett, J. 1995. "Adolescents' Uses of Media for Self-socialization." *Journal of Youth and Adolescence* 24: 519–533.

Ashcraft, N., and A. Scheflin. 1976. *People Space*. New York: Doubleday.

Austin, E., P. Bolls, Y. Fujioka, and J. Engelbertson. 1999. "How and Why Parents Take on the Tube." *Journal of Broadcasting and Electronic Media* 43: 175–193.

Bateson, G., D. Jackson, J. Haley, and J. Weakland. 1956. "Toward a Theory of Schizophrenia." *Behavioral Science* 1: 251–264.

Bavelas, J., and L. Segal. 1982. "Family Systems Theory: Background and Implications." *Journal of Communication* 32: 99–107.

Berger, P., and T. Luckman. 1966. *The Social Construction of Reality*. New York: Doubleday.

Bochner, A. 1976. "Conceptual Frontiers in the Study of Communication in Families: An Introduction to the Literature." *Human Communication Research* 2: 381–397.

Bochner, A., and E. Eisenberg. 1987. "Family Process." In C. Berger (ed.), *Handbook of Communication Science*. Beverly Hills, Calif.: Sage.

Brody, G., and Z. Stoneman. 1983. "The Influence of Television Viewing on Family Interactions." *Journal of Family Issues* 4: 329–348.

Brown, J., C. Dykers, J. Steele, and A. White. 1994. "Teen Room Culture: Where Media and Identities Intersect." *Communication Research* 21: 813–827.

Bryce, J. 1988. "Family Time and Television Use." In T. Lindlof (ed.), *Natural Audiences: Qualitative Research of Media Uses and Effects*. Norwood, N.J.: Ablex.

Bryce, J., and H. Leichter. 1983. "The Family and Television: Forms of Mediation." *Journal of Family Issues* 4: 309–328.

Calvert, S. L. 2000. Is Cyberspace for All Girls? Paper presented at the annual meeting of the American Psychological Association, Washington, D.C., August.

Calvert, S. 2002. "Identity Construction on the Internet." In S. Calvert, A. Jordan, and R. Cocking (eds.), *Children in the Digital Age*. Westport, Conn.: Praeger.

Cantor, J. 1999. "Ratings for Program Content: The Role of Research Findings." *Annals of the American Academy of Political and Social Sciences* 557(May): 54–69.

Carlson, M. 1999. "Do Not Enter: Filters, Monitoring Software Help Control Kids' Internet Use." *Hartford Courant* (May 27): F1/F4.

Comstock, G. 1991. *Television and the American Child*. San Diego, Calif.: Academic Press.

Connolly, C., and J. Schwartz. 1999. Gore lets parents in on children's Internet safeguards. *Washington Post* (May 5): A6–A7.

Dorr, A., P. Kovaric, and C. Doubleday. 1989. "Parent-Child Co-viewing of Television." *Journal of Broadcasting and Electronic Media* 33: 35–51.

Gershuny, J. 1992. "Revolutionary Technologies and Technological Revolutions." In R. Silverstone and E. Hirsch (eds.), *Consuming Technologies: Media Information in Domestic Spaces*. London: Routledge.

Gray, A. 1992. *Video Playtime*. New York: Routledge.

Guernsey, L. 2001. "Cyberspace Isn't So Lonely, After All." *New York Times* (July 26): G1.

Hall, E. 1959. *The Silent Language*. Greenwich, Conn.: Fawcett Press.

Hall, E. 1966. *The Hidden Dimension*. New York: Doubleday.

Hochschild, A. 1989. *The Second Shift*. New York: Viking.

Holz, J. 1998. Measuring the Child Audience. Survey No. 3. The Annenberg Public Policy Center, University of Pennsylvania, Philadelphia.

Huston, A., E. Donnerstein, H. Fairchild, N. Feshbach, P. Katz, J. Murray, E. Rubenstein, B. Wilcos, and D. Zuckerman. 1992. *Big World, Small Screen: The Role of Television in American Society*. Lincoln: University of Nebraska Press.

Jordan, A. 1990. The Role of the Mass Media in the Family System: An Ethnographic Approach. Unpublished doctoral dissertation, The Annenberg School for Communication, University of Pennsylvania, Philadelphia.

Jordan, A. 1991. "Social Class, Temporal Orientation, and Mass Media Use within the Family System." *Critical Studies in Mass Communication* 9: 374–386.

Kaiser Family Foundation. 1999. *Kids and Media @ the New Millenium*. Menlo Park, Calif.: The Henry J. Kaiser Family Foundation.

Kohn, M., and C. Schooler. 1983. *Work and Personality: An Inquiry into the Impact of Social Stratification*. Norwood, N.J.: Ablex.

Kraut, R., M. Patterson, V. Lundmark, S. Kiesler, T. Mukhopadhyay, and W. Scherlis. 1999. "Internet Paradox." *American Psychologist* 53: 1017–1031.

Larson, R. 1995. "Secrets in the Bedroom: Adolescents' Private Use of Media." *Journal of Youth and Adolescence* 24: 535–550.

Lawrence, F., and P. Wozniak. 1989. "Children's Television Viewing with Family Members." *Psychological Reports* 65: 395–400.

Liebert, R., J. Sprafkin, and E. Davidson. 1982. *The Early Window: Effects of Television on Children and Youth*, New York: Pergamon.

Leichter, H., D. Ahmed, L. Barrios, J. Bryce, E. Larsen, and L. Moe. 1985. "Family Contexts of Television." *Educational Communication Technology Journal* 33: 26–40.

Lin, C. 2001. "The VCR, Home Video Culture, and New Video Technologies." In J. Bryant and A. Bryant (eds.), *Television and the American Family*. Mahwah, N.J.: Erlbaum.

Lin, C., and C. Atkin. 1989. "Parental Mediation and Rulemaking for Adolescent Use of Television and VCRs." *Journal of Broadcasting and Electronic Media* 33: 53–67.

Lindlof, T., M. Shatzer, and D. Wilkinson. 1988. "Accommodation of Video and Television in the American Family." In J. Lull (ed.), *World Families Watch TV*. Newbury Park, Calif.: Sage.

Livingstone, S. 1992. "The Meaning of Domestic Technologies: A Personal Construct Analysis of Familial Gender Relations." In R. Silverstone and E. Hirsch (eds.), *Consuming Technologies: Media Information in Domestic Spaces*. London: Routledge.

Livingstone, S. 1999. "Personal Computers in the Home: What Do They Mean for Europe's Children?" *Intermedia* 27: 406.

Lull, J. 1980. "The Social Uses of Television." *Human Communication Research* 6: 197–209.

Maccoby, E. 1954. "Why Do Children Watch Television?" *Public Opinion Quarterly* (Fall): 239–244.

Medrich, E., J. Roizen, V. Rubin, and S. Buckley. 1982. *The Serious Business of Growing Up*. Berkeley: University of California Press.

Messaris, P. 1983. "Family Conversations about Television." *Journal of Family Issues* 4: 293–308.

Montgomery, K. 2000. "Digital Kids: The New On-line Children's Consumer Culture." In D. Singer and J. Singer (eds.), *Handbook of Children and the Media*. Newbury Park, Calif.: Sage.

Morley, D. 1980. *The Nationwide Audience*. London: British Film Institute.

Morley, D. 1986. *Family Television: Cultural Power and Domestic Leisure*. London: Comedia.

Murdock, G., P. Hartmann, and P. Gray. 1992. "Contextualizing Home Computing: Resources and Practices." In R. Silverstone and E. Hirsch (eds.), *Consuming Technologies: Media Information in Domestic Spaces*. London: Routledge.

Pollner, M., and L. McDonald-Wilker. 1985. "The Social Construction of Unreality." *Family Process* 24: 241–254.

Roe, K. 1987. "The School and Music in Adolescent Socialization." In J. Lull (ed.), *Popular Music and Communication*. Newbury Park, Calif.: Sage.

Rosenblatt, P. 1994. *Metaphors of Family Systems Theory*. New York: Guilford.

Schmitt, K. 2000. Public Policy, Family Rules and Children's Media Use in the Home. Report No. 35. The Annenberg Public Policy Center, University of Pennsylvania, Philadelphia.

Schramm, W., J. Lyle, and E. Parker. 1961. *Television in the Lives of Our Children*. Stanford, Calif.: Stanford University Press.

Seiter, E. 1999. *Television and New Media Audiences.* New York: Oxford University Press.

Stanger, J. 1997. Television in the Home. Survey No. 2. The Annenberg Public Policy Center, University of Pennsylvania, Philadelphia.

Stanger, J., and N. Gridina. 1999. Media in the Home 1999: The Fourth Annual Survey of Parents and Children. Survey No. 5. The Annenberg Public Policy Center, University of Pennsylvania, Philadelphia.

Steele, J., and J. Brown. 1995. "Adolescent Room Culture: Studying Media in the Context of Everyday Life." *Journal of Youth and Adolescence* 24: 551–576.

Struys, K., K. Roe, and V. van Rompaey. 2001. Children's Influence on the Family Purchase of Media. Paper Presented at the International Communication Association Conference, Washington, D.C., May.

Stroh, M. 1999. "Safeguarding Kids on the Net." *Sarasota Herald-Tribune* (May 27): 1E/4E.

Subrahmanyam, K., P. Greenfield, R. Kraut, and E. Gross. 2002. "The Impact of Computer Use on Children's and Adolescents' Development." In S. Calvert, A. Jordan, and R. Cocking (eds.), *Children in the Digital Age.* Westport, Conn.: Praeger.

Tichi, C. 1991. *Electronic Hearth: Creating an American Television Culture.* New York: Oxford University Press.

Turkle, S. 1995. *Life on the Screen.* New York: Simon & Schuster.

Turow, J. 1999. The Internet and the Family. The Annenberg Public Policy Center of the University of Pennsylvania, Philadelphia.

Valkenburg, P. M., M. Krcmar, A. Peeters, and N. Marseille. 1999. "Developing a Scale to Assess Three Styles of Television Mediation. *Journal of Broadcasting and Electronic Media* 43(1): 52–66.

Vetere, A., and A. Gale. 1987. *Ecological Studies of Family Life.* New York: Wiley.

Wartella, E., and S. Mazzarella. 1990. "An Historical Comparison of Children's Use of Leisure Time." In R. Busch ed. *For Fun and Profit.* Philadelphia, Pa.: Temple University Press.

Winn, M. 1977. *The Plug-In Drug.* New York: Viking Books.

Woolf, K., and J. Allen. 2001. The Fifth Annual Conference on Children and Media: A Summary. Washington, D.C., May. Available at ⟨www.appcpenn. org⟩.

8

The Internet and the Family: The Views of Parents and Youngsters

Joseph Turow and Lilach Nir

Overview

American parents and youngsters are often of very different minds when it comes to giving personal information to Web sites. Kids' release of information to the Web could well become a new arena for family discord.

• American 10–17 year olds are much more likely than parents to say it is OK to give sensitive personal and family information to commercial Web sites in exchange for a free gift. Examples of such information include their allowance, the names of their parents' favorite stores, what their parents do on weekends, and how many days of work their parents have missed.

• 41% of online parents with kids ages 8–17 and 36% of youngsters aged 10–17 report having experienced incidents of disagreement, worry or anger in their family over kids' release of information to the Web.

• Almost half of U.S. parents are not aware that Web sites gather information on users without their knowing it.

• 61% of parents say they are more concerned about 13 to 17 year olds than they are about younger children revealing sensitive information to marketers.

Adapted from the Annenberg Public Policy Report Series Number 33 (May 2000). This research was funded by the University of Pennsylvania's Annenberg Public Policy Center. The authors would like to particularly thank the Center's director, Kathleen Hall Jamison, for her wonderful encouragement and support. Reprinted with permission.

• It is wrong to think that simple discussions between parents and kids about what information to give to the Web can easily resolve these tensions. Fully 69% of parents and 66% of kids say they have had these sorts of discussions. But when we specifically interviewed pairs of parents and kids in the same family, we found that most didn't agree on whether these sorts of discussions had ever taken place.

These are highlights from a complex picture that we found in the second Annenberg National Survey on the Internet and the Family. The unprecedented comparison of the attitudes of youngsters and parents toward giving up family information to Web sites was conducted by a major national survey firm for the Annenberg Public Policy Center of the University of Pennsylvania. All the respondents belonged to households with at least one computer connected to the Web. 304 youngsters aged 10–17 and 1001 parents with at least one child between ages 8 to 17 were interviewed between January 13 and February 17, 2000.

One aim of this second survey was to track differences from last year's findings regarding what parents generally think and do about the Web. We found that more of them believe in the Web's power to help kids grow. In 2000, all but a small proportion of parents feel that the online world holds strong educational possibilities. Parents are rather evenly divided, though, on whether the Web will also powerfully harm young minds.

Our survey expanded into new territory in 2000 to focus on another topic of growing importance, family privacy and the Web. As teenagers have emerged as major users of the Web, commercial sites have increasingly been gleaning information from them for marketing purposes. We wanted to know whether parents and youngsters agree that releasing information to Web sites is a problem and, if so, whether they do anything about it.

The question ties into an issue that is currently the topic of much public policy discussion: the possibility that youngsters using the Web might give up information about themselves and their families to marketers that their parents would not want disclosed. On the Web, the smallest bits of information divulged by kids about their home life can be aggregated using increasingly sophisticated tracking tools. Web sites can bring the intelligence together to create detailed portraits of a family's lifestyle. Accurate or not, such portraits can profoundly influence how marketers, banks, insurance companies, government agencies and other organizations treat family members—what discounts they give them, what materials they send them, how much they communicate with them, and even whether they want to deal with them at all.

Congress responded to some of this concern about the leakage of family information when, in the 1998 Children's Online Privacy Protection Act, it ordered the Federal Trade Commission to regulate data collection on sites that target children under age 13. The Commission developed rules to ensure that Web sites get parents' permission before the sites request information from children under age 13 about themselves or their families. The FTC rules went into effect in April 2000.

Was Congress' decision to focus only on kids under 13 warranted, or should society expand the information disclosure debate to include youngsters 13 and over? We addressed the question in interviews with parents, teens, and tweens (a marketing term for 10–12 year olds). We created scenarios aimed at learning what the youngsters say would be OK for teens to reveal to Web marketers compared to what their parents say would be OK for teenagers to reveal. And we tried to understand whether those we interviewed are aware of the way Web sites track their visitors without them knowing it.

• We learned that 96% of U.S. parents with children aged 8 to 17 believe that teenagers should have to get their parent's consent before giving information online.

• 62% of tweens and teens agree, including, curiously, more than half of the youngsters who are consistently willing to give up sensitive personal and family information.

• When faced with the scenario of a free gift, though, caution seems to go out the window for many of the kids.

The study explores the concerns parents have about teens' release of information to the Web and how parents deal with this challenge. In the final section of this report, we argue for a social policy that helps families establish clear norms for information privacy and regulates the extent to which Web sites aimed at tweens or teens can elicit information from them.

The Study and the Population

In the 2000 research, we repeated key questions from the late-1998 benchmark study "The Internet and the Family: the View from Parents, the View from the Press." We also added new questions that explored notions of privacy on the Internet among parents and children.

According to Roper Reports and the Current Population Survey (CPS) for 1999, 71% of households with kids 8–17 now have computers and 67% of those households connect to the Internet. In all, then, 48% of US households with kids 8–17 have online connections. This year we focused on this group. In last year's survey (conducted in November and December 1998) homes with computers but no Internet connections were also included as part of an effort to better understand why some parents choose to connect to the Internet and some did not. A second important difference in 2000 is that children 10–17 were also interviewed, providing the opportunity to compare and contrast parents' and childrens' visions of the Internet—and the rising wave of concern over privacy and security issues.

Telephone interviews were conducted with a nationwide cross section of 1,001[1] parents of children 8–17 in homes with Internet connections. The Random Digit Dialing (RDD) sampling methodology was used to locate respondents. During the interviews parents were asked to answer questions while thinking about their child 8–17 that had the most recent birthday. When the child the parent had focused on during the interview was at least 10–17 years old, an attempt was made to also interview that child. When that child was not available, another child 10–17 in the household was interviewed. Approximately half of the 304[2] children 10–17 that were interviewed were selected from same households as the parents. The other half of the childrens' sample (for which parents were not interviewed) was located using the Random Digit Dialing (RDD) sampling methodology. All the interviews were conducted January 13 through February 17, 2000. Interviews with the adults averaged 20 minutes; the ones with the kids averaged 10 minutes.

The Parents and Youngsters

For the half of the children's sample whose parents we did not interview, we decided to limit our requests for background information for reasons of time. We know that the youngsters are scattered randomly across U.S. area codes. We also know that the average age is $13\frac{1}{2}$ and that 52% are girls, 48% boys.

We learned more about the parent population (and therefore about the 150 kids linked to them). As tables 8.1 and 8.2 indicate, the majority of parents of children 10–17 with online connections at home are white and between 30 and 40 years old. Seven in 10 (69%) have at least some college education; 38% have college or graduate degrees. Income distribution is hard to assess because so many parents—12% more than in our late 1998 study—refused to answer the question when it was presented toward the end of the interview. It may be that the interview's topic of information privacy sensitized many of the parents to a concern about divulging household income. Fortunately, the overwhelming majority of respondents were much more forthcoming in answering questions during the rest of the interview.

Table 8.3 shows that 37% of the youngsters in our study told us that they use the Web "a lot," while 37% said "some." Only 7% said that they don't go online at all. Boys and girls reported no difference in the use of the Web. Teenagers (aged 13–17) were substantially more likely than tweens (those aged 10–12) to say they use the Web a lot. Nevertheless, of the kids who don't go online at all, about half were teens and half tweens.

As the table shows, for virtually all the kids (91%) going online means visiting Web sites. Sending and receiving e-mail is another hugely popular activity, with visiting chat rooms and playing games with other people online far less common. Older kids are much more likely than younger ones to participate in chat rooms and game-playing with others. Boys are more likely than girls to involve themselves in cooperative game-playing online.

Tables 8.4 and 8.5 present answers to the questions we asked the parents about online use. The majority of parents have had the Web at home for over a year. Only 6% of our respondents say they have never gone online. Three quarters of the ones who do go online say they use both e-mail and the World Wide Web. Twenty-one percent say their Internet use is limited to e-mail. One quarter of the parents who go online consider themselves beginners, 44% see themselves as intermediates, and 31% view themselves as advanced or expert users.

Table 8.1
Characteristics of Parents with Children 8–17 and Online Computers at Home

	$(n = 1,001)$* %
Sex	
Male	41
Female	59
Age	
20–29	4
30–44	57
45–59	33
60 or older	6
Race	
White	76
African American	6
White Hispanic	4
Black Hispanic	1
Asian	2
Native American	2
Other	3
No answer	5
Marital status	
Married	79
Employment status	
Employed	83
"Not employed" homemaker	10
"Not employed" student	2
Retired	2
Disabled	1
Unemployed	2
Number of children, aged 8–17	
One	46
Two	37
Three	12
Four or more	5

Note: *When the numbers don't add up to 100% it is because of a rounding error.

Table 8.2
Last Education Degree and Household Income of Parents with Children Aged 8–17 and Online Computers at Home

	(n = 1,001)* %
Last education degree	
Grade school or less	1
Some high school	3
High school graduate	25
Some college	25
College graduate	31
Post graduate	14
No answer	2
Yearly income	
Less than $30,000	9
$30,000–$49,999	19
$50,000–$74,999	23
$75,000 or more	24
No answer	26

Note: *When the numbers don't add up to 100% it is because of a rounding error.

These percentages are almost exactly the same as the ones we found last year.

For parents in Web households, home rather than work is the place in which they report most of their online activity taking place. As table 8.5 indicates, fully 42% of our respondents said they have not gone online at all from work in the past month. Moreover, while 78% say they go online at home at least every few days, a smaller 45% say they go online from work that frequently. Table 8.5 shows that compared to last year, parent online use is up somewhat both at work and home.

Attitudes of Online Parents toward the Web, 2000 vs. 1998

One aim of our 2000 survey was to track differences from last year's findings regarding what parents generally think and do about the Web. We presented parents with fifteen of the most illuminating statements

Table 8.3
Patterns of Internet Use, Children Aged 10–17

	Total ($n = 304$)	Gender		Age	
		Boy ($n = 145$)	Girl ($n = 158$)	10–12 ($n = 101$)	13–17 ($n = 203$)
Frequency of Internet use					
A lot	37	38	36	21	45*
Some	37	35	39	37	37
Not Much	19	21	17	29*	14
Not at all	7	7	7	12*	4
Don't Know/ Refused	0	0	1	2*	0
Specific Internet usage Send/Receive e-mail?					
Yes	83	82	85	70	90*
No	17	19	15	30*	10
Visit chat rooms?					
Yes	43	40	46	32	49*
No	57	60	54	68*	51
Visit Web sites?					
Yes	91	92	89	86	93*
No	9	8	11	14*	7
Play online games?					
Yes	32	43*	26	23	40*
No	66	57	74*	77*	61

Note: *Means that the percentage difference is statistically significant from the percentages of the corresponding category in that variable (boys vs. girls, young vs. old children).

Table 8.4
Patterns of Online Use, Parents of Children 8–17

	$(n = 1,001)^*$ %
Percentage on the Internet	
E-mail only	21
Other Internet (with or without e-mail)	74
Neither	6
Ability to go online or navigate the Internet	
A beginner	24
An intermediate user	42
An advanced user	22
An expert user	8
Don't know	4
Length of online connection at home	
Less than six months	15
Between six months and a year	18
More than a year, but less than two years	21
More than two years	46
Don't know	0

Note: *When the numbers don't add up to 100% it is because of a rounding error.

from last year about the potential benefits and harms of the Internet for children. We asked them how much they agreed or disagreed with each of the assertions along a five-point scale, from agree strongly to disagree strongly.

As table 8.6 indicates, we found a remarkable continuity in the belief that the Internet is a useful and even critical component of a child's education while at the same time it gives youngsters access to content with troublesome values. The one fairly substantial jump in agreement related to parents' view of the overall safety of the Web. While 40% agreed in late 1998 that "the Internet is a safe place to spend time," a majority—51%—agreed in the 2000 survey. Otherwise, the percentages of parents agreeing with the positive statements rose slightly while the percentages agreeing with negative statements regarding the Web remained the same.

• The statement that most parents agreed with in both 2000 and 1998 was that "access to the Internet at home helps my children with their

Table 8.5
Frequency of Web Use, for Parents of Children 8–17, Late 1998 vs. 2000

	1998 ($n = 676$) %	2000 ($n = 1,001$) %
Frequency of going online in the past month from work		
Every day	26	30
Every other day	7	7
Every few days	8	8
A few times	11	7
One or two days	6	5
Don't know	—	1
None	40	42
Frequency of going online in the past month from home		
Every day	30	37
Every other day	15	17
Every few days	21	18
A few times	17	12
One or two days	12	6
Don't know	—	—
None	4	10
Frequency of going online in the past month from other places		
Every day	3	3
Every other day	1	2
Every few days	4	3
A few times	5	7
One or two days	7	5
Don't know	—	1
None	79	79

Table 8.6

Percentage of Online Parents Who Agreed "Strongly" or "Somewhat" with Statements about the Internet (Late 1998 vs. 2000)

	1998 ($n = 676$) %	2000 ($n = 1,000$) %
Access to the Internet helps my children with their schoolwork.	84	89*
Online, my children discover fascinating useful things they never heard of before.	81	85*
Children who do not have Internet access are at a disadvantage compared to their peers who do have Internet access.	68	74*
I am concerned that my child/children give out personal information about themselves when visiting Web sites or chat rooms.	77	74
I am concerned my child/children might view sexually explicit images on the Internet.	76	72*
The Internet can help my children learn about diversity and tolerance.	60	66*
People worry too much that adults will take advantage of children on the Internet.	57	59
Going online too often might lead children to become isolated from other people.	60	59
The Internet is a safe place for my children to spend time.	40	51*
Families who spend a lot of time online talk to each other less than they otherwise would.	48	50
My children's exposure to the Internet might interfere with the values and beliefs I want to teach them.	42	43
Children who spend too much time on the Internet develop anti-social behavior.	40	41
I often worry that I won't be able to explore the Web with my children as well as other parents do.	21	26

Note: *Indicates that the difference between responses of online parents in 2000 and in late 1998 is statistically significant.

schoolwork": 89% agreed with this in 2000, compared to 84% in late 1998.

• Number two on the list is parents' agreement that "online, my children discover fascinating things they have never heard of before": 86% of parents agreed somewhat or strongly with this statement in 2000, compared to 81% a year earlier.

• Seventy-four percent of parents in 2000 agree that "children who do not have Internet access are at a disadvantage" compared to 68% in late 1998.

This assessment that the Internet is not an interesting luxury but a near necessity is undercut, however, by concerns. For example:

• About seven in ten parents (71%) in 2000 agree with the statement "I am concerned that my children might view sexually explicit images on the Internet." Seventy-six percent agreed with this in 1998.

• 51% (compared to 48%) agreed that "families who spend a lot of time online talk to each other less than they otherwise would."

• Sixty-two percent of parents agreed with the new statement this year "I am concerned that my children might view violent images on the Internet."

The Parents' Web Attitude Clusters

Last year, we used a statistical technique known as cluster analysis to group parents in on-line households according to their attitudes about the Internet. Three groups of parents emerged:

• *The Online Worriers*—parents who are most concerned about bad effects that the Internet might have on their children and their families, though they also see the Web's positive qualities.

• *The Disenchanteds*—on-line parents who are not convinced about the Internet's educational value for their children even as they are concerned about its negative consequences.

• *The Gung Ho*—online parents who are highly positive about the Web and reject assertions about the negative effects of the Internet.

In 2000 we attempted to see whether and to what extent these groups of online parents still exist.[3] We found that they do, in percentages quite similar to those we saw last year, as the table below notes.

	Online Worrier	Disenchanted	Gung Ho
Jan–Feb 2000	40%	16%	43%
Nov–Dec 1998	39%	22%	39%

Comparing 2000 and 1998, we see a stable proportion of on-line worriers who are concerned about the negative social effects of Internet use. We see fewer disenchanted parents who are skeptical about the real benefits the Internet can bring for children. And we see a very slight increase in the proportion of gung ho parents, the ones who reject many concerns about the Internet.

Last year we noted that gung ho parents tended to have had an online connection longer than other online parents. We noted the same relationship this year, though the association was not as strong. The tendency for people who remain online for more than two years to stay positive (or develop positive inclinations) toward the Web would suggest that the stable percentage of online worriers is to some extent being replenished by newcomers.

The decline in the percentage of disenchanted parents suggests that relatively few people with youngsters discount the potential positive power of the Web for kids. Parents' thinking about the Web appears to be dividing along two views on its role in society. Both gung ho's and online worriers believe in the online world's strong educational possibilities, while online worriers insist the Web can also powerfully harm young minds.

Families and Information Privacy on the Web

We move now to the new topic that we addressed in the 2000 survey: the attitudes of parents and children in online households toward giving up information to Web sites. One major question we had was whether the attitudes parents hold generally toward the Web—for example, whether they are online worriers, disenchanteds or gung ho's—are reflected directly in the attitudes they hold to information privacy in the digital domain. Or, we wondered, do parents see information privacy separately from the way they see the Web as a whole because of a special concern that their children might release sensitive family information?

We also wanted to know whether American parents and children 10–17 are similar or different in the ways that they think about family privacy and report their interactions around it.

Background: The Web's Interest in Teens' Information

Our interest in comparing parents and youngsters in this age group grew out of awareness that commercial sites have increasingly been pursuing teens. As an article in *Forbes Digital Tool* noted, "the disposable income and tech-friendly instincts of teenagers have made [this segment] the hottest target for revenue generation among web companies."[4] "There's a "frenzy over teens," agreed Dan Pelson, chief executive of Bolt Media Inc., a Web "community" for teenagers.[5]

Like commercial sites aimed at adults, teen-oriented commercial domains gather information about their visitors for advertising, market research and electronic commerce. They use visitor data to attract sponsors who will pay for *banners* and other ads on the site to reach such individuals. Sites also sell information to marketers who need to know about the interests and habits of people whose profiles fit the visitors to the site. In addition, sites use the information themselves to help them sell products or services directly to their visitors. (Teenagers can purchase online by using their own bank cards, their parents' credit cards or money pre-deposited through *digital wallets* that some online retailers have instituted.)

Information about visitors can be gathered on the Web in basically two ways. One is by requesting data from visitors when (and if) they register to use the site. The other is by tracking what users do on a site. To track, Web sites place tags, called *cookies*, on the visitor's computer disk drive. Cookies can note how often (and when) a visitor comes to a site and where the visitor clicks the mouse when there. The Web site can retrieve this *clickstream* information for an analysis called *digital profiling*. The profiling can merge information from the online registration and clickstream as well as from other information gleaned from the visitors—for example e-mails. Merchandising sites have been active in merging online data they have about their customers with "offline" (sometimes called *legacy*) data they have developed about them through such activities as telephone inquiries and credit card purchases.

To allay consumers' concerns that Web sites are selling far and wide what they know about individuals, many Web sites post privacy policies that attempt to assure their users. The standard approach is to promise that the information will not be shared or sold to others in ways that allow an association of the individual's name with the data. A careful reading of many Web-site privacy policies, however, will reveal a number of important loopholes in this promise. Chief among them is a disclaimer that information gleaned by or given to advertising banners on the site are not covered by the privacy policy. By placing a banner on a site, in fact, an advertiser can quietly insert its own cookie on the visitor's computer and follow the clickstream. If the banner encourages the visitor to fill his or her name and address on a sweepstakes form in the banner ad, the marketer now has an easy way to link the cookie to a real person with online and offline activities.

Privacy advocates have worried strenuously about the gathering of all sorts of data about individuals on the Web. They claim that although customer records always have been collected, the Web is unique because it makes it easy to connect information within and across databases and to use that data instantly. The concern that has resonated most with lawmakers is the possibility that youngsters using the Web might give up information about themselves and their families to marketers that their parents would not want disclosed. Congress responded to some of this concern about this leakage of family information when, in the 1998 Children's Online Privacy Protection Act, it ordered the Federal Trade Commission to regulate data collection on sites that target children under age 13. The Commission developed rules to ensure that Web sites get parents' permission before the sites request information from children under age 13 about themselves or their families. The FTC rules went into effect in April 2000.

FTC rules consider youngsters over 13 to be adults when it comes to the disclosure of information on the Web. We tried to zero in on what parents think of this notion and, in general, how they and youngsters differ in thinking about and dealing with information privacy.

Parents' Approach to Family Information Privacy

Parents' stance on treating youngsters 13 and over as adults on the Web comes through quite clearly in our survey: they don't agree. As noted at the beginning of the report, fully 96% of the parents interviewed believe that "teenagers should have to get their parent's consent before giving out information online." In fact, 84% of the parents agree "strongly" with the statement. Moreover, 60% of parents agree that they "worry more about what information a teenager would give away to a Web site than a younger child under 13."

These answers are part of a strong pattern of concern for information privacy that we found among most parents. Table 8.7 presents the percentages that agree or agree strongly with fifteen statements on the subject. Second on the list—just under the statement about requiring parents' consent—is parents' belief that they should have a legal right to know "everything" that a Web site knows about them; 95% agree, with 87% agreeing "strongly" with the statement.

While the overwhelming number of parents agrees with these statements, there is a fair divergence in answers to the others. We used the computer technique called cluster analysis to discover if all the parents fit one profile in their answers or if there is diversity among them regarding their attitudes toward information privacy on the Web. The technique determines whether there are patterns among respondents in the extent to which certain statements deviate strongly from the average reply ("the mean"), based on a scale in which "agree strongly" is 5 and "disagree strongly" is 1. When the deviation from the mean of responses to a particular statement is strongly positive, it means that the people in the group agree or agree strongly with the statement more than most of the people in the sample. When the deviation from the mean of responses to a particular statement is strongly *negative*, it means that the people in the group disagree or disagree strongly with the statement more than most of the people in the sample.

As figure 8.1 shows, we found three groups of parents with important differences in the way they state their attitudes toward family information privacy. We label the groups *wary*, *cavalier*, and *selectively trusting*.

• The wary make up 38% of the parents. They express a greater distrust of Web sites than the other two groups. It shows up in their stronger than average nervousness about Web sites having and sharing information about them; increased concern since going online that outsiders are learning sensitive information about them; disbelief that sites will adhere to privacy promises; and a sense that privacy policies are not easy to understand.

• The cavalier (30% of the parents) are much more likely than the others to reject specific concerns about Web privacy. They tend to disagree that since going online they have become more concerned about outsiders learning sensitive information about them; to dismiss worries about family members giving information to Web sites; and to deny worrying that a teen would give away more personal information on the Web compared to a child under age 13. Cavalier parents are also quite a bit less likely than wary and selectively trusting ones to know that web sites collect information about them even if they don't fill out information on the sites—a fact that perhaps suggests some naivete on the part of the Web cavaliers.

• The selectively trusting (32%) have characteristics of both groups. Like the wary, they have a higher than average concern about aspects of Web privacy—in their case, that family members might give away inappropriate information and that a teen would give away more information than a child under 13. Quite different from the wary, however, is the tendency of selectively trusting parents to say that Web sites' privacy policies are reliable and that sites will live up to their promises about not sharing information. Selectively trusting parents also stand apart from the other two groups in stating that they like to barter information for offers or compensation on the Web and in claiming that privacy policies are easy to understand.

Being wary, cavalier, or selectively trusting has no association with a person's self-reported expertise with the Web, or with the amount of time the household has been online. We also found that these privacy clusters are unrelated to a parent's gender. Mothers are just as likely as fathers to report cavalier, wary, or selectively trusting attitudes toward Web privacy.

We noted, too, that concern about information privacy on the Web is not the same as general concern about the Web. When we examined the association between parents' Web attitude clusters—online worriers, disenchanteds and gung ho's—to these privacy clusters, we saw no statistically significant relationship between the two groups. It turns out that people who are worried, enthusiastic or disenchanted about the

Table 8.7
Percentage of Parents Who "Agreed" or "Agreed Strongly" to the Privacy Statements

	Total (n = 1,001)	Wary (n = 375)	Cavalier (n = 303)	Selectively Trusting (n = 323)
Teenagers should have to get their parent's consent before giving out information online.	96	98#	91	98#
I should have a legal right to know everything that a Web site knows about me.	95	99#	89	97#
I am nervous about Web sites having information about me.	73	90#+	43	81#
I am more concerned about giving away sensitive information on-line than about giving away sensitive information any other way.	63	79#	29	79#
My concern about outsiders learning sensitive information about me and my family has increased since we've gone online at home.	59	82#+	22	66#
I worry more about what information a teenager would give away to a Web site than a younger child under 13 would.	61	63#	33	81*#
I look to see if a Web site has a privacy policy before answering any questions.	72	69	61	86*#
When I go to a Web site, it collects information about me even if I do not register or fill in information about myself.	54	64#	37	59#
Web site privacy policies are easy to understand.	41	18	50*	60*#
When a Web site has a privacy policy, I know that the site will take proper care of my information.	41	14	37*	76*#

I sometimes worry that members of my family give information they shouldn't about our family to Web sites.	36	46#	6	54#
I trust Web sites not to share information with other companies or advertisers when they say they won't.	37	7#	29	80*#
I like to give information to Web sites because I get offers for products and services I personally like.	18	5	14*	36*#
I will only give out information to a Web site if I am paid or compensated in some way.	9	3	5	21*#

Notes:

*Notes that the percentage of respondents who agreed with this statement was significantly different form the group of "wary" parents.

#Notes that the percentage of respondents who agreed with this statement was significantly different form the group of "cavalier" parents.

+Notes that the percentage of respondents who agreed with this statement was significantly different form the group of "selectively trusting" parents.

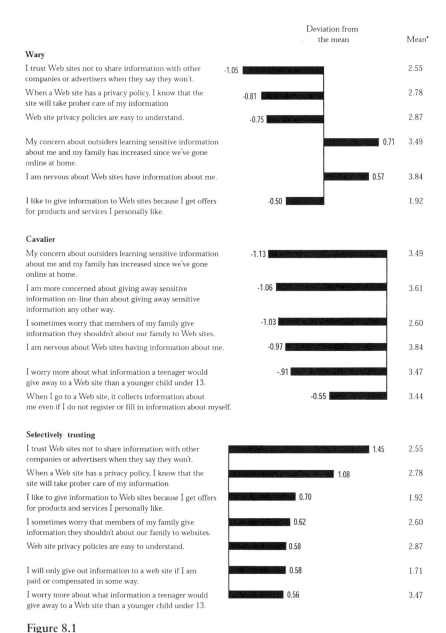

Figure 8.1
Groups of parents based on their privacy views.
Note: *This is the mean (average) of responses to the statement by the entire sample of parents. See text.

Web feel that way for reasons that may or may not include their opinions about information privacy on the Internet. They may, for example, be more or less concerned about Web violence, or more or less enthused about great learning sites.

Parents and Supervision Regarding Information

We did find statistically significant associations between the way parents talk about Web privacy (as seen in the clusters) and the ways they say they act or would act regarding their family's information. Wary parents respond differently from cavalier ones, and they in turn answer differently from those who are selectively trusting. At the same time, the pattern of answers suggests that the cavalier and selectively trusting parents are more conservative in their actions than their stated attitudes might predict.

Table 8.8 provides one illustration of this tendency. It presents parents' experiences and approaches to teaching their children about information privacy. We see that wary parents are more likely than others to say that they have had unhappy experiences with information loss through theft or children's release of data. Wary parents are also more likely to say they chose not to register for a Web site that wanted personal information and that they have not read a privacy policy.

Though these findings show statistically significant differences among these parent respondents, the table also reveals important similarities. Overall the reported experiences and actions of cavalier and selectively trusting parents reflect a caution about privacy that is not so very different from the caution that wary parents exhibit. Moreover, the groups are not statistically different on a number of key actions: buying something over the Web (only half of even the cavalier parents have done it); reporting tension around issues of Web information (about 40% in all groups recall it); and saying they talked to their kids about how to deal with Web requests for information (nearly two thirds in each group say they have done it). The picture that emerges generally is that selectively trusting parents are more selective than their privacy attitudes suggest and that even the cavalier parents are really not so cavalier about giving out information or letting their children do it.

This picture is reinforced in the parents' responses to questions based on our two scenarios. We designed each scenario to place the parent in a

Table 8.8
Experiences of Parents Regarding Information Privacy

	Total (n = 1,001)	Wary (n = 376)	Cavalier (n = 303)	Selectively Trusting (n = 323)
Person or company used information about them in an improper way	10	15#+	5	10
Person or company used information about them in an improper way specifically on the Web	3	4	1	3
Had incident where parent was worried about something his/her child told both a telephone marketer	4	7+	3	2
Had incident where parent was worried about something his/her child told a Web site	5	5	3	5
Had incident where parent was worried about something his/her child told a telephone marketer and Web site	3	5	0.5*+	3
Generally reports tension over his/her child giving information to the Web[6]	41	44	38	40
Bought something over the Web	53	52	54	54
Never read a site's privacy policy	16	20#	13	14
Read a site's privacy policy one time to a few times	53	54	55	50
Read a site's privacy policy many times	24	19	25	29*
Doesn't know what a privacy policy is or whether read one	6	6	6	6
Registered on a Web site	41	38	41	44
Chose not to register on a Web site at least once because was asked for personal information	65	73	59*	62*

Talked with his/her child about how to deal with requests
for information from Web sites   66   67   66   65

Notes:
*Notes that the percentage of respondents who agreed with this statement was significantly different form the group of "wary" parents.
#Notes that the percentage of respondents who agreed with this statement was significantly different form the group of "cavalier" parents.
+Notes that the percentage of respondents who agreed with this statement was significantly different form the group of "selectively trusting" parents.

situation that encouraged the exchange of information for a free, rather valuable "gift" from a favorite store. The scenarios became our major vehicles for comparing the parents' sensitivities with those of youngsters aged 10 to 17 on concrete instances of information exchange.

Scenario 1 The first scenario aimed to assess the tendency of the parents to say they would give out their name, address and other information under realistic conditions of a Web privacy policy considered standard in the industry. The scenario reflects what the industry-supported organization Privacy & American Business says "three out of four adult Web users" want before they give up personal information on the Web: a benefit, notice about how the firm will use their information, and an industry-accepted privacy policy.[7]

The interviewer posed the scenario in the following manner:

I'd like you to pretend that you visit the Web site of your favorite store and see that you can earn a *great* free gift if you answer some questions. In order to get the free gift, you must give your name, home address, and answer some questions about what you like and don't like. The store clearly promises not to give out the names or home addresses of people who register for the free gift—but the store may give out answers to any of the other questions to other stores or advertisers.

Would *you* answer these types of questions in return for a great free gift, or not?

If the parent said no or "it depends," the interviewer asked, "What if the product was worth $25?" A no to that led to a raising of the product's value to $50, then to $100.

Table 8.9 lists the initial answers of respondents as well as the percentage of total respondents who were ultimately swayed. Clearly, the wary parents were most immediately likely to say no (80%), followed by the cavalier (66%) and then the selectively trusting (56%). The somewhat higher tendency of selectively trusting parents to say *yes* or *it depends* rather than *no* probably relates to that group's greater-than-average belief in the truth of Web sites' privacy policies. In the final tally, 43% of selectively trusting parents were swayed to yes, compared to 33% of cavaliers and only 17% of the wary. In all 29% of the parents said that they would accept the offer of the free gift in exchange for identifying data and "other" information.

Table 8.9
Parents' Answers to Scenario 1

	Total (n = 1,001)	Wary (%)*	Cavalier (%)#	Selectively Trusting (%)+
Would you answer these types of questions in return for a great free product?				
Yes	18	9	21*	26*
No	68	80#+	66+	56
Depends on the product	4	4	3	4
Depends on the information they want	5	3	3	4
Depends on the product and information	4	2	4	7*
Don't know/No answer	2	3	2	2
Total additional parents who said "yes", if the product were worth $25, $50, or $100 (n = 1,001)	7	9	12	17*
Total who said yes** (n = 1,001)	29	17	33*	43*#

Notes:

**The total is based on the accumulated number of parents who said yes to the offer, including those who said "no" or "depends" the first time. See text.

*, #, +Means that the percentage is different from the percentage in the column designated by the mark.

Scenario 2   Our goal for the second scenario was to learn what kinds of specific personal and family information parents believe is acceptable for teens to give up to Web sites. We constructed fifteen items that varied along lines of relatively public and relatively private elements involving the teen or the family. For this scenario we left the privacy policy ambiguous. The interviewer said the following:

Now (whether you currently have a teenaged child or not) suppose a Web site asked a teenager 13 to 17 years old to answer the following questions in order to get a great free gift. Do you think it is completely OK, OK, not OK or not at all OK for a teenager to give the following information to a Web site to get a free gift? If you are not sure, please just tell me.

Please remember that we are not asking for you to answer these questions now—just to tell us if you think it is OK for a teenager to answer questions like these on a Web site.

Parents' responses to the fifteen items are ranked in table 8.10 from the items that they feel are most OK to reveal to a Web site to those they feel are least OK. Overall, it appears that parents consider information about things parents or teens do out of the home and in public most acceptable to reveal. Knowledge about the teen's personal space, embarrassments, or body are intermediate items, while disclosures about *parents'* personal space, embarrassments or body are least acceptable to reveal.

The privacy clusters roughly follow this arrangement and the pattern that we have seen previously: The wary are least likely to state that giving up the information is acceptable. The selectively trusting and cavalier dovetail each other in their somewhat more accepting responses, but in percentages that are quite a bit more conservative than their stated privacy attitudes would lead one to suspect. In fact, the average number of selectively trusting and cavalier parents who said it was acceptable to give up the personal and family information was 24% and 23%, respectively. These numbers are not all that different from the 21% "OK" rate in the sample as a whole, and not wildly different from the 16% average of the wary parents. Clearly, the great proportion of individuals in all three parent privacy groups found the notion of teenagers giving out virtually all of this information to Web sites highly problematic.

Statistical procedures allowed us to construct a *parents' information disclosure scale* that indicated the extent of a person's sensitivity to the release of information.[8] The higher a person's score, the more likely the person was to find it acceptable for a teen to release sensitive personal and family information. Curiously, we found no significant associations between sensitivity to information disclosure and a variety of characteristics, including parents' education, income, gender, expertise with the computer, and the length of time the household has been connected to the Web. We did find that the younger the parent, the more accepting he or she is to a child's disclosure of information. However, all of these characteristics (including age) taken together were not strong enough to comprise the major factors that predict parents' answers regarding teenagers' disclosure of information. Finding these predictors is a challenge for further research.[9]

Comparing Kids and Parents on Information Privacy

Our interviews with the 10 to 17 year olds aimed to see if their attitudes toward privacy and their decisions in the scenarios are substantially different from those of parents.

We found a striking pattern: In the attitudes they express, youngsters seem quite concerned about protecting their information privacy and nervous about Web sites' having information about them. Yet when we give them specific opportunities to get a free gift in exchange for personal or family information, a much larger proportion of kids than parents are ready to do it. Their approach is the opposite of the tendency shown by the cavalier and selectively trusting parents. These parents often express relatively blasé attitudes toward information privacy but turn out to be quite conservative when confronted with the specific scenarios. By contrast, many of the youngsters express conservative general Web privacy attitudes but turn out to be quite liberal with their information when confronted with the scenarios.

Because our time with the youngsters was much shorter than our time with the parents, we tapped into the kids' privacy attitudes using only five of the fourteen privacy statements we read to the parents. As table 8.11 shows, more parents than kids express nervousness about Web sites holding information about them and agree that teens should have to get parents' permission before giving out information online. More parents than kids also disagree that they trust sites' promises about information and reject the notion that they like to give Web sites information in return

Table 8.10

Percentage of Parents Who Feel It Is "Completely OK" or "OK" for Their Teenager to Give This Information to a Web Site, in Exchange for a Free Gift

	Total (n = 1,001)	Wary (n = 375)	Cavalier (n = 303)	Selectively Trusting (n = 323)
Give out names of his or her favorite stores	44	38	43	52*#
Give out names of his or her parents' favorite stores	33	27	35*	38*
Give out whether his or her parents talk a lot about politics	25	20	28*	29*
Give out how many times his or her parents have gone to a place of worship in the past month	25	20	28*	29*
Give out whether he or she has skin problems	24	19	26	29*
Give out what types of cars the family owns	21	15	24*	27*
Give out what he or she does on the weekends	19	13	19	24*
Give out how many days of school he or she missed in the past year	19	12	22*	24*
Give out whether the family drinks wine or beer with dinner	17	13	21*	18
Give out how much allowance he or she gets	17	11	20*	21*
Give out whether he or she cheated in school during the past year	16	11	20*	17*
Give out whether his or her parents have skin problems	16	10	20*	18*
Give out whether his or her parents speed when they drive	14	12	17	14
Give out how many days of work his or her parent missed in the past year	10	7	13*	11
Give out what his parents do on the weekends	10	6	12*	12*

Notes:
*Notes that the percentage of respondents who agreed with this statement was significantly different form the group of "wary" parents.
#Notes that the percentage of respondents who agreed with this statement was significantly different form the group of "cavalier" parents.
+Notes that the percentage of respondents who agreed with this statement was significantly different form the group of "selectively trusting" parents.

Table 8.11
Parents' vs. Kids' Agreement with Privacy Statements

| | Parents (n = 1,001) | | Kids (n = 304) | |
	Agree Strongly (%)	Agree Somewhat (%)	Agree Strongly (%)	Agree Somewhat (%)
Teenagers should have to get their parent's consent before giving out information online	84	12	60	19
I am nervous about Web sites having information about me	41	31	38	25
I look to see if a Web site has a privacy policy before answering any questions	50	19	50	23
I trust Web sites not to share information with other companies or advertisers when they say they won't	15	21	19	22
I like to give information to Web sites because I get offers for products and services I personally like	4	14	10	18

for products and services. The higher parent percentages should not, however, obscure our finding that far more than half of the youngsters gave cautious answers that paralleled those of the parents. Only 41% of the kids say they trust Web sites. Seventy-three percent say they "look to see if a Web site has a privacy policy before answering any questions." Seventy-nine percent agree that teens should get parents' consent before giving out information online.

Scenarios 1 and 2

This aura of caution was much less evident in the responses many of the 10 to 17 year olds gave to the first scenario. The interviewer posed the situation in the same way it was posed to the parents. That led to the question, "Would you [give name, address and answer some other questions about what you like or don't like] in return for a great free gift, or not?" As with the parents, if the youngster said no or "it depends," the interviewer asked, "What if the product was worth $25?" A no to that led to a raising of the product's value to $50, then to $100.

Straight off, 22% of the youngsters said they would be swayed to exchange the information for a free gift. Recall from table 8.9 that the proportion of parents who said they would be swayed was similar— 18%. (In fact, that difference is not statistically significant.) The real divergence between kids and parents came when the interviewer asked if the person would do it if the gift were worth different amounts of money. By $25, 30% of the kids had said yes to the initial offer or the offer that mentioned the cash value. By $50 the proportion was 38%, and by $100 it was 45%. With parents, the accumulated proportions saying yes at the $25, $50 and $100 offers were 21%, 24% and 29% respectively. (The differences between kids and parents *were* statistically significant at each of the money values.)

Table 8.12 lays out the initial and final results. As a result of the enticements, a total of 29% of parents and 45% of kids ended up saying they would exchange the information for a free gift. Part of the reason that the kids were attracted to the cash value more than the parents may be that their sense of a lot of money is different from that of adults. What parents may consider a relatively small amount for important information may seem like a gold mine to a youngster.

Table 8.12
Answers of Youngsters Aged 10–17 to Scenario 1

	(%)
Would you answer these types of questions in return for a great free product? ($n = 304$)	
Yes	22
No	63
Depends on the product	3
Depends on the information they want	4
Depends on the product and information	5
Don't know/No answer	3
Total additional kids who said "yes," if the product were worth $25, $50, or $100 ($n = 304$)*	23
Total who said yes ($n = 304$)	45

Note: *The total is based on the accumulated number of youngsters who said yes to the offer, including those who said "no" or "depends" the first time. See text.

Fitting the pattern we have suggested, the youngsters who say the scenario would sway them nevertheless say they are concerned about privacy. On three of the privacy-attitude statements, they reveal the same strong level of caution about revealing personal information as the youngsters who would not be swayed. The same high percentages say they are nervous about Web sites knowing about them, agree that teens should have to get their parents' consent, and look for a privacy policy before answering any questions.

The two items on which the kids who would and would not barter information for a gift differ reflect a kind of enthusiasm combined with trust that begins to explain why many of the youngsters accepted the blandishment of scenario 1. Forty-six percent of the kids who say they would barter information for a gift agree that they like to go to Web sites because they get attractive offers, but only 16% of the kids who wouldn't barter said that. Similarly, 60% of the bartering group say they trust web sites to keep promises not to share information. Only 27% of those who wouldn't barter say that.

This interest in attractive offers certainly shows up in the way the kids who were swayed by the first scenario responded to scenario 2, as table 8.13 shows. This "will barter" group, representing almost half of all kids, is willing to give up personal and family information in percentages far higher than the parents.

Youngsters' Reported Experiences with the Web

Perhaps not surprisingly, the "will barter" group is substantially more likely than the "won't barter" group to report giving personal information to a Web site, as table 8.14 shows. Youngsters willing to barter are also less likely than their unwilling counterparts to say that they have spoken with their parents about how to deal with Web requests for information. In addition, the table shows that "barter-willing" youngsters are less likely to believe that their parents trust them "completely" to do the right thing on the Web.

At the same time, the barter willing and unwilling groups do not differ when it comes to reporting tensions with parents over information. Overall, 36% of youngsters aged 10–17 report that they have experienced tension—that is, that they have disagreed with their parents frequently or sometimes over what they say in chat rooms or email, or that they have gotten their parents angry at them for giving out information elsewhere on the Web that their parents considered inappropriate. As table 8.14 indicates, this number is consistent not only with respect to the barter groups but also when it comes to gender and age. Girls, boys, older children and younger children do not differ in reporting tensions with their parents over giving information to the Web.[10]

In general, gender does not associate with many of answers that the youngsters gave about their experiences with the Web. Girls *are* somewhat more likely than boys to say they have talked to their parents about how to deal with Web requests for information. In the case of other reported activities and knowledge about the Web—including their level of expertise—boys and girls have the same confidence level.

When it comes to information-privacy attitudes and the scenarios, however, girls are quite different from boys. Girls are less likely than boys to say they would barter their name, address and information about tastes for a free gift worth up to $100. 39% of the girls are barter-willing compared to 54% of the boys. Similarly, as table 8.15 shows, boys are substantially more willing than girls when answering scenario 2 to say

Table 8.13
Percentage of Youngsters Saying It Is "OK" or "Completely OK" for a Teenager to Give Out Information for a "Great Free Gift"

	Total Kids (n = 304)	Will Barter[1] (n = 136)[2]	Won't Barter (n = 158)[2]	Parents (n = 1,001)
Give out names of his or her favorite stores	65#	82*	53	45
Give out the names of his or her parent's favorite stores	54#	70*	45	33
Give out what types of cars the family owns	44#	57*	34	22
Give out how much allowance he or she gets	39#	52*	30	17
Give out whether his or her parents talk a lot about politics	39#	51	31	26
Give out what he or she does on the weekends	39#	51*	32	18
Give out how many days of school he or she missed in the past year	35#	44*	27	18
Give out how many times his or her parents have gone to a place of worship in the past month	30	39*	23	25
Give out what his or her parent's do on the weekends	26#	36*	20	10
Give out whether he or she has skin problems	24	33*	20	24
Give out whether his or her parents speed when they drive	24#	33*	18	14
Give out whether the family drinks wine or beer with dinner	23#	31	18	16
Give out whether he or she cheated in school during the past year	22#	22	23	16
Give out how many days of work his or her parent missed in the past year	21#	28*	15	10
Give out whether his or her parents have skin problems	19	24	16	15

Notes:

1. "Will barter" are those who said they would accept the free gift in scenario 1. See text.

2. The percentages in the table do not include "no answer" or "don't know."

*Indicates a significant difference between the percentages of teens who agreed to the statement, in a comparison between "will barter" and "won't barter."

#Indicates a significant difference between the percentage of teens and the percentage of parents who said it is "OK" or "completely OK" to give out information in exchange for a gift.

Table 8.14
Experiences of Youngsters Regarding Information Privacy

	Total Kids (n = 304)
Never read a site's privacy policy	25
Read a site's privacy policy one time to a few times	42
Read a site's privacy policy many times	25
Doesn't know what a privacy policy is or whether read one	19
Has given information to a Web site about self	31
Say parents trust them completely to do the right thing when it comes to using the Internet	69
Say parents trust them some or a little to do the right thing when it comes to using the Internet	28
Talked to parents about how to deal with requests for information on the Web	69
Experience tension with parents over giving information to Web	36

Notes:
1. "Will barter" are those who said they would accept the free gift in scenario 1. See text.
2. These are valid responses, the percentages in the table do not include "no answer" or "don't know".
*Indicates that the percentage difference is statistically significant from the percentages of the corresponding category in that variable (will barter vs. won't barter, boys vs. girls, young vs. old children).

they would give out certain types of family or personal information for a free gift. Gender also makes a difference when it comes to trusting Web sites "not to share information" with other firms. Half of the boys agree that they can trust Web sites, while only 35% of the girls accept the proposition.

We found no link between age and gender in the answers the youngsters gave. Age alone, however, was more consistently associated than gender with Web experiences as well as with attitudes toward giving up sensitive information.

Table 8.14 shows that kids age 13–17 are more likely than tweens to say they have read a privacy site and to have given personal informa-

Will Barter[1]		Gender		Age	
Yes ($n = 136$)[2]	No ($n = 158$)[2]	Boys ($n = 145$)	Girls ($n = 158$)	10–12 ($n = 101$)	13–17 ($n = 203$)
23	26	28	22	36	19*
44	40	42	41	29	44*
14	17	15	17	7	20*
19	17	14	18	27	12*
40	24*	32	31	16	39*
60	77*	69	69	74	63
37	20*	25	30	23	34
62	75*	63	75*	67	70
39	34	35	37	34	37

tion to the Web. Table 8.15 shows that young age was consistently, and often strongly, associated with accepting the release of personal and family information in scenario 2. Kids 13–17 were far more likely to say it was OK to disclose the answers to 11 of the 15 statements presented to them in exchange for a free gift. Through a different type of analysis, we learned that the higher the age of the youngster (from 10 to 17), the more likely he or she would be to say it is OK to give out personal and family information as measured in a *kid information disclosure scale* that we constructed from the 15 statements.[11]

Table 8.15 suggests that on several responses 10–12 year olds are often as cautious as parents regarding personal and family information. Federal regulations refer to these children and younger ones when requiring a Web site to get parental permission when wanting to ask for, or track, information about a youngster. Ironically, though, it is the older kids, the ones who are fair game for Web sites, who are far more likely than parents to give up the kinds of information the parents would not want released.

Table 8.15

Percentage of Youngsters Saying It Is "OK" or "Completely OK" for a Teenager to Give Out Information for a "Great Free Gift"

	Total Kids ($n = 304$)
Give out names of his or her favorite stores	65[#]
Give out the names of his or her parent's favorite stores	54[#]
Give out what types of cars the family owns	44[#]
Give out how much allowance he or she gets	39[#]
Give out whether his or her parents talk a lot about politics	39[#]
Give out what he or she does on the weekends	39[#]
Give out how many days of school he or she missed in the past year	35[#]
Give out how many times his or her parents have gone to a place of worship in the past month	30
Give out what his or her parents do on the weekends	26[#]
Give out whether he or she has skin problems	24
Give out whether his or her parents speed when they drive	24[#]
Give out whether the family drinks wine or beer with dinner	23[#]
Give out whether he or she cheated in school during the past year	22[#]
Give out how many days of work his or her parent missed in the past year	21[#]
Give out whether his or her parents have skin problems	19

Notes:

*Means that the percentage difference is statistically significant from the percentages of the corresponding category in that variable (boys vs. girls and young vs. old teens).

[#]Means that the percentage difference is statistically significant from the percentage of parents who agreed to that statement.

Gender		Age		Total
Girls (*n* = 158)	Boys (*n* = 145)	10–12 (*n* = 101)	13–17 (*n* = 203)	Parents (*n* = 1,001)
60	71*	51	72*	45
48	58	43	59*	33
37	53*	37	48	22
33	46*	27	45*	17
33	45	17	49*	26
35	43	29	44*	18
29	41*	30	37	18
26	34	21	34*	25
23	30	18	31*	10
23	26	11	31*	24
23	26	11	31*	14
22	25	16	27*	16
20	24	12	27	16
19	23	17	23	10
23	25	11	31*	15

Although we found rather strong associations between age and the answers to scenario 2, we found no relationship between age and a willingness to give up name, address and information about likes and dislikes as described in the first scenario. The reason is probably not the clearer mention of a privacy policy in scenario 1 than 2, because we found no difference between the age groups in the trust of privacy policies. Perhaps younger children consider topics such as whether their parents drink wine, what they do on weekends, and whether they cheat on tests to be more obviously sensitive than giving out one's name and address to a Web site. Moreover, both parent and child respondents may have thought that somehow the Web site could find out their names and addresses and associate them with scenario 2's answers.

Despite the basic associations we found between age and a youngster's sensitivity to releasing information, more complex regression analyses revealed the same frustrating lack of predictability that we found with parents. We failed to find any background or attitudinal characteristic—whether age, gender, attitudes toward Web privacy, or any details regarding the child's attitude or experience—that could statistically predict answers on either scenarios 1 or 2. What this means is that while we have found some key associations between age and a youngster's privacy attitude as well as between gender and a kid's privacy attitude, trying to get at the cluster of attitudes and background characteristics that can together predict a youngster's (or parent's) response to information-privacy scenarios remains a challenge.

Parent-Child Communication and the Web

The findings we have reported for our entire sample of 300 youngsters held up when we looked at the 150 in this group whose parents we also interviewed. While the larger sample of kids was generally more useful to test for statistical associations, the linked pairs of parents and children allowed us to see specifically if youngsters and parents tended to be on the same page when they spoke about information privacy and the Web.

When we interviewed pairs of parents and kids in the same family, we found chance rather than pattern in key communication areas. We found that kids and their parents don't necessarily hold the same attitudes or even remember the same family interactions.

• It was only a matter of chance that the parents and the kids who said they would barter information for free gifts in scenarios 1 and 2 were related.

• Whether parents agreed with their kids on whether they trusted them "completely" was also merely a matter of chance.

• Similarly, although over 60% of all the parents and kids we interviewed (including the youngsters who were open to information barter) said that they have had discussions about how to deal with Web information requests, we found in our pairs that most parents and kids didn't agree on whether these sorts of discussions had ever taken place!

The findings are sobering for those who believe that simple discussions between parents and their children can encourage a consistent family approach to dealing with requests for information on the Web. They suggest that parent-child conversations about Web privacy issues are fleeting at best, perhaps in the form of "don't give out your name" or "don't talk to strangers" that parents have traditionally urged upon their children. In view of the chance relationships between youngsters' and parents' approach to bartering information, it would seem that parent-child communication about family privacy policies is an area that deserves a great deal of attention.

Concluding Remarks

If there is one point that our study highlights it is that many—in fact, probably most—American families are filled with contradictions when it comes to the Internet. Parents fear that it can harm their kids but feel that their kids need it. Parents and kids individually say they have talked to each other about giving out information over the Web, but parents and kids in the same family don't remember doing it. Kids agree that parents should have a say on the information they give out over the Web but nevertheless find it acceptable to give out sensitive personal and family information to Web sites in exchange for a valuable free gift.

It should not be surprising that these sorts of contradictions lead to tensions. This year's Annenberg report on the Internet and the Family has focused on the contradictions and tensions surrounding the release of family information. We have found that three out of four parents say they are concerned that their children "give out personal information about themselves when visiting Web sites or chat rooms." Smaller, though still quite substantial, proportions of parents and youngsters report having experienced at least some incidents of disagreement, worry or anger in the family over kids' release of information to the Web. The proportions of families feeling such tensions will likely grow in coming years as new technologies for learning about individuals proliferate on the Internet. For media and marketers, information about teens is an increasingly valuable commodity. For logical business reasons they will pursue knowledge about youngsters and their families as aggressively as possible.

The task for civic society is to set up a counterbalance to their efforts that establishes norms about what is ethically and legally correct for media and marketers to do. We might note here that Federal and university research guidelines require academic investigators to get parents' permission to interview tweens and teens about something as benign as their general attitudes toward the Web. It is ironic that marketers can track, aggregate and store far more personal responses to questions by individuals in these age groups without getting any permission from parents at all.

Nevertheless, while one can agree (as almost all parents do) that teenagers should get permission from parents before giving information to sites, legislation that forces Web sites to get that permission raises complex issues. A clear drawback is that mandating Web sites to get parental permission from youngsters aged 10 to 17 is impractical in an era when youngsters can discover ways to get around such requirements or forge their parents' permission.

Even if it becomes possible for a site to verify whether a visitor is or is not a teen, we have to question whether this sort of verification is socially desirable. What might be the consequences of the "electronic carding" of tweens and teens? Would many Web sites simply prohibit teens from entering rather than go to the trouble to turn off their tracking and profiling software for them? More controversially, would it mean that teens could not participate in chat rooms or listservs where information about users is systematically collected? If so, would that be infringing on the right of the youngsters to express their opinions in open forums?

Clearly, the new digital technologies are creating circumstances where society's interest in encouraging parents to supervise their youngsters is colliding with society's interest in encouraging youngsters' to speak out and participate in public discussions. We hesitate to suggest that the FTC rules that guide Web sites regarding children under 13 should be applied to youngsters 13 and over. At the same time, we reject the notion that teens should be approachable by Web sites as if they are fully responsible and independent adults in need of no parental supervision. We believe that the best policy in this area lies in aggressively encouraging family discussions of privacy norms along with limited Federal regulation.

• Our study points to the importance of urging parents and their children to talk in detail about how to approach requests by Web sites for personal and family data. Parents should not take for granted that traditional cautions such as "don't give out your name" or "don't talk to strangers" will be enough for the Web. Family members need to understand how all sorts of information about their interests can be tracked through cookies and related software without their even knowing it.

• Many parents cannot develop norms about family privacy alone. Our study and others have found that parents simply do not know enough about the Web to be aware of the way Web sites gather information and what to do about it. Here is a terrific opportunity for community groups, libraries, schools, and state and Federal agencies to work together on campaigns aimed at making information privacy a hot family topic and bringing community members together to learn about it.

• One way to get family members talking about these issues when children are relatively young (say, aged 6 through 12) is to convince parents and kids to surf the Web together. Encouraging family Web surfing, and family discussions about Web surfing, ought to be a priority of government and nonprofit organizations that care about enriching Americans' Internet experiences.

• Logically connected to encouraging community and family discussions of information privacy is the need for individuals to know what

Web sites know about them. Our research shows that virtually all parents believe that they should have a legal right to that information. A Web Freedom of Information Act should be passed that allows every person access to all data, including clickstream data, that a Web site connects to his or her individual computer or name. Whether parents should have the right to access their youngsters' data should be a mater of public discussion.

• Our finding that youngsters are substantially more likely than parents to say they would give up personal information to a Web site when increasing values are associated with a free gift supports suggestions for another Federal regulation: Web sites aimed at tweens and teens should be prohibited from offering free gifts, including prizes through sweepstakes, if those gifts are tied in direct or indirect ways to the youngsters' disclosure of information.

We fully expect that some of these suggestions will be more controversial than others. All of them will take a lot of work. But then, it will take a lot of work from many quarters of society to help maximize the benefits of the Internet for the family.

Notes

1. The sampling error for percentages based on the entire sample of 1001 parents is approximately plus or minus 3.5 percentage points. The sampling error is larger for smaller subgroups within the sample.

2. The sampling error for percentages based on the entire sample of 304 children is approximately plus or minus 5.6 percentage points. The sampling error is larger for smaller subgroups within the sample.

3. A discriminant analysis was performed using the 1998 three-group online segmentation as the dependent variable; items which were used to derive the 1998 segmentation (also asked in the 2000 study) were used as independent variables. Classification rates were quite good (90% of respondents belonging to group 1 were correctly classified, 89% for group 2, 87% for group 3) with an overall cross-validated correct classification rate of 89%. The classification function coefficients were used to create an algorithm (a weighted formula) with which to classify respondents of the 2000 study into the online segments.

4. Regina Joseph, "It's time for handheld wireless devices: CollegeClub.com wants to offer gadgets to your kids They won't help Johnny's grades, but they sure are cool," *Forbes Digital Tool* (*www.forbes.com*), May 07, 1999.

5. Roger O. Crockett, "Forget the Mall. Kids Shop the Net. Soon they'll spend billions online. How should marketers and parents respond?" *Business Week*, July 26, 1999, p. EB 14.

6. We considered parents as having "experienced tension" with youngsters over kids' release of information to the Web if the parents answered any of four questions in specific ways. One question asked, "when it comes to chat rooms, or sending and receiving email, do you disagree with your children frequently, sometimes, rarely or never?" If the person said frequently or sometimes, we took that as a yes to having experienced tensions. The second question asked if the parent had ever been involved in a specific incident where the parent was worried about something that his or her child told a Web site. A third question asked "as far as you know, has any of your children been involved in a chat room or communicated with people you found unacceptable on the Web?" The fourth question asked, "Has any of your children ever given out information he or she shouldn't to Web sites?" We found that 41% of the parents answered yes to one or more of these questions.

7. Alan F. Westin, "'Freebies' and Privacy: What Net Users Think," *Privacy & American Business Survey Report*, (July 14, 1999). http://www.pandfab.org/sr990714.html.

8. The parents' information disclosure scale was scaled from fifteen different items in the data set. We employed principal components factor analysis, which is a test to assess whether the items belong to a single conceptual dimension. A principal components factor analysis of the fifteen variables yielded a single factor, explaining 58.4% of the variance in responses. The fifteen items were then examined for inter-item consistency, in unidimensional scaling (Cronbach's alpha = 0.95). A scale of the fifteen items, whose values represent the respondent's (parent) inclination to think it's OK for a teen to disclose private and sensitive information, was then computed. The higher the score, the more likely that respondent would say it's OK for a teen to disclose information. The scale mean across the total parents' sample (n = 957) was 2.19, and the standard deviation was 0.82.

9. We used multiple regression analysis here. We also attempted to find predictors of whether a parent would be swayed in the first scenario. Here too, we did not find demographics or Internet experiences to be strong enough predictors of a parent's intention to barter information for a free gift.

10. We considered youngsters as having "experienced tension" with parents over releasing information to the Web if they answered either of two questions in specific ways. One question asked, "when it comes to chat rooms, or sending and receiving email, do you disagree with your parents frequently (that is, a lot), sometimes, rarely (that is, not too much) or never?" If the person said frequently or sometimes, we considered him or her as having experienced tensions. The second question asked, "Have your parents ever been angry at you for giving information to a Web site that you shouldn't have given?" If the youngster said yes to that, we considered him or her as having experienced tensions.

11. Like the parents' scale, the kids' information disclosure scale was created from 15 different items in the data set. We employed principal components factor analysis, which is a test to assess whether the items belong to a single conceptual dimension. A principal components factor analysis of the 15 variables yielded two factors, explaining 58.9% of the variance in responses. A closer examination of the two items revealed they were equally correlated with the main dimension, and therefore they were not omitted from the scale. The 15 items were then examined for inter-item consistency, in unidimensional scaling (Cronbach's alpha = 0.92). A scale of the 15 items, whose values represent the respondent's (kid's) inclination to disclose private and sensitive information, was then computed. None of the items if deleted would have improved the alpha reliability coefficient. The higher the score, the more likely that respondent would disclose information. The scale mean across the total kids' sample (N = 290) was 2.66, and the standard deviation was 0.80.

9

Mediated Childhoods: A Comparative Approach to Young People's Changing Media Environment in Europe

Sonia Livingstone

Developing a Research Agenda

Two eight-year-old boys play their favourite multimedia adventure game on the family PC. When they discover an Internet site where the same game could be played interactively with unknown others, this occasions great excitement in the household. The boys choose their fantasy personae and try diverse strategies to play the game, both cooperative and competitive, simultaneously "talking" on-line (i.e., writing) to the other participants. But when restricted in their access to the Internet, for reasons of cost, the game spins off into "real life." Now the boys, together with their younger sisters, choose a character, don their battle dress and play "the game" all over the house, going downstairs to Hell, The Volcanoes and The Labyrinth, and upstairs to The Town, "improving" the game in the process. This new game is called, confusingly for adult observers, "playing the Internet."

This episode raises a host of questions concerning children and young people's engagement with media, many of which are addressed by this Special Issue. How do different media relate to each other: do some media displace others or depend on others; what determines interest in and selection of particular texts? How do the media fit into broader social contexts of leisure and, for children, into social contexts of play and learning? Are these media relations and social contexts themselves undergoing social change, and does this change give rise to new

Adapted from the *European Journal of Communication* 13, no. 4 (December 1998): 435–456. Reprinted by permission of Sage Publications Ltd from Sonia Livingstone, "Mediated Childhoods," Copyright © Sage Publications Ltd 1998.

opportunities and dangers for young people and their families? Is it still meaningful to distinguish between non-mediated and mediated leisure, as media reception merges with face-to-face interaction? What is the significance of virtual or fantasy participation in mediated interaction? And what are the consequences of inequalities in media access/use for social participation? Finally, given that adult and child perspectives diverge, how should all of this be researched?

The comparative project, "Children, Young People and the Changing Media Environment," whose work in progress is reported in this Special Issue, takes its inspiration from Himmelweit et al.'s (1958) seminal study, *Television and the Child*. That study examined many possible effects of television on children's lives following its introduction in Britain during the 1950s, informing policy-makers and parents as well as setting the agenda for research on children and television for decades to come. In the 1990s new forms of media are entering the lives of children and young people around Europe and research is again needed. As in that earlier study, we have conceptualized the likely impacts of new media as diverse but interconnected, requiring a broad-based description of media meanings, uses and impacts in their everyday social context together with a research design which facilitates comparisons between those with and without certain media and according to demographic or lifestyle categories. Researching "new media" means studying a moving target. In selecting the video recorder, multiple television channels, the personal computer, video games and the Internet for study, we assume that the electronic screen (which now encompasses broadcasting, print and computing) will remain central to the changing media environment. Within this, however, we recognize that new media may be defined in terms of technology (interactivity, digitalization, the convergence of telecommunication/broadcasting/computing) in terms of services (especially the convergence of information/entertainment/education/commerce); in terms of social diffusion and globalization processes; in terms of textual forms (genre hybridities, non-linear fiction, interactive audiences); and in terms of historical changes in social and cultural practices (Livingstone et al., 1997; Silverstone, 1997).

Having to resolve the question of "what's new" represents one of several differences between Himmelweit's study and the present research, highlighting ways in which new media—as well as the intervening 40 years of research—raise new challenges (Livingstone and Gaskell, 1995). A second difference concerns the move away from questions of "effect" to questions of meaning and use. This is in response to the sustained critique of the effects tradition (Livingstone, 1996) as well as to the practical impossibility of constructing a before-and-after research design given that multiple forms of media are gradually diffusing through society. Thus the shift from "television" to "the media environment" is significant: describing media access in the 1990s means mapping complex combinations of diverse media, and both the determinants and consequences of these combinations are of interest (e.g., Johnsson-Smaragdi et al., 1998). Broadening the project to encompass cross-national comparisons, however, allows some possibility for before-and-after, and have-and-have-not, comparisons.

This article argues that the focus on television viewing as a cause in children's lives is productively replaced by an enterprise which contextualizes media use—particularly new media use—within a broad analysis of children and young people's life worlds, including their use of traditional media. This shift is consonant with the recent attempt to open up audience studies by assuming more active, interpretative and participatory modes of engagement between audiences and media. However, mapping media environments, charting their determinants and consequences and investigating diverse modes of audience engagement all require a wider variety of research traditions than informed *Television and the Child*. This is reflected in the multidisciplinarity of the European research teams, including developmental and social psychology, cultural and sociological studies of childhood and youth, media uses and gratifications, the sociology of leisure/consumption, diffusion research and reception studies.

The awkward absence of a single term to cover our age range, extended to cover 6 to 17 years, signals a further difference—between "the child" and "children and young people" in the titles of Himmelweit et al. and the present project. The post-1950s emergence of youth culture, among other factors, has led to childhood and youth as connected but distinct (and separately theorized) phenomena. One challenge is to span analyses of both childhood and youth in researching the new media. The complementary challenge is to reveal the role played by the media in childhood and youth. Researchers in media studies hardly need persuading of the mediated nature of childhood and youth. But curiously perhaps, the sociology of childhood neglects this aspect of children's lives[2]—whether because its aim is to emphasize the cultures which children create for themselves or because of an implicitly elitist rejection of the media as uninteresting or unimportant. The rethought sociological child-as-agent (rather than child-as-object or child-as-outcome of social processes) lives a non-mediated childhood—a carefree child playing hopscotch with friends in a nearby park, not a child with music on the headphones watching television in her bedroom. Child psychology does acknowledge the media, but mainly in relation to cognitive development, and much of it remains, problematically, wedded to the effects tradition. More influential links exist between youth studies and media studies (e.g. Drotner, 1996; Fornas and Bolin, 1994), although these are often narrowly focused on certain media (e.g., music) or certain aspects of audiences (e.g., counter-cultures, resistance) to the neglect of other, more widespread and more ordinary media uses.

To sum up the guiding assumptions of our project in progress, we first contextualize new media in relation to older media, exploring uses of Internet and multimedia while not neglecting magazines, music or national television. The point is to complement—and thus to contextualize—studies of separate media.[3] Changes in the media environment both add to the leisure options and may also transform the meanings of older media; conversely, it is the social practices established for older media which set the parameters within which new media are appropriated into daily life. Second, we draw on research on children—itself divided into psychological, developmental studies of "the child" and sociological studies of "childhood"—and research on youth and youth culture. Researching across this age range allows us to work towards the integration of these different research traditions, to explore the transition from childhood and youth,[4] and to analyse childhood and youth within a unitary framework, for example investigating the common perception that characteristics of youth (e.g., the move towards independence, individualization and self-identity, engagement with consumer culture) are increasingly characteristic of younger children. A third guiding assumption is that media research needs more work specifically on children and youth: most media research focuses on adults, the family or the household, as if the life world of young people may be either assumed from or simply tacked onto an existing knowledge of adult society. Yet sociological and cultural studies of these age groups have been motivated by the recognition that childhood and youth are not simply stages through which individuals pass but are sociological phenomena in their own right, neither prior to nor separate from society as a whole.[5] Compared with the high levels of public concern over children and young people's use of new media, little research considers this group specifically—with notable exceptions from the cultural studies tradition (Buckingham, 1993; Kinder, 1991; Seiter, 1993). For certain media and certain European countries, research is particularly sparse.

Locating Media Use in the Context of Everyday Life

The idea of context provides a point of departure. On a descriptive level, our objective is to produce systematic and detailed accounts of the place of new media in childhood and youth. More theoretically, various approaches have been used to capture the idea of context, including those of social ecology, the social environment and the field. These direct us towards investigating the societal and social psychological ordering—or transformation—of practices, opportunities and problems for children, young people and their families in everyday life. Thus we consider "new" media in the context of older media, media use in the context of leisure, and leisure in the context of children and young people's world. The life world is itself conceptualized in terms of the expanding circles—the home, the school, the peer group, the community locale, the nation, the globe. Yet one can easily get lost describing the myriad details of particular media uses in different contexts by specific categories of children or young people, and conversely, in conducting comparative research, one must be wary of generating numerous "facts"—such as amount of time children spend watching television in different European countries—while forgetting their contexts. For example, while the findings emerging from our comparative project indicate that countries differ substantially in the amount of television viewed, our stress on "environment" leads us to attempt to contextualize these by document-ing access to diverse media (and the policies which regulate them), dis-posable leisure time (including length of school day, bedtime conventions, childcare practices), available places for leisure (including typical house size, public provision for leisure facilities, transport arrangements), and other significant aspects of young people's lives around Europe (family structure, patterns of parental employment, national languages, degree of urbanization, education system and so forth). As noted earlier, such an investigation requires a multidisciplinary study.

Without such contextualization, research on children and young peo-ple tends to transform the positives and negatives of their lives into pos-itive and negative children or young people, particularly negative ones (the Internet addict, the screen-zombie, the social isolate). Similarly, without contextualization research tends to pit "old" media against "new" media, failing to recognize the complex ways in which they are mutually entangled in everyday life. Furthermore, contextualization counters the tendency towards technological determinism evident within the literature on new media. Despite a widely shared sense of technolog-ical change, in which the screen in the family home is seen as the future site of a new multimedia culture integrating telecommunications, broad-casting, computing and video, researchers have learned to be sceptical of the assumption that social change follows equally rapidly (e.g., Miles et al., 1987; Silverstone, 1997). It is far from obvious whether playing Power Rangers in the playground is significantly new or just a new vari-ant on an age-old form of children's play. Similarly, while adolescents have retreated to their bedroom for privacy for as long as there have been adolescents with a room of their own, it is not obvious how much this experience is affected by their now having their own television set.[6] While new technologies are developed, entering the households of early adopters in part according to a technological agenda, more widespread use depends on their appropriation into pre-existing systems of meanings and practices (Neuman, 1991; Rogers, 1986; Schoenbach and Becker, 1989; Silverstone and Hirsch; 1992). Not only are these much slower to change, but their investigation demands a more user-centred—here a child-centred—focus.[7]

Approaching the contexts of media use through a child-centred focus is readily compatible with a cultural, constructionist approach to childhood and youth. Through his contextualized analysis within the sociology of childhood of the micro-workings of peer culture, Corsaro (1997) shows how the everyday activities of children reveal their participation in the production and reproduction of society. Drawing on Goffman's (1961) notion of secondary adjustments, Corsaro stresses that through such daily actions, often invisible to adult eyes, children contribute to the construction of social structures which have consequences for both children and adults. To develop my earlier example of children's play, the point would be that it is only from the viewpoint of—indeed only as a result of the activities of—the children playing the game that connections are created among a computer game, the Internet, dressing up, playing with friends, redefining personal space, the negotiation of gender-appropriate roles and parental regulation or facilitation of play. The daily practices which generate these connections mediate social relations within the family and peer group and have consequences for the space–time patterning of leisure.

In their everyday lives children and young people weave together a huge diversity of activities. This interconnection across activities may be deliberate, as in the intertextual integration of content themes across diverse media forms (e.g., Disney fans; see Drotner, in 2000). Or it may be more or less accidental (as when a child's leisure alters if a best friend moves in next door). The leisure environment affords access to certain kinds of activities and interconnections among activities, depending on social arrangements of time, space, cultural norms and values and personal preferences and lifestyle. Within these arrangements, children and young people (and their families) construct their own local contexts and it is within these that media use becomes meaningful (Qvortrup, 1995). Moreover, every choice is made meaningful by its mutual relation with all others: watching television means something different to the child with nothing else to do compared with the child who has a personal computer at home or friends knocking on the door. Thus conditions of access and choice within the child's environment are central to an understanding of the meanings of media use.

The point of a child-centred, constructivist approach is to argue that children and young people—both individually and as a market—not only respond to but also influence changes in their immediate environment, including their mediated environment. This argument can be developed to suggest that children and young people should be researched not only because they represent an audience neglected by the adult-centred focus on households as the unit of new media consumption but also because their uses of and experiences with new media are of specific analytical relevance to media theory. Children and young people represent the early users of new media (households with children lead in terms of media diffusion); possibly they are more flexible or creative users (having fewer already established patterns and routines of daily life; indeed, their main pattern is already that of change or development over time); they lack the conceptual baggage of many adults which leads them to fear new technologies and, more generally, the future; and last, research on youth in particular has shown us that while the media often serve as the very currency through which identities are constructed, social relations negotiated and peer culture generated, for adults this is more likely to be provided by work.

Contexts of Everyday Life in a Time of Social Change

In effect, we can conceptualize childhood and youth as themselves representing key contexts for media use—as occupying times and spaces whose contours are themselves part of wider trends. These trends are widely debated within social theory; and while claims for a radical break with tradition are overstated, any analysis of media use in context must consider these broader trends. Various authors (e.g., Reimer, 1995; Ziehe, 1994) have commented on the trend within western societies towards a separation of social structure and lifestyles. It is quite a task to map how far patterns of media use depend on traditional sociostructural distinctions (especially, social class divisions, traditional collective solidarities and standardized family structures). Yet to the extent that we are witnessing a shift away from, or a loosening of, the determining role of such distinctions, there are significant consequences for media research. For example, one can no longer presume a knowledge of media use from a knowledge of these distinctions (Reimer, 1995), giving a new twist to the notion of information-rich and information-poor households. It would seem that multiple factors lie behind media acquisition, including variation in both economic and cultural capital (Bourdieu, 1984), and in many European countries at least, acquisition of many leisure technologies is inversely related to socioeconomic status, although early adoption of information technology is a middle-class phenomenon (see van der Voort et al., 1998). Thus, the fluidity of contemporary links between social structure and lifestyles invites investigation of the place of the media in relation to each: instead of asking how traditional sociodemographic factors determine patterns of media use, research should also investigate processes of social participation or exclusion in society as a result of differential access to new forms of media or culture.

How should this new fluidity be thought of? Beck (1992) argues that the trend just described is not only away from traditional social formations but towards the individualization of social life—he stresses the diversification and individualization of life worlds and lifestyles which, potentially, introduce both new opportunities and new dangers. Applying this to the analysis of childhood, Buchner argues that:

every child is increasingly expected to behave in an "individualised way" ... children must somehow orient themselves to an *anticipated* life course. The more childhood in the family is eclipsed by influences and orientation patterns from outside the family ... the more independent the opportunity (and drive) to making up one's own mind, making one's choice ... described here as the *biographization* of the life course. (Buchner, 1990: 77–78)

Clearly childhood and youth is a key period for the construction of the self or identity, as young people are preoccupied with making the transition from their family of origin towards a wider peer culture (see Suess et al., this issue). As traditional structures, at all levels from the family to the nation-state, which confer identity are being undermined, others are actively sought by young people, and these are readily provided by the market. The integration of individualization and consumerism is also an increasingly globally structured process, transcending national boundaries. This makes for a heady context within which young people seek to construct a meaningful life project which is more or less shared with their peers, conceived locally and globally, in actuality and virtually

(Ziehe, 1994). However, against this context of new opportunities one should stress also the transformation of leisure culture into promotional culture as modern marketing directs flows of popular culture, identity is refashioned through consumption and the citizen (or viewer) is transformed into the consumer (e.g., Kinder, 1991). Clearly, whether conceived optimistically or pessimistically, the processes of globalization of media and culture are seen by many as the means par excellence by which such social changes are effected—for the detachment of meanings from their contexts of production is central to the conditions of late modernity, opening up possibilities for new contexts of consumption as market processes are increasingly freed (or refashioned) to infuse the life world of the family (Lash and Urry, 1994).

The analysis of individualization has implications both for the importance of media in everyday life and for our analysis of children and young people in terms of their autonomy vs their integration into social networks (whether traditional or new). Integrating these concerns raises questions about the role of media in the (possibly) changing balance between the relative independence or dependence of young people on their family, with implications in turn for policies informed by protectionism or liberalism.[8] Interestingly, the individualization thesis offers a historical account of the sociology of childhood as itself an outcome of a lengthy process of social change in which children, traditionally subordinated by or excluded from civic society, are repositioned as citizens in a democratic society and as partners within the home.[9] Changing patterns of media-related activities may have some very concrete consequences for the use of social place—in terms of the boundary between public and private, both within the community and within the household (Meyrowitz, 1985). At the level of community, research is needed to determine whether the information technologies in particular represent a means of social inclusion, with civic and cultural opportunities denied to those without access, or, perhaps, they represent an invitation to young people to withdraw from traditional leisure activities and, as a consequence, from social and political participation. At the level of the household, Giddens (1993: 184) suggests that we are seeing "a democratisation of the private sphere." Through the historical transformation of intimacy, children—like any other participants in a relationship—

have gained the right to "determine and regulate the conditions of their association" (Giddens, 1993: 185); and parents have gained the duty to protect them from coercion, ensure their involvement in key decisions, be accountable to them and others and to respect and expect respect.

Arguably, we are witnessing contradictory trends—both towards the autonomy of children, domestic democracy and individualization of childhood and towards increased regulation and risk management of children by adults. Rather than interpreting these as contrary trends towards independence and dependence respectively, Rose (1990) suggests that childhood is undergoing more a process of bureaucratization than of democratization, through a combination of strategies which constrain children's participation in public while capturing their private, individual world of identity and agency.[10] The ways in which the media particularly become caught up in these processes remain to be disentangled. If there is a new responsibility to construct an explicit project of the self[11] in socially regulated and approved ways—and for even younger children—the media may play a part in both facilitating and undermining this process, as perceived by parents, teachers and children/ young people. Moreover, the anxieties produced by these changes tend to lead many to hold new forms of media directly responsible, together with the globalization and consumerism which accompany them. While one can bracket off these anxieties as a sociological phenomenon with their own history and conditions of existence (Drotner, 1992), it is also the case that they not only reflect but also affect the social reproduction of childhood and patterns of media consumption.

Children, Young People, and the Media Environment across Europe

Contexts of media use are elaborated in this article in two main ways. First, differences in social, cultural, economic and political structures both across and within European countries are likely to make a difference to children and young people's media use. Second, among western countries these structures are themselves subject to broader processes of modernization, processes which have particular significance for young people. For both these reasons, comparisons across different European countries will be invaluable to the contextualizing of media use by children and young people. To the extent that different countries represent different positions on these broad structural variables, including the diffusion and appropriation of media, comparative analysis offers a kind of natural experiment for explaining the meanings, uses and impacts of new media within each country. To make such comparisons manageable in practice, the research should be restricted to modernized, western countries which are undergoing related sociopolitical changes;[12] overlarge national differences would prevent observations interesting in one country being informative for another.

The purpose of a comparative analysis is to improve the understanding of both one's own country and the countries with which comparison is made (Chisholm, 1995). In the context of developing European Union policy on a variety of fronts, comparative analysis also informs our understanding of European culture and society. Thus, by comparing a sizeable group of countries, broadly comparable in degree of modernization and global positioning, we hope to illuminate the ways in which specific dimensions of comparison (demographic, cultural and media-related) across European countries underpin the meanings and impacts of old and new media. To make the comparisons valuable, we must—counter-intuitively perhaps—beware of excessive caution. Chisholm (1995: 22) notes that a sensitivity to the difficulties of comparative analysis invites the adoption of a relativist framework which contends that "societies and cultures are fundamentally non-comparable and certainly cannot be evaluated against each other." The resulting "Tower of Babel" turns research into a collection of interesting "facts" which participants and observers must work hard at to draw valuable lessons. We have attempted to avoid the babble of non-comprehending voices by working within a broadly shared theoretical framework, rather than putting together, post hoc, different projects using non-comparable concepts and methods (see Blumler et al., 1992).

Within Europe there are marked differences in the structures of childhood and these affect the time–space relations of young people's media use. Age is a useful marker of social difference: for example, in Finland a seven-year-old is expected to be able to go to school and then return home to look after him/herself until a parent finishes work; in Britain and France both moral and welfare considerations make this unacceptable, with implications for parents' work practices, childcare provision, urban planning and leisure. Within Europe, there are also marked differences in media provision, especially but not solely with respect to newer forms of media—the Internet, home computing, multiple television channels and personal media goods. It is clear from the comparative project that these differences do not simply depend on national wealth or other straightforward socioeconomic indicators, but rather both reflect and affect structures of childhood and youth at all levels from domestic practices to national policy.

Within this broad orientation, a number of approaches can be taken when making cross-national comparisons. Perhaps the simplest approach explores hypothesized universal themes within diverse national contexts. The widespread social significance of gender in framing meanings and practices of media consumption would be an example, and in this case the results of comparative analysis might qualify the apparently universal features of gender according to their inflection in different cultural meaning systems (developmental trajectories provide another example; see Suess et al., 1998). A somewhat different approach would identify dimensions of cross-cultural difference—such as variations in family structure, or national wealth, or linguistic uniformity/diversity, asking what consequences this has for media use in each nation (see Pasquier et al., 1998). A third approach, more technologically led, starts with the provision of media in each country and asks about either or both of the determinants and the implications of differential patterns of media diffusion across Europe. As noted above, an example might be the sizeable variations in children's access to the Internet (and the different government and educational policies which in part determine this) and the consequences for children's access, meanings and use of the Internet both at home and in school (see van der Voort et al., 1998 and Johnsson-Smaragdi et al., 1998).

A fourth and final approach would hold that as Europe is subject to the conditions of late modernity, cultural variations in the processes of individualization, globalization, privatization and consumerism would have implications for the contexts within which different media are appropriated by different groups of children and young people (e.g., Buchner et al., 1995; Lemish et al., 1998). Earlier, we have suggested that the emergence of "bedroom culture" can be examined in this way (Livingstone et al., 1997). The observation that British children more than other European children own personalized media (e.g. two-thirds have a television in their bedroom) seems to be a matter neither of societal diffusion of media nor of cultural differences in religion, language or wealth. Rather, it suggests broader cultural differences in terms of privatization (a shift from community to household, from common leisure provision to personal/family ownership) and individualization (the trend towards living out one's project of the self independently of traditional defining structures of identity). Consequently, we suggest that the situation in any one country can be usefully understood in terms of the convergence or differentiation of national (or regional) cultures as part of such broader processes—particularly, globalization, privatization, individualization and consumerism.

While there are many specific hypotheses to be examined according to each of the three approaches outlined above, this fourth approach looks beyond the tendency of childhood and youth research to be framed by national concerns (Chisholm, 1995; although see Drotner, 1996). This is crucial as the media (or the "mediatization" of culture) clearly work at all levels from local to global (see Lemish et al., 1998). Indeed, not only does globalization arouse public anxieties—particularly regarding national identity, linguistic boundaries or moral tradition—but also globalization reframes age-old concerns over both "the child" and "youth" as children and young people are positioned as a target of these anxieties, being seen as the "weak link" through which external "threats" make their entry. A contrary, but also problematic, discourse of globalization can be detected beneath the notion of the so-called Information Society, for this assumes a kind of Whig history where everyone is supposedly marching in the same, technologically determined, progressive direction.[13] Our project attempts to avoid both these discourses—of threat and of progress. Unless children and young people's use of new media are understood in their cultural context, the host of statistical findings which research produces about the diffusion of media across Europe, for example, provides a kind of Rorschach blot on which to project potentially inappropriate assumptions (whether of opportunity or danger) about other nations. The advantage of cross-national research is that it challenges the decontextualizing, even ethno-centric assumptions easily made by research conducted in national contexts (especially in relatively large or powerful countries), as these often rest on presumptions about how other countries are similar, or opposite, to one's own. In terms of developing both theory and policy, the advantage is clearly that of facilitating an awareness of how things could be—and are elsewhere—arranged differently.

Notes

This article draws on a research project "Children, Young People and the Changing Media Environment" directed by the author in collaboration with George Gaskell and Moira Bovill at the London School of Economics and Political Science. The British project, conducted in association with the Broadcasting Standards Commission, is supported financially by the Advertising Association, the British Broadcasting Corporation, the Broadcasting Standards Commission, British Telecommunications plc, the Independent Television Association, the Independent Television Commission, the Leverhulme Trust and Yorkshire/Tyne Tees Television. The multinational project, directed by S. Livingstone and G. Gaskell at LSE, is supported financially by the Broadcasting Standards Commission, the Youth for Europe Programme (EC-DGXXII) and the European Science Foundation. The author would like to thank Jay Blumler, Kirsten Drotner, Johan Fornäs, Peter Lunt, Dominique Pasquier, Bo Reimer, David Scott and the participants in the European research project for their constructive discussion of an earlier version of this article.

1. While Israel is not part of Europe, it was included to strengthen the representation of Mediterranean countries (it is linked to the European Commission for scientific purposes).

2. Taking Qvortrup (1995), James et al. (1998) and Corsaro (1997) as indicative of this new approach to childhood, it is notable that none considers the media in any detail, if at all.

3. Previous research has tended to produce diverse but discrete studies—gender and the computer at school, heavy users of video games, soap opera viewers, children's understanding of the distinction between reality and fantasy, teenagers' music subcultures—while other areas of media uses are unaccountably neglected—reading books for pleasure (Boëthius, 1995) or counter-stereotyped media uses (girls as sports fans, boys as soap opera fans)—depending on the vagaries of academic fashion.

4. The age range studied is, of course, bisected by the transition from primary to secondary education. This occurs at somewhat different ages in different European countries and may be expected to have consequences in itself for leisure experience. To maximize comparability across national studies we selected the

following age breaks: 6–7 years (in most countries, the first year of school, though the third year in Britain and Netherlands), 9–10 (one or two years before the end of primary school for most countries), 12–13 (typically the first year of secondary school, with some exceptions) and 15–16 (in most cases the last, or penultimate year of compulsory education). About half of the national studies in fact included all years, and for comparisons involving these countries, the age breaks 6–8, 9–11, 12–14 and 15–17 are used.

5. More problematically, the concomitant critique of the concept of socialization results in an undertheorization of age and development, and thus the present project draws on developmental psychology as well as the sociology of childhood (e.g., Suess et al., 1998).

6. To the extent that new media open up new opportunities or dangers, today's parents, teachers and researchers may be the least appropriate people to drive the research questions: this generation is in the exceptional but temporary position of lacking the meaning-making frames of both the early adopters who have followed the development of technologies and their children who have grown up with "new" media (Livingstone et al., 1997).

7. Schoenbach and Becker (1989) surveyed the impact on households of media introduced in the 1980s (VCR and cable/satellite television) across a variety of western countries. They found little evidence of a reduction in time spent on non-media leisure, little evidence of reduction in time or money spent on print and auditory media, consistent evidence for increasing specialization in uses of all media, not just the new ones, and no evidence that new media create new audience interests, although they may provide new means of satisfying existing interests.

8. For example, in charting patterns of television use by the family from 1950 to 1990, Andreasen (1994) suggests that the shift from family co-viewing towards individual viewing was facilitated both by technological developments—the purchase of multiple sets, the individualizing effects of multichannel cable television and of the remote control, and by the emergence of more democratic families with non-traditional views about parent–child power relations.

9. Various kinds of support exist for this "democratization" of childhood, from historical accounts (following Aries, 1962) to international policy (notably, the UN Children's Committee concerned with Article 12 of the UN Convention of Human Rights which stresses the need to respect and listen to children, to act in the child's best interests, and not to discriminate against children). In England, the Children Act 1989 marked the shift from treating children as the passive objects of parental rights to being treated as legal subjects in their own right.

10. The contrary trends lead to paradoxes such as the way in which "play and spontaneity have also become parts of the curriculum of nursery schools" (Qvortrup: 1995: 195); in Britain we have noted the apparent coincidence of parental restriction of children's access to public spaces and their liberal provision of media within the private domain of the child's bedroom (Livingstone

et al., 1997). Rose's resolution is to argue that the more there is talk of children's rights, children's participation and children as agents, the more also is society moved to regulate the conditions of this participation.

11. "The reflexive project of the self, which consists in the sustaining of coherent, yet continuously revised, biographical narratives, takes place in the context of multiple choice as filtered through abstract systems" (Giddens, 1991: 5).

12. Even among western countries, certain factors—such as the strength of the public broadcasting tradition—are especially characteristic of Europe countries.

13. Consider the concerns behind most European governments' policies to keep up or get ahead in the race to produce the "digital generation."

References

Andreasen, M. S. (1994) "Patterns of Family Life and Television Consumption from 1945 to the 1990s," pp. 19–35 in J. Bryant and A. C. Huston (eds.) *Media, Children and the Family—Social Scientific, Psychodynamic and Clinical Perspectives*. Hillsdale, NJ: Lawrence Erlbaum.

Aries, P. (1962) *Centuries of Childhood: A Social History of Family Life*. New York: Vintage Books.

Beck, U. (1992) *Risk Society: Towards a New Modernity*. London: Sage.

Blumler, J. G., J. M. McLeod and K. E. Rosengren (1992) "An Introduction to Comparative Communication Research," in J. G. Blumler, J. M. McLeod and K. E. Rosengren (eds.) *Comparatively Speaking: Communication and Culture across Space and Time*. Newbury Park, CA: Sage.

Boëthius, U. (1995) "Controlled Pleasures: Youth and Literary Texts," pp. 39–57 in J. Fornas and G. Bolin (eds.) *Youth Culture in Late Modernity*. London: Sage.

Bourdieu, P. (1984) *Distinction: A Social Critique of the Judgement of Taste*. London: Routledge and Kegan Paul.

Buchner, P. (1990) "Growing up in the Eighties: Changes in the Social Biography of Childhood in the FRG," in L. Chisholm, P. Buchner, H.-H. Kruger and P. Brown (eds.) *Childhood, Youth and Social Change: A Comparative Perspective*. London: Falmer Press.

Buchner, P., M. Bois-Reymond and H.-H. Kruger (1995) "Growing up in Three European Regions," in L. Chisholm, P. Buchner, H.-H. Kruger and M. Bois-Reymond (eds.) *Growing up in Europe: Contemporary Horizons in Childhood and Youth Studies*. Berlin: Walter de Gruyter.

Buckingham, D. (1993) *Reading Audiences: Young People and the Media*. Manchester: Manchester University Press.

Chisholm, L. (1995) "European Youth Research: Tour de Force or Turmbau zu Babel?," pp. 21–32 in L. Chisholm, P. Buchner, H.-H. Kruger and M.

Bois-Reymond (eds.) *Growing up in Europe: Contemporary Horizons in Childhood and Youth Studies*. Berlin: Walter de Gruyter.

Corsaro, W. A. (1997) *The Sociology of Childhood*. Thousand Oaks, CA: Pine Forge Press.

Drotner, K. (1992) "Modernity and Media Panics," in M. Skovmand and K. C. Schröder (eds.) *Media Cultures: Reappraising Transnational Media*. London: Routledge.

Drotner, K. (1996) "Cross-over Culture and Cultural Identities," *Young: Nordic Journal of Youth Research* 4(1): 4–17.

Drotner, K. (2000) "Difference and Diversity: Trends in Young Danes' Media Uses," *Media, Culture and Society* 22(2): 149–166.

Fornäs, J. and G. Bolin (eds.) (1994) *Youth Culture in Late Modernity*. London: Sage.

Giddens, A. (1991) *Modernity and Self-identity: Self and Society in the Late Modern Age*. Cambridge: Polity Press.

Giddens, A. (1993) *The Transformation of Intimacy: Sexuality, Love and Eroticism in Modern Societies*. Cambridge: Polity Press.

Goffman, E. (1961) *Asylums: Essays on the Social Situation of Mental Patients and Other Inmates*. Harmondsworth: Penguin.

Himmelweit, H. T., A. N. Oppenheim and P. Vince (1958) *Television and the Child: An Empirical Study of the Effect of Television on the Young*. London and New York: Oxford University Press.

James, A., C. Jenks and A. Prout (1998) *Theorizing Childhood*. Cambridge: Cambridge University Press.

Johnsson-Smaragdi, U., L. d'Haenens and F. Krotz (1998) "Patterns of Old and New Media Use among Young People in Flanders, Germany and Sweden," *European Journal of Communication* 13(4): 479–501.

Kinder, M. (1991) *Playing with Power in Movies, Television and Video Games: From Muppet Babies to Teenage Mutant Ninja Turtles*. Berkeley: University of California Press.

Lash, S. and J. Urry (1994) *Economies of Signs and Space*. London: Sage.

Lemish, D., K. Drotner, T. Liebes, E. Maigret and G. Stald (1998) "Global Culture in Practice: A Look at Children and Adolescents in Denmark, France and Israel," *European Journal of Communication* 13(4): 539–556.

Livingstone, S. (1996) "On the Continuing Problems of Media Effects Research," pp. 303–324 in J. Curran and M. Gurevitch (eds.) *Mass Media and Society*, 2nd edn. London: Edward Arnold.

Livingstone, S. and M. Bovill (eds.) (2001) *Children and Their Changing Media Environment: A European Comparative Study*. Mahwah, NJ: Lawrence Erlbaum.

Livingstone, S. and G. Gaskell (1995) "Children, Young People and the Television Screen," pp. 297–319 in F. Guglielmelli (ed.) *Reinventing Television: The World Conference*. Paris: Association Television et Culture.

Livingstone, S., G. Gaskell and M. Bovill (1997) "Europäische Fernseh-Kinder in veränderten Medienwelten," *Television* 10(2): 4–12.

Meyrowitz, J. (1985) *No Sense of Place: The Impact of Electronic Media on Social Behavior*. New York: Oxford University Press.

Miles, I., J. Bessant, K. Guy and H. Rush (1987) "IT Futures in Households and Communities," pp. 225–242 in R. Finnegan, G. Salaman and K. Thompson (eds.) *Information Technology: Social Issues—A Reader*. London: Hodder and Stoughton.

Morrow, V. and M. Richards (1996) "The Ethics of Social Research with Children: An Overview," *Children and Society* 10: 90–105.

Neuman, W. R. (1991) *The Future of the Mass Audience*. Cambridge: Cambridge University Press.

Pasquier, D., C. Buzzi, L. d'Haenens and U. Sjoberg (1998) "Family Lifestyles and Media Use Patterns: An Analysis of Domestic Media among Flemish, French, Italian and Swedish Children and Teenagers," *European Journal of Communication* 13(4): 503–519.

Qvortrup, J. (1995) "Childhood and Modern Society: A Paradoxical Relationship," pp. 189–198 in J. Brannen and M. O'Brien (eds.) *Childhood and Parenthood*. London: Institute of Education, University of London.

Reimer, B. (1995) "Youth and Modern Lifestyle," pp. 120–144 in J. Fornäs and G. Bolin (eds.) *Youth Culture in Late Modernity*. London: Sage.

Rogers, E. M. (1986) *Communication Technology: The New Media in Society*. New York: Free Press.

Rose, N. (1990) *Governing the Soul: The Shaping of the Private Self*. London: Routledge.

Schoenbach, K. and L. B. Becker (1989) "The Audience Copes with Plenty: Patterns of Reactions to Media Changes," pp. 353–366 in L. B. Becker and K. Schoenbach (eds.) *Audience Responses to Media Diversification: Coping with Plenty*. Hillsdale, NJ: Lawrence Erlbaum.

Seiter, E. (1993) *Sold Separately: Children and Parents in Consumer Culture*. New Brunswick, NJ: Rutgers University Press.

Suess, D., A. Suoninen, C. Garitaonandia, P. Juaristi and R. Koikkalainen (1998) "Media Use and the Relationships of Children and Teenagers with their Peer Groups: A Study of Finnish, Spanish and Swiss Cases," *European Journal of Communication* 13(4): 521–538.

Silverstone, R. S. (1997) "New Media in European Households," pp. 113–134 in U. T. Lange and K. Goldhammer (eds.) *Exploring the Limits: Europe's Changing Communication Environment*. Berlin: Springer-Verlag.

Silverstone, R. S. and E. Hirsch (eds.) (1992) *Consuming Technologies: Media and Information in Domestic Spaces*. London: Routledge.

Van der Voort, T. H. A., J. W. J. Beentjes, M. Bovill, G. Gaskell, C. Koolstra, S. Livingstone and N. Marseille (1998) "Young People's Ownership and Uses of New and Old Forms of Media in Britain and the Netherlands," *European Journal of Communication* 13(4): 457–477.

Ziehe, T. (1994) "From Living Standard to Life Style," *Young: Nordic Journal of Youth Research* 2(2): 2–16.

10

Outlook and Insight: Young Danes' Uses of the Internet—Navigating Global Seas and Local Waters

Gitte Stald

Introduction

In September 2000, all young Danes aged 6 to 16 years had access to computers and Internet—either at home, at school or at the local library. Consequently, all Danish adolescents have, in principle, access to the services of the Internet ranging from information, communication, entertainment and trading. Access to these services provides opportunities to connect—locally and across any borders. Yet access is not the same as exploitation and use of the possible services. The uses of as well as attitudes towards Internet vary greatly among young people in the age range I focus on here, 12- to 16-year-olds. Access in practice (e.g., hanging the costs and possibly permission from parents or teachers), competence, literacy and usability are decisive factors in the extension and use of IT in the life-worlds of young Danes. From one theoretical viewpoint, the Internet may be perceived as the ultimate channel to advanced democratic worldwide communication and cultural exchange. From the grounded position of the majority of 12- to 16-year-olds, however, the Internet and the notion of the World Wide Web is, on the one hand, acknowledged as a possible means of connecting and having access to the world. On the other hand, thoughts on Net use are primarily focused on local usability and the transformation of internationally obtained information and connections to useful tools in one's daily social and cultural practices.

From Working Paper No. 7, Department of Media Studies, University of Copenhagen, Denmark, July 2001. Reprinted with permission of the author.

The aim of this paper is to discuss how young Danes' use of a variety of Internet services affects their thoughts and reflections on their dual identity as Danes and as world citizens. I shall put forward my findings on and analysis of the issues presented above by discussing three main themes: (1) Meaning of access. (2) Uses and experiences. (3) Thoughts on Internet use between the local and the global. Empirically, I draw primarily on findings from the Year 2000 study.[1] I have looked at the large group of broadly defined "average young people" and not in particular at the advanced or especially innovative young Internet users. By way of introduction, I shall put forward some preliminary theoretical thoughts on the relation between conception of experienced and perceived proximity and that between proximity and community.

The analysis indicates that adolescents who use the Internet for communication, information, entertainment and trading are conscious of the worldwide dimension of "being" and communicating in cyberspace. Still, they remain pragmatically focused on local usefulness. Using the Internet and reflecting on the outcome obviously has an impact on the balance between feelings of self-consciousness, national pride, local belonging and security, on the one hand, and orientation towards and curiosity about new experiences, cultures and people, on the other.

The discussion raises perspectives on the Internet as an important medium for possible global encounters and cultural transformation, which remain rooted in individual interests and experiences and develop collectively in cyberspace and "real life" communities.

Theoretical Approach

I find a duality in the ways we tend to think of our engagements in cyberspace. On the one hand, the vast universes of cyberspace can be conceptualised as open spaces. Our knowledge and experience informs us of the international extent of information technology and of the geographically and culturally dispersed users of the Internet. The metaphors of cyber*space* and *World Wide Web* guide our visualisation, on a symbolic level, in this direction. But in situations of use, the virtual rooms tend to be perceived as locally experienced. This is related to our need to identify our locality in the situation in order to determine the relations between the participants in a communicative activity or between the "here," which is our basis, and the "there," which is where sources of other information are situated. My suggestion is that information and communication in cyberspace promote a perception of proximity that is most intense during online interaction, exchange of information and recognition of formats, codes (not only in a technical sense), themes, etc.

As a construction of the mind, the virtual world is always with us in the physical world. That is, we experience the virtual in the context of the "real." The transcendence of the borders between the virtual and the physical world is most often metaphorically referred to as "going in/ being in" and "leaving/going out." Transcendence is taking place when the physical world demands the attention/"presence" or action of the individual or when the experiences in cyberspace are transferred to the physical world.

Even if the virtual is a construction or a conception, the apprehension of reality as well as of experiences, information and relations achieved in cyberspace is transferred to and transformed in the "real world" and becomes real. By "becomes real" I mean that the experiences, information and relations achieve meaning, importance, and value or just get "listed" in the life-world of the individual.

Figure 10.1 illustrates, in a very simple way, how the virtual world—symbolised by the dotted quadrangle—exists in the realm of the physical world—illustrated by the inner, light-grey circle. The conception of the

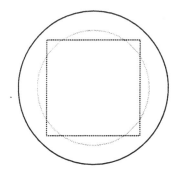

Figure 10.1
Conception of the transcendence between the virtual world and the physical world.

virtual and the "real" and of the relation between them is symbolised by the largest circle, which encircles the other figures. The chosen forms are not important as such, but merely illustrative. At this point, I have not completed my speculations about the figurative representation of the relation between the virtual and the "real" world. In the figure, I have chosen to let the borders of the virtual transcend those of the "real" world. I have done so because the intention of the figure is to illustrate the concept (the outer circle) of the relation, and the general concept demonstrates a notion of the virtual as intertwined with the "real" in what I would call a dialectic of experiences and exchange. The meaning of the spaces (corners and bows) where the quadrangle and the inner circle do not overlap should be discussed. What is in there? Following the logic of the figure, it must be empty spaces or bits of "the virtual" and "the real." I choose to tone down the problem of "empty spaces" or "islands" in this context, however, as the basic purpose of the figure is to demonstrate, in a simple way, how "the real" and "the virtual" are interrelated and how both are encompassed by the theoretic concept of a dialectic process.

Proximity is imagined and experienced psychologically. The experience of proximity has two major origins. First, some presentations in all media constitute experienced and well known universes, where surroundings, themes, atmosphere, style, and "language" (here: mode of communication as well as tongue) are familiar to the Net user. Parallel to this basic, practical and local use of the Internet, a virtual dimension of transformation of universal information and exchange into satisfaction of local needs and purposes can be distinguished. Second, cyberspace enhances the perception of "closed" or intimate rooms to be compared to physical or psychological rooms experienced in everyday life outside the mediated experience. Intellectually, as mentioned above, the adolescent users acknowledge the international connection—"after all, it *is* called the World Wide Web" (boy, 15 years). New experiences on the Net, be they surfing or browsing randomly or trying new possibilities, can be perceived as expeditions to new universes, not knowing exactly what might turn up around the corner or what the reactions of the natives in these "strange" and foreign cultures might be. At the same time, in the situation there is a sense of the well known and safe. Very quickly, the codes, behaviour and procedures are well known and the new universe can be added to the rank of familiar "rooms" in cyberspace.

The general conception of cyberspace among the present target group might be related to the specific self-reflectivity and introversion characterising the period of youth. The centre of interest and reflection is the self, which also guides the functions and experiences (intellectual and emotional) that serve the purposes and fulfil the immediate needs in the social, cultural and aesthetic practices of the individual or of the collective. Only few reflect on globality as a realisation of the symbolically endless universes of cyberspace or the reverse, of cyberspace as a symbolic representation of the world. The adolescents are, at the same time, heavy consumers of the possibilities in all aspects of their life-worlds (which include cyberspace) for the purposes mentioned above, and they move easily between diverse spheres and levels of social and cultural interaction. Johan Fornäs discusses this in relation to adolescence in general: "Young people move rapidly between family, school and public spaces, and they are eager to explore alternative ideals and norms found in communication through media or peers" (Fornäs 1995, p. 245). At the same time, however, they try to overview their world and define their individual and collective identity by sorting and excluding in their practices. Fornäs expresses the point as follows: "Their raids into the public arena are balanced by a fierce protection of their private territories, the agents of which are the peer group as well as the individual, in individuating preparation for adult personal autonomy" (Fornäs 1995, p. 245). This notion is valid also in relation to the young people's behaviour in cyberspace.

The Meaning of Access

In 1996 and 1997, when I conducted my first large-scale study on young Danes media uses and media cultures, very few had access to the Internet at home, let alone in their bedrooms. Some schools and some libraries had one or two computers with Internet access. In March 2000, when I conducted my second study, 6 out of 10 of my informants had access at home and all had access at schools, libraries, Internet cafes or at friends' homes. All my informants in the Year 2000 study, covering the age group 12 to 16 years, had tried surfing, information seeking or visiting a chat group.[2]

Statistically, 50% of the Danish population had *access to Internet in the home* in September 2000, while 63% of the population had access at home, at work or elsewhere. Fifty-eight percent between 16 and 29 years had access at home and 75% at home, at work or elsewhere. Sixty-five percent of two-parent families with children had access at home compared to 31% of single-person households. Statistics show that, proportionally, access depends on educational background and income. More than 50% of those who do not have access plan to buy a modem/connection within the following year (Danmarks Statistik, September 2000). The percentage of persons with access at home has risen dramatically, from 8% in spring 1997 to 50% in September 2000 and with the prospects of increased numbers. Pragmatically, part of the explanation is economic, as the costs have decreased during the same period, while another part of the explanation is that people in all groups of society have found uses for the Internet. On the psychological road from scepticism to purchase, the influence of the general hype around IT—especially in relation to school, education and future prospects—that has dominated the public as well as political debate has been substantial (Stald 2000). The scepticism of the average Danish parent has been transformed by the integration of multimedia computers and Internet in the homes as well as in most public fields where citizens meet the institutional level of society. Not least, however, the attitudes have changed because of the growing numbers of accessible services that are immediately practical, from timetables and price indexes to e-mail and online communication. I describe this development as a transformation from parental concerns about usability and intellectual degeneration to concerns about Net addiction and moral degeneration, and from scepticism about usability to awareness of the potentials of and demands for IT individually as well as collectively in the future national and international society. The parental change in attitudes towards IT can be read tentatively as one element in the change in attitudes among young people, from anxious interest to predominantly practical as well as mental integration of IT into the everyday lives of young Danes.

In 1998, 25% of the participants in the survey conducted in connection with the European comparative project had access to Internet at home, while only 4% had access in their bedroom. The survey from 1998 showed, first, a tendency towards access to media in the bedroom increasing the frequency and amount of time spent on media uses and, second, that home access is important. In my study from spring 2000, 84 out of 146 participants had access to Internet at home and 22 had a modem in their bedroom. The qualitative data do not counter these findings, but the discussion is put into perspective by including more examples of "super-users"[3] who do not have Internet access at home, but spend hours at school, the library or at Net cafes in order to satisfy their interest and need for the uses of the Internet.

Ethnic Minorities

The findings from the 2000 study also indicate that some children from *ethnic minorities* do not have Internet or computers at home due to negative attitudes towards IT or for ideological reasons. Other reasons are economic difficulties or family members' lack of the competence necessary to exploit the computer and Internet services. The latter part of the explanation also applies to the population as a whole, that is that social and/or educational background is decisive to some groups' access to and uses of IT and Internet.

Reflections on Uses and Usability

During these four years, the experiences of and *reflections on the uses and usability* of the Internet have obviously developed as well. The proportions falling into the categories "super-users", "users" and "non-users" have changed. At first the group of "super-users" was very small, now it contains more members. The group of "users" has grown from some to most of the adolescents, and the group of "non-users" has decreased to very few. As the Internet has become accessible to all young Danes, it has become integrated into their everyday lives with media and information technology. Along with this development, the notion of novelty has ceased to be one of the main reasons for using the Internet: "You know, the Internet, and chat, you know, has become very common now. It is so common. At first it was really popular and then it has just become rather boring, really" (Asger, 12 years, boy).[4]

Gender-Divided Use

A field of certain interest is the *gender-divided uses* of the Internet. Statistically, more boys than girls have access to multimedia PCs and Internet at home and in their bedrooms. Also boys use the Internet more frequently and for longer time periods. What is significant, however, is that, during the past four years, girls in the target group have found that the Internet could offer them many services and information of use in their social and cultural practices. In 1996 and 1997, when I conducted my first study, many of the girls had no interest at all in computers or Internet. Many of the girls had used computers or Internet so little—or had never tried using the Net—that they felt uncomfortable with or even frightened by the technique (Stald 1998). Mobile phones were also very rare among young people at that time. From 1996 to 2000, the interest in and usability of ICT among young girls has seen a dramatic shift. Even if my empirical data from 2000 still point towards a smaller group of female than male "super-users," many more girls can be defined as rather skilled and frequent "users." In my target group, the girls who use the Internet focussed on communication (primarily e-mail and chat) and on information seeking, while relatively few played online computer games, downloaded programmes or shopped on the Net. The boys communicated online or via e-mail in cyberspace, but were generally less interested in random chat than were the girls. The boys also spent time in cyberspace playing online games, downloading music or moving pictures, etc., and they were more frequently designers of their own Web page or perhaps producers of web-pages for friends, family members or other acquaintances.

Figure 10.2 illustrates the presence of the Internet in the media universe of a 15-year-old girl.[5] The computer is situated next to the television set and logged on the Internet, specified as "chat." The girl is watching a football match (note the banner advert) comfortably seated in the sofa, remote control within reach, while her father, sitting next to her, is studying the newspaper. On the front page, the Danish Prime Minister is quoted for a famous and often repeated sentence (also in other drawings in the study): "Couldn't we do it a *little* better?" The drawing is a comment on Internet as obviously accessible, but it also illustrates differences in parental and adolescent media uses. Of course,

Figure 10.2
Susie, 15 years.

the father *could* be the user of the computer/Internet as well. But he probably would not leave it switched on.... The notion of the Internet as difficult to use has ceased to be one of the main reasons for not using it. There are still, however, some girls—especially in the group of 12- to 13-year-olds—who claim rather flirtatiously that they can barely switch the computer on or off, let alone master Windows or move around in one of the popular Web rooms. Signe, a girl of 13 years, says: "I don't know why you would want to have a computer. I think it is *absolutely* dreadful. I only use the computer at school when we absolutely *have* to. I hardly know how to shut it down (giggles)." The very few boys who said that they do not use the Internet and do not know how to use it explain that they lack interest or at least that it is a matter of little importance.

Risks
Theoretically, *risk* in relation to new media in modern society is used in the sense of the uncertainty caused by the complex consequences of technological progress for society and for the individual. James Slevin

says, inspired by Anthony Giddens, that "New kinds of risk feature as both unacknowledged conditions and unintended consequences in the process of connecting the local and the global by means of modern communication technology" (Slevin 2000, p. 13). Transformed to the empirical micro perspective, this risk is to be understood as a common mode of uncertainty related to possible negative personal experiences in day-to-day media uses. These are fears of actual threats as described below, of uncertainty as to how to comprehend the potential universality of the information and communication in cyberspace, and of the individual's own position in the juxtaposition between global networking and local transformation and meaning.

Chris Abbott says, in a discussion on young people making connections on the Internet, that: "In particular young people have been constructed as potential victims of this aspect of the Net," by which he refers to "inappropriate material" (Abbott 1998, p. 85). The young users themselves do not, however, think of themselves as victims, but parallel the uncertainty and—seen from the viewpoint of a teenager—challenges of the Net with the uncertainty and challenges of everyday life. Risk is part of living and you deal with it according to your experience and circumstances. It should be mentioned that none of my informants mentioned having had really bad or frightening experiences, only disturbing or stupid ones.

While the use of Internet is an obvious possibility for most of my informants, they also find reasons for thinking twice before entering chat rooms or other situations where you meet other persons in cyberspace. And at least you must be very careful about revealing your identity to just anybody. "The Internet is ok, it's just that—there are so many paedophiles on the Net, that's what I heard. There are many stories about paedophiles who look up girls who have been chatting with them and so on, right? So ... I never identify myself as me on the Net" (Anna, 13 years, girl).

The notion of identity play—or cheating—in cyberspace is wide spread. For many of my informants, the fact of never knowing to whom you are talking (as several informants put it) spoils the fun and excitement of communicating with new people. But the threat of having someone "out there" laugh at you is not the only risk. The majority of my informants are very much aware of the risks of abuse and misuse being perpetrated by persons with sinister purposes. The substance of the following quote is found in various forms in most of the interviews: "I like to be able to see the person I am talking to, you know, it is not exactly fun to sit and write.... You never know if the nice person with whom you are talking is actually a 40-year-old paedophile who is sitting at home masturbating because he thinks you are cool to talk to" (Daniel, 15 years, boy).

The following quote illustrates the notion held by many of the adolescents, that one must *see* another person in order *to know* him or her: "They are nice on the phone but when you meet them their personality changes" (Monika, 15 years, girl).

The experiences are often locally orientated, that is, they take place in Danish chat rooms: "I have experienced—well, I haven't called anybody, but I was talking to someone, having a really good talk, you know. And then suddenly I found out that he was 43 and not 16. It was ... He was sitting in his office and ... Well" (Jeanette, 15 years, girl).

Communicating in cyberspace is obviously a matter of trust if you want the full joy and advantage of it (Clark 1998, Giddens 1991). "The pure relationship depends on mutual trust between partners, which in turn is closely related to the achievement of intimacy.... What matters in the building of trust in the pure relationship is that each person should know the other's personality and be able to rely on regularly eliciting certain sorts of desired responses from the other. This is one reason (not the only one) why authenticity has such an important place in self-actualization" (Giddens 1991, p. 186, also quoted in Clark 1998). Lynn S. Clark points to the fact that trust and "authenticity" are not central to teen chat room relationships (Clark 1998, p. 179). Since you can be whoever you want to be, there is a certain freedom and openness in the chat rooms, which is stated by some of my informants. But in general, I suggest that part of the frustration with chat and the validity of the communication and possible established personal relations lies in the fact that the young people are actually looking for trust and authenticity in the chat room relations. The novelty of chat ceased to evoke fascination, and most of my informants are looking for some quality not found in the occasional "chat-for-fun" and "chat-to-tease" games.

Thus, the fear of meeting someone really disagreeable or threatening or of just being cheated is related to experiences and fears in real life and in "the neighbourhood." For those who unworriedly but cautiously go on chatting, the possibility of playing with your identity is challenging in the interaction with another person and a shield you can hide behind. If you bond very well over time, you can start revealing bits of the truth and consider the possibility of meeting outside cyberspace.

The few informants who communicate with "unknown" persons in other countries do not express any fears of being abused, threatened or cheated. The general opinion of the informants is that, when you choose to make the effort of finding and writing to someone who lives far away in a foreign place, there is a common interest in exchanging experiences and thoughts. This is one area where physical distance is simultaneously noted—as a guarantee of sincerity and interest—and overcome. It is sometimes overcome by the shared experience of proximity in the communicative situation, which takes place in a room established for the situation. The increased duration and intensity (among other thing how much you tell each other) of the relationship promote the perception of proximity and community.

Risk must also be discussed from the viewpoint of the parents and other adults. For many adults, access to certain types of texts or information is just as threatening to their children and teenagers as potential paedophiles. Porn sites, violence, Web sites of satanic cults, nazis, etc. have caused many parents to try to restrict use of the Internet and perhaps even to choose technical (or rather: software) solutions to prohibit access to sites that could have a negative influence on children and young people. Some of the boys state, e.g. in the mini-survey, that their favourite Web page is "pornworld" or the like and they joke about porno, finding recipes for bomb production, the latest new on Marilyn Manson, etc. Most of the young people, however, dissociate themselves from such uses—in the presence of an adult. Hence, secret visits on forbidden Web sites seem to equal other explorations in the period of youth. I shall not go deeper into this discussion here. I just wish to describe the parental fear of uncontrollable (leaving out the new effective programmes for sorting accessible Web sites) access to all sorts of information, activities and communication in cyberspace. When the media—

first the stereo, then the TV-set, then the video and finally the computer, the phone and the Internet—moved into children's and young people's bedrooms, parents lost control and influence (by debating the uses) of large parts of children's media uses. Concerning young people's activities in cyberspace, the parents can't even knock on the door and enter the private room in order to study what is going on, they must have access to a symbolic room as well. This is also the case with other media, as interactivity and virtual experience are found in relation to media use in general, though more or less explicitly. In relation to cyberspace, however, the lack of mass communicated information makes it more difficult to share the experience. Access to the virtual room is particularly difficult to gain in relation to Internet use, as the room is largely created in the mind of the user. In this respect, young people who in this period of life are detaching themselves from the parents have the opportunity to create private rooms in cyberspace and decide where and with whom or what they wish to spend time. The parents, on the other hand, feel a lack of control in yet another area, and the invisible borders of the virtual private rooms cannot be transcended by the curious, worried, moralising—or perhaps even interested—parent.

The Integration of Internet

Along with the extension of Internet access, the Internet has been integrated into young people's social, cultural and aesthetic practices as one among many media/channels. A few of the "super-users" claim the Net is *the medium*, above and beyond all other media: "The Internet? I use it for … well everything. You can find anything on the Net" (Alex, 15 years, boy). For most of the adolescents, the Internet is an obvious choice in many daily situations, but in general Internet use has not ousted other media in the everyday lives of teenagers. Internet is used along with all other media, each time the result of making choices in the situation among a rank of possible channels for information, communication or entertainment. Sometimes the media work together in a sort of figurative convergence: information on a movie is found on the Net, telephone calls on the mobile phone are followed up by return calls on the parental stationary phone (to decrease the costs) or by an entire series of exchanges of e-mail messages. Telephone calls and SMS messages fly between friends in a group. Also a certain intertextual reference codex has become integrated into media communication. For instance, references to www links in television or radio programmes, online interaction between participants on TV or Net programmes with invitations to join the dialogue or to "send us an e-mail" in many popular radio or television programmes (e.g., MTV). According to findings in the present study, the tendency is broadly significant, but especially in youth media universes.

The drawing below is one among many that illustrate the integration of more media in the adolescent daily life. It can be read as Lasse's satirical illustration of his daily life with media. They are all important in his universe. Note the clock on the wall, which symbolises the connection between media use and time management. The tripling of the artist pictured in the drawing illustrates the level of activity in his daily life, but also the equality of the media's role in his life. The football and the single boot next to the television set symbolise non-media activities (see figure 10.3).

Figure 10.3
Lasse, 15 years.

Literacy and Competence

Access to all the possible uses of the Internet is not solely dependent on access in a technical sense. To exploit the possible practical unlimited sources of information and to participate in social and cultural exchange and communication, certain *literacy* is demanded. Julian Sefton-Green raises the question of whether children are actually as *hyper-literate* in the digital world as is often presumed, and concludes that more research is needed and that new literacies must be analysed in relation to traditional ones. "The range of different kinds of 'reading' and 'writing' activities facilitated by the computer and its various multimedia forms suggest that very different levels of skill and understanding at both psychological and social levels, may be necessary to participate in digital culture" (Sefton-Green 1998, p. 9).

Even if very small children who do not read or write can have fun exploring certain web pages or browsing for the joy of it, the full (or optimal) exploitation of the Internet demands reading and writing skills at a certain level, as most of the Net is text-based—even if the visual presentations and animations are many. This prevents most children up to nine or ten years from participating at an advanced level. Also, those among the older children and teenagers who do not read and write well will either have to break the traditional boundaries here or find other ways of joining the youth culture universe and of obtaining the necessary knowledge, experience and communicative exchange. There are, however, many examples showing that strong motivation enables these potentially "illiterate" adolescents to overcome the obstacles of reading and writing, and perhaps to even improve, by jumping into it. Others, who are not very visible in the target group, decline use of the Internet, sometimes with the stated explanation that the Internet is not interesting, useful or entertaining.

Skills in English

Finally *skills in English* are necessary in order to use large parts of the Net and in order to form personal relationships outside Denmark. English is the first foreign language taught at school from the fourth grade, and children and young people meet English every day in movies, TV-serials, cartoons, music and computer games. They are also familiar with English as a tool for most communication when abroad on holidays. All in all, they consider knowledge of English very important for present and future management of various situations and functions. English is perceived as the potential world language that could enable a worldwide cultural exchange and social connectivity: "Well, English is, what's it called, an international language. It is very important to know how to speak English. . . . What I think is, English, if it was worldwide it would be good" (Mounir, 15 years, boy, ethnic minority). It is one thing, however, to recognise English as a familiar language and as a representation of perceived quality and exciting/entertaining mediated stories, and quite another to be able to use English in a communicative exchange or assimilate most of the information in English. The establishment and maintenance of personal relations via the Net with persons in other countries is difficult for many young Danes, also those in the group of 12- to 16-year-olds who consider themselves rather skilled in English. If they communicate with English-speaking persons, they very soon become aware of their own limitations. If they communicate with other persons who do not have English as their native language, the chances of communication and interesting exchange of experiences are rather limited: "It's one thing that it's difficult to get to know a new person, you haven't met, it is really difficult. And if it's someone from another country so you don't master the language fully, then it's even more difficult. And then it might become rather shallow talk. Then it really doesn't matter . . ." (Julie, 15 years, girl). Some are able to overcome this—e.g., one of my informants wanted so much to communicate with a boy in the U.S. that he had the dictionary stationed next to the computer. All in all, reading English is possible; communicating in English at an advanced level is most often difficult.

Uses and Experiences

Most of the adolescents in the age range I study use the Internet regularly for downloading information for schoolwork and various fields of interests, for e-mailing friends and families or sending SMS messages. They visit popular chat groups, download programmes and MP3 files, etc. The fact is, however, that young people primarily use the Internet for local purposes, whether the purpose is writing an essay at school, communicating with friends and family or supplementing their cultural practice and personal participation in their local networks of friends. This could involve, for example, finding the best and hottest homepage on your favourite music group, or being the one who knows most about the most popular soccer teams or who has downloaded the latest versions of, or the main codes for, a game.

Communication

Communication is to be understood as exchange of information, knowledge, experiences, thoughts, attitudes and emotions. Part of young people's use of the Internet is comparable to the way in which they use traditional media for information seeking and entertainment; most Internet use, however, can be described as some sort of exchange or communicative interaction. The findings from my interviews show that the adolescents generally rank interpersonal communication at the top of their list of Internet uses. That is, they view the Internet as a medium of communicative interaction and as a system of local and global networking.

Among my forty-eight informants, only very few girls said that they had tried to communicate with persons in foreign countries. These cases were more or less obligatory pen pal e-mails to hosts from an exchange visit in Finland. Or the relations were established in Denmark (e.g., family members, exchange student living with the family) and e-mail was used to keep in contact. None of the girls mentioned having actively tried to get in contact with adolescents abroad. Some of the boys had tried to find new friends in cyberspace, for example by checking out the pen pal sites on international teenage Web pages. Some of the boys have established personal relations—some of them lasting, others passing—through online games. For many, however, the reason for not seeking friends internationally in cyberspace is their rejection of the possibility of making friends and getting to know each other in cyberspace.

Only two among my informants mentioned explicitly had they had joined international chat rooms.

In the intellectually reflexive situation of the interview, some of my informants expressed a rather strong opinion that chat is an impersonal way of communicating—a 15-year-old girl says that it is a sort of "closed contact, just to write"—because of the lack of sensory impressions. I would add to this that part of the explanation lies in a lack of tradition of expressing oneself intellectually or emotionally in writing. Many things can be expressed in short form or even in Internet language (abbreviations and symbols). But this is still a far cry from putting impressions and expressions into text.[6] The enthusiasts, or those who happen to have had very positive experiences, of course reverse this quite common attitude. This opposite position, primarily expressed by 15- to 16-year-olds, is the experience that "you can say a lot of things, you know, in writing" (girl, 15 years), compared to the intimacy of telephone calls where a virtual private room is constructed by the participants. The scepticism among many in the target group concerning the quality, validity and durability of Net-based relations is striking, however. At this point in the paper, it is appropriate to remind the reader that the study covers representatives from a broadly defined group of the 12- to 16-year-olds. If the target group had been "super-users" and advanced "users," the scepticism and division of the qualities in RL and in VR would have been less explicit, but not absent.

Many of the informants in my year 2000 study say that they are no longer very interested in chat on the Net—chat belongs to a period two or three years ago when Internet and the various possible ways of using the Net were new and exciting. In 2000, many of those who no longer chat frequently and dedicatedly tend to parallel chat to occasional watching of dull TV serials or zapping—the motivation is "nothing else to do," that is, chatting and browsing are used to prevent boredom. Another motivation for reducing the time spent on free chat in the most popular chat rooms is connected to the much-discussed play with identity in chat rooms and other virtual rooms. Romantic or sexual interest as motivation for active search for interesting chat partners is of interest to some—now and then.

The boys might find it interesting to have private conversations with girls on the Net, but they are generally more sceptical regarding the possibility of finding "the one and only" than are some of the girls. "I don't chat—I really don't want to talk to complete strangers, I think it is, well, absolutely ridiculous. I don't see any point in doing it—You could go down to the local youth club and meet some new people there" (Lars Peter, 15 years).

An important function of computer-mediated communication is the use of e-mail for maintaining relations with friends and family: "I don't know, ... in my family it is like that, well we are scattered in all directions, actually. One of my older sisters lives in Brighton in England and my older brother lives in Aarhus, and I have one in Odense, and one is in New Zealand for the time being, so it—there is so much e-mailing because it is also cheapest. Well, I could make a phone call if it was really important, but mostly I write for fun. Then I have some friends, well some I just met on the Net but also some of my old friends whom I write with at the weekends if I cannot get in touch with them" (Lars Peter, 15 years, boy). Communication with friends is either with those far away or those in "the neighbourhood." E-mailing with friends whom you probably meet everyday in various situations can be compared to telephoning or using SMS messages, as they are likely to be short, for fun or with the purpose of arranging activities and exchanging news.

Communication in cyberspace also involves discussions in news groups of all kinds. Some join specific groups of interest, some join occasionally or randomly when they happen to meet an interesting discussion or feel like commenting on something. Examples are discussions on Web sites of sport groups, pop-groups, online computer games, and fan clubs. But only few actively take part in discussions of this kind, and very few visit international newsgroups. This matches the findings of preferences for local Web sites, where information on various topics is found and exchange of news and thoughts takes place.

The informants were asked to write down their favourite chat room as well. Sixty-four out of 146 did so and all chat rooms mentioned were Danish. This indicates that chat is indeed a local activity, to be seen as one among many where young people come together, try out their identity and mirror themselves in others. Other places to meet are schools— even if the formal institutional frames around the groups and possible activities cannot be compared to the virtual frames of chat rooms in cyber-space—youth clubs, sports clubs, parties, concerts, etc.

Information

In my mini-survey, I asked the 146 participants to write the name of their favourite Web site. Eighty mentioned one, while the remaining 66, primarily girls, had no specific preference. The 80 answers represented sport groups and other fan sites or interest sites, Web stations, music, television stations and a few private Web sites. Out of these, 13 were international web pages, ranking from the Web pages of the soccer fan clubs of Ajax Amsterdam, Juventus and Manchester United to Brad Pitt, 2Pac, and porn sites (I have a suspicion that the references to porn sites are provocations of the interviewer—though it is not unlikely that my informants visit such sites). The 67 Web pages of local origin all serve to update the level of information on what is going on in the various fields of interest in youth culture.

Generally the young users are aware of the vast amounts of information than can be found on the Net—awareness not least supported by the searches that are met by thousands of "hits." "You can find so many things, so some of it must be useful. If I find 7,400 pages I take the first ten, then I don't bother to do more" (Ulli, 16 years, boy). Another way of finding information and surfing in cyberspace is to follow links, which is used especially when searching for new information on specific topics; in such cases, the users are quite often operating in international waters.

But what about the perceived validity of the information: "I think it is about the same as when it comes to television and newspapers and things like that.... Because, you see pages that are falsified and pages that are valid, so, oh ..." (Rasmus, 15 years, boy).

Playing and Gaming

None of my informants mentioned having participated in MUDs and MOOs, but it seems obvious that there are some parallels between participating in these role-playing games and those of online computer games, particularly regarding the ways in which participants adopt and develop identity and the concept of community (Turkle 1995). Abbott describes how most of the work in this area discusses older college students, while his own target group is 12- to 25-year-olds. His data were collected in 1993 and 1994, and I think one of the reasons why not even the "super-users" in my study mention MUDs or MOOs is that, since the early nineties, online computer games have become better and more popular. Another reason is obviously that the extensive Internet access has promoted the online gaming cultures among a more broadly represented group of adolescents (Abbott 1998, pp. 89–91).

Apart from the entertaining functions of chat, browsing, and searching for news in your fields of interest, there is a growing interest in using the Internet as a network for playing and gaming. I mentioned one of the informants who had tried to play chess with a Greek boy and others have played cards over the Net. Some of the girls mention "playing identity" together with friends, that is sitting together at the computer having fun by creating a virtual identity and playing it out in the chat room. Online computer games, however, are mentioned by some of the boys as an exciting and challenging activity. Often the games take place physically in Net cafes, and either you belong to an established group of gamers and play frequently and seriously, or you randomly arrange a game with a group of friends. The players participate in quite unique communities in and around the games. What is of specific interest in this connection is that the most popular games are worldwide networks, and you can play with others from all over the world (that is where there is general access to the Net, primarily the U.S., Europe, Australia and parts of Asia). The impact on the conception of globality and locality, and hence of collective and individual identity, made by this global networking has apparently not yet been studied specifically in relation to online computer games. Based on my findings from the year 2000 study, my preliminary suggestion would be that, for engaged players, the world of games establishes new, virtual spheres where the normative, moral, social and cultural codex of the communities in and around the games is laid down by the participants. For the players in the situation and outside the game, the virtual world is the point of departure for identity formation and establishment of personal relations. The platform, so to speak, is not the world but "the world." Obviously, the players constantly transgress the borders between the virtual world and the world, but at this stage in my analysis, I tend to think that the virtual world is more related to the locality of the life-world than to globality. One argument is that the players, as represented by my informants, talk about localities in the games as recognisable and well known. Another argument derives from the experiences in the games, where patterns of interpersonal relations and social mobility from "the real world" shine through. I touch on related aspects of this discussion in the section Theoretical Approach above and in the section below, Thoughts on Internet Use between the Local and the Global.

Trading/Shopping

Shopping on the Net is still not very common among Danish Internet users. According to the latest statistics, only 15% of Danish Internet users have been Net shopping during the month prior to the survey. The goods purchased are primarily books, music/CDs, and electronics (TNS Interactive Global eCommerce Report—July 2000). Scepticism concerning security as well as lack of knowledge on how to find the shops and how to pay are the main reasons (of the parents who would have to consent) for not shopping. Some of the boys, however, had ordered especially CDs, Cd-roms, DVDs or computer magazines on the Net and paid by invoice. Others had bought clothes using their parents' visa or master card. Most of the trading was with American or English companies, and a driving force for choosing to shop on the Net was partly the cheaper prices but also, importantly, the ability to purchase something not yet available on the Danish market.

Ethnic Minorities

One example of particular uses that I analyse more closely in my study is the case of children of ethnic minorities and refugees whose families are scattered over large parts of the world. They use the Internet to keep in contact with the family and to maintain bonds and their cultural identity. Telephoning is still the most common mode of interpersonal communication with the family back home. Some of my informants from ethnic minorities tell about very long talks on the phone, where news and family matters at each end of the line are exchanged. I have described the intimate symbolic rooms created especially by teenagers who exchange confidential and private information (Stald 2000). This apprehension of actual and symbolic intimacy and proximity must be applicable to the situation of relatives living far apart—in different "worlds." The voice, the tone, and the privacy of conversation can add a feeling of proximity between the two speaking persons. The talk might enforce the sense of longing and cause the cultural roots of belonging to adhere firmly to the ground of the home country. The Internet is used in much the same way by those Danish citizens with immigrant backgrounds who have access to e-mail and online communication, many of whom are adolescents, especially those with family and friends in the mother country who also have access. As e-mail and online communication are cheaper than telephoning, contact can be more extensive and frequent. However, in e-mail and online communication, the tone of voice and the senses must be replaced by sensitive use of words.

The Internet is also used locally to communicate with members of the same cultural minority. For instance, Rosa, a 13-year-old girl from Albania, chats in Albanian in a private room with her cousin, and they sometimes "talk" to other Albanians in a popular chat room. They all live in or around Copenhagen. These "talks" make the girl feel good, especially about her cultural identity, because she senses belonging to a group and a community where her "otherness" is non-existent.

Telephone and Internet communication train the native language, which to all members of the Diaspora is one of the most important symbols of cultural belonging.

"Speeding Up Things"

The Internet has "speeded up things for most young Danes," as one of my informants puts it, thinking of data seeking and communication. Access to information, visual or textual, on practically all issues and subjects and in all parts of the world is achievable within seconds. At the same time, connecting in interactions between persons is almost instantaneous. The amount of data, the speed of distribution and the speed of downloading have increased the demand for information of all sorts in many situations. For instance, information seeking for educational purposes (in school) has risen dramatically, with resulting difficulties in sorting the information in terms of relevance and in evaluating the quality of the data. Also, by "speeding up things," the Net is conducive to rapid changes in youth cultures, especially regarding cultures of taste and aesthetic representation, and to exploitation of various youth culture universes.

Thoughts on Internet Use between the Local and the Global

Young Danes think of democracy, civil rights and a certain living standard as matters of course in Denmark and our part of the world. They also think of access to media as obvious as well as the right to communicate, speak and exchange opinions on all issues. The Internet is felt by many to be the perfect tool to maintain democracy, as it enables everyone to participate in communication and exchange and supplies everyone with access to endless information.

When discussing the potential uses of the Internet, however, some consider the fact that large parts of the world do not have access to IT. Some reflect on the possible democratic aspects of the Internet and on whether it is, in fact, world wide, as the discussion among these 15-year-old boys illustrates:

Paolo: I use it to find information, right, and it could be something from China …

Sune: Well, it couldn't!

Gitte: Why not?

Sune: It could hardly be something from China

Paolo: No, you couldn't read it, then, but …

Lasse: They have a dictatorship there …

Sune: Yer, well, they don't release that much from China yet, that was more what I meant.

Paolo: (mumbling) Well, then it could be from Japan

Again these observations were made in the interview situation. The general discussion on the use of Internet shows a lack of interest in these matters. The evaluation of the potentials of Internet use is focused on everyday life and local communities.

It is quite obvious that, to the young Danes I have been studying, the Internet is generally not the most important source of information and experiences concerning global and local matters. The adolescents get their mediated experiences primarily from television *and* from the Internet, movies, magazines, radio, music, newspapers and books. Young Danes' attitudes towards locality and globality and their notions

of Danishness versus being world citizens are formed by their mediated experiences, but also by their personal experiences either in their
everyday lives—for example encounters with ethnic minorities and other
cultures—or from travelling, which is frequent among young Danes.
Most of my informants who do use the Net for communication and
information seeking state urgently that they think it is quite important
to get first hand experiences—to be present in the physical world and
encounter people as well as places in real life and real time. Almost
all feel that personal encounters are more valuable than mediated
experiences—even though this is how they have acquired a large part of
their knowledge and experiences. Sometimes these youngsters become
almost poetic describing how much it means to be present and smell the
ocean, taste the strange food, hear the sounds of foreign places and languages and sense the new impressions:

I think that it has something to do with ... I would like to be able to feel the
wind, and, oh, if I go to, well, the Atlantic Ocean, I could smell the salty water,
and altogether all those senses that you can't have via a computer.... (Lars-Peter,
15 years, boy)

It is much more fun to be somewhere where you can swim instead of sitting here
with swim pants and goggles and swim belt and fins and sit like this (make
swimming movements) on the Internet, right. As if you swim in warm water ... it
is not the same as swimming. (Jesper B, 12 years old, boy)

And a last example is from a girl who comments on the possible use of
Web-cams to improve the mediated experiences in interpersonal communication as well as of other places:

You have to see it with your own eyes, right, I think it is important because then
you are more persons who ... you see another sight (picture). (Karen, 15 years,
girl)

The focus on local use as well as the downplaying of the general
importance and influence of Internet use among the adolescents in my
target group does not mean, however, that the Internet is not perceived
as a useful and innovative medium for global encounters and cultural
outlooks. Some of my informants state that they find it useful or even
exciting to communicate in cyberspace with young people around the
world: "I should like to talk (on the Net, GS) to someone in the U.S.
Then you could talk about what it is like over there and things like that
..." (Bjarke, 12 years, boy).

There is certain ambivalence in the argument on the local uses of globally pursued information, experiences and personal relations. Obviously also adolescents pursue information and exchange globally as well as locally, even if local origin and orientation predominate. A global orientation was already established in adolescents' general media use and is therefore not exotic or strange. But the conclusion is also quite simply that the globally pursued information/relations must be transformed into the cultures of the proximate and real life-world, which to young people is more "here-and-now," with emphasis on "here" both symbolically and in practice.

The ambivalence that can be deduced analytically, but that is not very explicitly expressed by the informants, can be illustrated by the following example of the *juxtaposition* of a 15-year-old girl. The example is not about Internet use, but still useful. Foreign cultures have been met, experiences of other places reflected upon and worked through from the position of a young Dane. Longing for new encounters collides with the locally transformed experiences and expectations:

Well, I guess I think of myself as ... Ah, a world citizen somehow or how to put it, mostly because ... I feel that, of course I was born in Denmark and that is the language I feel most at ease with, and I really do like our Danish culture—or the way it is—I love Denmark, but I ... I would like to see the rest of the world as well, and when I do that I don't want go out with the attitude, that "I am Danish and if your culture is not like ours at home, then it is no good," or, you know.... I don't want to have an attitude like that, right? I would like to be open to ..., but well, of course, I think ... I could imagine myself living in another country than Denmark, but it wouldn't be ... then it would have to be a country where the culture is quite like Danish culture. I couldn't live for example in Arabia or somewhere like that, because the culture is so different from Danish culture. (Julie, 15 years, girl)

Digital Divide and Democratic Potential

Over the past decade, alongside the development of computer technology and integration of IT in society as well as in common people's everyday lives, fascination with the potentials of IT has grown, as has an increasing fear of its possible negative effects. As Don Tapscott puts it, "the most widely feared prediction surrounding the digital revolution is that it will splinter society into a race of information haves and have-nots, knowers and not-knows, doers and do-nots—a digital divide. This revolution holds the promise of improving the lives of citizens but also the threat of further dividing us" (Tapscott 1998, p. 255).

It seems relevant—in light of the varieties of uses of and attitudes towards IT as a tool in everyday lives now and in the future—to discuss the threats of a possible digital divide. There are differences that have their origin in social, educational, cultural divides. Power play is something that takes place not only among gaming children and adolescents, but is also a practice related to external and deeply rooted structures and traditions. In Denmark, gender division might be one area in which to find the most significant gap. In general, boys and girls have different skills and ways of exploiting the potentials of the Internet—which does not mean that girls cannot or do not use and exploit the Internet extensively. But the gap between the few female "super-users" and female "non-users" is perhaps more significant in relation to the prospects for the future. The influence of social and educational background on access and use is another area of interest.

On the other hand, the traditionally rather homogenous social and cultural patterns of Danish culture,[7] typified by sociability and communication—compared to other nations and other parts of the world—do come through in the field of IT uses as well. Interest and usability in everyday lives reinforce the will to overcome traditional hindrances for advanced media uses, such as literacy and specific skills (competence). A very good example is the growing interest in communicating on web sites related to special interests, e.g., online computer games or other cultural products. A scroll view of the listed participant groups and of the inputs in discussion groups and in chat groups shows a broad representation in terms of age, background (social, educational, ethnic), and experience. Bad spelling (not to be confused with Net language) is no hindrance to participation, and behaviour does not have to match the expected norms of middle class social meetings as long as the local "netiquette" and culture are observed. The users that, in other past contexts, might have been thought of as "outcasts" or "not suitable" or "lower graded" feel at home in and at ease with the familiar rooms in cyberspace. This is perhaps more applicable to adolescents than to Danes in general, which raises interesting perspectives for the meaning of the Internet in a future continuous process of democratisation on various levels in society. The question is, then, how the normative, social and cultural codex that is forming in Internet societies transcends the borders between cyberspace and reality and what the effect of this will be.

The notion of familiarity is related to the personal relations and cultural and aesthetic practices established in various rooms in cyberspace. The culture of the Internet quickly enables the average user to feel at home, whatever the purpose of the activity might be. Sometimes you do find "closed" environments for "in" persons with access permitted only by the acceptance of others, be they news services, shops/trading, covert sites or simply groups or domains for members only. Sometimes you are just met as an intruding or dumb newbie; sometimes you are met by welcoming committees for newcomers. Because of the anonymity of the real life identity, many adolescents do not hesitate to try out new possibilities and rooms in cyberspace.

Perspectives from Users' Viewpoint(s) and Author's Comments

My ambition is to continue this study by looking at 18- to 25-year-olds, as my present findings and analysis indicate that, in at least a part of the group, the patterns of Internet uses and of advanced use change with age. This relates to one of my conclusions, namely that the ability and need to use the Internet for more than local purposes is connected to growing up, finding oneself and getting a better or wider view of the world in general. One of my "super-user" informants says that he has been thinking of something very true that his teacher once said: "your consciousness grows and the world gets smaller" (Asbjoern, 15 years). He said this in a discussion about the influence of the Internet, but his point was that to him what makes the world get smaller is not so much being able to go global on the Net as growing older, more experienced and more reflective. It is the sum total of experiences, including the mediated ones, that forms the way you think of yourself as a citizen in the cross-point of local and global communities.

The presence of information technology in the everyday lives of young Danes and a notion of the possible universal reach of cultural exchange and social communion in cyberspace make adolescents aware of the globality and entity of our world and of their own position as world citizens. But, as most activities and experiences in cyberspace are perceived as local or have a local purpose, the perspective of the world-wide community or the global village, as referred to by some of the informants, is of less importance and interest—momentarily and in this period of life.

Another point is that adolescents in year 2000 no longer perceive IT and the World Wide Web as the digital revolution. Young people in Denmark more or less grew up with the technologies, and even if the development has been overwhelming in Denmark during the past five years, young people's memories are rather short and the fascination shifts rather quickly. There is still some fascination with the extensive possible uses of the Internet, especially those owing to new services (e.g., many free, online possibilities), technical development (e.g., speed and graphics), and to constantly improved possibilities for interaction in personal relations as well as in various activities such as online gaming or participation in debates and news groups. There is also, however, a resigned, blasé attitude among the "super-users" and "users" and a less worried position among "the non-users." The "users" have either caught up with the technologies on an advanced level that enables them to exploit and develop their uses and enjoyment of IT or adjusted their skills, uses and needs to the technical and virtual demands and possibilities. The non-users are quite often (but not always) non-users by choice, as they find no need for and usability in the present state of IT. As they, with a few exceptions, have tried to use the Internet, they are less worried about their prospects in the future society regarding education, employment and integration in society than the young non-users were four years ago (Stald 1998).

I shall conclude with another drawing by 15-year-old Asbjoern, whom I quoted above (see figure 10.4). He is one of the advanced users of the Internet, but he also reflects quite a lot on the ways we use the Internet and on the possible consequences. The drawing is a satirical portrait of the artist himself, isolated with his computer and drifting in open but anonymous space on an island, torn away from the mainland, but connected via ICT. He has depicted his self-ironic comment on the general concern regarding young people's uses of computers and Internet. The

Figure 10.4
Asbjoern, 15 years.

boy had been living with his parents in the Far East for one year, and there he established local friendships and experienced the local culture mixed with his experience of being someone who belonged to the group of socially and economically superior visitors from the West. He gives close consideration to the relations between local and global cultures, which results in some insecurity on his part concerning the prospects and potentials of future global progress and concerning the individual's possible influence and place in this future prospective world. Where does he land the island and is it a landing of his own choice and/or the result of a conglomeration of external conditions?

Notes

1. This chapter is based primarily on empirical data from an ongoing project on *Global Media, Local Youth* (working title). The project is a Ph.D. thesis and part of the research programme *Global Media Cultures*, situated at the Institute of Film & Media Studies, University of Copenhagen. Secondly, I draw on findings

from a large qualitative study of Danish children's and young people's media uses that was part of the European, comparative project *Children, Young People and the Changing Media Environment*. I conducted the qualitative part of the Danish study in 1996/97. Kirsten Drotner was co-ordinator of the Danish project.

2. These numbers are findings from a mini-survey on access and preferences conducted in the classes I visited in March 2000. The result was 146 answers from pupils in 8 classes on four different locations. The data are not statistically valid or representative of all Danes between 12 and 16 years. The findings are representative of the local groups I interviewed and support the qualitative findings.

3. In my first study, I divided the computer users in three main categories: "super-users," "users" and "non-users" (Stald 1998). I find this division useful and applicable to Internet users, as there is an obvious relation between being a "super-user" of computers and of Internet. "Super-users" should not automatically be equated with "heavy-users," even though the amount of time spent on computer use in this group is perhaps high. "Super-users" are interested not only in the usability of Internet services but in exploiting the potentials of the technique as well as of the various services and in experimenting with being creative and constructive in fields of specific interest. "Users" are focused on the immediate usability in everyday life—be it for communication, information seeking or entertainment. This group includes users who are quite skilled and those who are not so skilled, heavy users as well as light users. "Non-users" do not find any use for the Internet in their everyday lives. Only very few among the 12- to 16-year-olds, however, have never tried using the Internet, or do not feel they could manage it. This is a decisive change from four years ago.

4. The identity of all quoted informants of as well as interviews and drawings has been disguised.

5. All children made drawings as a part of the group interview sessions. They were asked to draw themselves while using one or more media, alone or with family or friends, in a place of their own choosing. In the 2000 study, they were asked to choose a title for their drawing. Of the resulting 164 drawings, 112 were made by the target group of my present study, the 12- to 13- and 15- to 16-year-old participants, 48 from the 1996/97 study and 64 from the 2000 study. The drawings present many themes, experiences, attitudes and emotional conceptions of media uses and everyday life. Most are skilfully made and coloured, and some are humoristic or even satirical comments on the meaning of media in general or the specific uses of media.

6. Letter writing in historic periods could perhaps inspire a revitalisation of writing.

7. The traditionally perceived homogeneity of Danish culture and society is becoming history due to the impact of people from other cultures who have come to Denmark since the 1960s. Danes in general and young Danes in particular

advance the attitude that people from ethnic minorities must adjust to Danish norms and culture, while also stating that they respect the rights of the minorities to maintain their religious and cultural traditions. Denmark is, however, adjusting to a new era of a multicultural society—slowly but with no way back.

References

Abbott, Chris (1998) "Young People and the Internet," pp. 84–105 in Julian Sefton-Green (ed.) *Digital Diversions: Youth Culture in the Age of Multimedia*. London: UCL Press.

Anderson, Benedict (1991, 2nd ed.) *Imagined Communities: Reflections on the Origin and Spread of Nationalism*. London & New York: Verso.

Blauenfeldt, Anders and Mikkel B. Stegmann (1999) *Danskernes Internetvaner—brugersurvey, April 1999* (Internet-use in Denmark—user survey, April 1999). Znail, ⟨www.znail.com⟩.

Clark, Lynn Schofield (1998) "Dating on the Net: Teens and the rise of 'pure' relationships," pp. 159–183 in Steve Jones (ed.) *Cybersociety 2:0*. London: Sage.

Danmarks Statistik (2001) *Pc'ere og adgang til Internet 2000 (Pc's and access to Internet 2000)*. ⟨http://www.dst.dk⟩.

Drotner, Kirsten (2000) "Difference and diversity: trends in young Danes' media uses," in *Media, Culture & Society*. London: Sage, vol. 22: 149–166.

Fornäs, Johan (1995) *Cultural Theory & Late Modernity*. London: Sage.

Groebel, Jo (1999) "Taking off for the virtual world," pp. 131–145 in Paul Löhr & Manfred Mayer (eds.) *Children, Television and the New Media*. Munich: Televizion & University of Luton Press.

Jones, Steve (1998) (ed.) *Cybersociety 2:0*. London: Sage.

Morley, David and Kevin Robins (1995) *Spaces of Identity. Global Media, Electronic Landscapes and Cultural Boundaries*. London: Routledge.

Schmidbauer and Paul Löhr (1999) "Young People Online," pp. 146–169 in Paul Löhr & Manfred Mayer (eds.) *Children, Television and the New Media*. Munich: Televizion & University of Luton Press.

Sefton-Green, Julian (ed.) (1998): *Digital Diversions: Youth Culture in the Age of Multimedia*. London: UCL Press.

Slevin, James (2000): *The Internet and Society*. Cambridge: Polity Press.

Stald, Gitte (1998) "Living with computers. Young Danes' Uses of and Thoughts on the Uses of Computers," in *SEKVENS. Yearbook of Film & Media Studies*, København: Institut for Film- & Medievidenskab, pp. 199–227.

Stald, Gitte (2000) "Telefonitis: unges danskeres brug af telefonen i IT-tidsalderen" ("Telephonitis: Young Danes' Uses of the Telephone in the age of IT"), in MedieKultur, Særnummer September 2000, pp. 4–22.

Tapscott, Don (1998) *Growing up Digital: The Rise of the Net Generation*. New York: McGraw-Hill.

TNS Interactive Global e-Commerce Report—July 2000. ⟨http://worldwide. tnsofres.com/ger/denmark.htm⟩.

Turkle, Sherry (1995) *Life on the Internet: Identity in the Age of the Internet*. New York: Simon & Schuster.

Wellman, Barry (1999) (ed.) *Networks in the Global Village*. Boulder: Westview Press.

11

Sex on the Internet: Issues, Concerns, and Implications

Mark Griffiths

The rapid growth of the Internet has led to the re-examination of many areas of behaviour. One such area concerns issues surrounding sexual behaviour and excessive Internet usage, particularly as some academics have alleged that social pathologies are beginning to surface in cyberspace. This chapter examines the concept of "Internet addiction" in relation to excessive sexual behaviour and Internet pornography, as well as examining newer areas of Internet sexuality such as "online relationships" and sex-related Internet crime (e.g., cyberstalking").

Sex-Related Uses of the Internet

Before examining the "addictiveness potential" of the Internet and its relationship with sexuality, it would appear wise to examine all the different ways that the Internet can be used for sexually-related purposes as it is probably the case that only some of these activities may be done to excess and/or be potentially addictive. The Internet can (and has) been used for a number of diverse activities surrounding sexually motivated behaviour. These include the use of the Internet for:

• seeking out sexually-related material for educational use. This includes those seeking information regarding (i) sexual health promotion (e.g., information about contraception, sexually transmitted diseases, etc.), (ii)

Reprinted from *Children in the New Media Landscape*, ed. Cecilia von Feilitzen and Ulla Carlsson (Göteberg, Sweden: UNESCO International Clearinghouse on Children and Violence on the Screen, 2000), pp. 169–184. Reprinted with permission from the Nordic Information Centre for Media and Communication Research at Göteborg University, Sweden.

self-help/diagnosis (e.g., advice about sexual dysfunctions, sexual diseases, etc.), and (iii) scientific research (e.g., reports of studies in the area of sexology, national reports on sexual behaviour, etc.). These may take the form of either stand-alone web pages or may be incorporated within Usenet discussion groups.

• buying or selling sexually-related goods for further use offline. This includes the buying or selling of goods for (1) educational purposes (e.g., books, videos, CD-ROMs, etc.), (2) entertainment/masturbatory purposes (e.g., magazines, books, videos, CD-ROMs, etc.), and (3) miscellaneous purposes (e.g., sex aids/toys, contraception, aphrodisiacs, etc.).

• visiting and/or purchasing goods in online virtual sex shops. Visiting a virtual sex shop may be done for either voyeuristic purposes ("window shopping") or for the sole intention of actually buying goods for use offline.

• seeking out material for entertainment/masturbatory purposes for use online. This can either be primarily image-based (e.g., pornographic Web sites offering picture libraries, video clips, videos, etc., live online strip shows, live voyeuristic Web-Cam sites, etc.) or text-based (e.g., chat rooms, Usenet discussion groups, etc.).

• seeking out sex therapists. This may involve either individuals or couples seeking out an online sex therapist for advice about sex and/or relationship problems.

• seeking out sexual partners for an enduring relationship (i.e., a monogamous partner) via online dating agencies, personal advertisements/ "lonely hearts" columns and/or chat rooms.

• seeking out sexual partners for a transitory relationship (i.e., escorts, prostitutes, swingers) via online personal advertisements/"lonely hearts" columns, escort agencies and/or chat rooms.

• seeking out individuals who then become victims of sexually-related Internet crime (online sexual harassment, cyberstalking, paedophilic "grooming" of children).

• engaging in and maintaining online relationships via e-mail and/or chat rooms.

• exploring gender and identity roles by swapping gender or creating other personas and forming online relationships.

• digitally manipulating images on the Internet for entertainment and/or masturbatory purposes (e.g., celebrity fake photographs where heads of famous people are superimposed onto someone else's naked body).

On first examination—and by evaluating the relatively sparse literature in this area—it would appear that excessive, addictive, obsessive and/or compulsive Internet use only applies to some of these behaviours. The most likely behaviours include the use of online pornography for masturbatory purposes, engaging in online relationships, and sex-related Internet crime (e.g., cyberstalking). Before looking at these three areas in more detail, a brief overview of Internet addiction will follow.

Internet Addiction

One area where Internet sexuality has been discussed academically is that of "Internet addiction". Despite opposition to the concept of behavioural (i.e., non-chemical) addictions, such as Internet addiction, there is a growing movement (e.g., Orford, 1985; Marks, 1990; Griffiths, 1996a) which views a number of diverse behaviours as potentially addictive, including gambling, overeating, sex, exercise, shopping, and computer game playing. Internet addiction is another such area since it has been alleged by some academics that social pathologies (i.e., technological addictions) may be beginning to surface in cyberspace (e.g., Griffiths, 1996b; 1998a; Brenner, 1997; Cooper, 1998; Scherer, 1997; Young, 1998a; 1998b).

Technological addictions are non-chemical (behavioural) addictions which involve excessive human-machine interaction. They can either be passive (e.g., television) or active (e.g., computer games) and usually contain inducing and reinforcing features which may contribute to the promotion of addictive tendencies (Griffiths, 1995a). They also feature the core components of addiction, including salience, mood modification, tolerance, withdrawal, conflict and relapse (Griffiths, 1996a; 1996c). It has been argued by Griffiths (1996c) that any behaviour (e.g., Internet use) which fulfils these criteria can be operationally defined as addictions. These core components are expanded upon below in relation to Internet sex of whatever type it happens to be (e.g., downloading pornography, cybersex relationships, etc.):

Salience   This occurs when Internet sex becomes the most important activity in the person's life and dominates their thinking (preoccupations and cognitive distortions), feelings (cravings) and behaviour (deterioration of socialized behaviour). For instance, even if the person is not actually on their computer engaged in Internet sex they will be thinking about the next time they will be.

Mood modification   This refers to the subjective experiences that people report as a consequence of engaging in Internet sex and can be seen as a coping strategy (i.e., they experience an arousing "buzz" or a "high" or paradoxically tranquilizing feel of "escape" or "numbing").

Tolerance   This is the process whereby increasing amounts of Internet sex are required to achieve the former mood modificating effects. This basically means that for someone engaged in Internet sex, they gradually build up the amount of the time they spend in front of the computer engaged in the behaviour.

Withdrawal symptoms   These are the unpleasant feeling states and/or physical effects which occur when Internet sex is discontinued or suddenly reduced, e.g., the shakes, moodiness, irritability, etc.

Conflict   This refers to the conflicts between the Internet user and those around them (interpersonal conflict), conflicts with other activities (job, social life, hobbies and interests) or from within the individual themselves (intrapsychic conflict and/or subjective feelings of loss of control) which are concerned with spending too much time engaged in Internet sex.

Relapse   This is the tendency for repeated reversions to earlier patterns of Internet sex to recur and for even the most extreme patterns typical of the height of excessive Internet sex to be quickly restored after many years of abstinence or control.

Young (1999a) claims Internet addiction is a broad term which covers a wide variety of behaviours and impulse control problems. She claims it is further categorized by five specific subtypes:

Cybersexual addiction   Compulsive use of adult web sites for cybersex and cyberporn.

Cyber-relationship addiction   over-involvement in online relationships.

Net compulsions   obsessive online gambling, shopping or day-trading.
Information overload   compulsive Web surfing or database searches.
Computer addiction   obsessive computer game playing (e.g., *Doom, Myst, Solitaire*, etc.).

Only two of these specifically refer to potential sexually-based addictions (i.e., cybersexual addiction and cyber-relationship addiction) but Young's classification does raise the question of what people are actually addicted to? On a primary level, is it the sexually-related behaviour or is it the Internet? In reply to Young, Griffiths (1999a) has argued that many of these excessive users are not "Internet addicts" but just use the Internet excessively as a medium to fuel other addictions. Griffiths argues that a gambling addict or a computer game addict is not addicted to the Internet. The Internet is just the place where they engage in the behaviour. The same argument can be applied to Internet sex addicts. However, there are case study reports of individuals who appear to be addicted to the Internet itself. These are usually people who use Internet chat rooms or play fantasy role playing games—activities that they would not engage in except on the Internet itself (some of which are sex-related). These individuals to some extent are engaged in text-based virtual realities and take on other personas and social identities as a way of making themselves feel good about themselves.

In these cases, the Internet may provide an alternative reality to the user and allow them feelings of immersion and anonymity (which may lead to an altered state of consciousness). This in itself may be highly psychologically and/or physiologically rewarding. The anonymity of the Internet has been identified as a consistent factor underlying excessive use of the Internet (Young, 1998b; Griffiths, 1995b). This is perhaps particularly relevant to those using Internet pornography. There may be many people who are using the medium of the Internet because (1) it overcomes the embarrassment of going into shops to buy pornography over the shop counter, and (2) it is faster than waiting for other non-face-to-face commercial transactions (e.g., mail order). Anonymity may also encourage deviant, deceptive and criminal online acts such as the development of aggressive online personas or the viewing and downloading of illegal images (e.g., pornography) (Young, 1999).

There have been few studies of excessive Internet use which have found that a small proportion of users admitted using the Internet for sexual purposes (e.g., Morahan-Martin & Schumacher, 1997; Scherer, 1997; Young, 1998b). None of the surveys to date conclusively show that Internet addiction exists or that Internet sex addiction is problematic to anyone but a small minority. At best, they indicate that Internet addiction may be prevalent in a significant minority of individuals but that more research using validated survey instruments and other techniques (e.g., in-depth qualitative interviews) are required. Further to this, Griffiths (1999a) has also noted other problems with the criteria used in most of the surveys to date. They (1) have no measure of severity, (2) have no temporal dimension, (3) have a tendency to overestimate the prevalence of problems, and (4) take no account of the context of Internet use. Case studies of excessive Internet users may provide better evidence of whether Internet sex addiction exists by the fact that the data collected are much more detailed. Even if just one case study can be located, it indicates that Internet sex addiction actually does exist—even if it is unrepresentative. Griffiths (1998a) has argued that excessive usage in a majority of cases appears to be purely symptomatic but that for what appears to be an exceedingly tiny minority, the Internet may be addictive.

Pornography on the Internet

From the earliest days of photography to the latest innovations in real-time, e.g., one-to-one video conferencing, sex has played a defining role in the development and advance of new communication technology (Sprenger, 1999). Although the pornography industry cannot be credited with inventing these new technologies, they were certainly the first to put them to profitable use. Pornographers have always been the first to exploit new publishing technologies (e.g., photography, videotape, Internet, etc.). It is estimated that the online pornography industry will reach $366 million by 2001 (Sprenger, 1999) though other estimates suggest it is already worth $1 billion (*The Guardian*, 1999). Further to this, the research company Datamonitor reported that over half of all spending on the Internet is related to sexual activity (*The Guardian*,

1999). This includes the conventional (e.g., Internet versions of widely available pornographic magazines like *Playboy*), the not so conventional (Internet versions of very hardcore pornographic magazines) and what can only be described as the bizarre (discussion groups on almost any sexual paraphilia). Further to this, there are also pornographic picture libraries (commercial and free-access), videos and video clips, live strip-shows, live sex shows and voyeuristic Web-Cam sites.

Research has also revealed that Internet surfing has many parallels with road traffic. There appear to be identical patterns of congestion and "solid block motion" where everyone is forced to advance at the same speed (Brooks, 1999). One Web-traffic researcher, Bernardo Huberman (who works for Xerox Palo Alto Research Center) analyzed more than 500,000 visits to a major web portal and came to the conclusion that the Internet sex sites are the "undisputed kings" in selling advertizing space. Huberman noticed that Internet surfers typically click once or twice and then get out of a site. However, Huberman noted that some people were clicking up to 200 times and that nearly all of these instances were people accessing Internet sex sites. Further investigation revealed an amazingly sophisticated structure which led surfers deeper and deeper into the site (Brooks, 1999). The "click counts" data collected by Huberman suggests that there is an almost compulsive element in accessing online pornography and that some people are very heavy users of these services. Such research cannot show that Internet pornography addicts exist but is at the very least indicative of repetitive, habitual and/or pathological behaviour. Further to this, the Internet offers 24-hour constant access and has the potential to stimulate excessive use. In some cases this may become an addictive and/or compulsive activity.

One of the main reasons why the pornography industry has such a vested interest in this area is that in the online world the buying of most products is hassle-free and anonymous. However, buying pornography in the offline world may be embarrassing or stressful to the consumers particularly if they have to go to venues deemed to be "unsavoury". If pornography consumers are given the chance to circumvent this process, they invariably will. Pornography and its distribution are now widespread on the Internet—but how prevalent is Internet pornography? Academic researchers also claim that "sex" is the most searched for topic on the Internet (Cooper, Scherer, Boies & Gordon, 1999) and as many as one third of all Internet users visit some type of sexual site (Cooper, Delmonico & Burg, 2000). In the U.K. a survey carried out by University of Middlesex in 1995, and replicated in 1997, analysed a million word searches on an Internet search engine and reported that over half of them were aimed at locating pornography (Sparrow & Griffiths, 1997). However, these studies were carried out using word searches from only one search engine and the situation may have changed slightly in the last few years. Furthermore, the study reported that the pornography was more than just pictures of naked people but also included more worrying material. For instance, there was information for paedophiles on how to entrap and (in some instances) kill children.

Children and Internet Pornography

One of the biggest fears among parents who are thinking of using the Internet is that their children will be exposed to pornography, particularly because over 17 million children are using the Internet world-wide (Thompson, 1999). Issues surrounding censorship are high on the moral agenda but preventing access to such sites is difficult. A major U.S. survey undertaken in 1998 by the Annenberg Public Policy Center (Lillington, 1999) reported that 75 percent of parents were anxious about what their children might be exposed to on the Internet. To what extent is this fear justified? The media has certainly played a role in heightening parents' fears as two-thirds of all newspaper articles about the Internet highlight negative aspects and one in four mentioned child pornography (Lillington, 1999).

Internet pornography is not difficult to access—especially with the development of powerful yet easy-to-use search engines. In fact, a survey by the National Opinion Poll (NOP) in June 1999, found that a third of U.K. children had found content on the Internet that upset or embarrassed them—up from 20 percent in the previous survey (Thompson, 1999; Lillington, 1999). Of this material, 58 percent was described as being "rude". Given that the same NOP poll found that one in four U.K. children aged seven to sixteen years old (i.e., 3 million children) are regular Internet users with half of them doing it from home (Thompson, 1999), it therefore appears there may be widespread cause for alarm.

There are many steps a parent can take to prevent their child from accessing pornography including:

• reading guidelines for parents which run through issues and possible approaches for overseeing Internet use by children. These include those produced in offline versions (see table 11.1) or those that can be found online. These include such sites as the Netparents resource collection (www.netparents.org/parentstips/resources.html), NCH Action for children site (www.nchafc.org.uk/internet/index.html) and Schoolzone's resources (www.schoolzone.co.uk/resources/safety_frame.htm).

• being with your children at all times when they access the Internet.

• joining an Internet service provider that prevents its users from accessing such things.

• installing one of the many different types of blocking package on the market that filter content in some way (Griffiths, 1997b; 1998b). These include those which use lists of key words that you can define (e.g., Net

Table 11.1
Guidelines for Children on How to Be Safe on the Internet

---

1. Never tell anyone that you meet on the Internet your home address, telephone number or school's name unless you are given permission by a parent or caregiver.
2. Never send anyone your picture, credit card or bank details (or anything else).
3. Never give your password to anyone—even your best friend.
4. Never arrange to meet anyone in person that you have met on the Internet without first agreeing it with your parent or caregiver.
5. Never stay in a chat room or in a conference if someone says or writes something which makes you feel uncomfortable or worried. Always report it to your parent or caregiver.
6. Never respond to nasty, suggestive or rude e-mails or postings in Usenet groups.
7. If you see bad language or distasteful pictures while you are online, always tell your parent or caregiver.
8. When you are online, always be yourself and do not pretend to be anyone or anything you are not.
9. Always remember that if someone makes you an offer which seems too good to be true—then it probably is.

Source: NCH Action for Children: Children on the Internet. Opportunities and Hazards, 1998.

Nanny), software packages that can block certain areas of the Internet, such as Usenet groups, or which restrict access at certain times (e.g., Cyber Patrol), packages which have a built-in censor to certain categories as defined by the maker of the package (SurfWatch), or packages which block access to certain file types, like GIF and JPEG which are lot of pornographic images use. However, there may be a "technological generation gap" as the recent poll by NOP reported, that children knew more about filtering software than their parents (Thompson, 1999).

Despite packages like SurfWatch and Net Nanny which block access to pornographic sites, such packages can still be circumvented. There are also other packages like Babewatch which do the exact opposite (i.e., locate nothing but pornographic sites for the user) (Griffiths, 1997b; 1998b). It appears to be the case that parents are not as vigilant about their children's Internet use as they could be. For instance, a survey of 500 online households by the U.S.-based National Center for Missing and Exploited Children found that 20 percent of parents did not supervise their children's Internet use. It was also reported that 71 percent of parents with children aged 14 or older said they had stopped monitoring their children's Internet use (Thompson, 1999).

Online Relationships

Probably one of the most unexpected uses surrounding the growth of the Internet concerns the development of online relationships and their potentially addicting nature. It is hard to estimate the number of online relationships but in the U.K. it was reported in the media that there had been over one thousand weddings as a result of Internet meetings. Media commentators claim that cyberspace is becoming another singles bar as there are now numerous sites aimed at those who want romance and/or a sexual liaison. Some of these are aimed at single people (e.g., Widows, Thirtysomething U.K. and Married with Kids) while others appear to encourage and facilitate virtual adultery (e.g., MarriedM4Affair, Cheating Wife or Lonely Husband).

Young, Griffin-Shelley, Cooper, O'Mara and Buchanan (2000) define an online relationship (a "cyberaffair") as a romantic and/or sexual relationship that is initiated via online contact and maintained predominantly through electronic conversations that occur through e-mail and in virtual communities, such as chat rooms, interactive games, or newsgroups. Young et al. report that what starts off as a simple e-mail exchange or an innocent chat room encounter can escalate into an intense and passionate cyberaffair and eventually into face-to-face sexual encounters. Further to this, those in online relationships often turn to mutual erotic dialogue (often referred to as "cybersex"). In this instance, cybersex involves online users swapping text-based sexual fantasies with each other. These text-based interactions may be accompanied by masturbation. Online chat rooms provide opportunities for online social gatherings to occur almost at the push of a button without even having to move from your desk. Online group participants can—if they so desire—develop one-to-one conversations at a later point either through the use of continuous e-mails or by instant messages from chat rooms. It could perhaps be argued that electronic communication is the easiest, most disinhibiting and most accessible way to meet potential new partners.

Infidelity Online—How and Why Does It Occur?

There are a number of factors that make online contacts potentially seductive and/or addictive. Such factors include the disinhibiting and anonymous nature of the Internet. This may be very exciting to those engaged in an online affair. Disinhibition is clearly one of the Internet's key appeals as there is little doubt that the Internet makes people less inhibited (Joinson, 1998). Online users appear to open up more quickly online and reveal themselves emotionally much faster than in the offline world. What might take months or years in an offline relationship may only take days or weeks online. As Cooper and Sportolari (1997) have pointed out, the perception of trust, intimacy and acceptance has the potential to encourage online users to use these relationships as a primary source of companionship and comfort.

Some researchers have made attempts to explain how and why infidelity occurs online. Cooper (1998) proposed the "Triple A Engine"

(Access, Affordability, and Anonymity) which he claimed help to understand the power and attraction of the Internet for sexual pursuits. Young (1999) also claimed to have developed a variant of the "Triple A Engine" which she called the "ACE model" (Anonymity, Convenience, Escape). Neither of these are strictly models as neither explains the process of how online relationships develop. However, they do provide (in acronym form) the variables involved in the acquisition, development and maintenance of emotional and/or sexual relationships on the Internet (i.e., anonymity, access, convenience, affordability and escape). It would also appear that virtual environments have the potential to provide short-term comfort, excitement and/or distraction.

Types of Online Relationships

A number of researchers have forwarded typologies of the different kinds of Internet users in relation to sexual and/or relationship activity (Cooper, 1998; Young, 1999; Griffiths, 1999b). Cooper, Putnam, Planchon and Boies (1999) suggest there are three types of cybersexual user (recreational, at risk, and compulsive) but this tells us little except about frequency of use. However, Griffiths (1999b) has outlined three basic types of online relationship in relation to actual online behaviour. The first one is purely virtual and involves two people who never actually meet. They engage in an online relationship which goes further than being pen-pals as the exchanges are usually very sexually explicit. Neither person wants to meet the other person and are engaged in the interaction purely for sexual kicks. It is not uncommon for these individuals to swap gender roles. The "relationships" may be very short-lived and the people involved will usually have real-life partners. These people prefer the distance, relative anonymity and control offered by the Internet and will prefer to confine the relationship to cyberspace. As far as these people are concerned, they do not feel they are being unfaithful.

The second type of online relationship involves people meeting online but eventually wanting the relationship to move from the virtual to the actual after becoming emotionally intimate with each other online. The shared emotional intimacy often leads to cybersex and/or a strong desire to communicate constantly with each other on the Internet. For many, the online relationship will progress after sending photographs of each other into secret phone calls, letters, and offline meetings. Once they have met up, and if they are geographically near each other, their Internet use will usually decrease considerably as they will spend far more time actually (rather than virtually) with each other.

The third type of relationship involves two people first meeting offline but then maintaining their relationship online for the majority of their relationship. This is usually because they are geographically distant and may even be living in separate countries. These people only meet up a few times a year but may spend vast amounts of time "talking" to their partners on the Internet most nights. As they are geographically distant, the relationship only continues for those who have the time, the budget and the travel opportunity to maintain the nominal physical contact. With regards to "addiction," it is only the first type outlined here that may be addicted to the Internet. The latter two types are more likely to be addicted to the person rather than the activity—particularly as their Internet usage stops almost completely when they meet up offline with their partner.

Although many people who have not engaged in an online relationship fail to understand the pull and attraction of such an activity, it quite clearly can have detrimental consequences for some people who do. An online relationship can lead to a loving and compassionate individuals to become uncaring towards their partner and/or family, evasive, and demanding privacy online. In an effort to help both couples and therapists, Young et al. (2000) produced a list of early warning signs in the detection of a suspected online relationship. These include (1) a change in sleep patterns, (2) a demand for privacy, (3) ignoring other responsibilities, (4) evidence of lying, (5) personality changes, (6) loss of interest in sex, and (7) declining investment in the relationship.

Sex-Related Internet Crime

Despite the seemingly marked absence of serious consideration, sex-related Internet crime seems set to become increasingly important to all those involved in the administration of criminal justice. Sexually-related Internet crime is on the increase and some of the perpetrators may be addicted to the criminal activity in question and/or develop obsessions about their Internet victims. In the broadest possible sense, sexually-related Internet crime can be divided into two categories—(1) display, downloading and/or the distribution of illegal sexually-related material, and (2) the use of the Internet to sexually procure and/or intimidate an individual in some way (e.g., online sexual harassment, cyberstalking, paedophilic grooming).

Charlesworth (1995) noted that criminal law and those who enforce it have taken time to come to terms with the implications of change with regards to Internet crime. Those in the criminal justice system continue to rely on their own familiar scheme of reference when attempting to comprehend the criminal behaviour. For the most part, they have some understanding of the mode of operation, likely benefits to the offender and costs to the victim of the criminal activity presented before them. However, the unfamiliarity of sexually-related Internet crime denies those in the criminal justice system all important access to their own scheme of understanding. The advancements in computer technology generally (and the increased availability of the Internet in particular) have provided for new innovations in, and an expansion of, the field of criminality (and more specifically in the area of sexually-related Internet crime) (Durkin, 1997; Durkin & Bryant, 1998; Griffiths, Rogers & Sparrow, 1998; Deirmenjian, 1999).

Most people's perceptions about sexually-related Internet crime are probably based on media reports. These usually concern:

• Distribution of illegal pornography on the Internet.

• Use of the Internet for paedophilic purposes (i.e., paedophiles distributing child pornography or pretending to be a child to make contact with children).

• High profile prosecutions of Internet pornographers (such as the recent imprisonment of the U.K.'s largest pornography operator who was given an 18-month prison for designing Web sites (e.g., Farmsex, Europerv and School-girls-R-Us) featuring extreme pornography, bestiality, coprophilia and torture (Wilson, 1999).

However, one of the main problems with Internet pornography is that any country's attempt to interdict cross-border flows of pornography would be defeated by advances in communication technology—especially data transmission (Millar, 1996; Sprenger, 1999). The police crackdown on Internet pornography has been argued by some to be futile as it could drive it underground (Booth, 1996). Part of the Internet's appeal is its subversive nature, for it crosses frontiers, language barriers and is not policed by any one country.

Online Harassment and Cyberstalking

Stalking has been a high-profile crime in the 1990s leaving victims with a shattered sense of security and well-being. It now seems to be the case that stalkers are moving with the times and starting to harass and stalk in cyberspace. As a direct result of the increased accessibility of the Internet world-wide, the incidence of cyberstalking will almost certainly increase. Very recently the first prosecution case of cyberstalking or harassment by computer occurred in Los Angeles, when a 50-year old security guard was arrested for his online stalking activities (Gumbel, 1999).

In 1998, Novell (one of the world's leading providers of network software) began a U.K. study into "spamming" (i.e., the receiving of unwanted and unsolicited cyber junk mail). The focus of the study was to estimate the cost in business terms of time and money wasted. However, one of the unexpected findings of the research was that a large minority of women, 41 percent of the regular Internet users, had been sent pornographic material or been harassed or stalked on the Internet (Gumbel, 1999). Three percent of these messages were highly personal and sexual, and 35 percent of the messages were unsolicited pornography. Such unwarranted attention is intrusive and is a serious cause for concern.

CyberAngels (www.cyberangels.org) is a branch of the Guardian Angels and was set up in 1995. To date, it has dealt with over 200 cases of cyberstalking—two of which ended in the rape of the victims according to their Senior Director, Colin Gabriel Hatcher (Griffiths, Rogers & Sparrow, 1999). The organization claims that cyberstalking usually occurs with women who are stalked by men, or by children who are stalked by adult predators. Typically the victim is new online and therefore ignorant of "netiquette." In most cases, people just receive unsolicited junkmail but it can turn sinister. The risk of harassment intensifies if someone enters an Internet chat room. In most instances, the online harassment and stalking have eventually escalated offline (by tracing the victim's telephone number and address). Hatcher makes the point that cases such as these should not be trivialized as the paranoia of a small group of computer users (Griffiths, Rogers & Sparrow, 1998). In the U.S. libel and defamation are taken very seriously but stalking is sometimes perceived as a crime related to women's hysteria.

One of the problems with Internet use is that there are always more novices than those experienced, so the novices are not being taught the ways that they can protect themselves from being exploited. At least with obscene phone calls there is a voice and with letters there is handwriting; with e-mails there is nothing to go on, no clue as to the personality of the person involved. To some this makes the whole thing creepier. What's more, these "new" criminals perhaps would never have interfered in other people's lives and committed such acts in a face-to-face scenario.

Cyberstalking: What Can Be Done to Combat the Problem?

The development of computer technology is producing new categories of crimes in which the perpetrators believe they can hide behind the seemingly anonymous computer screen in an attempt to intimidate, threaten and spread hatred. These people appear to be naïve about exactly how anonymous they can be since specialists in this field can trace almost any electronic trail back to a computer. Every time a person visits a web site, they are leaving their e-mail address behind as a calling card. If that person takes part in any Internet discussions on a Usenet site, he or she is again leaving his/her identity. Where new crimes occur, new methods are used to combat it. For instance, a police officer was recently caught attempting to solicit minors over the Internet when a police officer pretended to be a 13-year old girl (Gumbel, 1999). This was a lot easier to do over the computer than it would have been in real life. The International Web Police (www.Web-Police.org) are well placed to fight this relatively new type of crime.

At present very few cases of cyberstalking have reached U.K. courts although U.K. law is adequately equipped to deal with such scenarios because of the recent 1997 Protection From Harassment Act. There is no specific mention of computers in the Act but the definition of harassment is based on the "reasonable man" test, i.e., any action which would reasonably be considered to be harassment are caught within the Act. This so-called "stalking act" sets out to create both criminal and civil sanctions for harassment, and in so doing, builds upon existing common law nuisance actions (Griffiths, Rogers & Sparrow, 1999). Criminal law and those who enforce it must come to terms with the implications of change with regards to computer crime. It could be argued that the technical complexity associated with cybercrime combined with the limited number of prosecutions has permitted criminal justice practitioners the luxury of ignorance. Sparrow and Griffiths (1997) have stated if computer-related crime is to occupy a position of increasing importance in the range of offending behaviour, then criminal justice practitioners must be willing to familiarize themselves with such activities in order to make judgements about the offender and the nature of their offending. In the future, cyberstalking may be viewed in the same way as other more "traditional" criminal acts are currently viewed.

Internet Sexuality: Conclusions

One of the objectives of any future research should be to determine the object of the Internet sex addiction. If some people appear addicted to the Internet, what are they addicted to? Is it the medium of communication (i.e., the Internet itself)? Aspects of its specific style (e.g., anonymity, disinhibition, etc.)? The information that can be obtained (e.g., hard-core pornography)? Specific types of activity (gender-swapping, role-playing games, playing sex computer games, cyberstalking)? Talking/fantasizing to others (in chat rooms or on Internet Relay Chat)? Perhaps it could even be a complex interaction between more than one of these. It is most likely that the Internet provides a medium for the "addiction" to flow to its object of unhealthy attachment (i.e., a secondary addiction to more pervasive primary problems).

The Internet can easily be the focus of excessive, addictive, obsessive and/or compulsive behaviours. One thing that may intensify this focus are the vast resources on the Internet available to feed or fuel other addictions or compulsions. For example, to a sex addict or a stalker, the Internet could be a very dangerous medium to users and/or recipients. There is also the problem that the Internet consists of many different types of activity (e.g., e-mailing, information browsing, file transferring, socialising, role-game playing, etc.). It could be the case that some of these activities (like Internet Relay Chat or role-playing games) are potentially more addictive than some other Internet activities. It is also worth noting that there has been no research indicating that sexually-related Internet crimes such as cyberstalking are addictive. However, the small number of case studies that have emerged do appear to indicate that cyberstalkers display addictive tendencies at the very least (salience, mood modification, conflict, etc.) although further research is needed to ascertain whether these excessive behaviours could be classed as bona fide behavioural addictions.

With regard to online relationships and affairs, these behaviours present a new dimension in couple relationships. These sex-related Internet behaviours appear as though they can be used from the healthy and normal through to the unhealthy and abnormal (i.e., use, abuse, and addiction) (Cooper, Putnam, et al., 1999). The Internet is anonymous, disinhibiting, easily accessible, convenient, affordable, and escape-friendly. These appear to be some of the main reasons for online infidelity. The detection of online affairs may be difficult but that does not mean it should not be given serious consideration in either an academic or practitioner context. These groups, along with those who engage in or who are on the receiving end of such behaviours, need to recognize that the Internet adds a new dimension to relationships. This has implications for assessment and treatment of couples who may, knowingly or unknowingly, undergo a relationship breakdown due to the impact of excessive online communication. However, as was noted earlier, text-based relationships can obviously be a positive and rewarding experience for many people. It is also an area in need of future research.

Interestingly, there is no clear evidence about the effects of pornography on users (Barak, Fisher, Belfry & Lashambe, 1999). However,

Young et al. (2000) assert that future research is needed to more clearly delineate the identification and classification of problematic online sexual activities. Further to this Cooper, Putnam, et al. (1999) proposed a continuum of Internet sexual activities from life enhancing to pathological needs to be replicated and further refined. There are very few areas surrounding excessive Internet use and its relationship with sexuality that do not need further empirical research (e.g., online sexual addiction, Internet and computer addiction, and online relationship dependency and or virtual affairs). More remains to be done in cyberspace to more clearly understand both the risks and benefits for Internet users, couples and society as a whole.

There is no doubt that Internet usage among the general population will continue to increase over the next few years. Social pathologies relating to Internet sexual behaviour do exist. This is certainly an area that should be of interest and concern not only to psychologists but to all those involved in clinical health issues. Excessive use of the Internet is not problematic in most cases, but the limited case study evidence available does suggest that for some individuals, excessive Internet usage is a real addiction and of genuine concern.

References

Barak, A., Fisher, W. A., Belfry, S. & Lashambe, D. R. (1999). Sex, guys, and cyberspace: Effects of Internet pornography and individual differences on men's attitudes toward women. *Journal of Psychology & Human Sexuality, 11*, 63–91.

Booth, N. (1996). Clampdown can easily be beaten, say net experts. *The Times*, August 16, p. 2.

Brenner, V. (1997). Psychology of computer use: XLVII. Parameters of Internet use, abuse and addiction: The first 90 days of the Internet usage survey. *Psychological Reports, 80*, 879–882.

Brooks, M. (1999). Sex site surfers teach traffic watchers. *The Guardian* (Online), September 30, p. 3.

Charlesworth, A. (1995). Never having to say sorry. *The Times Higher Educational Supplement (Multimedia Section)*, May 10, p. viii.

Cooper, A. (1998). Sexuality and the Internet: Surfing into the new millennium. *CyberPsychology and Behavior, 1*, 181–187.

Cooper, A., Delmonico, D. & Burg, R. (2000). Cybersex users, abusers, and compulsives: New findings and implications. *Sexual Addiction & Compulsivity: The Journal of Treatment and Prevention, 7*(2), 5–30.

Cooper, A., Putnam, D. E., Planchon, L. A. & Boies, S. C. (1999). Online sexual compulsivity: Getting tangled in the net. *Sexual Addiction & Compulsivity: The Journal of Treatment and Prevention, 6,* 79–104.

Cooper, A., Scherer, C., Boies, S. C. & Gordon, B. (1999). Sexuality on the Internet: From sexual exploration to pathological expression. *Professional Psychology: Research and Practice, 30,* 154–164.

Cooper, A. & Sportolari, L. (1997). Romance in Cyberspace: Understanding online attraction. *Journal of Sex Education and Therapy, 22,* 7–14.

Deirmenjian, J. M. (1999). Stalking in cyberspace. *Journal of the American Academy of Psychiatry and the Lau, 27,* 407–413.

Durkin, K. F. (1997). Misuse of the Internet by pedophiles: Implications for law enforcement and probation practice. *Federal Probation, 61*(3), 14–18.

Durkin, K. F. & Bryant, C. D. (1998). Propagandizing pederasty: A thematic analysis of the on-line exculpatory accounts of unrepentant pedophiles. *Deviant Behavior, 20,* 103–127.

Griffiths, M. D. (1995a). Technological addictions. *Clinical Psychology Forum, 76,* 14–19.

Griffiths, M. D. (1995b). Netties anonymous. *Times Higher Educational Supplement,* April 7, p. 18.

Griffiths, M. D. (1996a). Behavioural addictions: An issue for everybody? *Employee Counselling Today: The Journal of Workplace Learning, 8*(3), 19–25.

Griffiths, M. D. (1996b). Internet "addiction": An issue for clinical psychology? *Clinical Psychology Forum, 97,* 32–36.

Griffiths, M. D. (1996c). Nicotine, tobacco, and addiction. *Nature, 384,* 18.

Griffiths, M. D. (1997a, August). Technological addictions: Looking to the future. Paper presented at the 105th Annual Convention of the American Psychological Association, Chicago, Illinois.

Griffiths, M. D. (1997b). Children and the Internet. *Media Education Journal, 21,* 31–33.

Griffiths, M. D. (1998a). Internet addiction: Does it really exist? In J. Gackenbach (Ed.), *Psychology and the Internet: Intrapersonal, Interpersonal and Transpersonal Applications.* Pp. 61–75. New York: Academic Press.

Griffiths, M. D. (1998b). Children and the Internet: Issues for parents and teachers. *Education and Health, 16,* 9–10.

Griffiths, M. D. (1999a). Internet addiction: Internet fuels other addictions. *Student British Medical Journal, 7,* 428–429.

Griffiths, M. D. (1999b). All but connected (Online relationships). *Psychology Post, 17,* 6–7.

Griffiths, M. D. (in press). Gambling technologies: Prospects for problem gambling. *Journal of Gambling Studies.*

Griffiths, M. D., Rogers, M. E. & Sparrow, P. (1998). Crime and IT (part II): 'Stalking the Net'. *Probation Journal, 45,* 138–141.

The Guardian (1999). Blue money. *The Guardian* (Online), May 27: p. 5.

Gumbel, A. (1999). Techno detectives net cyber-stalkers. *Independent on Sunday*, January 31, p. 17.

Joinson, A. (1998). Causes and implications of disinhibited behavior on the Internet. In J. Gackenback (Ed.), *Psychology and the Internet: Intrapersonal, Interpersonal, and Transpersonal Implications.* Pp. 43–60. New York: Academic Press.

Lillington, K. (1999). Web life: Parenting. *The Guardian* (Online), September 9, p. 5.

Marks, I. (1990). Non-chemical (behaviourial) addictions. *British Journal of Addiction, 85,* 1389–1394.

Millar, S. (1996). Police curb on Net porn 'impossible'. *The Guardian*, September 2, p. 6.

Morahan-Martin, J. M. & Schumacher, P. (1997, August). Incidence and correlates of pathological Internet use. Paper presented at the 105th Annual Convention of the American Psychological Association, Chicago, Illinois.

Orford, J. (1985). *Excessive Appetites: A Psychological View of the Addictions.* Chichester: Wiley.

Scherer, K. (1997). College life online: Healthy and unhealthy Internet use. *Journal of College Development, 38,* 655–665.

Sparrow, P. & Griffiths, M. D. (1997). Crime and IT: Hacking and pornography on the Internet. *Probation Journal, 44,* 144–147.

Sprenger, P. (1999). The porn pioneers. *The Guardian* (Online), September 30, p. 2–3.

Thompson, B. (1999). New kids on the net. *The Guardian* (Online), June 24, p. 2–3.

Wilson, J. (1999). Net porn baron escapes jail. *The Guardian*, October 7, p. 5.

Young, K. (1998a). Internet addiction: The emergence of a new clinical disorder. *CyberPsychology and Behavior, 1,* 237–244.

Young, K. (1998b). *Caught in the Net: How to Recognize the Signs of Internet Addiction and a Winning Strategy for Recovery.* New York: Wiley.

Young, K. (1999a). Internet addiction: Evaluation and treatment. *Student British Medical Journal, 7,* 351–352.

Young, K. (1999b, August). Cyber-disorders: The mental illness concern for the millennium. Paper presented at the 108th Annual Meeting of the American Psychological Association, Boston, MA.

Young, K. S., Griffin-Shelley, E., Cooper, A., O'Mara, J. & Buchanan, J. (2000). Online infidelity: A new dimension in couple relationships with implications for evaluation and treatment. *Sexual Addiction and Compulsivity: The Journal of Treatment and Prevention, 7,* 59–74.

III

The Wired Homestead and Online Life

What is disrupted and what is enhanced in our home spaces and family relations by computer networking? Connectivity to everything outside the home becomes ubiquitous and continuous—which would seem to be an enhancement. But since the medium of the internet is two-way, the outside world also has greater access to us in our homes. That could be a problem for some people.

The articles and essays in this section examine the implications of internet use for structures and processes of family activities and relationships, as well as the use of the physical space in the home. Are family dynamics affected by the location of the computer, or by the presence of multiple access points?

Accessing information online that we want or need from outside the home is usually a major convenience for us (comparative shopping online, researching medical information, downloading that last minute tax form). If the computer is centrally located—say, in the family room or kitchen—family members might gather around to compare collectively diverse products and prices on an item of general interest, such as a fish aquarium or summer vacation packages. Surely, if the fish aquarium search were conducted in the study or the parents' bedroom, fewer family members would participate in the review of choices. Are we designing our homes differently these days in order to accommodate this technology or to make it amenable to family gathering and collective use?

Steven Izenour examines these questions in his chapter and concludes that computer technology will not have a big impact on architectural design. He argues that technology is so miniaturized today that it blends easily into the existing structure of our homes, our rooms and our pockets. For example, computers have been set up in the kitchen or the contiguous family room. With that and other new technologies, the kitchen has become the center of many homes, as it was over a hundred years ago. Izenour sees the consistent shape of the house, uninterrupted in basic shape by most high technology, as consistently harkening to a rural ideal, in which we imagine families were more close-knit and collaborative.

Can the location of a computer bring families together? In their chapter on computer use by family members, David Frohlich, Susan Dray, and Amy Silverman report that location might facilitate or inhibit family interaction. The placement of the computer in the kitchen or another common gathering area such the living room facilitates family interaction and collective decision making. But also important is the design of the computer itself. Aptly named the "personal" computer, not the "group" computer, it inhibits collective use. A single chair in front of a "personal" computer encourages an isolated individual's interacting with the machine. Frohlich, Dray, and Silverman bemoan the "rampant featurism" that pervades today's computers and predicts a burgeoning of many smaller, simpler digital communication tools around the house that facilitate intermittent casual and collective use. This trajectory is apparent from the launch of such tools as mini-computers, like Notepad, and personal digital assistants, mobile phones with web access, and WebTV. These smaller, decentralized tools (in the children's bedroom, the den, the kitchen, and so on) will be interconnected—probably wirelessly—to a central server (looking like our current desktop computers). It is a return to the mainframe computer model of the 1960s and 70s, whereby the intelligence was built into a central computer, and content was distributed to users through remote "dumb" terminals and monitors. From a central networked server, we can stream (through speakers in a designated room) daily news or music selections from our favorite web sites. Onto a large wall or screen in the family room we can project a slide show or home videos from a stored file in the server. According to Frohlich, Dray, and Silverman, these are some of the kinds of casual "background" communication activities that families are seeking from their home computers. The technology should be minimalist, usable, and transparent; the content should be collectively viewed or easily shared. Parents, they report, feel uncomfortable with their children having a networked computer in their bedroom. A central server not only would manage content and traffic for a home area network, it would also monitor web connections of remote devices (such as a networked PC or WebTV in the children's bedroom).

When the computer moved out of the study and into the kitchen or other common areas, it became more accessible to mothers as well as to fathers and kids. Catherine Burke examines how the domestic arrangements of space and time with home computers affect women's access and use of these resources. Surveying the experiences and attitudes of 150 women in the United States, Canada, the United Kingdom, Australia, and Asia, she finds that women with families tend to feel guiltier about using the home computer than women without families. She concludes that women with families need more time, their own personal computer and a redistribution of domestic chores to increase access and use of online resources.

By investigating the daily needs and interests of women (and girls), we are better able to understand how and why they use computer networks. Lisa-Jane McGerty warns us in her chapter of the dangers of separating women from the context of their daily lives offline when we study their internet use. She suggests, too, that "the intrusion of these technologies into the home is having an impact on constructions of gender, while simultaneously constructions of gender are doubtless impacting on Internet use in those domestic spaces and elsewhere." Moreover, she argues, we must realize that gender interacts with other aspects of a woman's environment—for example, social class, occupation, education, and age. McGerty asks for research that explores how these various factors affect "the gendered dynamics" of internet use at home and elsewhere, and what it means for women's daily lives.

Decreasing contact and communication with family members are among the disruptions to household relationships that Robert Kraut, Sara Kiesler, Bonka Boneva, Jonathon Cummings, Vicki Helgeson, and Anne Crawford found in a 1998 exploration of internet use. In their re-examination of these issues in a follow-up study, though, the Carnegie Mellon University researchers note that most of the negative outcomes initially associated with internet use—including increased isolation and addictive behavior—have dissipated. They speculate that the earlier findings may be attributable to participants being new users of the internet. Moreover, few of the family and friends of participants also had internet access at that time. Therefore, participants could not use the internet to increase communication and contact with family and friends. In this sense, access to the internet may have disrupted their existing social relationships.

The follow-up work involved a subset of the original sample and a new sample of families in the Pittsburgh area. Kraut and his colleagues found that in both groups more use of the internet associated with positive outcomes related to social involvement and psychological well-being. Moreover, as we learn from impact studies of earlier communication technologies, there are dual or reinforcing social effects. Kraut notes that people differing in extraversion and social support are likely to use the internet in different ways. They are also likely to have different social resources available in their offline lives.

The point is a refrain throughout these articles on the homestead and online life: we need to examine the use and impact of the internet in the context of people's daily needs and interests. That is one point of Sherry Turkle's "Virtuality and Its Discontents." Though not referring to the family directly, the piece addresses the phenomenon of people using the internet in the home to search for interpersonal connections outside it. Turkle sees the development as a poignant reflection on our atomized society, and she sees both positive and negative aspects to it. She sees many ironies in people trying to discover themselves and close relationships in a "culture of simulation." What, we can ask, might the implications be for real family members who might not be getting the close attention (and even love) that virtual links are receiving? At the same time, Turkle notes that "virtual personae can be a resource for self-reflection and self-transformation" so that we can use the communities we build inside our machines to improve the ones outside of them. It is a comment that sets us up perfectly for the book's final part, "The Wired Homestead and Civic Life."

12

The Internet's Implications for Home Architecture

Steven Izenour

I thought it might be instructive to do a short virtual history of the American home and the American everyday environment just to see if, in fact, the internet is such a a gigantic new thing. There have, of course, been other gigantic things that have happened to us technologically in 200 years. And considering the effect of all those things in their time and their place might tell us something about the ultimate effect of the internet.

If we look back 200 years, we probably all lived on a farm or over a shop, and maybe we trudged off to the general store once a month for a little entertainment and to get a few things. But then, thanks to manifest destiny and all that space we found when we got here, we attributed all positive moral, social, and esthetic virtues to that farm that we started on or to that little store. The "rural ideal" became a kind of driving force for the way we live, for all intents and purposes. In reality, we all know that we took the first chance we had to get away from the farm and head to the city. There's always been this contradiction between symbol and reality.

In the nineteenth century, with the first Industrial Revolution, things began to fragment and become specialized, thanks to technology. The train and the streetcar came along, so we could live in a row house or a tenement or in a suburb. We could work in a factory or an office building. And we could shop on Main Street. Lots of big changes.

But we still aspired to that rural ideal. Our houses, the symbols that we used to live every day, came from that farm or that little shop. The typical American suburb is little different, symbolically, from that farm.

It's just that piece of that farm that we can afford in terms of time and distance.

And from the nineteenth century, the farmers who were left out there had the Sears Roebuck catalogue, which was the Amazon.com of the nineteenth and early twentieth centuries. The train could bring them stuff despite the distance. In the twentieth century, things get really interesting. We add the car to the mix and we get not the internet, but the interstate. The row house becomes Levittown. Main Street becomes the strip mall. Things move further apart. It works, after a fashion, because a lot of us can live our suburban-rural ideal at four houses to the acre and spend our life in our cars going from the 'burb to the mall to the office park. But thanks to the cell phone, the TV, the radio, and all of that, we still remain more or less interconnected one way or another.

Which brings us to the internet. And lo and behold, we can now live, work, and shop on that farm again—or go back 200 years—and so everything, in a sense, becomes almost back to the future. To understand the internet you probably ought to look at the effect of technology on the home itself. Home technology didn't start with TV. Before the TV, you had the effect of technology on the bathroom, which was a radical shift to the design of the American house.

Plumbing came indoors. The effect of technology on the kitchen was immense. In the house of 200 years ago, everybody lived to a great extent in one room, which was the kitchen. Thanks to technology, we've gone all the way around and come right back to that. We've miniaturized the kitchen and made it practical for the kitchen to be part of the family room. In fact, we live in one room again with our TV in our kitchen.

So, there's this constant effect of technology to kind of go back to the past, if you will, and reinvent the past. A classic example of this could be a working-class Philadelphia living room in the 1950s or 1960s, where the TV becomes a great piece of baroque furniture, almost a symbolic center of the house instead of the fireplace. After that, the TV invents a new room for us: the "rec" room, or family room.

But what happens very quickly with the TV, and even more quickly with the internet now, is we can miniaturize all of this stuff and, suddenly, it no longer becomes an "architectural driver" anymore. It isn't a big enough thing that requires architectural planning. It becomes personalized. You put in your pocket. It becomes the Watchman, the Walkman, the cell phone. Suddenly, much of that domestic form-making from the technology becomes purely part of our personal space and not something that particularly affects the way—the physical way—in which we live or the house we live in.

Put all that together with the computer and it seems to me we see the same acceleration: really, once you go to the laptop and the Palm Pilot and all of that, it really is going to have very little effect other than what invisibly happens in the wall or an antenna on top of the house to the actual house that we live in. Our house is still going to be generated by all those symbols and rural ideals that we all aspire to.

You know, our home is still all about our love affair with that rural ideal. We still love our cars. We still want to be entertained or achieve community now and then. We turn on the TV, the net. Or if worse comes to worst, we jump in the car and head to the new urbanism Main Street down the road.

Surprise—again, the symbols have remained the same. The way we combine them and access them changes, but they're still the same old symbols. It may seem odd, but there it is: The net will have an immense effect on our lives, but not necessarily on the form and the spaces that we actually live in every day.

13

Breaking Up Is Hard to Do: Family Perspectives on the Future of the Home PC

David M. Frohlich, Susan Dray, and Amy Silverman

13.1 Introduction

13.1.1 The Domestic Computing Debate

There are number of good reasons for *not* wanting to use a home computer. It is big and expensive, unstable and unreliable, overly complicated and imperfectly designed for the tasks it supports, and it suffers from "rampant featurism" to justify upgrades nobody needs (Norman 1998). Given the provision of alternative devices which could package computing more simply, conveniently and stylishly for particular tasks, why would anyone choose to use a general purpose computer? Longer term, if computers can eventually become small and pervasive enough to disappear into the furniture (Weiser 1991; Birnbaum 1997), why would any home of the future have one left exposed on a desktop?

This debate is essentially one about the "disaggregation" or break up of the home PC into specific computing functions which can be relocated around the home and family. Some of these functions might be embedded in familiar devices such as televisions, telephones and radios, while others might appear in novel but connected information appliances. This is very much an active debate at present with a large number of stakeholders in the computer, telecommunications and entertainment industries trying to figure out what it will mean for them and their products as different kinds of domestic technology "converge". It has meant that in addition to the pronouncement of industry gurus such as

Reprinted from *International Journal of Human-Computer Studies* 54 (2001): 701–724, by permission of the publisher Academic Press.

those cited above, there are a large number of market research reports addressing the concerns of stakeholders from a technology point of view. While these constitute a good starting point for understanding the domestic computing marketplace, their narrow technology focus makes them blind to broader social and cultural trends affecting technology uptake and to its fit with individual and family life. Consequently, they often generate conflicting predictions of the future, and rarely identify radically new market requirements.

In this chapter, we want to promote an alternative approach to understanding this debate through what might be called user research. User research as the name suggests takes an explicitly user-centric focus in order to understand the personal and social impact of technology from the consumers point of view. In the context of designing domestic technology user research involves going into homes in order to observe, talk to and interact with families on their own terms and in their own space. Although user research has its own limitations stemming from the use of smaller scale and more qualitative research methods, it is particularly sensitive to the interplay of disparate old and new technologies in peoples lives. Consequently, it tends to generate new requirements, insights and questions which are independent of particular technologies. Combined with traditional market studies, user research can be very powerful. As we hope to show in this case, it provides a way of injecting a sense of realism into overly utopian technology predictions.

The chapter begins with a brief review of market research data on the domestic computing debate and goes on to introduce relevant findings from a number of existing user research studies. A new study is then described, before relating its findings back to the debate.

13.1.2   Domestic Market Research

Market research reports undoubtedly give a good indication of what is really going on in the domestic computing market and some indication of what will happen in the future. Typically, these reports draw on a number of data sources to identify future trends in specific markets: including sales and market penetration figures, interviews with technology providers about their future marketing strategies, with "channel" partners who sell the technology to consumers, and with consumers themselves about reasons for purchase, current uses and future purchasing intentions.

In general, most recent reports confirm the growth of new-category computing devices in the home which are challenging the superiority of the home PC. According to Dataquest, these devices are enabled by the internet and break down broadly into internet televisions (NetTV), internet telephones (Screenphones), and internet data terminals comprising Network computers (NetPC) and application-based devices (Weiner 1997; Sheppard 1998). Other market research companies add internet gaming consoles (IDC—Kaldor, Card, Hwang & Zinsmeister 1997), appliance peripherals and home networking products to this collection (Forrester—Rhinelander & Mines 1998).

However, these reports disagree about the rate of adoption of the new devices and the size of the ultimate markets available. For example, IDC predict that the worldwide shipments of NetTVs in 2001 will be 6.65 million units amounting to $1.025 billion (Kaldor et al. 1997), whereas Dataquest predict shipments of the same product in the same year to be about half that: 3.67 million units worth $490 million (Sheppard 1998). One source of confusion in these predictions may be the recent upturn of home PC sales as a result of falling PC prices (Rhinelander, Bluestein, Van BosKirk, Vernier & Gerber 1997). Cheap PC prices undermine the information appliance market because consumers will tend to favour a proven general-purpose device over an unproven restricted function device at roughly the same price. Some reports even point out that this trend could continue until PC prices fall to zero (Green, McCarthy & Bernoff 1996). This would require adoption of a new business model for PCs, akin to that for mobile phones, where PC vendors make money not from selling hardware but by internet service revenue which follows from using it. This would surely change the prospects for focused function appliances, unless they too could switch to the same model (cf. Yankee Group 1997).

Finally, several reports point to the emergence of an intermediate future between PC domination and appliance takeover: co-existence. They note a rise in the number of multiple PC households, the development of home networking technology and the possibility of networked appliances running off a central PC hub. Thus, an Intel white paper pointed out that 14 million of the 40 million US households owning a PC in 1997 (35%) had more than one PC, and that this proportion is set to rise further (Intel 1998). Furthermore, PC-owning families are also more likely to be purchasers of the new internet appliances because they spend more time on-line to appreciate the value of increased internet access (Morrisette, Bernoff, Walsh & Sheppard 1999). As soon as families have more than one internet access device in the home they face problems of sharing programs, data, services and connections. These would be alleviated by using the home PC as a central internet gateway and storage repository and linking other devices to it via an in-home network (Miller & Baker 1998; Staten 1997). This is a compelling vision since it would allow consumers the choice of using internet appliances as "PC companions" as well as standalone devices. Whether or not it will come true, in place of the other two possibilities of continued PC domination or appliance takeover is not clear from the market research data alone.

13.1.3   Domestic User Research

A number of existing studies of home consumers themselves throw further light on the future of domestic computing as discussed above. They begin to show how people relate to technology, what the home PC has come to be used for over the years, and how far it has become domesticated so as to fit into modern family homes and routines.

One of the earliest and most innovative studies of home technology predates the personal computer and home PC, but is nevertheless relevant to its adoption today. In visits to 82 three-generation families in the Chicago area in the late 1970s, Csikszentmihalyi and Rochberg-Halton (1981) asked people about the meaning of things in their homes. They found that the significance of many "special" objects in the home lay not so much in their functionality (i.e., what they did) but in their style and appearance, in their past association with important people and events in their lives, and in their ability to reflect something of their own personalities. The importance given to these various attributes differed by age and gender, leading to very different attitudes to the same possessions and technologies by different members of the family (see also Silverstone 1992).

The first "personal" computers to be taken home had very few of these attributes: being impersonal, of uniform style and appearance, limited in functionality and without a past history. Not surprisingly, the first reports of their use at home stressed a lack of impact and integration with family life. Hence, an ethnographic study of 20 U.K. families in the late 1980s showed that many home PCs were lying unused or were only operated sporadically by the men and boys of the household for work or games (Silverstone 1991). This was despite a household penetration rate of 20% at the time.

A similar picture emerged from user research in the U.S. around the same time (Vitalari, Venkatesh & Gronhaug 1985). However, this work was carried on longitudinally throughout the 1980s and early 1990s, and showed an increasing use of the home computer by additional members of the household and for a wider range of tasks (Venkatesh 1996). These tasks included family communication, reading, family recreation, family record keeping and finances, home shopping, children's schoolwork and adult education. The most recent phase of this work carried out in 1999 (Project NOAH II) has involved telephone interviews with 905 computer households and 300 non-computer households, and home PC diary logging with 120 of the computer households. Early results suggest that aside from a distinct segment of teleworking households where the home PC is used primarily for work, the top recreational uses of the home PC are now e-mail and web surfing followed by entertainment (Venkatesh 1999). Consequently, the home PC is now seen as a more essential technology than it used to be; on a par with the television and microwave and more important than a stereo or VCR.

Further detail on internet use at home comes from the HomeNet project at Carnegie Mellon University. This project has been monitoring the uptake and social impact of the internet since 1995 when it gave out free Macintosh computers and internet connections to about 100 families in the Pittsburgh area. Despite frustrations with maintaining and using internet services families have made increasingly diverse use of them to supplement existing practices of information management in the home (Kraut, Scherlis, Mukhopadhyay, Manning & Kiesler 1996). By far the most popular use of the internet was for social communication through a combination of e-mail, newsgroups, chat groups and Web publishing.

This kind of internet use is engaging to women and girls as well as men and boys, although paradoxically, it can lead them to experience increasing levels of social isolation and depression (Kraut, Patterson, Lundmark, Kiesler, Mukhopadhyay & Scherlis 1998). Whatever the cause of these effects, it is clear from this study that the home computer has assumed new significance for families at the end of the 1990s because of its connection to the internet, and that it is becoming an integral part of family life for better or worse.

Evidence for how that integration might be taken further comes from two studies of technology layout and home-life routines. In one study, 10 U.S. families were visited at home and asked to show the interviewers around the house and describe a typical day (Mateas, Salvador, Scholtz & Sorensen 1996). These interviews revealed the importance of the kitchen/dining area as a key social and information centre for the home, and its disconnection from the home PC which tended to be located in private study areas. They also revealed widespread distribution of other activities that might be supported by computer technology if it were available in other rooms of the house, and the need for people to interact with this technology together and for brief periods of time. Similar conclusions emerged from a recent set of visits to 10 homes in the North-West of England (O'Brien & Rodden 1997). Families were observed and interviewed about their patterns of home life and the use of different rooms and spaces. They found conflicts over the use of private and public spaces in the home which tended to get overloaded with functions provided by the technology located in them. The authors suggest that mobile or distributed technology which can be re-configured for its location might ease this tension and improve its fit to family life.

Taken together, these latter findings suggest a real need for distributing home computing and internet access around the house, although they are neutral about whether this is best supported by PCs, appliances or a mix of both.

13.1.4   Motivation for the Current Study

In order to address these questions more directly, we decided to carry out a new study of home PC use. Our main concern was to examine the need for relocation of home PC functions around the house, and whether or not this implied more focused-function devices for specific rooms. If possible we hoped to identify which *clusters* of functions were appropriate to each room, thereby revealing how much a device designed for each room would have to do. Building on previous user research, we also wanted to attend to differences in the perception and use of the home PC by different members of the household, and to understand how family members share time and access to the home PC today. This led to the following research questions for the study:

• How do individual members of a family *use and share* the home PC?

• How do family members want to *relocate* their favourite applications and services?

• What implications does this have for the *functionality* of additional computing devices in the home?

13.2   Methods

In-home interviews with complete families were chosen as the primary research method over standard focus groups with family representatives. This allowed us to uncover the viewpoints of all members of a family on PC use, to record and discuss the precise location of the PC and other technology inside a variety of homes and to stimulate family discussion of home life and related technology.

A profile of the 11 participating families is shown in table 13.1. All families lived in and around the Boston area and were essentially multimedia PC owners in which at least one parent and child actively used the PC and could be present to talk to us at the visit. To be included in the study, these individuals had to use the PC at least once a week. The set of families were recruited to represent a spread of income levels, geographical locations and housing types. In all they comprised 20 adults and 21 children (between 6 and 18 years) of varying interest and experience in home computer use. Each family was provided with a meal at the start of the visit and paid an incentive for taking part in the study.

Each visit lasted about 3 hours, and consisted of the following.

• A pre-visit questionnaire for each family member about PC uses and locations (see table 13.2).

Table 13.1
Profile of Families Visited in the Study

Family	Adults	Kids	Internet?	Days Use/Week	Annual Income (in thousands)	Housing	Location
1	2	1	Yes	2–3	$50–70	Private house	Suburban
2	2	1	No	2–3	$100+	Condominium	Urban
3	2	1	Yes	2–3	$100+	Private house	Urban
4	1	2	No	7	<$20	Apartment	Urban
5	2	4	Yes	4	$20–40	Rented house	Suburban
6	2	2	Yes	7	$70–100	Private house	Rural
7	1	1	Yes	7	$50–70	Rented house	Suburban
8	2	2	No	7	$45	Private house	Rural
9	2	3	Yes	7	$20–40	Apartment	Urban
10	2	2	Yes	2–3	$50–70	Private house	Suburban
11	2	2	Yes	7	$100+	Private house	Suburban

Table 13.2
Pre-visit Questionnaire

	Name of Favourite PC Application	Room I Use it in Now	Room I Would Like to Use it in
1st			
2nd			
3rd			

• Hour 1: A shared meal in which we got to know the family and went on to collect and discuss their questionnaires.

• Hour 2: A discussion of PC use at the PC with parents and children separately.

• A tour of the house with parents and children separately.

• Hour 3: The presentation of a number of new product concepts for reaction and feedback (not reported here).

Two or three of the authors were present at each visit to conduct the interviewing, carry out the data recording and help the younger children. Different types of data were recorded in different parts of the visit. In general, we tried to use the least invasive recording method for each part without unduly compromising the analysis. For example, the questionnaire discussions and the adult home tours were audio taped, while the PC interviews, the child home tours and the product concept reactions were video taped. Photographs of each room were also taken during the adult home tour and debrief conversations between the authors were audio recorded after each visit.

Applying this method with 11 families generated about 22 hours of audio interview data, 6 hours of home tour video data, 20 rolls of film and additional samples, drawings, notes and debrief tapes. In the next section, we summarize the key findings from the first 2 hours of each visit, insofar as they relate to the research questions outlined in section 13.1.4. To do this we worked mainly from transcripts of the audio and video records, making collections of comments on key topics in order to extract themes and patterns of responses. We returned to the original tapes or ancillary materials primarily to clarify and extend our understanding of the transcripts.

In reporting our analysis we attempt to remain faithful to the spirit of the responses made by families, citing quotes we feel illustrate that spirit in different ways. As in any qualitative analysis, this requires an element of trust from readers in our selection of quotes and reporting of themes. We warn against trying to infer themes simply from the given quotes. That would be like trying to conduct the analysis out of context and from a tiny fraction of the data we have surveyed. In fact, themes which are reported in the text with words like "generally" and "typically" are based on consistent responses made by more than half the families in our sample (i.e. six or more out of eleven). Quotes are then used to illustrate aspects of the themes.

13.3   Results

13.3.1   Current Uses and Values

13.3.1.1   The home PC quickly becomes an established part of family life.   In all families it was striking how much the home PC had become a routine part of family life, even where the family had purchased their first PC in the last year or two. It was typical for people to report a wide range of uses within a single household on a regular basis. This can be seen in the quote below from the mother of Family 5 (M5). [In subsequent quotes, the following notation is used to identify speakers: I = Interviewer, M1 = Mother of Family 1, F2 = Father of Family 2, S3 = Only son of Family 3, D4c = Third daughter of Family 4].

M5:   Like t' e kids use it for games but they also—its August right now so we're in the middle of summer holiday, but once school starts the kids get on it, they have homework projects, they type their papers, you know they play games to break up the boredom or whatever of school work, but they use the internet for research, instead of going to an encyclopaedia they throw in the encyclopaedia disk that came with the system, its just automatic for them to do that. So yeah definitely if this was gone they wouldn't want to resort to books!

Another indication of the acceptance of the PC in the home was that in all the families we visited we did not find a single non-PC user. Even the youngest child in the sample (aged 6) liked to play games with her older sister (aged 9). None of the families could imagine ever being a non-PC household again. This was underlined by one mother of a family whose PC had recently stopped working:

M4:   I miss it so much when it's broken down, I really enjoy it.

13.3.1.2   A single application delivered a range of values.   To begin to characterize the key values of the home PC more precisely we asked each member of the family to write down their three favourite applications and to tell us about why they liked and used them. From these answers and discussions it became clear that there is no simple mapping between applications and values. The same application may be used for quite different *purposes* by different people or by the same person on different occasions. For example, the same word processing package was the favourite of a father in the study to compose work reports on, of a mother to type letters to her friends, and of a daughter to write essays for enjoyment. We also found that different applications could be used to deliver the same values. For example, people reported using games, reference CDs and audio CDs for fun and relaxation.

Because of these effects and our interest in values rather than applications, we re-classified each favourite application in terms of the primary reported reason for using it. In fact, we selected from seven primary reasons or uses which appeared to cover the collection well:

Organization: Used to run household schedules and affairs.

Interest: Used to support a personal interest or hobby.

Self-expression: Used as an artistic medium.

Learning: Used as a means of self-improvement, training or education.

Communication: Used to interact with others.

Work: Used to carry out either an adult's work-at-home or a child's homework.

Fun: Used as a method of relaxation as an end in itself.

This classification of primary uses of the PC led us to the following findings.

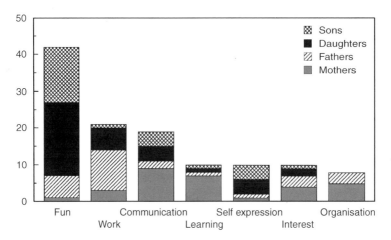

Figure 13.1
Primary uses of the PC by different members of the family.

13.3.1.3 The PC offered something for everybody in the family. One of the great strengths of the PC seemed to be its multi-purpose nature, and the resulting ability to offer something for everybody in the household. Typically, each member of the family found about 2 or 3 things which they like to use the PC for, although these differ systematically between generations and individuals (see figure 13.1).

From figure 13.1, we can see that these mothers used and valued the PC most for communication, fathers for work and children for the fun it can provide. Indeed, a full half of all the reasons cited by children for using the PC were fun-related. Beyond these simple preferences other patterns were apparent. For example, only the adults reported using the computer for household organization tasks, while it was mainly the children who reported using it for creative self-expression. Mothers used the PC more than others as a learning and self-development tool and daughters rate it as more useful for homework than sons.

In general, the children seemed to use the machine more playfully and creatively than their parents, who used it mainly as a tool for the support of work, communication, self-improvement and household management. The exception to this is seen in the fathers' attraction to fun/game applications, and in both parents modest use of the PC to support existing personal interests. For example, one father was interested in collecting old artefacts and regularly monitored archaeological web sites including one for the current Boston road excavations for tips on where to dig. Another father ran an ice cream factory and often chatted to other "ice cream people" over the newsgroups.

13.3.1.4 PCs were bought for one thing and used for others. The discovery of new things to do on the PC was a constant experience reported by families. For example, the ice cream factory father had bought the PC to do his accounts on and only discovered later that he could also use it to communicate with others in the industry. As in previous studies, we found that the home PC is often purchased initially for work use by one of the adults but then becomes a shared family resource for a variety of recreational, practical, communication and learning purposes by all members of the family. Alternatively, it may have been bought to support a child's homework and general education but then became useful for adult work at home as well as recreation, communication and domestic business. The two biggest "bonus" uses to most families were games for the children and e-mail for the adults.

The process of discovering new uses for the PC involves a certain amount of time wasting on applications which are eventually "discarded" by some. However, this often has the side effect of building up new PC skills and understanding which may be used in other contexts in the future:

F5: Its like when we first got SIM city it was new to everyone and everybody wanted a turn at it and slowly some people really liked it and other ones didn't find as much interest in it. So the conflict kinda worked itself out

M3: When my son first got us on the internet I guess last fall it was like a new toy and I was on a couple of news groups related to my job my professional life. I would come back and correspond with people and then I realised I was giving all this free advice and here I was at work thinking I don't get paid enough for what I do and why was I giving it away on the computer?

I: Yeah

M3:   It was about a month or so when I was into those news groups and I'm really not anymore. Sometimes when I have more time I would like to do more research. I would like to, you know, use the internet more

M6:   I'm feeling a little, what's the word, distanced from it. I used to work with computers but things were so different. That was seven years ago.

13.3.1.5 Parents worried about controlling their children's use of the PC.   An overriding concern of most parents in the study was how best to control the children's use of the PC. The strength of this feeling initially surprised us and later became understandable as we discussed the levels and types of control involved. Some kinds of control stemmed from straight-forward and justifiable concerns about children accessing unsuitable content on the web. Some children were banned from using the internet (including e-mail) for this reason. The cost of internet connection was a concern for some parents who wanted ways of setting time or budget limits for their family. Another concern was for the security of work documents that might be deleted by young children. One father insisted on being present when his children switched on the PC, so that he could steer them into the right area and type of application. A further type of control was of the limited time for sharing the PC which, if left uncontrolled, would result in the most dominant members of the household winning out. As one mother told us:

M9:   I've seen people literally pushed off that (computer) chair.

The children themselves recognized the need for parents to arbitrate between them but were plainly puzzled about some of the other controls imposed:

D1:   Sometimes he (father) is not on it and nobody's on it, and he won't let me play with it. I don't know why.

D6:   It would be great to have a Kid's Internet and we didn't have to ask parents to use it, because there are things we aren't supposed to get into. I don't understand why they don't let us go into the internet. My Dad is always hiding the password.

A more subtle concern parents had about the PC was that it should not begin to dominate either an individual family member's life or the life of the family as a whole. This sentiment was extended to all kinds of technology in the home. In its simplest form, it emerged as a legitimate concern about the addictive power of the latest games on children's behaviour. A less obvious form of containment of the effect of the PC was a family who had spent hundreds of dollars on stylish cabinets to hide away the PC from view when not in use. These concerns are best summed up in the words of one family who point out the extensible, addictive quality of the PC:

F6:   What do I think of computers?

I: Yeah

F6:   They are very useful. They are, um you know, there is this almost like they have this city inside of them

M6:   A world

F6:   And um I can get my work done and be entertained

M6:   They offer a lot as long as you know when to put the brakes on. Because you could spend your whole life, day after day (on it).

13.3.2   Contention for PC Time

13.3.2.1   There was widespread competition for PC time.   We found widespread competition for concurrent use of the PC. This was naturally more severe in the larger households where more people were competing for the single resource. Conflict was between all combinations of family members: children with children, children with parents and parents with each other:

M4:   We'd get into a fight

M4:   All of us would be on a different computer if they were in each room in the house

M5:   I wouldn't say we have a problem with conflict but it does arise just in the manner of seven of us using the same computer

M11:   We'd all like our own computers. I'd like one in the car for Pete's sake

The peak time for using the PC was in the early evening after dinner when children needed to research or type up school projects and parents needed to catch up with home accounts or work. Younger children wanted to play games at the same time while older children and adults also wanted to check e-mail and discussion groups. A typical pattern of use was for the mother to use the PC during the day in-between house-work, childcare or part-time work, and for the father to use it later in the evening when the children have gone to bed. Alternatively if both parents worked during the day, then they had to negotiate between themselves who got first turn at the PC after the children. Again priority usually went to the person who goes to bed earlier:

M3:   Usually what happens if I'm on it at night I'm usually not on it for very long since I go to bed usually a lot earlier than he does. Marc will say "let me know when your off it"

F3:   I'll say when your off it let me know and leave it on

13.3.2.2   Adults gave way to children unless their task was more urgent.   It became clear from these conversations that adults generally let the children go first and would delay their own PC use until later in the evening; often working into the early hours of the morning as a result. Aside from the obvious effect of tiredness on them this also seemed to be inhibiting their recreational use of the PC, since they had to do their most urgent work-related jobs on it first, leaving little time for games or casual browsing of the World Wide Web, etc. The exception to this rule of "children first" was if one of the parents had a greater need to use the PC than the children. For example, urgent adult work took precedence over game time for children:

M2:   But Becky sometimes we will have to say to her "You have to stop playing that game we need a phone number". Somebody will call in and if somebody calls in and we've got some information in here …

13.3.2.3   Adults arbitrated between children on the basis of task priority, bedtime and total time on the PC.   The same metric of task priority was often used to decide which child goes first. The usual bedtimes of each child were also taken into account. In cases where priorities are equal, the parents often administered a system of time limits for competing users. For example, young children were sometimes given turns of half an hour each:

M4:   So like I said what I do is I say "OK nobody will use the computer. We will decide who needs it and which is more important

I: Yeah so it goes on who needs it the most

M4:   Right who needs it the most. If it's to play a game then no. Then if it's to do school work then fine then he gets the priority

F5:   When they're playing the games we set time limits so everyone has a turn

These rules were taken very seriously by families and cheating was heavily sanctioned:

F11:   My son gets priority because he goes to bed earlier. She stays up later so she can have it later, but when he's typing and we come down and we find out he's playing on AOL so we have a yell and a scream session and that's the end of that (his session)

13.3.2.4   Duration of use varied but can be very short.   The duration of sessions at the PC appeared to vary greatly within and between individuals. These could be as short as a few minutes or as long as a few hours, depending on the type of application being used and the kind of external pressures from people waiting to use the PC next:

F3:   If I want to do something like this (a memo) ... I'll be on for doing something like this for 10 or 15 minutes you know to revise it but if I'm doing book keeping which is about once a week I'll be a couple of hours

M4:   Probably an hour or 45 minutes (for typing). You know the games were longer. They'd consist of like 2, 3 or 4 hours

However, in addition to the usual practice of sitting down at the PC to use it, people described numerous attempts to dip in and out of the PC for very short periods time. These usually took the form of multitasking PC use with making phone calls and coffee, chatting to others and even watching TV. This was easier in some houses than others where the PC was located close to other technology or people. For example, having the PC in the kitchen supported much more casual use than having it in an office:

F2:   I like Saturday morning or Sunday morning. If I come down and make a pot of coffee and I'm waiting for it to perc' I might play a fast game of bridge just cos I'm waiting for the coffee pot to perc through

13.3.2.5 Joint use of the PC was common.   We also heard reports of considerable joint use of the PC by more than one user. These were usually associated with playing/watching games and browsing the World Wide Web, but could also arise in cases of parents helping children with homework, or parents collaborating over creative projects, domestic letters and accounts. Particularly common were accounts of older children helping younger children in the household to use the computer, and of two or more people trying to solve a usage problem:

F6:   Yeah that's true, you wanted to look at butterflies in Mexico and we used the internet looking for that.

M4:   Then we've got the bowling and that was real fun 'cos you could have four players

I: OK play together

M4:   Yeah right so we would team off, you know, my three sons and myself would team off, and we would play bowling which that would be for a few hours too

M6:   Saturday or sometimes in the evenings the kids wanted to play a game or you know they like to have a turn playing with dad on the computer so then there's a little bit of

F6:   We take turns. I sit with either one or the other and take some time

M5:   They like to play together so they'll bring in an extra chair and they'll sit and play either interactive games or watching what the other one is doing

F5:   Because Briana is not really familiar with the operation

M5:   She's still learning

I: So Alicia coaches her

M10:   And also sometimes we're just trying to figure something out and we sit here and he's showing me or he'll say hey look at this and we'll come over its kinda fun

In all these cases, people felt that the current PC is not set up to allow easy access to more than one person at a time. [...]

13.3.2.6 Passive PC watching was also common. Because of the high levels of contention for the PC in many households, some people ended up literally queuing for their turn next to someone who was currently using the computer. Alternatively, because some PCs were in public rooms, non-users were sometimes drawn into conversation with users about what they are doing. Both situations led to a kind of passive PC watching behaviour which some families described as rewarding in its own right—for learning about other people's interests and pulling the family together:

M5: Sometimes they're watching me. Sometimes Ryan and Peter will come in if I'm working on a project whether its on the internet looking at something in particular they'll watch me, or if they're interested in what I'm doing with work or whatever, or sometimes they'll just be waiting for me to get off. Or they'll sit there, they'll discover something and they'll be like "Mom mom" you know, and I'll come in and I'll sit down and Ryan will sit down and we'll watch Peter or something with this great discovery that he's made, whether its a city he's building or something he's found on the internet. So we'll just watch. Its a way to interact and do something together which really goes beyond what you can do with the television

13.3.3 Location and Relocation of the Home PC

13.3.3.1 The PC was found in only a few specific room locations. Across the 11 families we visited, we found the PC in only three main rooms. Six families had located the PC in a dedicated office area, two had put it in a dining room or kitchen/dining area, while three had put it in the parent's master bedroom. Talking to the parents about these choices it became apparent that a dedicated office was usually the preferred location if the household had one. If it did not have one, then finding a suitable alternative location was difficult because it had to be quiet enough for people to be able to concentrate but accessible enough for everyone to use when they need to. The living room was rejected on the grounds of being too noisy, and children's bedrooms were rejected on the grounds of being too inaccessible to parents—especially after the children had gone to bed. This left the dining areas and parent's own bedrooms, usually as "second best" choices:

F5: Its in the bedroom, well considering our limitations here I think that's the best room

I: So if you could have a PC in every room now if space wasn't an issue?

F5: If space wasn't an issue?

I: Lets just say a PC in every room where would you most enjoy surfing the web

F5: In a study type room that I could that could just lock myself away sometimes

13.3.3.2 Current PC location did not strongly predict use. In general, we did NOT find that the location of the PC in the home constrained its use, and there was only a weak relationship between rooms and PC activities performed in those rooms (see figure 13.2). In general, there was a good spread of activities performed on the PC wherever it was located, as might be expected for a single access point in any one home. With multiple access points we believe this would change somewhat to

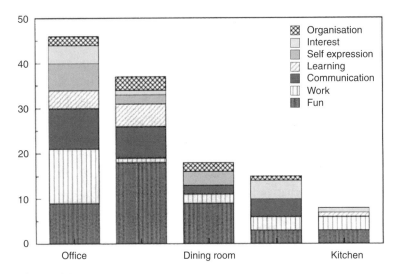

Figure 13.2

reflect a desire to vary what you do where and when in the home, as with other activities, and indeed to incorporate PC use *into* those other activities in a way which is not possible today (see below).

13.3.3.3 There is great demand for PC relocation. The pre-visit exercise form asked each member of the family to say explicitly where they would relocate the PC to perform their favourite applications. Figure 13.3 shows the resulting answers. Essentially, there was great demand for PC relocation. This differed between children and adults. Because the parents had usually chosen the current location of the PC to be convenient to them, most of the children wanted to move it to their bedroom for their convenience. However, in cases where the PC was in a public room such as a large kitchen, the parents expressed a wish to move it to a more personal space for them, such as an office. Once the essentials of privacy had been met, adults were also interested in relocating parts of their PC use to particular rooms for convenience and relaxation.

13.3.3.4 Children wanted to relocate the entire PC to their own private room. In general, the key new rooms in which people expressed a

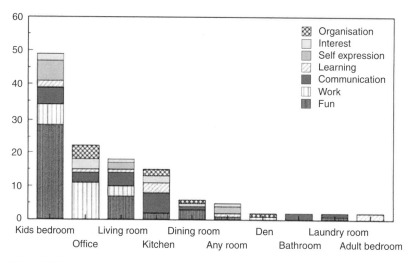

Figure 13.3

desire for the PC were the kid's bedroom, living room and kitchen. Of these, the kid's bedroom was by far the most popular. Almost all the children in the study registered this location next to each of their favourite applications; leading to the large number of votes shown in the first bar of figure 13.3. A typical conversation went as follows:

I: And where would you choose to do it in the house

D10b: In my room

I: All of those?

D10b: Yes

This pattern was only broken by children who did not have their own rooms as such because they shared them with brothers or sisters. In these cases the children would vote for alternative quiet corners of the house such as the laundry room or even, in one case, the bathroom:

I: OK and how about which room in the house would you like to do those?

D10c: At the end of the laundry room

I: Oh why?

D10c: Its so cool down there and quiet

I: Your room and how about the chat?

S4b: Lets see the bathroom

M4:   I knew he was going to say that

I: Why?

S4b: Because like its like I don't want no one bothering me because like they aggravating me

I: And your e-mail would you do that in the bathroom?

S4b: Yeah

I: OK

M4:   Half his life he spends in the bathroom

13.3.3.5   Adults wanted to relocate selective aspects of PC use for convenience and relaxation.   While most adults and children alike wanted to base the PC in a location they could call their own, several adults spoke of wanting additional access to the PC from other parts of the house. This was usually to improve the convenience of casual or intermittent access:

F11: It would be nice if I wanted to type something or review some budgets, rather than have to get up and go downstairs, which is all of thirty seconds to get there, just to flip on a remote control screen typewriter here (family room) and be able to access it

M11: I get tired of going downstairs and all of a sudden I think gee I'd better e-mail Lauren in Singapore, so I have to all the way downstairs, and basically I live on this floor because I'm doing the dishes

M11: Its just like people build and they put the washer dryer on the second floor so they don't have to go all the way down to the basement to put the clothes in one machine

13.3.3.6 There was some association between activities and locations. One element of convenience of access was the association between what people were already doing in a location and what related things they could do on the computer if it was "to hand." Figure 13.3 shows some loose associations people made between PC activities and locations. For example, people mentioned wanting to use games and internet services in the family room where they could be shared more easily, using scheduling, address book and communication applications in the kitchen where household planning was done, and using household accounting software in the dining room where bills got paid:

M5: The kids want to play in the bedroom, we want to play in the living room

I: Would there be a range of different types of things you'd use a computer in the dining room for?

M1: Um well although we don't have any program that would make use of book keeping or cheques, we have something where you can quicken or find the actual kind of thing

I: Domestic banking

M1: I kinda fits that usage in a room like this

I: Is this where you pay your bills and stuff like that out here on the table

M1:   Usually yes come out here and write the cheques

I: How about the kitchen could you see yourself—

M1:   Jeepers. um The first thing that would come to my mind I guess would be some use for keeping a list of recipes like a database type thing … Or telephone numbers instead of leafing through pieces of paper "Where's so and so's telephone number?"

M6:   Kaboodle has a couple of neat things, though it had something you would use in the kitchen. Like you could do your grocery list, you could put recipes in it, and then say which recipes you'd be cooking, and then you would have a grocery list things like that. You could make your daily schedule, your weekly schedule, your monthly schedule, you could put the kids chores on it, you could make cards, um you know sort of a drawing thing, and um it had just a little writing thing, and um it had games on it I loved it. I think I wore it out

13.3.3.7   Mood and privacy of location were key influencing factors. Throughout our conversations about location of the home PC two important factors emerged. One was the mood of a room in terms of its orientation to work or play and the other was the privacy of a room in terms of its orientation to personal or shared activities:

F11:   You'll see when you go downstairs (office) you're in a different mood you're not relaxed like you are up here (family room)

M4:   The typing I would do in my bedroom where its quiet and personal and I cannot be disturbed

M11:   I was just thinking that sometimes I'd like to run myself completely because here the phones are ringing, the kids are calling, you know you never have any real peace

Some rooms like the office had a distinctly private and work-oriented feel to them and were therefore most suitable for work and organization type uses. Other rooms like the living or family rooms were more public and playful in character and therefore suitable to shared uses relating to fun, interest and self-expression. In between these extremes were more ambiguous rooms like the kitchen and dining room which, though public and associated with relaxation, were also used for work related purposes like organization and communication. Probably the most ambiguous room in the house was the child's bedroom which was used for both private and shared activities relating to both work and play which may explain the attraction to children of relocating all PC activity there.

13.4   Summary and Discussion

13.4.1   Answers to Initial Research Questions

Returning to the research questions that motivated the study we can now provide some answers (see again section 13.1.4).

Regarding the current *use and contention* for the home PC we have found, like Venkatesh (1996), that the versatility of the PC-now offers something for everyone in active PC-owning households. This leads to a situation of high contention for PC time, especially in larger households and where adults and children cannot use the PC during the daytime. The consequence of this contention is that families evolve rules and patterns of shared PC use which give greatest access to those with the greatest need; where need is usually equated with the instrumental use of the PC to accomplish work-related or family organization-related tasks. Only after these needs have been met can family members begin to enjoy more recreational uses of the PC, involving fun, communication, personal interests and self-expression. This is despite the fact that these are the uses which people report deriving the most enjoyment from.

Many of the findings on the desired *location and functionality* of home computing facilities stem from this tension. For example, children ask unanimously for their own computer in their own room, rather than for sophisticated ways of performing their favourite applications in different locations around the house. This can be seen as a request for greater access and control over *what* they do on the computer and *when* they do it, since the current situation of shared PC use is naturally restrictive and closely regulated by their parents. From the child's point of view this is a much greater need than re-packaging the PC in simpler and easier to use forms, or providing multiple access points around the house. In contrast, adults who have chosen the current location of the home PC, are more interested in accessing their favourite applications from a variety of *additional* locations, especially in rooms which have a more public or recreational feel to them. In general, they want to do "serious" PC stuff in a private office area, and to perform more "casual" PC activities selectively in other parts of the house, such as the living room and kitchen.

The picture which emerges is one of families wanting to realize more of the recreational uses of the PC whilst protecting its value as a serious "work" tool. At the moment they are constrained from doing this by having to timeshare with each other for a single computing resource fixed in a single, office-oriented, location. Given the opportunity of concurrent access to computing resources around the home, children ask for a fixed dual-purpose (work/play) platform designed for their bedroom, while adults choose broadly to keep the main box where it is for office use, and to relocate their recreational PC activities to the more public rooms of the house.

13.4.2   Additional Discoveries

Two additional discoveries have emerged from the study and are worthy of future attention.

First, we have been surprised by the strength of feeling expressed by adults over *controlling their children's use of the PC*, and by the number of resulting restrictions on the children. Part of this concern derives from parents having to administer a fair system of PC sharing within the household and might diminish with improved PC access. However, another part derives from the very success of the PC in engaging young people in a range of time-consuming activities. Parents worry about the intrinsic value of some of these activities for their children's well being, but also about the overall periods of time children are spending on the computer in relation to time spent on other things. This concern is likely to increase rather than diminish with improved PC access. Indeed, the central shared PC can be seen as both an excuse and a mechanism today for parents to constrain their children's computer-based activities. With distributed access to the PC, or with more personal appliances for each member of the family, parents will struggle to keep track of what their children are doing with computers in the home, and will no longer be able to control this with something as simple as a chair. Kraut et al. (1998) pick up on the same point in their discussion of the negative side effects of internet use. They suggest that these might stem from the overall time taken away from existing family activities by internet use, and that one way of minimizing them is to cite the PC in a public room where others can sanction extended use.

Second, we have found that there is a strong latent desire to interact with the home PC in a variety of new ways which allow for *joint, brief, intermittent and casual encounters.* Home users are already trying to use the PC like a TV where they can walk-up and switch to specific applications instantly, sit back and watch the interaction of others, or get something going to monitor as a background activity. This is currently difficult and frustrating because the home PC is still designed essentially for use by an individual user sitting up at the monitor for extended periods of time. This finding resonates strongly with that of Mateas, Salvador, Scholtz and Sorensen (1996), who observed that families ordinarily organize their non-PC activities into many small blocks of time, the majority of which are spent in the presence of others.

13.4.3   Implications for the Domestic Computing Debate

The above levels of enthusiasm for and use of the home PC should not be too surprising in a sample of families selected to be active PC users. However, the number of such families is likely to have increased considerably since 1997 when the interviews were carried out, and their experience may be indicative of what lies further along the general trend towards "domestication" of the PC (e.g., Venkatesh 1996). In this context, we have observed several major forces operating in the home to preserve the home computer and prevent it from being broken up into separate devices.

First, the computer itself is highly valued by all members of the family for the broad functionality it provides. Norman's (1998) account of the home PC is only partially right, and is best seen as one-half of a modern love/hate relationship with the machine. On the positive side, people love being able to communicate more easily with family and friends, to play exciting games, to learn and make discoveries, to be creative and to save themselves time and money. On the negative side, we found more comments about access and control than about usability and reliability. If these issues can be addressed by better PC design and in-home networking then the status quo may be a much more satisfactory option than is usually assumed.

Second, children in particular like the computer and express a strong preference for having one in their bedroom, over and above having easier access to individual applications around the house. Furthermore, there is already an established process for at least partial satisfaction of this need in the PC upgrade process. When families get a new PC they tend to hand down the old one to the children; hence, the rise in multiple PC households. Ironically, this can be seen as a positive side effect of the "rampant featurism" that makes the main family PC obsolete at regular intervals. Note also that PC inheritance by children has the additional benefit of increasing parental access to the main PC, thereby suppressing one part of their need for further computer access around the house.

Beyond these forces, we have found that adult needs for additional computing in the home do not necessarily imply an attraction for single-function appliances. Their need for relocation is to deliver greater convenience and enjoyment from whole clusters of "recreational" applications. These did not map neatly onto a single technology such as "internet services" or onto single activities such as "home photography," "cooking" or "gardening" as figure 13.3 shows. Furthermore, gender differences between clusters further complicate the set of applications that any shared adult device would need to run. What seems to be required is a shared multifunctional device, *more* focused in function than a PC but *less* restricted in function than an application-based appliance.

Finally, our findings imply a strong need for in-home networking between any mix of PC and non-PC devices. Families related easily to questions about relocating PC functionality around the home, and consistently assumed that additional devices would run all their own applications, services and data. Furthermore, the concern of parents to exercise control over their children's use of the computer constitutes another reason to network so that access controls can be set centrally and children's activity monitored.

Otherwise, parents will be reluctant to allow at least their younger children access to additional devices. All this leads us to believe in the kind of PC-Appliance co-existence suggested by Miller and Baker (1998), at least for PC households like the ones in our study, where appliances can be networked to a main PC server which is itself a single home gateway to the internet.

13.4.4   New Requirements for a Better Home PC

At the same time as reinforcing the value of the home PC, our findings also suggest a number of ways of improving it.

The current home PC is being used intermittently by multiple family members with different interests and abilities, and often by more than one member at a time. An added complication is that parents express a strong desire to monitor and control their children's use of the PC and internet at various levels. We believe this implies that the home PC needs to be more explicitly designed as a *multi-user* rather than a single-user machine. It should behave more like a *Family Computer* (FC) than a *Personal Computer* (PC). This would mean that individual members of the family should be able to personalize the behaviour and appearance of the machine to their own taste, thereby reducing complexity and reflecting personality. This would bring more meaning and sentimentality into the ownership of computers, and move them onto a par with other kinds of objects in the home (see again Csikszentmihalyi & Rochberg-Halton 1981). At the same time it should be possible to quickly change between users and behaviours, or incorporate additional users into an ongoing interaction. Setting up different desktops within Windows and requiring users to log in and out of them is a step in this direction. However, we found that very few families used these tools, and believe that more elegant and radical methods of personalization are still required. In fact, the flexible morphing of one general-purpose machine into a number of restricted function virtual machines can itself be seen as an alternative approach to the problem of an overspecified PC.

Industrial design is another dimension of the home PC requiring improvement. As families begin to acquire more than one PC for their home, the second and subsequent machines are being sited in children's bedrooms and public areas such as the family room or kitchen. Less space is available in these rooms for standard boxes, and there is much more concern about external appearance and style, especially to visitors.

Smaller more stylish PCs are required here, as the success of the Apple iMac has shown. However, this could be taken further, by tailoring functionality and design to key members of the household such as children, or key rooms of the house such as the bedroom, kitchen or family room. This leads to the idea of a kind of personalization to locations as well as people in the home.

An extension of this design trend would be to further reduce the overall size of the PC so that it becomes *mobile*. If this could be done without significant increase in cost, the result would be highly attractive as a satisfaction of adult desires for more recreational computing around the house. Sacrificing functionality for cost might be acceptable here for families who already have a main PC, as long as the clusters of functionality on the second device matched adult expectations.

Finally, a real opportunity exists to *broaden the range of interaction styles* available on both conventional and novel home computing platforms. Since the CRT monitor and keyboard is already designed for sit-up use by an individual user at a desk, the need from our data is for more relaxed sit back use by individuals or groups. The use of remote control input devices and speech interfaces would be obvious enhancements to explore here, together with button, pen and other kinds of input on less conventional variants or companion devices.

13.5   Future Research

This study has focused on the question of redistributing the functionality of the PC and internet around the homes of PC-owning families. Within this framework we are aware that our sample of families is very small, and situated in a particular time and place; namely 1997 and Boston, Massachusetts. Already home PC and internet use has moved on in America, and even within America there are large variations in family behaviours and attitudes towards technology. Outside America the cross-cultural and technological differences are much larger and likely to dramatically affect the answers to questions about what computing is appropriate to particular rooms or people in the household. So the first priority for future research must be to validate or refute these findings with a broader population of families.

Beyond these scaling and cross-cultural considerations, two other future directions for user research on domestic computing would be to examine the attractiveness of different *forms* of computing devices at home, and to interview *non-PC*-owning families from an entirely different perspective.

In PC families, we have discovered needs for a children's bedroom "PC" and a more focused-function recreational device for adults. There are a variety of existing computing platforms that might support these needs, including all-in-one PCs, NetTVs, Screenphones, Wall Displays, Laptops, Handheld PDAs and Tablets. Two big factors in selecting between them is the extent of mobility and connectivity required. Are people happy to keep such home devices in one place, do they want to be able to transport them between locations occasionally, or do they want full portability both inside and outside the home? If these are second or third devices, do people want continuous or intermittant connection to the main PC, independent or shared connections to the internet? Three related factors are the kinds of functionality and interaction styles required, and whether or not family members are prepared to share the device.

It may turn out that the particular blend of all these factors required by children or adults in the home cannot be satisfied by any existing platform or in-home networking architecture. In this case, completely new devices with novel interfaces and different interaction paradigms will be needed. Whatever the outcome, we believe such innovation is best driven from a principled understanding of user needs than by technical trial and error.

In non-PC families the computing landscape is different. It is most likely to build up in alternative ways through TV or telephone-related devices, including games consoles, fax machines and mobile phones. Additional sources of computing include all manner of personal portable products such as organizers, cameras, walkmans and toys. New studies of these households are required to understand their computing needs and desires in the absence of a general purpose device, and their relationship to the variety of other technologies available.

Given the rapid incorporation of computing and internet functions into many of these alternative technologies, it will ultimately be irrelevant to think in terms of which family happens to have a PC in the house. However, for the time being, this study has shown PC-ownership to be an important factor in choosing additional computing for the home.

13.6   Conclusions

Addressing the future of domestic computing from the user's point of view has led to new insights on technology needs. We have found that in families who already own a computer, its replacement by focused-function appliances is unlikely in the short term. The immediate need is for a second computer in the children's room, and then for a more relaxing and recreational computing experience around the house. While both these needs entail some restriction in PC functionality, through parental controls and recreational interests, they continue to point to shared multifunctional devices rather than personal uni-functional ones. We also detected a strong underlying desire to share data, programs and internet connection between multiple devices in the home; suggesting the need for in-home networking to connect secondary devices to a central PC.

Acknowledgments

We gratefully acknowledge the internal sponsorship and support of HP Labs Bristol, Home Products Division and Vancouver Division for this study. We would also like to thank all the families who welcomed us so warmly into their homes, and all members of the Home PC Futures Team for extensive discussions on the findings. These include: Chris Pedersen, Nick Haddock, Tom Solyga, Cath Sheldon, Shirley Bunger, Dick Grote, Dave Reynolds, Roger Gimson, Phil Neaves, Royston Selman, Mark Bailey and Ian Dickinson.

References

Birnbaum, J. (1997). Toward pervasive information systems. *Personal Technologies*, 1, 11–12.

Csikszentmihalyi, M. & Rochberg-Halton, E. (1981). *The Meaning of Things: domestic Symbols and the Self*. Cambridge: Cambridge University Press.

Green, E. N., McCarthy, J. C. & Bernoff, J. (1996). Unlocking PC potential. *Forrester Report (People an Technology Series)*, 3.

Intel (1999). Emerging trends in home computing: the home network. ⟨www.intel.com/home/network⟩.

Kaldor, S., Card, D., Hwang, D. & Zinsmeister, W. (1997). *IDC's forecast of the worldwide information appliance marketplace, 1996–2001*. IDC Bulletin No. 15080 (Consumer Devices).

Kraut, R., Patterson, M., Lundmark, V., Kiesler, S., Mukhophadhyay, T. & Scherlis, W. (1998). Internet paradox: a social technology that reduces social involvement and psychological well-being? *American Psychologist*, 53, 1017–1031.

Kraut, R., Scherlis, W., Mukhopadhyay, T., Manning, J. & Kiesler, S. (1996). HomeNet: a field trial of residential internet services. *Proceedings of CHI'96*, pp. 284–291. New York: ACM SIG-CHI.

Mateas, M., Salvador, T., Scholtz, J. & Sorensen, D. (1996). Engineering ethnography in the home. *Companion Proceedings of CHI'96*, pp. 283–284. New York: ACM Press.

Morrisette, S., Bernoff, J., Walsh, E. O. & Sheppard, A. H. (1999). Net devices ascend. Forester Report, June 1999.

Miller, S. & Baker, V. (1998). *Building the home information infrastructure*. Dataquest Focus Report, No. PCIS-WW-FR-9802.

Norman, D. (1998). *The Invisible Computer*. Cambridge, MA: MIT Press.

O'Brien, J. & Rodden, T. (1997). Interactive systems in domestic environments. *Proceedings of the Conference on Designing Interactive Systems: Processes, Practices, Methods and Techniques*. 18–20 August, pp. 247–259, ACM.

Rhinelander, T. & Mines, C. (1998). The PC era winds down. *Forester Report (People and Technology series)*, 42.

Rhinelander, T., Bluestein, W. M., Vanboskirk, S., Vernier, B. & Gerber, S. (1997). Cheap PC thrills. *Forester Report (People and Technology Series)*, 4.

Shepperd, G. (1998). Internet appliances transform the TV and the telephone. Dataquest Market Analysis No. CSAM-WW-DP-9803.

Silverstone, R. (1991). *Beneath the bottom line: households and information and communication technologies in an age of the consumer*. PICT Policy Research Paper No. 17. Brunel University.

Silverstone, S. M. (1992). The meaning of domestic technologies: a personal construct analysis of familial gender relations. In R. Silverstone & E. Hirsch, Eds. *Consuming Technologies: Media Information in Domestic Spaces*, pp. 113–194. London: Routledge.

Staten, J. (1997). The evolution of the home PC: from personal computer to home information center. Dataquest Market Analysis No. PCIS-WW-DP-9708.

Venkatesh, A. (1996). Computers and other interactive technologies for the home. *Communications of the ACM*, 39, 47–54.

Venkatesh, A. (1999). *Project Noah preliminary results.* Personal communication.

Vitalari, N. P., Venkatesh, A. & Gronhaug, K. (1985). Computing in the home: shifts in the time allocation patterns of households. *Communications of the ACM*, 28, 512–522.

Weiner, A. (1997). Getting out of the box: future internet access trends. *Dataquest Perspective* No. IEST-WW-DP-9702.

Weiser, M. (1991). The computer for the 21st centuary. *Scientific American*, 265, 94–104.

Yankee Group (1997). The consumer internet appliance: a market in the making. *Consumer communications White Paper*, 14.

14

Women, Guilt, and Home Computers

Catherine Burke

Introduction

It is generally agreed that women are less likely to become involved with computers than men. The attempts to explain this phenomenon have focussed predominantly around the question of differences between the sexes in their approach, attitude towards, and cognitive ability with computers. For example, the theory that men have "focussed worlds" while women cover more than one activity at one time and have "diffuse worlds" has been offered to explain gender differences in this context.[1] Sadie Plant has posed an alternative viewpoint in suggesting that "the notion that IT (information technology) is all masculine is a convenient myth sustained by the present power structures"[2] (p. 229).

Different capacities for "autonomy" between the sexes have been discussed in relation to women's supposed reluctance to relate with a machine.[3] Often discussion relies on stereotypical notions of women's "natural" preferences and inclinations as measured in terms of the style, quantity, and purpose of communication online.[4] The suggestion that "women's talk centres on experience and feelings, men's on analysis and logic"[5] (p. 76), is obviously contentious and I would suggest that over-concentration on this area of concern might be counterproductive.

David Boud, in his piece "Moving Towards Autonomy,"[6] suggests that the context in which learning occurs is all important. The notion of freedom in learning is an interesting one in relation to the woman student who may be studying at home. Autonomy itself is problematic for

From *CyberPsychology and Behavior* 4, no. 5 (2001): 609–615. Reprinted with permission of the author and Mary Ann Liebert, Inc.

women whose time and space is so often constricted and limited. Boud's discussion of student development based on various studies in this area outline descriptions of the stages which an individual might pass through in engaging with learning. Differences among individuals are acknowledged; that students may take varying amounts of time and energy passing through these various stages. However, gender differences are unacknowledged. The added complexity of familial relationships is the primary context for many mature women learners, and one might construct a parallel series of positions outlining the nature of changes occurring through struggle both in the ways in which the student views her powers in relation to her own learning, and in relation to the space she occupies in the familial context. Moving toward autonomy is an essential part of the learning process, but one that is shaped and altered by gender relations and space for learning, not merely by institutional and pedagogic factors. Contemporary feminism has drawn attention to the diversity of women's experience:

Women is a hugely diverse and complex categorisation and we cannot speak about education and training opportunities for women as though all women were the same.[7] (p. 9)

However, it is generally acknowledged in the field of women's education that there are common obstacles affecting women regardless of the content or nature of their learning. These have been summarized as:

practical and material constraints related to a woman's domestic and personal situation; psychological constraints such as lack of confidence; structural and institutional constraints such as lack of suitable education and training courses; lack of finance, access to transport and child care; and women's feelings, expectations and attitudes, arising from their position in society.[7] (p. 37)

These factors are of central importance within any debate around increasing access, and there is a danger that consideration of computer-supported learning can become focussed to such an extent on the use of the technology that the sociocultural context is neglected.

A mild revolution has taken place in the public world of work in terms of the development of women's skills in using information technology, but this has been tempered by the fact that women are in the main precluded from positions of power and authority. In the private world of the home, computers have become commonplace and facilitate the leisure, learning, and employment pursuits of household members. But who is playing, who is working, and who is studying? Since most computer use is geared around play the distribution of free time within the family will have a bearing on access. In addition, there exist cultural and ideological understandings and discourses that underpin domestic power relations, which have to date not been researched or considered. Sherry Turkle has talked about the "holding power" of computers. This is the degree to which computers have "the ability to fascinate—to hold or command users' attention for long periods—to involve him or her personally."[8]

But arguably, this holding power is not neutral. This power is exerted differently on men and women according to the context in which it is created. Put simply, for men or boys, the computer will hold attention because the distraction of domestic responsibility is minimal. For women, and especially mothers, the computer will hold attention within the dialectic of family responsibility. Consequently, for women, time and space in relation to the computer in the home will be tempered and qualified, regardless of the nature of the pursuit.

In my experience of working with women adult learners in community education over the past 15 years, I have recognized how frequently women's educational pursuits have triggered tensions in familial relationships. This kind of experience has been documented by McGivney.[7] She recognizes that many women who stay at home to care for families experience restrictions on their social and spatial autonomy. McGivney quotes Stott and Pill, who report that

research on decision making within families in western societies has demonstrated that the balance of power usually resides with the husband. The ability to maintain authority and influence others within marriage depends on the resources which each partner brings to the relationship ... factors such as education, income and occupational status will increase a partner's autonomy and provide him or her with more leverage when engaging in effective decision making.[9] (p. 18)

When women pursue an interest or activity that does not relate directly to their domestic role, and effectively exposes and challenges unequal power relations within the family, they can often meet with strong, sometimes violent resistance from male partners. This has been researched in relation to women's activities outside of the home where male partners are said to take on a gate-keeping role.[10] How much more challenging to male partners might women's active pursuit of education and self-development via computer technology in the home be? Much computer competence develops from spending time playing around, poking about and seeing what happens. A mother sitting in front of a PC having fun, playing games for as long as it takes, and spending time not earning or formally learning will necessarily impact on the family environment differently than if the person was a father or a child.

An Investigation of Women's Access to Home Computers: Background to the Present Study

The experiences of mature men and women students have been compared in recent studies, which have found that student mothers often felt they had to reassure the family of the minimal repercussions their studies would have on family life in order to get approval.[11] Women had to manage feelings of guilt at not fulfilling the domestic role as well as before, while mature male students found it easier than women to opt out of parenting and other domestic responsibilities. Kirkup and Abbott[12] have examined differences between men's and women's access to a computer necessary for study in the home. Women students often perceived the computer as a family resource and their needs for study use were not a priority. Men were more likely to see the computer as theirs.

The cultural feminist commentator Leonie Rowan, who has examined the impact of learning technologies within a postmodernist framework, has suggested the importance of considering the "gendered local" in her appraisal of the challenges and opportunities arising through current changes in open and distance learning.[13] She explains that within the context of an increasingly wide and complex global framework, "The local ... is of interest, not because it provides a framework for thinking about what women 'really' do or are, but rather because it is a site with immediate impact upon the situation within which the construction of identity occurs"[13] (p. 124).

In examining in some detail the domestic as a space for the construction of identity, the massive increase in the numbers of households with at least one computer is of interest. Arguably, the location of the home computer is significant. Whether it is placed in the living room, bedroom, study, or garden shed, a decision has been made collectively or individually. The relative power of decision making in the household, related to earning power and ideological constructs as well as practical considerations, is revealed in the act of placing the computer.

Methodology

These issues formed the focus of a survey designed to elicit information detailing the experience of women in accessing computers in their own households. During the spring of 1999, an online questionnaire collected information in the form of quantitative and qualitative data. A total of 150 women contributed information for the survey. Most completed the questionnaire; some contributed lengthy personal histories, and an interest in having this area brought out into the public domain was characteristic of their responses. Participants were recruited via the Internet by means of academic discussion lists in the field of computer-supported learning and through a network of academics who teach women's studies or teach women students information technology (IT). It is acknowledged that the participants do not represent a scientific sample and were never intended to be so. Rather, the sample was to enable a pilot study to take place in order that the parameters of a larger study might begin to take shape.

Findings and Discussion

The participants, a self-selecting group of women from the U.K. (50%), the U.S.A. (28%), Australia (17%), and Canada and Asia (5%) are arguably a selection of individuals with access to networked computers at home or at work and might be thought of as a relatively privileged sample. It is acknowledged here that this is the case, but even more remarkable then is the fact that access limitations do currently feature in the lives of 25% of participants.

The majority, 112 women (75%), reported good levels of access to computers in their households. A large proportion of respondents (46%) were in full-time employment, many working as academics or in the computer industry. Of those women who reported feelings of guilt or restricted access (25%), by far the majority (83%) were living with children ranging from single infants through to four or five older children or teenagers. Out of this group, access to time and space and change in the distribution of household chores was considered to have the most bearing on increasing access. The survey findings illustrated that it indeed was not possible to generalize about women as a category. There were considerable differences revealed in terms of own attitude and awareness of the attitude of others toward use of computers. A larger sample would be needed to examine differences in relation to social and economic status, ethnicity, level of education, and occupation.

Ownership and Control

Control is usually associated with ownership. Many women who participated in the online survey were living in households with more than one computer. Often one was slower or older and competition for access related to the faster or networked machine. In a number of cases, women specified the fact of ownership as one aspect of control, as in "The computer is mine; I permit the children limited access" and "I bought the PC and I sort out everybody's else's problems." One case showed an interesting dilemma around ownership:

I used to live with my partner, who when I first met him was something of a Luddite. He then became very interested in computers (or should we say my computer). I found at times that it was difficult to get him off MY computer. Paradoxically, laptops whose location is nonspecific are nevertheless located and access delineated through notion of ownership. Thus, interestingly, the survey revealed a distinct gender association with use of laptops, as in "Laptop is mainly used for my husband's work" or "I have priority on desktop; partner has priority on laptop."

Space and Location

Location makes a statement about the expectations for use within the home. The number of computers and their relative and different functions, capabilities, and sophistications throw up new questions and assumptions about their utilization by the different members of a household.

Of the online participants in the survey, most shared access with others in a study or part of a living room or bedroom. Only 24 out of the total number (17%) had sole use of a study room. Explanations for choice of location were offered, including "We put the computer in the living room because we wanted the kids to be able to use within shouting distance of the kitchen, so's we wouldn't have to keep running up and downstairs to sort out problems." But use of living space posed problems: "When I am using the computer in the evening, specially to work or study, I get distracted by my partner watching the telly." Shared use of a computer as part of a bedroom and another in a separate study area in certain contexts is still limiting, while the predominant determinant is one of attitude as illustrated by another participant.

My partner is also in academia. He prioritises his work over mine every time even when I am working to a deadline. I work at college as much as I can although child care responsibilities mean I can't often work during the evening or weekends because my partner has the computer.

Home computers hold the potential for enhancing and expanding women's space within and beyond the household. Internet and e-mail communication provide opportunities to widen women's sphere of influence and broaden networks almost without limit. For single women, living with very young children, the networked home computer, if affordable, provides a means of escape and creative outlet during years of confinement.

Guilt

Feelings of guilt are often experienced by women who return to study as partners, wives, daughters, and mothers. The survey asked specifically if participants ever experienced feelings of guilt when spending time using the home computer. A further study, which might examine responses from men in households, would begin to illustrate any gender differences which exist in relation to guilt. However, the current survey certainly revealed that some women do experience guilt when using computers in the home.

Respondents were asked to indicate whether or not they "often" felt guilty about spending time at the computer. A minority (15 or 10%) recorded in the affirmative. One participant commented,

A woman can have a private study area; a computer of which she has sole access, but my own experience is that I always feel guilty: I should be spending time with my husband and son.

However, on closer examination, all but two of these women were mothers and perhaps even more significantly, a large proportion of the 15 had 2 or more children: 9 women who often felt guilty had more than 2 children living in their household; 5 of these had more than 3 children. It is clear that having school-age children in the household has an impact. As one respondent put it,

I can gain access easily during school hours but then I tend to spend too long and neglect other things; it's probably just as well I am not a person who feels she has to clean every day, being untidy does not bother me; however, sometimes things build up a little too much and I feel guilty.

Women who reported enjoying sole use of a computer within a room of their own (24 or 36%) could be considered to have the most privileged situation. One noted how her partner's anxiety interfered with her sense of privacy and reminded her of her responsibilities toward the relationship.

I have noticed that if I pop upstairs for a few minutes to check my private e-mail, a little voice floats up the stairs asking what I am doing. It is as though he is scared I will disappear all night and we will revert to hardly seeing each other again.

Tolerance of access is conditional on length of time spent and potential neglect of relationships and responsibilities. For many women, their computer skills had developed over an intense period of study which may have been accepted or tolerated by partners, but on the understanding that this was an aberration. Some women felt obliged to "pay back" this tolerance through restricting time spent and normalizing relations.

Through the last three years my husband has been very supportive even during the times where we have only seen each other for a few minutes each day. It has, however, been hard on him and now I feel I must restrict my time using the computer or I will be neglecting him.

In another context, it is the wider family that creates and sustains emotional barriers to access. However, for one respondent, the source of guilt was experienced differently:

Using the computer is low on my list of priorities. In contrast to the question above, I feel guilty at not spending more time at the computer.

For many women, the use of the internet has revealed to them new aspects of their own creativity. Private passions for creating, maintaining, and improving personal spaces on the Web take women away from their partners for long periods of time. Sometimes, this leads to feelings of guilt and distancing within familial relationships.

I feel that a large problem is my keen interest in IT. Being a large part of my degree and now my job means that using a computer for me is an end as well as a means. I enjoy actually using the things and finding out things about them rather than just using the applications to produce a letter or spreadsheet. I have my own Web site and although my husband is interested in the content he does not understand why I can spend hours producing and improving it.

The computer pulls and attracts and a partner can experience anxiety owing to the extent to which they are alienated from this new technological attraction in women's lives.

Although my husband understood why I was spending so much time in my room comments started to sneak into the conversation. Mainly he commented on how my cockatiel (who is a mummy's bird) had stopped coming out of her cage unless I was downstairs. I felt that this concern for my bird was a way of telling me that I was neglecting HIM.

Women build relationships with computers which are said to "blossom" and "flourish" and which have an intensity that can be threatening to other members of a household, particularly if they do not understand or share the attraction.

Male partners' attitude toward women's time spent accessing home computers varies considerably, but some participants in the survey wished to comment directly on the actions and attitudes of partners.

I feel that my time spent at the computer is grudgingly accepted ... I believe that men still see this machine as their own and there is deep resentment that a woman should be able to use it let alone understand it. I feel I am a threat to my partner's knowledge which is limited in some aspects ... secretly he is working on this, he has to get the upper hand.

However, conversely, the following statements indicates shifts of gender identification currently being formulated within the intimate spaces of households.

I get the feeling that because I am using the computer he views it as a domestic appliance along with the washing machine and the cooker—i.e., it is something women "know" and men don't need to.

Intensity of use is an important issue in relation to the use of home computers. Intensity is a subjective and relative term and for some women, the measure of that intensity is determined through a dynamic linked to intimate and familial obligations and responsibilities.

During this time I spend a huge amount of time in the "back" bedroom and turned it into "my" room—to the extent that my husband knocks on the door before entering. After 2 years of studying the ironing pile had grown to an incredible size and I had forgotten how to use the vacuum cleaner.

Inner Computer Time Scheduling

Accessing home computers, taking up space within the household (and indeed within the computer), and using time in pursuit of personal interest or education can be problematic. For women for whom access is not currently a problem, hurdles have been overcome or the problem is managed through a process of quiet unobtrusive manoeuvring. A process one participant named as "Inner Computer Time Scheduling" occurs. Decision making goes on internally.

I notice that when he expresses an interest in using the computer I automatically place his request above my own. Unfortunately, I don't seem to include the fact that he may be playing a game or surfing the Web rather than doing programming work as part of my inner computer time scheduling process.

It can seem that access is not an issue as many women and their partners do not formally sort out the distribution of time. But it could be argued that the "inner computer time scheduling" which occurs is carried out predominantly by women.

In general I don't have a problem with computer access. But I think that is largely because I self-regulate my time so as not to intrude on the rest of the family.

And perhaps the sense of guilt experienced by some women is an essential part of the inner computer time scheduling which prevents full occupancy of time and space—something experienced occasionally by some women such as this participant living with her child and no partner:

"There are times when I get wrapped up in my own world whilst using the computer, especially when I am using the Internet. I also forget to take a break and therefore lose track of time."

Freedom of access may be only partial or temporary, and therefore somewhat illusive.

I think that the idea of working any time any place bringing freedom may be something of a myth. I felt that when I was heavily involved in October and November my involvement in the family was a bit less than usual and this was problematic. I felt conscious all the time that I shouldn't be working at the computer.

Futures

In his discussion "Distance education in a post-industrial society," Otto Peters poses some interesting predictions.[14] In suggesting that the post-industrial era will bring about broad shifts in culture and values, he provides a scenario where a new type of man (sic) will emerge as the postmodern self. This person will have to face the future that what counts is no longer raw muscle power, or energy, but information. The changes in the economy of industrialized countries will have implications in the world of work both outside the home, where the service sector will become even more important, and inside the home, where leisure as a commodity will assume a greater significance. But unless changes in family structure and ideology correspond, the burden of domestic labor and consequent lack of leisure time will continue to rest with post-modern woman, and it is unlikely that the hedonistic tendencies of the new era will distract them from carrying this burden. For many women, as the survey has revealed, the breadwinner ideology of the modern industrialized era is becoming broken down and women no longer position themselves within the family according to social and cultural status or economic earning power. However, the survey has also revealed considerable tension in this important site of self-determination and change.

References

1. Bright, G. W. (1983). In: Bostock, S. J., Seifert, R., (eds) *Microcomputers in adult education*. London: Croom Helm, p. 65.

2. Plant, S. (1995). In: Spender, D. *Nattering on the Net: Women, power and cyberspace*. Melbourne: Spinifex, p. 229.

3. Gilligan, (1983). In: Bostock, S. J., Seifert, R. (eds.) Microcomputers in adult education. London: Croom Helm.

4. McConnell, D. (1994). *Implementing computer supported cooperative learning*. London: Kogan Page, pp. 75–76.

5. Hardy, G. & Hodgson, V. (1991). Gender and knowledge: An Exploration. Present at Women and Management Learning Conference.

6. Boud, D. (1988). Moving towards autonomy. In: Boud, D. (ed) *Developing student autonomy in learning*. London: Kogan, pp. 17–39.

7. McGivney, V. (1993). *Barriers to access, informal starting points and progression routes*. Leicester, U.K.: N.I.A.C.E., pp. 9, 17, 18, 37.

8. Turkle, S. (1984). *The second self: Computers and the human spirit*. London: Granada, p. 4.

9. Stott, N. & Pill, R. (1990). In *Barriers to access, informal starting points and program routes*. p. 18.

10. Wimbush, E. (ed) (1988). Relative freedoms: women and leisure. Milton Keynes: Open University Press.

11. French, S., & Richardson, H. (1999). Unpublished paper. *OK, I'll give it a go. Gender and the cyber classroom*. University of Salford, U.K.: I.T. Institute.

12. Kirkup, G., & Abbott, J. (1997). The gender gap: a gender analysis of the 1996 computing access survey. Milton Keynes: PLU.

13. Rowan, L. (1997). *Shifting borders: Globalisation, localisation and open and distance education*. Geelong, Victoria: Deakin University Press.

14. Peters (1993). In Keegan, D., (ed) *Theoretical principles of distance education*. London: Routledge.

15

"Nobody Lives Only in Cyberspace"[1]: Gendered Subjectivities and Domestic Use of the Internet

Lisa-Jane McGerty

"If I have no body, what is my gender? Is there a need for, or even an explanation for, gender in a place where our bodies are not?"[2]

Introduction

The Internet is much more than hardware and software. Using the Internet is a much more expansive act than at first it seems; like every human act it can be considered a social act as much as it is anything else. Theories abound suggesting that all technologies embody social relations (in many forms) as much as technical ones[3,4] and that the Internet is inevitably as entangled in the social arrangements of everyday life as we are.[5] Given the breadth of academic dialogue around these issues it is surprising then that the minutiae of daily life remain almost unexamined empirically for evidence of how information and communication technologies (ICTs) actually form part of our lives. What do we know of exactly why people (particularly women) go online, what they really do when they are "there" and most importantly, how this fits with their offline lives?

Researchers such as Kendall[1] and Markham[6] have begun to suggest that we currently know very little about these processes, and that this may stem from our tendency to consider Internet users as either online or offline, but rarely as both. Extending this, I would like to suggest that it

From *CyberPsychology and Behavior* 3, no. 5 (2000), 895–899. Reprinted with permission of the author and Mary Ann Liebert, Inc. The research from which this material is drawn has been generously supported by the University of Bradford.

is because theorists have tended to follow this "false dichotomy" of on/offline,[6] that we have failed to locate Internet users firmly within the context of their use and have singularly failed therefore to locate ICTs adequately within fundamental relations of gender, race and class. Further, I suggest that this separation of on and off line hampers our attempts to fully understand the gender dynamics of the Internet (specifically) at a time when the domestic environment in particular is becoming an increasingly important focal point for Internet use.

The Online/Offline Dichotomy

The tendency to consider Internet users as being either online or offline but not as simultaneously being both is rooted in the prominent notion of the Internet as a virtual space. Commentators have frequently emphasized the potential importance of the absence of physical bodies in cyberspace,[7,8] often suggesting that users project some kind of virtual self online. This virtual identity, it is often implied, can bear as much or as little relation to the "real" self as the user desires, in terms of gender, age, profession, disability, sexuality and even race. Much has been made of this in particular by cyberfeminists who highlight the liberatory potential of this freedom from the "meat" of the body and its visible and audible markers, by which we judge others and are judged ourselves.

It is only more recently that researchers have begun to suggest that Internet users may not, in fact, leave the "meat" behind when they are online. Sherry Turkle[9] in particular has interrogated in depth how online and "real" selves interact with each other and Annette Markham[6] has pointed to the futility of conceptualizing the experience of the online and offline in terms of "reality" and "virtuality," maintaining that although such a conceptualization allows us to integrate new technologies into conventional modes of thought, this is not how it is experienced by Internet users. And to quote Steve Jones on a similar point:

Not only is it important to be aware of and attuned to the diversity of on-line experience, it is important to recognize that on-line experience is at all times tethered in some fashion to off-line experience.[10]

Lori Kendall[1] has framed this debate most concisely by proposing that Internet use does not have the degree of independence from offline contexts that is often assumed. She suggests that while online participants do have greater choice in how to present themselves online than they do offline, "gendered, raced and classed identities continue to have salience in online interactions."[5] Her simple aphorism that "nobody lives only in cyberspace,"[1] which I have taken for the title of this article, sums up this view more than adequately. If relations of gender, race, and class have similar importance in online and offline contexts, then the online/offline realms can be seen to be less distinct than perhaps they first appear and pursuing this dichotomy in research seems fallacy indeed when we know so little empirically about the dynamics involved in gender relations, whether in cyberspace or in "real" space. Persisting with a polarized on/offline view does not help us to understand how structured gender relations might retain their efficacy in online contexts. What we really need to know is how the "real" and the "virtual" constitute each other with regard to gender, as the two realms are not distinct and theory should not pretend that they are by disregarding the fact that an individual can never be online without being offline too.

Of course, there is a feminist paradigm that views gender as performative and I would suggest that it is still possible to subscribe to this view while advocating the materially grounded approach to Internet research proposed here. Starting to unpack the on/offline dichotomy exposes an important and complex difficulty at the level of individual identity that further warns against falling into a dualistic on/offline view. This is because often inherent in the dichotomous approach is the problematic notion of the "virtual" self as eminently performative while the real self is something immutable and enduringly rooted within the wider context of structured relations of gender, race, and class. This is highly problematic not only because it implies that issues of gender, race, and class might have import only in real space and not in cyberspace but also because one can consider offline, so-called real identity, to be performative in the same way that online, so-called virtual identity, so clearly can be.

While agreeing with the proposition that gender, race, and class do have an impact in cyberspace, at the level of the individual one could validly maintain that these characteristics are tenuous performances both online and off. Feminist work has for many years argued the performative nature of gendered, raced and classed identities[11,12] and this applies equally to our "real" and our "virtual" selves. If the characteristics of our "real" selves and our "virtual" selves are both performances then the irrelevancy of the on/offline dichotomy is all the more apparent. Seeing these characteristics as performative constructs does not make their impact on individuals' lives any less real, and in fact adds additional credence to the view that the on/offline dichotomy is fallacy. If identity is tenuously constituted alike in both online and offline contexts then if we are to begin to fully understand gender processes at the level of the individual then we must investigate the online and the offline together, exploring how Internet users concurrently rationalise both. It is this kind of materially grounded analysis of the performance of gendered Internet use that will begin to illuminate the processes by which gender works in practice in people's everyday lives.

The Processes of Gender, Domestic Space, and Internet Use

I have begun to suggest here the reasons why pursuing a dichotomous on/offline approach to researching Internet phenomena does not aid much in understanding the gender dynamics of Internet use in the daily lived experience of users. What is urgently required is a greater understanding of how the gender (and other) processes of individuals' daily lives impact on their use of the Internet. Such research would go some way to rectifying the overconcentration in much academic (and other) writing on virtuality, on the separation of mind and body during Internet use, by focusing instead on how online "virtuality" and offline "reality" constitute each other. This research may well illustrate that recent predictions about the potentially liberating nature of online spaces, particularly for women, have indeed been premature.

That there are gender dynamics to Internet use seems highly likely, although this is currently an area that is grossly undertheorized. Past research has established that there are gender processes involved in the use of almost all technologies (including those not traditionally labeled as technological)[13-15] and there is no evidence to suggest that the Internet is any different in this respect to other technologies. Research has already indicated differences between men and women (and, importantly, between young boys and girls) in terms of online communication styles,[16] use of multiuser domains (MUDs),[9,17] attitudes to computing and the Internet more generally[18,19] and a variety of other gendered aspects of online spaces.

Research into Internet use in the domestic environment is, however, particularly scarce, and almost no work published to date examines the relatively mundane aspects of everyday domestic life in relation to the use individuals make of the Internet at home. The domestic market is fast becoming the major growth area for Internet usage, particularly here in the United Kindom where both government and the information and communications industries are currently prioritizing policies motivating citizens to take Internet technologies into their homes. It is not inconceivable that before long the majority of homes (in the Western world at least) will be capable of participating in cyberspace in whatever form it takes and this may well influence the traditional social construction of the home and the household as nontechnological.[20] Domestic spaces thus offer us a valuable context for exploring the interplay of gender dynamics with Internet use and without adequate detailed research into Internet use in the home I would argue we can not even begin to fully understand how men and women use and relate to this technology.

The important point with regard to domestic Internet use is that these new technologies are being integrated into existing household relations, and these relations we know to be highly gendered.[4,20,21] The evidence indicates that as the Internet becomes part of existing patterns of domestic time and space then it will be within these "domestic rituals and resistances that the battle for our information futures will be won or lost."[22] This scenario may well prove to be particularly pertinent in relation to women's use of these increasingly important Internet technologies because it is women who often choose to prioritize their role in sustaining family relationships at home at the expense of claiming time for themselves.[4] When the personal time that they sacrifice is time that could otherwise be spent online, and is being spent online by others, then the ground for inequalities will be reinforced.

As far back as 1996, Silverstone[22] was arguing for research into the "complex, diverse, perverse reality of the everyday worlds of those who live with media and information technologies" yet I would contend that this has not been achieved. Research into households and families of all types to discover how the Internet forms part of their lives remains largely elusive. Although we do know that there is a consistent relationship between ownership of ICTs and household income and class,[4] we do not yet know how domesticity functions when technologies as powerful as the Internet intrude into it. Although we do know that the screen has begun to replace the street as the focus of leisure,[4,23] we are not yet fully able to theorise how patterns of ICT use are related to gender and then to domestic leisure and work processes on the micro level.

I am suggesting here that addressing the impact on Internet use of the gender processes of households (and vice versa) is a worthwhile strategy for increasing understanding of the gender dynamics of this technology. Such research would illuminate the processes by which gendered subjectivities and technologies are achieved[14] and would explore the interplay of the two in the lived experience of domestic Internet users. The research would probe how gendered identities affect the perception and use of the Internet as these identities are negotiated with other aspects of identity (class, race, sexuality, age, education, [dis]ability, employment), and with the inevitable effects of these on disposable income, domestic arrangements and access to technology. Findings of such research could contribute to ongoing debates about what constitutes gender, home and leisure in contemporary Western society while also highlighting the necessity of including considerations of the gendered nature of ICT use in public and commercial policy decisions and in the provision of content and services online.

Conclusion

The startling omission in the body of work to date on the social impact of the Internet is not just empirical evidence of what the differences might be between women and men in terms of their use (or nonuse) of the Internet, but more importantly why those differences might exist. Just as specific patterns of gender relations constitute all technologies so this may be manifesting itself as day to day, and seemingly mundane, disparities between women and men in how, when and why they use the Internet. That is, disparities in the decision to go online, in the perception of the technology, in the type of online activity pursued, the frequency and length of time spent engaging in online activities, the motivations for those activities and, crucially, in the relationship of those activities with offline activities and identities. Every aspect of this will be gendered and the processes by which this is occurring are only likely to be successfully illuminated through the kind of research advocated here, that is by small scale, detailed, qualitative research into the minutiae of individuals' daily domestic lives. Such research recognises that users of both sexes, and of all skin colors, sexualities, abilities, classes, and ages interact with Internet technologies but that their experiences vary enormously, as does their level of inclusion or exclusion. It also recognises that the intrusion of these technologies into the home is having an impact on constructions of gender, while simultaneously constructions of gender are doubtless impacting on Internet use in those domestic spaces and elsewhere. Recognizing that online and offline experiences are materially one and the same, i.e., that they are just that—experiences—and pursuing a materially grounded analysis of technology use by situating Internet users firmly in the gendered context of their use, enables us to improve our understanding of how the gender dynamics of this technology work in practice in people's everyday lives. And only by improving understanding can we begin to reduce inequalities and thereby exclusion.

Acknowledgments

The author would like to thank Dr. Anne Scott for invaluable comments on previous drafts of this article.

References

1. Kendall, L. (1999). Reconceptualizing "Cyberspace": Methodological considerations for on-line research. In: Jones, S., (ed.) *Doing Internet research: Critical issues and methods for examining the Net.* Thousand Oaks: Sage, pp. 57–74.

2. McAdams, M. (1996). Gender without bodies. *CMC Magazine* 1996; 3. Online document: ⟨http://www.december.com/cmc/mag/1996/mcadams.html⟩.

3. Curry Jansen, S. (1989). Gender and the information society: A socially structured silence. *Journal of Communication*, 39: 196–215.

4. Green, E., & Adam, A. (1998). On-line leisure, gender, and ICTs in the home. *Information Communication and Society*, 1: 291–312.

5. Kendall, L. (1998). Meaning and identity in "Cyberspace": The performance of gender, class and race online. *Symbolic Interactions*, 21: 129–153.

6. Markham, A. (1998). *Life online: Researching real experiences in virtual space*. Walnut Creek: AltaMira Press.

7. McRae, S. (1995). Coming apart at the seams: Sex, text and the virtual body. In: Cherny, L., Weise, E. R., (eds.) *Wired women: gender and new realities in cyberspace*. Seattle: Seal Press, pp. 242–263.

8. Star, S. L. (1995). Introduction. In: Star, S. L., (ed.) *The cultures of computing*. Oxford: Blackwell, pp. 1–28.

9. Turkle, S. (1995). *Life on the screen*. New York: Simon & Schuster.

10. Jones, S. (1999). Preface. In: Jones, S., (ed.) *Doing Internet research: Critical issues and methods for examining the Net*. Thousand Oaks: Sage, pp. ix–xiv.

11. Wakeford, N. (1996). Sexualized bodies in cyberspace. In: Chernaik, W., Deegan, M., Gibson, A., eds. *Beyond the book: Theory, culture, and the politics of cyberspace*. Oxford: Office for Humanities Communication, Oxford University Computing Services, pp. 93–104.

12. Butler, J. (1990). *Gender trouble: Feminism and the subversion of identity*. New York: Routledge.

13. Rothschild, J. (1983). Technology, housework, and women's liberation: A theoretical analysis. In: Rothschild, J., (ed.) *Machina ex dea: Feminist perspectives on technology*. New York: Teachers College Press, pp. 79–93.

14. Cockburn, C. (1992). The circuit of technology. In: Silverstone, R., Hirsch, E., eds. *Consuming technologies: Media and information in domestic spaces*. London: Routledge, pp. 32–45.

15. Ormrod, S. (1995). Feminist sociology and methodology: Leaky black boxes in gender/technology relations. In: Grint, K., Gill, R., (eds.) *The gender-technology relation: Contemporary theory and research*. London: Taylor & Francis, pp. 31–47.

16. Herring, S. (1993). Gender and democracy in computer-mediated communication. *Journal of Communication*, 3: 1–17.

17. Kendall, L. (1998). "Are you male or female?": Gender performances on MUDs. In: O'Brien, J., Howard, J. A., (eds.) *Everyday inequalities: Critical inquiries*. Oxford: Blackwell, pp. 131–153.

18. Durndell, A., Glissov, P., & Siann, G. (1995). Gender and computing: persisting differences. *Educational Research* 37: 219–227.

19. Ford, N., Miller, D. (1996) Gender differences in Internet perceptions and use. *Aslib Proceedings*, 48: 183–192.

20. Cockburn, C. (1997). Domestic technologies: Cinderella and the engineers. *Women's Studies International Forum*, 20: 361–371.

21. Cockburn, C., & Furst Dilic, R., (eds.) (1994). *Bringing technology home: Gender and technology in a changing Europe.* Buckingham: Open University Press.

22. Silverstone, R. (1996). Future imperfect: Information and communication technologies in everyday life. In: Dutton, W., (ed.) *Information and communication technologies: Visions and realities.* New York: Oxford University Press, pp. 218–226.

23. Rojek, C. (1993). After popular culture: Hyperreality and leisure. *Leisure Studies*, 12: 277–289.

16

Internet Paradox Revisited

Robert Kraut, Sara Kiesler, Bonka Boneva, Jonathon Cummings,
Vicki Helgeson, and Anne Crawford

With the rapidly expanding reach of the Internet into everyday life, it is important to understand its social impact. One reason to expect significant social impact is the Internet's role in communication. From the early days of networked mainframe computers to the present, interpersonal communication has been the technology's most frequent use (Sproull & Kiesler, 1991). Over 90% of people who used the Internet during a typical day in 2000, sent or received e-mail (Pew Internet Report, 2000), far more than used any other online application or information source. Using email leads people to spend more time online and discourages them from dropping Internet service (Kraut, Mukhopadhyay, Szczypula, Kiesler, & Scherlis, 2000). Other Internet communication services are increasingly popular—instant messaging, chat rooms, multi-user games, auctions, and myriad groups comprising "virtual social capital" on the Internet (Putnam, 2000, p. 170).

If communication dominates Internet use for a majority of its users, there is good reason to expect that the Internet will have positive social impact. Communication, including contact with neighbors, friends, and family, and participation in social groups, improves people's level of social support, their probability of having fulfilling personal relationships, their sense of meaning in life, their self-esteem, their commitment to social norms and to their communities, and their psychological and physical well-being (e.g., Cohen & Wills, 1985; Diener, Sul, Lucas, & Smith, 1999; Thoits, 1983; Williams, Ware, & Donald, 1981).

From *Journal of Social Issues* 58 (2002): 49–74. Reprinted with permission from Blackwell Publishing Ltd.

Through its use for communication, the Internet could have important positive social effects on individuals (e.g., McKenna & Bargh, 2000; McKenna, Green, & Gleason, 2002), groups and organizations (e.g., Sproull & Kiesler, 1991), communities (e.g., Wellman, Quan, Witte, & Hampton, 2001; Borgida, Sullivan, Oxendine, Jackson, Riedel, & Gang, 2002), and society at large (e.g., Hiltz & Turoff, 1978). Because the Internet permits social contact across time, distance, and personal circumstances, it allows people to connect with distant as well as local family and friends, co-workers, business contacts, and with strangers who share similar interests. Broad social access could increase people's social involvement, as the telephone did in an early time (e.g., Fischer, 1992). It also could facilitate the formation of new relationships (Parks & Roberts, 1998), social identity and commitment among otherwise isolated persons (McKenna & Bargh, 1998), and participation in groups and organizations by distant or marginal members (Sproull & Kiesler, 1991).

Whether the Internet will have positive or negative social impact, however, may depend upon the quality of people's online relationships and upon what people give up to spend time online. Stronger social ties generally lead to better social outcomes than do weaker ties (e.g., Wellman & Wortley, 1990). Many writers have worried that the ease of Internet communication might encourage people to spend more time alone, talking online with strangers or forming superficial "drive by" relationships, at the expense of deeper discussion and companionship with friends and family (e.g., Putnam, 2000, p. 179). Further, even if people use the Internet to talk with close friends and family, these online discussions might displace higher quality face-to-face and telephone conversation (e.g., Cummings, Butler, & Kraut, 2002; Thompson & Nadler, 2002).

Research has not yet led to consensus on either the nature of social interaction online or its effects on social involvement and personal well-being. Some survey research indicates that online social relationships are weaker than off-line relationships (Parks & Roberts, 1998), that people who use email regard it as less valuable than other modes of communication for maintaining social relationships (Cummings et al., 2002; Kraut & Attewell, 1996), that people who use email heavily have weaker social relationships than those who do not (Riphagen & Kanfer, 1997) and that people who use the Internet heavily report spending less time communicating with their families (Cole, 2000). In contrast, other survey research shows that people who use the Internet heavily report more social support and more in-person visits with family and friends than those who use it less (Pew Internet Report, 2000). Because this research has been conducted with different samples in different years, it is difficult to identify central tendencies and changes in these tendencies with time. Further, the cross-sectional nature of the research makes it impossible to distinguish self-selection (in which socially engaged and disengaged people use the Internet differently) from causation (in which use of the Internet encourages or discourages social engagement).

A longitudinal study by Kraut, Patterson, Lundmark, Kiesler, Mukhopadhyay and Scherlis (1998) was one of the first to assess the causal direction of the relationship between Internet use and social involvement and psychological well-being. The HomeNet field trial followed 93 households in their first 12–18 months online. The authors had predicted that the Internet would increase users' social networks and the amount of social support to which they had access. The consequence should be that heavy Internet users would be less lonely, have better mental health, and be less harmed by the stressful life events they experienced (Cohen & Wills, 1985). The sample as a whole reported high well-being at the start of the study. Contrary to predictions, however, the association of Internet use with changes in the social and psychological variables showed that participants who used the Internet more heavily became less socially involved and more lonely than light users and reported an increase in depressive symptoms. These changes occurred even though participants' dominant use of the Internet was communication.

These findings were controversial. Some critics argued that because the research design did not include a control group without access to the Internet, external events or statistical regression could have been responsible for participants' declines in social involvement and psychological well-being (e.g., Gross, Juvonen, & Gable, 2002; Shapiro, 1999). However, these factors would have affected heavy and light Internet users similarly, so could not account for the differences in outcomes between them.

A more pertinent problem noted in the original HomeNet report is the unknown generalizability of the results over people and time. The participants in the original study were an opportunity sample of families in Pittsburgh. In 1995 and 1996, when they began the study, they initially had higher community involvement and more social ties than the population at large. In addition, they had little experience online, and few of their family and friends had Internet access. One possibility is that using the Internet disrupted this group's existing social relationships. Had the study begun with a more socially deprived sample or more recently, when more of the population was online, the group's use of the Internet for social interaction might have led to more positive effects. In addition, some critics questioned the particular measures of social involvement and well-being deployed in this study (e.g., Shapiro, 1999).

The present article addresses these issues of generalizability through a follow up of the original HomeNet sample and a new longitudinal study. The rationale for both studies is similar. If use of the Internet changes the amount and type of interpersonal communication people engage in and the connections they have to their friends, family, and communities, then it should also influence a variety of psychological outcomes, including their emotions, self-esteem, depressive symptoms and reactions to stressors being (e.g., Cohen & Wills, 1985; Diener, Sul, Lucas, & Smith, 1999; Thoits, 1983; Williams, Ware, & Donald, 1981). The follow-up study examined the longer-term impact of Internet use on those in the original HomeNet sample, providing a second look at a group for whom initial Internet use had poor effects. It retained the outcome measures collected in original HomeNet study.

The second study followed a new sample in the Pittsburgh area, from 1998 and 1999. It compared an explicit control-group of those who had recently purchased a television set with those who purchased a computer. It also examines the impact of the Internet on a broader variety of social and psychological outcome measures than did the original Home-Net study. The goal was not to make differentiated predictions for each measure, but to see if using the Internet had similar consequences across a variety of measures of social involvement and psychological well-being. The sample was sufficiently large to permit an analysis of the impact of individual differences in personality and social resources on Internet usage and outcomes. In particular, the research examines whether using the Internet had different consequences for people differing in extraversion and in social support. As discussed further in the introduction to Study 2, people differing in extraversion and social support are likely use the Internet in different ways. In addition, they are likely to have different social resources available in their off-line lives, which could change the benefits they might gain from social resources they acquire online.

Study 1:   Follow-up of the Original HomeNet Sample

The data are from 208 members of 93 Pittsburgh families, to whom we provided a computer and access to the Internet in 1995 or 1996. The families were recruited through four high school journalism programs and four community development organizations in 8 Pittsburgh neighborhoods. The sample was more demographically diverse than was typical of Internet users at the time. Details of the sampling and research protocol are described in Kraut et al. (1996).

  The analyses of social impact reported in Kraut et al. (1998) were drawn from Internet usage records and from surveys given just before participants began the study and again in May 1997. Server software recorded participants' use of the Internet—hours online, email volume, and Web sites visited per week. The surveys included four measures of social involvement (time spent in family communication, size of local social network, size of distant social network, and perceived social support [Cohen, Mermelstein, Kamarck, & Hoberman, 1984]), and three well-established measures of psychological well-being: the UCLA Loneliness Scale (Russell, Peplau, & Cutrona, 1980), the Daily Life Hassles Scale, a measure of daily-life stress (Kanner, Coyne, Schaefer, & Lazarus, 1981), and the Center for Epidemiological Studies' Depression Scale (Radloff, 1977). It included the demographic characteristics of age, gender, household income, and race as control variables, because there is evidence that these factors influence both the amount of Internet use and the social and psychological outcomes (e.g., Von Dras & Siegler, 1997; Magnus, Diener, Fujita, & Payot, 1993). We also included the personality trait of extraversion (Bendig, 1962) as a control variable, because extraversion is often associated with well-being (Diener, et al., 1999) and

Table 16.1
Descriptive Statistics for Variables in Studies 1 and 2

Variable	Study 1		
	Mean	Std	*n*
Adult[a]	.66	.48	208
Male[a]	.42	.50	208
White[a]	.72	.45	208
Income[b]	5.53	1.27	197
Education[c]			
Computer sample[a]			
Extraversion[g]	3.54	.77	204
Social support[g]	4.02	.57	206
Internet use[h]	.72	.76	206
Local circle (log)[d]	3.01	.81	206
Distant circle (log)[e]	3.01	1.15	206
Family communication (log)[f]	4.31	.78	193
Face-to-face communicaton[h]			
Phone communication[g]			
Closeness near friends[g]			
Closeness distant friends[g]			
Community involvment[g]			
Stay in Pittsburgh[g]			
Trust[g]			
Anomie[g]			
Stress[j]	.24	.17	208
Loneliness[g]	1.93	.68	204
Depression[i]	.65	.40	205
Negative affect[g]			
Positive affect[g]			
Time pressure[g]			
Self-esteem[g]			
Computer skill[g]			
U.S. knowledge[k]			
Local knowledge[k]			

Notes: All variables are coded so that higher numbers indicate more of the variable.
a. Dicotomous variable (0/1)
b. 6 categories, from under $10,000 to over $75,000
c. 6 categories, from less than 11th grade to graduate-level work
d. Truncated at 60 and logged
e. Truncated at 100 and logged

Study 2			
Alpha	Mean	Std	*n*
NA	.88	.32	446
NA	.47	.50	446
NA	.92	.27	438
NA	4.91	1.55	443
NA	4.06	1.23	446
NA	.72	.45	446
.80	3.22	.65	389
.81	3.80	.54	389
.86	.00	.78	406
NA	2.56	.79	375
NA	2.21	1.05	361
NA	4.10	1.63	389
.55	−.01	1.00	406
.83	4.69	1.15	387
NA	3.54	.76	434
NA	2.94	1.10	286
.70	2.83	.75	390
NA	3.69	1.38	388
.74	3.17	.83	391
.57	2.66	.63	391
.88	.22	.14	382
.75	2.10	.66	389
.88	.53	.47	389
.88	1.67	.64	390
.88	3.49	.72	388
.82	3.02	.76	390
.85	3.70	.62	389
.90	3.26	.93	389
.41	.71	.33	388
.34	.68	.26	388

f. Sum of minutes communicating with other household members, logged
g. 5-point Likert response scale, with endpoints 1 and 5, where 5 is highest score.
h. Hours per week using the Internet (logged) in Study 1; Mean of standardized variables in Study 2
i. 4-point Likert scales, with endpoint 0 and 3, where 3 is highest score.
j. Mean of dichotomous response scales (0/1)
k. Proportion correct on multiple choice questions

may also influence the way people use the Internet. However, the sample was too small to examine statistical interaction involving the extraversion measure. See table 16.1 for basic statistics and other information about these variables.

Kraut et al. (1998) used a regression analysis of the effect of hours of Internet use on social involvement and psychological well-being in 1997 (Time 2), controlling for scores on these outcome measures at the pretest (Time 1) and the demographic and personality control variables. The follow-up study re-examines the impact of use of the Internet by adding a third survey, administered in February 1998 (Time 3). For about half the participants, the final survey came nearly 3 years after they first used the Internet; for the other half, the final survey came nearly 2 years later.

Method

All longitudinal research faces the potential of participant attrition. Our research was especially vulnerable because we had not planned initially to follow the participants for more than one year. Many of the high school students in the original sample graduated and moved to college. Further, technology changed rapidly during this period, and some participants changed Internet providers, ending our ability to monitor their Internet use. Of the 335 people who qualified for participation in the original study, 261 returned a pretest survey at Time 1 (78%), 227 returned a survey at Time 2 (68%), and 154 returned a survey at Time 3 (46%). Because this research is fundamentally about changes in social and psychological outcomes, we limit analysis to 208 participants who completed a minimum of 2 out of 3 surveys.

We used a longitudinal panel design to examine the variables that influenced changes in social involvement and psychological well-being from Time 1 to Time 2, and from Time 2 to Time 3. The measure of Internet use is the average hours per week a participant spent online between any two surveys, according to automated usage records (i.e., weekly use between Times 1 and 2 and between Time 2 and 3). Because this variable was highly skewed, we used a log transformation. When assessing the impact of Internet use on social involvement and psychological well-being at one time, we statistically controlled for the prior level of social involvement and psychological well-being by including the lagged dependent variable as a control variable in the model. Since this analysis controls for participants' demographic characteristics and the lagged outcome, one can interpret the coefficients associated with Internet use as the effect of Internet use on changes in these outcomes (Cohen & Cohen, 1983, pp. 417–422). (For example, when examining the effect of Internet use on loneliness at Times 2 and 3, we included the lagged variable for loneliness at Times 1 and 2, respectively, in the model to control for the effects of prior loneliness on Internet use and on subsequent loneliness.

As demographic control variables, we included adult status (0 if age $<= 18$; 1 if age > 18), gender (0 = female; 1 = male), race (0 = nonwhite; 1 = white) and household income. Because teens use the Internet substantially more than adults and in different ways (Kraut et al., 1998), we included the generation × Internet use interaction to determine whether the Internet had similar effects on both generations. Because the personality trait of extraversion is likely to influence social involvement, Bendig's (1962) measure of extraversion was included as a control variable when predicting social support and the size of local and distant social circles. Because daily-life stress is a risk factor for psychological depression, we included Kanner, Coyne, Schaefer, & Lazarus's (1981) hassles scale as a control variable when predicting depressive symptoms.

The analyses were conducted using the xtreg procedure in Stata (StataCorp, 2001) for cross-sectional time series analyses with independent variables modeled as a fixed effects and participant modeled as a random effect. For the dependent measures listed in Table 16.2, the basic model is Dependent Variable$_{Tn}$ = Intercept + Demographic Characteristics$_{T1}$ + Time Period + Dependent Variable$_{Tn-1}$ + Control Variables$_{Tn}$ + Log Internet Hours$_{Tn-1}$ + Log Internet Hours$_{Tn-1}$ × Time Period + Log Internet Hours$_{Tn-1}$ × Generation$_{T1}$. In the model Dependent Variable$_{Tn}$ is a measure of social involvement or psychological well-being at the end of the first or second time period and Dependent Variable$_{Tn-1}$ represents the same measure administered in the previous time period. The analyses of particular interest are the main effects of Internet use on subsequent measures of social involvement and psychological well-being and the statistical interactions of Internet use and time period on these outcomes. The main effect of Internet use assesses the cumulative impact of Internet use over the two or three years of the study, and the interaction of Internet use with time period assesses whether this impact is the same in the early period (previously reported in Kraut et al., 1998) and in the more recent period.

Results

Table 16.2 shows results from the analyses. Kraut et al. (1998) showed Internet use was associated with declines in family communication, in the number of people in participants' local and distant social circles, and with increases in loneliness, depressive symptoms, and daily-life stress. Of these effects, Internet use over the longer period tested in the current analyses is associated only with increases in stress. Two significant Internet use × time period interactions suggest that Internet use had different effects early and late in respondents' use of the Internet. In particular, depressive symptoms significantly increased with Internet use during the first period but significantly declined with Internet use during the second period (for the interaction, $p < .05$). Loneliness significantly increased with Internet use during the first period but was not associated with Internet use during the second period (for the interaction, $p < .01$). Whether these differences in results over time reflect participants' learning how to use the Internet as they gain more experience or whether they reflect changes in the Internet itself over this period is a topic we will return to in the discussion.

Because teenagers use the Internet more than their parents and because teens and adults differed on several of the outcomes reported in table 16.2, we tested the differential effects of Internet use with age. There was only one marginally significant interaction: Adults' stress increased more than teens' stress with more Internet use ($p < .10$).

Study 2: A Longitudinal Study of Computer and Television Purchasers

Study 2 is a replication of the original HomeNet research design in a sample of households that had recently purchased new home technology—either a computer or TV. We added controls to the design and new measures. First, we attempted to manipulate Internet use to create a true experiment, with participants randomly assigned to condition. We recruited households who recently bought a new home computer and randomly offered half free Internet service; households in the control condition received an equivalent amount of money ($225) to participate. Unfortunately, this experimental procedure failed when, by the end of 12 months, 83% of the control households obtained Internet access on their own (versus 95% of the experimental households who took advantage of free Internet service). Because this attempt to conduct a true experiment failed, we combined the groups for analyses of the effects of using the Internet.

Another design change was to add a comparison group—recent purchasers of a new television set. Study 1 had only compared heavier and lighter users of the Internet, all of whom had access to it. The addition of a TV-purchaser comparison group in Study 2 (of whom just 29% obtained Internet access after 12 months) provides a sample that was unlikely to use the Internet and helps to rule out explanations of change based on external events. In analyses of the effects of Internet use, we included participants from the television purchaser group, but controlled for sample selection bias by creating a dummy variable indicating whether participants were recruited for buying a television or computer.

We also increased the number of dependent variables, to examine the generalizability of the effects of using the Internet across outcomes and measures. The original study contained four measures of personal social involvement and three of psychological well-being. We added measures of personal social involvement (spending time with family and friends, use of the telephone, perceived closeness to a random sample from of the respondents' social networks). In response to Putnam's (2000) concerns that the Internet might undercut community participation as well as interpersonal contact, we added measures of involvement with and attitudes toward, the community at large. To measure psychological well-being, we added scales measuring the experience of negative and positive affect, perceived time pressure, and self-esteem. Because the Internet is a source of information as well as social contact, we added knowledge tests and a scale to measure computing skill. To test whether the distance-minimizing properties of the Internet blur traditional distinctions between geographically close and distant regions, our measures

Table 16.2
Analysis of the Original HomeNet Study after 3 years ($n = 208$)

Independent variables	Social Support[a]			Local Social Circle[b]			Distant Social Circle[c]		
	beta	se	p	beta	se	p	beta	se	p
Intercept	0.00	0.04		3.76	3.37		8.85	6.74	
Adult (0 = teen; 1 = adult)	−0.13	0.09		−19.37	7.41	**	−49.02	14.70	***
Male (0 = female; 1 = male)	−0.16	0.08	*	−2.74	6.89		6.57	13.70	
Household income	0.00	0.00		−0.20	0.15		0.14	0.29	
White (0 = other; 1 = white)	0.15	0.09		−8.26	8.23		−6.74	16.38	
Time period[h]	0.10	0.06		0.97	2.52		−4.04	4.66	
Stress[e]									
Extraversion[i]	0.07	0.05		1.04	2.74		−5.28	5.21	
Lagged dependent variable	0.45	0.07	***	0.21	0.06	***	0.33	0.10	***
Internet hours (log)	0.02	0.05		−1.15	3.29		−5.14	6.27	
Internet* period	0.10	0.08		−0.37	3.06		2.88	5.62	
Internet* adult	0.06	0.09		5.44	6.08		7.52	11.57	
n	189			189			187		
R^2	.29			0.26			0.17		

Notes: $^+p < .10$, $^*p < .05$, $^{**}p < .01$, $^{***}p < .001$; variables were centered before analyses.
a. Cohen, et al., 1984
b. Number kept up with monthly, living in the Pittsburgh area
c. Number kept up with annually, living outside of the Pittsburgh area
d. Log of the minutes communicating per day
e. Kanner, et al., 1981
f. Radloff, 1977
g. Russell, et al., 1980

Family Communication (log)[d]			Stress[e]			Depression[f]			Loneliness[g]		
beta	se	p	beta	se	p	beta	se	p	beta	se	p
−0.03	0.05		0.01	0.01		−0.01	0.03		0.03	0.04	
0.34	0.11	**	0.00	0.02		−0.14	0.06	*	0.04	0.09	
−0.08	0.10		0.00	0.02		0.02	0.05		0.27	0.08	**
0.00	0.00		0.00	0.00	*	0.00	0.00		0.00	0.00	
0.11	0.13		0.04	0.02	+	−0.14	0.07	*	−0.22	0.10	*
−0.34	0.10	***	0.06	0.01	***	0.01	0.04		0.12	0.06	+
						0.61	0.17	***			
0.37	0.08	***	0.54	0.06	***	0.18	0.06	***	0.44	0.05	***
0.05	0.07		0.03	0.01	*	−0.01	0.03		0.00	0.05	
0.16	0.12		−0.01	0.02		−0.13	0.05	*	−0.21	0.08	**
−0.02	0.13		0.04	0.02	+	−0.08	0.06		−0.09	0.10	
177			195			187			186		
0.15			0.46			0.20			0.36		

h. Period 1 is 12–18 months, from 1995 or 1996 to 1997 and period 2 is from the first post-test in 1997 to the second post-test in 1998
i. Bendig, 1962
j. The dependent variable measured approximately 12–18 month previously

of social involvement and knowledge differentiated between these, for example, asking separately about local and distant social circles and about knowledge of the Pittsburgh region and broader areas.

Finally, we extended the HomeNet study conceptually by examining the differential effects of individual differences in extraversion and perceived social support on the effects of Internet use. Extraversion is the tendency to like people, to be outgoing, and to enjoy social interaction; it is a highly stable personality trait, predictive of social support, social integration, well-being, and positive life events (e.g., Von Dras & Siegler, 1997; Magnus, Diener, Fujita, & Payot, 1993). The perception of social support refers to feelings that others are available to provide comfort, esteem, assistance, and information or advice; perceived social support buffers the effects of stress (e.g., Cohen, 1988).

We offer two opposing models of the relationship between extraversion and social support and Internet use. A "rich get richer" model predicts that those who are highly sociable and have existing social support will get more social benefit from using the Internet. Highly sociable people may reach out to others on the Internet and be especially likely to use the Internet for communication. Those who already have social support can use the Internet to reinforce ties with those in their support networks. If so, these groups would gain more social involvement and well-being from using the Internet than those who are introverted or have limited networks. They can gain these benefits both by adding members to their social networks and by strengthening existing ties.

By contrast, a "social compensation" model predicts that those who are introverted or lack social support would profit most from using the Internet. People with fewer social resources could use the new communication opportunities online to form connections with people and obtain supportive communications and useful information otherwise missing locally (see McKenna & Bargh, 1998). At the same time, for those who already have satisfactory relationships, using the Internet might interfere with their real-world relationships, if they swap, strong real world ties for weaker ones online. Analogous to the finding that cancer patients with emotionally-supportive spouses can be harmed by participating in peer-discussion support groups (Helgeson, Cohen, Schulz, & Yasko, 2000), it is possible that people with strong local relationships might turn away from family and friends if they used the Internet for social interaction.

Method

Sample   We recruited participants through advertisements placed in local newspapers, soliciting people for a study of household technology who purchased a new computer or new television within the previous six months. We obtained agreement from all adults and children in the family above age 10 to complete surveys. Half of the computer purchaser households were randomly offered free Internet access to participate in the study; the other participants were offered payments to complete surveys. After the initial telephone contact, we mailed consent forms and pretest surveys with return envelopes. Unlike the procedures used in Study 1, we did not encourage Internet use or provide technology support.

Measures   We administered surveys three times during the study, in February 1998, 6 months later, and a year later, February 1999. Because we had automated measures of Internet usage only for the group randomly given Internet access, our main independent variable is an index of self-reported Internet use (e.g., "I use the World Wide Web very frequently"; "Time per day spent using e-mail"; "Frequency per month of using a computer at home." The full text of for unpublished measures is available at http://HomeNet.hcii.cs.cmu.edu/progress/research.html.) Within the group randomly given Internet access, the Pearson correlations between the self report index of Internet use and the automated count of the number of sessions logged into the Internet in the 8 weeks surrounding the questionnaires was moderate ($r(112) = .55$ at Time 2 and $r(104) = .42$ at Time 3). These correlations reflect moderate validity of the self-report measure, although they are far from perfect because there is error in both the self-reports and in the server data (e.g., the usage records do not include Internet use at work and include cases where one family member uses another's account).

   We used self-report measures to assess demographic characteristics of the participants, and measures from the original HomeNet study, including perceived social support (Cohen et al., 1984), size of local and distant social circles, and time talking with other family members. We used the same measure of extraversion (Bendig, 1962). We added new measures of anomie (Srole, 1956), trust in people (Rosenberg, 1957, revised from Survey Research Center, 1969), community involvement (adapted from Mowday and Speers's 1979 measure of organizational commitment; e.g., I spend a lot of time participating in community activities; I feel part of the community in Pittsburgh), and intentions to stay in the Pittsburgh area ("Even if I had a chance to move to another city, I would very much want to stay in the Pittsburgh area"). We also assessed respondents' relationships with specific family and friends by asking them "How close do you feel?" to five individuals living in the Pittsburgh area and five living outside of the area who were closest to them in age. Participants described closeness to each nominee 5-point Likert scales.

To assess well-being, we again used the CES-D to measure depressive symptoms (Radloff, 1977), the daily life stresses scale (Kanner, Coyne, Schaefer, & Lazarus, 1981), and the UCLA Loneliness Scale (Russell, Peplau, & Cutrona, 1980) from the original HomeNet study. We added measures of self-esteem (Heatherton & Polivy, 1991), positive and negative affect (Watson, Clark, & Tellegen, 1988), perceived time pressure (adapted from Kraut & Attewell, 1997) and physical health (subscale from the SF-36; Ware, Snow, Kosinski, & Gandek, 1993).

Finally, because the Internet is a source of information as well as communication, we added measures of knowledge. We included a self-report measure of skill using computers, expanded from the original HomeNet study (e.g., "I am very skilled at using computers"; "I don't know much about using computers", (R)). We also added a test of knowledge, including multiple choice items on national current events, Pittsburgh current events, and general knowledge from a high school equivalency test (Research & Education Association, 1996). The knowledge test contained different items at different time periods.

Analyses   Data come from 216 households. Of the 446 individuals who were eligible to be in the sample, 96% completed survey 1, 83% completed survey 2 and 83.2% completed survey 3. Analyses are based on

406 respondents (91% of the original sample) who completed at least two surveys. The analyses were similar to those for Study 1. We used Stata's xtreg procedure, with participant as a random effect, (StataCorp, 2001) to analyze the panel design. In the Study 2 models, social involvement, well-being, and knowledge outcomes at the second and third time period were regressed on self-reported Internet use during that period, controlling for demographic characteristics and the lagged dependent variables. The models control for whether the respondent came from the TV purchaser or computer purchaser sub-sample and whether the dependent variables were collected at the second or third time period. To test whether levels of extraversion and social support moderated the effects of using the Internet, we included the main effects for the Bendig (1962) measure of extraversion and Cohen et al.'s (1984) measure of social support and the interaction of these variables with Internet use. We included adult status, gender, race, education and household income as demographic controls. Because teenagers use the Internet quite differently from adults, we also included the interaction of generation with Internet use.

Results

Table 16.2 shows scale reliabilities and descriptive statistics for variables in the sample, averaged over the three time periods. A table of correlations is available at http://HomeNet.hcii.cs.cmu.edu/progress/research.html.

Effects on Interpersonal and Community Social Involvement   Models testing the effects of using the Internet on interpersonal communication and community involvement are shown in tables 16.3 and 16.4, respectively. The main effects of Internet use on these measures of social involvement were generally positive. As table 16.3 shows, participants who used the Internet more had larger increases in the sizes of their local social circle ($p < .01$) and distant social circle ($p < .01$) and their face-to-face interaction with friends and family increased ($p < .05$). As table 16.4 shows, they also reported becoming more involved in community activities ($p < .10$) and felt greater trust in people ($p < .05$). The only significant reversal to the positive trend is that those who used the

Table 16.3

Predicting Interpersonal Social Involvement as a Function of Use of the Internet over Time and Individual Difference Variables. Study 2

Independent variables	Social support[a]			Local social Circle (log)[b]			Distant Social Circle (log)[c]			Family Communication (log)[d]		
	beta	se	p	beta	se	p	beta	se	p	beta	se	p
Intercept	−0.01	0.02		−0.02	0.03		0.01	0.04		0.29	0.01	***
Adult (0 = teen; 1 = adult)	0.18	0.05	***	−0.04	0.10		0.31	0.12	*	0.00	0.03	
Male (0 = female; 1 = male)	−0.09	0.03	**	0.03	0.06		−0.08	0.07		−0.01	0.02	
Household income	0.15	0.06	*	0.37	0.12	**	0.28	0.15	+	−0.03	0.04	
White (0 = other; 1 = white)	0.02	0.01	*	−0.01	0.02		0.01	0.03		−0.01	0.01	
Education	0.01	0.01		0.00	0.03		0.06	0.03	+	0.00	0.01	
Computer sample (0 = no; 1 = yes)	0.02	0.04		0.12	0.07		0.07	0.09		−0.01	0.02	
Time period (0 = first 6 months; 1 = second six months)	0.01	0.02		−0.05	0.04		−0.12	0.05	*	0.00	0.01	
Lagged dependent variable	0.53	0.03	***	0.33	0.04	***	0.46	0.03	***	3.86	0.04	***
Extraversion[f]	0.15	0.03	***	0.09	0.05	*	0.09	0.06		0.02	0.01	
Social support[a]				0.17	0.05	***	0.13	0.07	+	0.04	0.02	*
Internet use[e]	−0.01	0.02		0.12	0.04	**	0.15	0.05	**	0.00	0.01	
Internet* extraversion	0.01	0.03		0.02	0.06		−0.05	0.07		−0.01	0.02	
Internet* support				0.01	0.07		0.02	0.09		0.05	0.02	**
Internet* adult	−0.11	0.06	+	−0.13	0.11		−0.02	0.15		−0.06	0.03	+
n	406			385			365			373		
R^2	.51			.42			.47			.95		

Notes: [+]$p < .10$, *$p < .05$, **$p < .01$, ***$p < .001$; variables were centered before analyses.
a. Cohen, et al., 1984
b. Number kept up with monthly, living in the Pittsburgh area
c. Number kept up with annually, living outside of the Pittsburgh area
d. Minutes communicating per day
e. See table 16.2
f. Bendig, 1962

Face-to-Face Communication[e]			Phone Communication[e]			Closeness to Local Friends[e]			Closeness to Distant Friends[e]		
beta	se	p	beta	se	p	beta	se	p	beta	se	p
0.02	0.03		−0.02	0.03		−0.01	0.06		−0.01	0.04	
−0.55	0.11	***	0.12	0.10		0.27	0.17		0.15	0.16	
−0.19	0.07	**	−0.30	0.07	***	−0.29	0.12	*	−0.02	0.09	
−0.11	0.13		−0.04	0.13		−0.41	0.25	+	−0.16	0.20	
−0.01	0.02		0.03	0.02		−0.09	0.04	*	0.01	0.03	
−0.04	0.03		−0.02	0.03		0.00	0.05		−0.01	0.04	
−0.22	0.08	**	−0.03	0.08		−0.10	0.13		−0.10	0.10	
0.03	0.05		0.08	0.04	+	0.00	0.00		−0.04	0.06	
0.28	0.03	***	0.50	0.03	***	−0.99	0.00	***	0.50	0.04	***
0.14	0.05	**	0.16	0.05	**	0.00	0.00		0.01	0.07	
0.28	0.07	***	0.11	0.06	+	0.00	0.00		0.30	0.08	***
0.09	0.04	*	0.05	0.04		0.00	0.00		0.07	0.06	
−0.02	0.07		0.10	0.06		0.00	0.00		0.01	0.08	
−0.11	0.08		−0.08	0.07		0.00	0.00		0.15	0.10	
0.30	0.13	*	0.04	0.12		0.00	0.00		0.35	0.18	*
406			391			351			285		
.31			.51			.16			.44		

Table 16.4
Predicting Community Social Involvement as a Function of Use of the Internet over Time and Individual Difference Variables. Study 2

Independent variables	Community Involvement[a]			Stay in Pittsburgh[b]		
	beta	se	p	beta	se	p
Intercept	0.00	0.02		−0.02	0.04	
Adult (0 = teen; 1 = adult)	0.11	0.07		−0.01	0.14	
Male (0 = female; 1 = male)	−0.09	0.04	*	0.11	0.08	
Household income	−0.10	0.09		0.47	0.18	**
White (0 = other; 1 = white)	−0.05	0.02	**	−0.06	0.03	*
Education	0.05	0.02	**	0.01	0.04	
Computer sample (0 = no; 1 = yes)	0.09	0.05	+	0.11	0.10	
Time period (0 = first 6 months; 1 = second six months)	0.01	0.04		−0.07	0.06	
Lagged dependent variable	0.51	0.03	***	0.55	0.03	***
Extraversion[f]	0.17	0.04	***	0.13	0.07	*
Social support[g]	0.17	0.04	***	0.19	0.08	*
Internet use[e]	0.05	0.03	+	−0.13	0.06	*
Internet* extraversion	0.10	0.05	*	0.09	0.09	
Internet* support	0.02	0.05		−0.08	0.10	
Internet* adult	−0.01	.09		0.10	0.17	
n	403			402		
R^2	.50			.49		

Notes: $+p < .10$, $*p < .05$, $**p < .01$, $***p < .001$; variables were centered before analyses.
a. See table 16.2
b. See table 16.2
c. Srole, 1956
d. Rosenberg, 1957
e. Bendig, 1962
f. Cohen, et al., 1984

Trust[c]			Anomie[d]		
beta	se	*p*	beta	se	*p*
−0.01	0.02		0.00	0.02	
0.30	0.08	***	−0.24	0.06	***
−0.01	0.05		0.07	0.04	*
0.22	0.10	*	−0.12	0.08	
−0.02	0.02		−0.03	0.01	+
0.04	0.02	+	−0.03	0.02	*
0.07	0.06		−0.07	0.05	
−0.01	0.04		0.04	0.03	
0.51	0.03	***	0.43	0.03	***
0.07	0.04	+	−0.06	0.03	+
0.21	0.05	***	−0.16	0.04	***
0.07	0.03	*	−0.01	0.03	
0.00	0.05		−0.01	0.04	
0.02	0.06		0.02	0.05	
−0.12	0.10		−0.04	0.08	
405			405		
.48			.47		

Internet more became less committed to living in the Pittsburgh area ($p < .05$).

The interaction with extraversion shows that the association of Internet use with changes in community involvement was positive for extraverts and negative for introverts. Figure 16.1a illustrates these effects. Holding constant respondents' prior community involvement, extraverts who used the Internet extensively reported more community involvement than those who rarely used it; on the other hand, introverts who used the Internet extensively reported less community involvement than those who rarely used it. Interactions of Internet use with social support show that Internet use was associated with larger increases in family communication for those who initially had more social support. Each of these interaction effects supports the "rich get richer" hypothesis.

Finally, interactions of age with Internet use suggest different positive effects for adults and teens. Teens, as compared with adults, increased their social support and family communication with more Internet use, whereas adults increased their face-to-face interaction with family and friends and their closeness to distant relatives and friends with more Internet use.

Effects on Psychological and Physical Well-being   Table 16.5 shows the effects of Internet use on psychological well-being. These results are mixed, showing that, overall, both stress and positive affect increased with Internet use. The several interactions of Internet use with extraversion indicate that Internet use was associated with better outcomes for extraverts and worse outcomes for introverts. In particular, extraverts who used the Internet more reported increased well-being, including decreased levels of loneliness, decreased negative affect, decreased time pressure, and increased self-esteem. In contrast, these same variables showed declines in well-being for introverts. Figure 16.1b illustrates these effects. Holding constant prior loneliness, extraverts who used the Internet extensively were less loneliness than those who rarely used it, while introverts who used the Internet extensively were more loneliness than those who rarely used it. There were no interactions with social support or with age, and no effects on measures of physical health (not shown in the table).

(a)

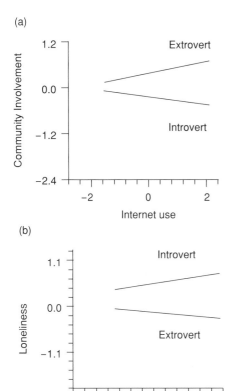

(b)

Figure 16.1

Interaction of internet use and extroversion on community involvement and loneliness.

Note: The plot shows the effects of community involvement and loneliness of Internet use for people differing in extroversion. The plots show predictions from the models reported in tables 16.4 and 16.5 as Internet use and extroversion move through the range appearing in the sample. Internet use varied from 1.12 standard deviations units less than the mean to 2.54 standard deviation units greater than the mean. The Introvert line represents the most introverted respondent, with an extroversion score −2.12 units below the mean, corresponding to a value of 1.10 on the original 5-point Bendig extroversion scale (1962). The Extrovert line represents the extroverted respondent, with a score of 1.78 units greater than the mean, corresponding to a 5 on the original scale.

Table 16.5
Predicting Psychological Well-Being as a Function of Use of the Internet over Time and Individual Difference Variables. Study 2

Independent variables	Stress[a]			Loneliness[b]			Depression[c]		
	beta	se	p	beta	se	p	beta	se	p
Intercept	0.00	0.00		0.00	0.02		0.01	0.01	
Adult (0 = teen; 1 = adult)	0.04	0.02	**	0.08	0.06		0.01	0.05	
Male (0 = female; 1 = male)	−0.01	0.01		−0.01	0.03		0.02	0.03	
Household income	0.00	0.02		−0.10	0.07		0.01	0.06	
White (0 = other; 1 = white)	0.00	0.00		−0.01	0.01		−0.02	0.01	+
Education	0.01	0.00		0.01	0.02		−0.01	0.01	
Computer sample (0 = no; 1 = yes)	−0.02	0.01	+	−0.06	0.04		−0.03	0.04	
Time period (0 = first 6 months; 1 = second six months)	0.01	0.01		−0.04	0.03		−0.04	0.02	+
Lagged dependent variable	0.54	0.03	***	0.27	0.03	***	0.48	0.03	***
Extraversion[f]	0.00	0.01		−0.21	0.03	***	0.03	0.02	
Social support[g]	−0.02	0.01	*	−0.59	0.04	***	−0.21	0.03	***
Internet use[e]	0.01	0.01	*	0.03	0.02		0.01	0.02	
Internet* extraversion	−0.01	0.01		−0.08	0.03	*	−0.05	0.03	
Internet* support	0.01	0.01		0.01	0.04		0.01	0.04	
Internet* adult	−0.02	0.02		−0.10	0.07		−0.09	0.06	
n	398			406			405		
R^2	.51			.66			.48		

Notes: $+p < .10$, $*p < .05$, $**p < .01$, $***p < .001$; variables were centered before analyses.
a. Kanner, Coyne, Schaefer, & Lazarus, 1981
b. Russell, Peplau, & Cutrona, 1980
c. Radloff, 1977
d. Watson, Clark, & Tellegen, 1988

Negative Affect[d]			Positive Affect[e]			Time Pressure[f]			Self-Esteem[g]		
beta	se	p	beta	se	p	beta	se	p	beta	se	p
0.01	0.02		0.00	0.02		0.00	0.02		−0.01	0.02	
−0.12	0.07	+	0.05	0.08		0.23	0.09	**	0.06	0.05	
−0.02	0.04		0.07	0.05		−0.18	0.05	***	0.11	0.03	***
−0.03	0.09		−0.15	0.09	+	0.12	0.10		−0.01	0.07	
−0.03	0.02	*	0.02	0.02		0.03	0.02		0.01	0.01	
0.03	0.02		0.00	0.02		−0.02	0.02		−0.01	0.01	
−0.08	0.05		−0.02	0.06		−0.03	0.06		0.07	0.04	+
−0.04	0.03		0.07	0.03	*	−0.06	0.04	+	0.03	0.02	
0.39	0.03	***	0.32	0.03	***	0.41	0.03	***	0.58	0.03	***
0.01	0.04		0.09	0.04	*	−0.15	0.04	***	0.05	0.03	+
−0.23	0.04	***	0.41	0.05	***	−0.12	0.05	*	0.28	0.03	***
0.04	0.03		0.14	0.03	***	0.05	0.03		0.02	0.02	
−0.12	0.04	**	0.04	0.05		−0.14	0.05	**	0.09	0.03	**
−0.08	0.05		−0.08	0.06		0.06	0.06		0.04	0.04	
−0.13	0.09		0.10	0.09		−0.06	0.10		0.01	0.07	
405			405			406			406		
.40			.43			.42			.63		

e. Watson, et al., 1988
f. See table 16.2
g. Heatherton & Polivy, 1991
h. Bendig, 1962
i. Cohen, et al., 1984

Effects on Skill and Knowledge   Table 16.6 shows the effects of Internet use on self-reported computer skill and multiple choices tests of world knowledge. Computer skill increased with more Internet use ($p < .001$); this increase was larger among those with more social support ($p < .05$). Knowledge of general knowledge (not shown in the table) and national current events did not change with Internet use. In contrast, those who used the Internet more became less knowledgeable about the local Pittsburgh area ($p < .05$).

Different Uses of the Internet   Because the way people choose to use the Internet could strongly influence its effects, we asked participants to report how often they used the Internet for various purposes. We conducted an exploratory factor analysis of these items to create four scales reflecting different uses of the Internet: (1) for communication with friends and family; (2) for acquiring information for school, work, news, and other instrumental purposes such as shopping; (3) for entertainment such as playing games, downloading music, and escape and (4) for meeting new people and socializing in chat rooms. These uses of the Internet were moderately interrelated (mean $r = .51$). Using the Internet for communication with family and friends ($r = .69$) and for information ($r = .62$) had the highest association with the Internet use index in reported in table 16.2, followed by use for entertainment ($r = .51$) and meeting new people ($r = .38$). Those with more extraversion were more likely than those with less extraversion to use the Internet to keep up with friends and family ($r = .10$, $p < .05$) and to meet new people online and frequent chat rooms ($r = .12$, $p < .05$), but the associations were weak. Those with stronger initial social support were less likely than those with weaker support to use the Internet to meet new people or use chat rooms online ($r = .11$, $p < .05$) or for entertainment ($r = −.14$, $p < .05$). Adults were more likely than teens to use the Internet for meeting new people ($r = −.41$, $p < .001$) and for entertainment ($r = −.29$, $p < .001$).

To test whether particular ways of using the Internet were more beneficial than others, we conducted a mediation analysis, by adding the measures of specific Internet use to the models in tables 16.3–16.6. These additions did not significantly affect the interactions between overall Internet use and extraversion or social support.

Discussion

The original HomeNet sample began using the Internet in 1995 or 1996. Our follow-up of participants remaining in the sample in 1998 showed that most of negative outcomes initially associated with use of the Internet dissipated, except for its association with increased stress. The statistical interactions of loneliness and depressive symptoms with time period suggest that use of the Internet led to negative outcomes during the first phase of the study and more positive outcomes later.

In Study 2, conducted from 1998 to 1999, more use of the Internet was associated with positive outcomes over a broad range of dependent variables measuring social involvement and psychological well-being—local and distant social circles, face-to-face communication, community involvement, trust in people, positive affect, and unsurprisingly, computer skill. On the other hand, heavier Internet use was again associated with increases in stress. In addition, it was associated with declines in local knowledge, and declines in the desire to live in the local area, suggesting lowered commitment to the local area.

Having more social resources amplified the benefits that people got from using the Internet on several dependent variables. Among extraverts, using the Internet was associated with increases in community involvement and self-esteem, and declines in loneliness, negative affect, and time pressure; it was associated with the reverse for introverts. Similarly, among people with more rather than less social support, using the Internet was associated with more family communication and greater increases in computer skill. Adults and teens gained somewhat different benefits from more Internet use, with adults more likely to increase their face-to-face interactions locally and their closeness to geographically distant relatives and friends.

What accounts for the differences between the original HomeNet research, showing generally negative consequences of using the Internet, and the follow-ups, showing generally positive consequences? Maturation of participants between the early and late phases of Study 1, differences in samples between Studies 1 and 2, and changes in the Internet itself are all potential explanations for this shift in results. Although our research cannot definitely choose among these explanations, a change in the nature of the Internet is the most parsimonious explanation.

Table 16.6
Predicting Knowledge as a Function of Use of the Internet over Time and Individual Difference Variables. Study 2

Independent variables	Computer Skill[a]		
	beta	se	p
Intercept	0.02	0.02	
Adult (0 = teen; 1 = adult)	−0.11	0.07	
Male (0 = female; 1 = male)	0.05	0.04	
Household income	−0.01	0.08	
White (0 = other; 1 = white)	−0.01	0.02	
Education	0.03	0.02	
Computer sample (0 = no; 1 = yes)	−0.10	0.05	+
Time period (0 = first 6 months; 1 = second six months)	0.04	0.03	
Lagged DV	0.65	0.03	***
Extraversion[f]	0.02	0.03	
Social support[g]	0.03	0.04	
Internet use[e]	0.31	0.03	***
Internet* extraversion	−0.02	0.04	
Internet* support	0.10	0.05	*
Internet* adult	0.14	0.08	
n	400		
R^2	.71		

Notes: $+p < .10$, $*p < .05$, $**p < .01$, $***p < .001$; variables were centered before analyses.
a. See table 16.2
b. Russell, Peplau, & Cutrona, 1980
c. Radloff, 1977
d. Watson, Clark, & Tellegen, 1988

U.S. Knowledge[a]			Local Knowledge[a]		
beta	se	p	beta	se	p
0.00	0.01		0.00	0.01	
0.18	0.04	***	0.13	0.03	***
0.04	0.02	+	0.04	0.02	*
0.09	0.04	*	0.06	' 0.04	
0.00	0.01		0.00	0.01	
0.03	0.01	***	0.03	0.01	***
0.01	0.03		0.02	0.02	
−0.04	0.02	*	−0.09	0.01	***
0.22	0.04	***	0.11	0.04	**
−0.02	0.02		0.00	0.01	
0.05	0.02	*	0.01	0.02	
0.00	0.01		−0.03	0.01	*
0.01	0.02		0.03	0.02	
0.00	0.03		0.00	0.02	
−0.01	0.04		0.01	0.04	
403			403		
.15			.15		

e. Watson, et al., 1988
f. See table 16.2
g. Heatherton & Polivy, 1991
h. Bendig, 1962
i. Cohen, et al., 1984

Maturation of participants and changes in the way they used the Internet could potentially account for the shift in results between the early and later phases of Study 1. For example, as the novelty of using the Internet wore off, participants may have jettisoned unrewarding Internet activities and adopted or increased their use of more personally rewarding ones. However, the first phase of Study 1, with its negative outcomes, occurred during participants' first year on line. Study 2, with its positive outcomes, also occurred during a one-year period, when most participants' were new to the Internet. Thus, while maturation could account for differences between the early and late phases of Study 1, it cannot account for differences between Studies 1 and 2.

Participants in Studies 1 and 2 came from separate opportunity samples. These sample differences make comparisons between the two studies problematic and could potentially account for differences in results between them. For example, the original sample included a larger proportion of teens and minorities. Although teenagers and adults gained somewhat different benefits from using the Internet, teenagers did not fare worse overall than adults from using the Internet. Similarly, supplementary analyses (not shown in tables 16.3–16.6) do not reveal racial differences in outcomes that can account for difference between the two studies. Participants in Study 1 had more social support and were more extraverted than those in Study 2, probably because they were recruited from families with organizational memberships. However, the statistical interactions with extraversion and social support reported in Study 2 would lead one to expect that outcomes would be more positive in Study 1 than Study 2, but this was not the case. While other, unmeasured differences in the samples might account for the differences in results between Study 1 and Study 2, differences in age, race, and social resources do not appear to do so.

The similarity of findings comparing the early and later phases of Study 1 and comparing Studies 1 and 2 suggest that changes in the Internet environment itself might be more important to understanding the observed effects than maturation or differences between samples. Simply put, the Internet may have become a more hospitable place over time. From 1995 to 1998, the number of Americans with access to the Internet at home more than quadrupled. As a result, many more of participants' close family and friends were likely to have obtained Internet access. Similarly, the services offered online changed over this period, increasing the ease with which people could communicate with their strong ties. For example, new communication services, such as American Online's instant messaging allow users to subscribe to a list of family and friends and be notified when members of their "buddy lists" came online. In addition to these changes to the online social environment, over the span of this research, the Internet provided a richer supply of information, with more news, health, financial, hobby, work, community, and consumer information available. It began to support financial and commercial transactions. Together, these changes could have promoted better integration of participants' online behavior with the rest of their lives.

Our finding from Study 2, that extraverts and those with more support benefited more from their Internet use, is consistent with this idea. That is, the Internet may be more beneficial to individuals to the extent they can leverage its opportunities to enhance their everyday social lives. Those who are already effective in using social resources in the world are likely to be well positioned to take advantage of a powerful new technology like the Internet.

Research shows that people can form strong social bonds online, and relationships formed online can carry over to the off-line world (e.g., Parks & Roberts, 1998; McKenna, Green, & Gleason, 2002). However, research also suggests that strong relationships developed online are comparatively rare. Most studies show that people use the Internet more to keep up with relationships formed off line than to form new ones (e.g., Kraut et al., 1996; Pew Internet and American Life Project, 2000). In addition, online relationships are weaker on average than those formed and maintained off-line (e.g., Cummings, Butler, & Kraut, 2002; Gross, Juvonen, & Gable, 2002). Gross, Juvonen, and Gable (this issue) also report that adolescents who feel socially anxious and/or lonely are especially likely to communicate online with people with whom they do not feel close. Thus one would expect that a diet filled with online relationships would be harmful to the social and psychology health of Internet users. Fortunately, people don't seem to use the Internet this way. Rather they mingle their online and offline worlds, using the Internet to keep up with people from their off-line lives and calling and visiting people they initially met online (Kraut et al., 1996; McKenna et al., 2002).

Although the impact of using the Internet across the two studies was generally positive, some negative outcomes remained. Across both studies, as people used the Internet more, they reported increases in daily life stress and hassles. Supplementary analyses did not identify any single stressor that occurred more frequently with Internet use, even though the cumulative increase with Internet use was statistically significant. One explanation is that the time spent online leaves less for many other activities, and that this time drought may lead to a generalized perception of stress.

In addition, to increases in stress, heavier Internet use was also associated with declining commitment to living in the local area and less knowledge about it. These declines may come about because the Internet makes available an abundance of online information (and social relationships) outside of the local area. Unlike regional newspapers, for example, the Internet makes news about distant cities as accessible as news about ones hometown.

The mechanisms by which the Internet has its impact on social involvement and psychological well-being remain unclear. One possibility is that the effects of using the Internet depend upon what people do online. For example, one might expect that interpersonal communication with friends and family would have more beneficial effects than using the Internet for downloading music, playing computer games or communicating with strangers. Another possibility is that all uses of the Internet are equivalent in this regard, and that the important factor is not how people use the Internet, but what they give up to spend time online. Thus the effects of using the Internet might be very different if it substituted for time spent watching TV or time spent conversing with close friends. No research to date, however, including our own, can distinguish between these two possibilities. Our own attempts to identify the unique effects of using the Internet for different functions were unsuccessful. Self-report measures may be too insensitive to track true differences in use.

Understanding the mechanisms for the Internet's impact is essential for informing private, commercial, and public policy decisions. People need better information to know whether to ration their time online or to decide which uses of the Internet are in their long-term interests. As experience with television suggests, enjoyable uses of new technology may be harmful in the long term (e.g., Huston et al., 1992; Putnam, 2000). Service providers need to decide what applications to offer online. School and libraries need to decide whether to offer email and chat capabilities along with their information-oriented services.

Experiment are a standard way to assess the impact of an intervention. While laboratory experiment can identify short-term consequences of Internet use, they are too limited to illuminate how the Internet affects slowly emerging phenomena, such as social relationships, community commitment, or psychological well-being (Rabby & Walther, 2002). Unfortunately, it is probably late in the evolution of the Internet to carry out true long-term experiments, at least in North America. We tried to conduct such an experiment on Internet use for Study 2, but in less than 12 months, 83% of the households in the control group had acquired Internet access on their own.

Nonetheless, researchers should continue to attempt to discern how using the Internet is affecting people's lives with the best designs possible. Although cross-sectional designs are most common in research on the impact of the Internet (e.g., Cole, 2000; Parks & Roberts, 1998; The Pew Internet & American Life Project, 2000; Riphagen & Kanfer, 1997), they cannot distinguish pre-existing differences among people who use the Internet from consequences of using it. Therefore, we believe longitudinal designs are essential to understanding the effects of Internet use and the differences in these effects as the Internet changes. In addition, we need better and more detailed descriptions of how people spend their time, both online and off, to relate these detailed descriptions to changes in important domains of life. The diary measures used by Gross, Juvonen, and Gable (2002) is a step in this direction.

Acknowledgments

Correspondence concernng this chapter should be addressed to Robert Kraut (e-mail: robert.kraut@andrew.cmu.edu). This research was funded by the National Science Foundation (Grants IRI-9408271 and 9900449). In addition, initial data collection was supported through grants from

Apple Computer Inc, AT&T Research, Bell Atlantic, Bellcore, CNET, Intel Corporation, Interval Research Corporation, Hewlett Packard Corporation, Lotus Development Corporation, the Markle Foundation, The NPD Group, Nippon Telegraph and Telephone Corporation (NTT), Panasonic Technologies, the U.S. Postal Service, and U.S. West Advanced Technologies. Tridas Mukhopadhyay and William Scherlis participated in designing and carrying out the original HomeNet studies.

References

Bendig, A. W. (1962). The Pittsburgh scales of social extraversion, introversion and emotionality. *The Journal of Psychology, 53,* 199–209.

Borgida, E., Sullivan, J. L., Oxendine, A., Jackson, M. S., Riedel, E., & Gangl, A. (2002). Civic culture meets the digital divide: The role of community electronic networks. *Journal of Social Issues, 58*(1), 125–141.

Cohen J., & Cohen, P. (1983). *Applied multiple regression/correlation analysis for the behavioral sciences.* Hillsdale, NJ: Lawrence Erlbaum Associates.

Cohen, S., & Wills, T. A. (1985). Stress, social support, and the buffering hypothesis. *Psychological Bulletin, 98,* 310–357.

Cohen, S., Mermelstein, R., Kamarck, T., & Hoberman, H. (1984). Measuring the functional components of social support. In I. G. Sarason & B. R. Sarason (Eds.), *Social support: Theory, research and applications* (pp. 73–94). The Hague, Holland: Martines Niijhoff.

Cole, J. (2000). Surveying the digital future: The UCLA Internet report. Downloaded from ⟨http://WWW.CCP.UCLA.EDU/pages/internet-report.asp⟩. November 17, 2000.

Cummings, J., Butler, B., & Kraut, R. (2002). The quality of online social relationships. *Communications of the ACM, 45*(7), 103–108.

Diener, E., Suh, E. M., Lucas, R. E., & Smith, H. (1999). Subjective well-being: Three decades of progress. *Psychological Bulletin, 125,* 276–302.

Fischer, C. S. (1992). *America calling.* Berkeley, CA: University of California Press.

Gross, E., Juvonen, J., & Gable, S. (2002). Internet use and well-being in adolescence. *Journal of Social Issues, 58*(1), 75–90.

Heatherton, T. F., & Polivy, J. (1991). Development and validation of a scale for measuring state self-esteem. *Journal of Personality and Social Psychology, 60,* 895–910.

Helgeson, V. S., Cohen, S., Schulz, R., & Yasko, J. (2000). Group support interventions for people with cancer: Who benefits from what? *Health Psychology, 19,* 107–114.

Hiltz, S. R., & Turoff, M. (1978). *Network nation: Human communication via computer.* Reading, MA: Addison Wesley.

Huston, A. C., Donnerstein, E., Fairchild, H., Feshbach, N. D., Katz, P. A., Murray, J. P., Rubinstein, E. A., Wilcox, B., & Zuckerman, D. (1992). *Big world, small screen: The role of television in American society.* Lincoln, NE: University of Nebraska Press.

Kanner, A. D., Coyne, J. C., Schaefer, C., & Lazarus, R. S. (1981). Comparisons of two modes of stress measurement: Daily hassles and uplifts versus major life events, *Journal of Behavioral Medicine, 4,* 1–39.

Kiesler, S., Lundmark, V., Zdaniuk, B., Kraut, R., Scherlis, W., & Mukhopadhyay, T. (2000). Troubles with the Internet: The dynamics of help at home. *Human-Computer Interaction, 15*(4), 223–352.

Kraut, R. E., & Attewell, P. (1997). Media use in a global corporation: Electronic mail and organizational knowledge (pp. 323–342). In S. Kiesler (Ed.) *Culture of the Internet.* Mahwah, NJ: Erlbaum.

Kraut, R., Mukhopadhyay, T., Szczypula, J., Kiesler, S., & Scherlis, B. (2000). Information and communication: Alternative uses of the Internet in households. *Information Systems Research, 10,* 287–303.

Kraut, R. E., Patterson, M., Lundmark, V., Kiesler, S., Mukhopadhyay, T., & Scherlis, W. (1998). Internet paradox: A social technology that reduces social involvement and psychological well-being? *American Psychologist, 53*(9), 1017–1032.

Kraut, R., Scherlis, W., Mukhopadhyay, T., Manning, J., & Kiesler, S. (1996). The HomeNet field trial of residential Internet services. *Communications of the ACM, 39,* 55–63.

Magnus, K., Diener, E., Fujita, F., & Payot, W. (1993). Extraversion and neuroticism as predictors of objective life events: A longitudinal analysis. *Journal of Personality & Social Psychology, 65,* 1046–1053.

McKenna, K. Y. A., & Bargh, J. A. (1998). Coming out in the age of the Internet: Identity "demarginalization" through virtual group participation. *Journal of Personality and Social Psychology, 75,* 681–694.

McKenna, K. Y. A., & Bargh, J. A. (2000). Plan 9 from cyberspace: The implications of the Internet for personality and social psychology. *Personality and Social Psychology Review, 4,* 57–75.

McKenna, K., Green, A., & Gleason, M. (2002). Relationship formation on the internet: What's the big attraction? *Journal of Social Issues, 58*(1), 9–31.

Parks, M., & Roberts, L. (1998). Making MOOsic: The development of personal relationships on line and a comparison to their off-line counterparts. *Journal of Social and Personal Relationships, 15,* 517–537.

The Pew Internet & American Life Project (2000, May 10). Tracking online life: How women use the Internet to cultivate relationships with family and friends. Downloaded May 15, 2000 at ⟨http://www.pewinternet.org/reports/⟩.

Putnam, R. D. (2000). *Bowling alone.* NY: Simon & Schuster.

Rabby, M., & Walther, J. B. (2002). Computer-mediated communication impacts on relationship formation and maintenance. In D. Canary & M. Dainton (Eds.), Maintaining relationships through communication: Relational, contextual, and cultural variations. Mahwah, NJ: Lawrence Erlbaum Associates.

Radloff, L. (1977). The CES-D Scale: A self-report depression scale for research in the general population, *Applied Psychological Measurement, 1,* 385–401.

Research & Education Association (1996). The best test preparation for the GED (General Educational Development). Piscataway, NJ: Author.

Riphagen, J., & Kanfer, A. (1997). How does e-mail affect our lives? Champaign–Urbana, Illinois: National Center for Supercomputing Applications. Retrieved October 15, 1999 from ⟨http://www.ncsa.uiuc.edu/edu/trg/e-mail/index.html⟩.

Rosenberg, M. (with the assistance of E. A. Suchman & R. K. Goldsen) (1957). *Occupations and values.* Glencoe, IL: Free Press.

Russell, D., Peplau, L., & Cutrona, C. (1980). The revised UCLA loneliness scale: Concurrent and discriminant validity evidence. *Journal of Personality and Social Psychology, 39*(3), 472–480.

Shapiro, J. S. (1999). Loneliness: Paradox or artifact? *The American Psychologist, 54*(9), 782–783.

Sproull, L., & Kiesler, S. (1991). *Connections: New ways of working in the networked organization.* Cambridge, MA: MIT Press.

Srole, L. (1956). Social integration and certain corollaries. *American Sociological Review, 21,* 709–716.

StataCorp (2001). Stata Statistical Software: Release 7.0. College Station, TX: Stata Corporation.

Survey Research Center (1969). *1964 election study.* Ann Arbor, Michigan: Inter-University Consortium for Political Research, University of Michigan.

Thoits, P. (1983). Multiple identities and psychological well-being: A reformulation and test of the social isolation hypothesis. *American Sociological Review, 48,* 174–187.

Thompson, L., & Nadler, J. (2002). Negotiating via information technology: Theory and application. *Journal of Social Issues, 58*(1), 109–124.

Von Dras, D. D., & Siegler, I. C. (1997). Stability in extraversion and aspects of social support at midlife. *Journal of Personality & Social Psychology, 72,* 233–241.

Ware, J. E., Snow, K. K., Kosinski, M., & Gandek, B. (1993). *Health Survey: Manual and interpretation guide.* Boston: Nimrod.

Watson, D., Clark, L. A., & Tellegen, A. (1988). Development and validation of brief measures of positive and negative affect: The PANAS scales. *Journal of Personality and Social Psychology, 54,* 1063–1070.

Wellman, B., Quan, A., Witte, J., & Hampton, K. (2001). Does the Internet Increase, Decrease or Supplement Social Capital? Social Networks, Participation, and Community Commitment. *American Behavioral Scientist, 45*(3), 436–455.

Wellman, B., & Wortley, S. (1990). Different strokes for different folks: Community ties and social support. *American Journal of Sociology, 96*(3), 558–588.

Williams, A. W., Ware, J. E., & Donald, C. A. (1981). A model of mental health, life events, and social supports applicable to general populations. *Journal of Health and Social Behavior, 22,* 324–333.

17

Virtuality and Its Discontents: Searching for Community in Cyberspace

Sherry Turkle

The anthropologist Ray Oldenberg has written about the "great good place"—the local bar, the bistro, the coffee shop—where members of a community can gather for easy company, conversation, and a sense of belonging. Oldenberg considers these places to be the heart of individual social integration and community vitality. Today we see a resurgence of coffee bars and bistros, but most of them do not serve, much less recreate, coherent communities and, as a result, the odor of nostalgia often seems as strong as the espresso.

Some people are trying to fill the gap with neighborhoods in cyberspace. Take Dred's Bar, for example, a watering hole on the MUD LambdaMOO. MUDs, which originally stood for "multi-user dungeons," are destinations on the Internet where players who have logged in from computers around the world join an on-line virtual community. Through typed commands, they can converse privately or in large groups, creating and playing characters and even earning and spending imaginary funds in the MUD's virtual economy.

In many MUDs, players help build the virtual world itself. Using a relatively simple programming language, they can make "rooms" in the MUD, where they can set the stage and define the rules. Dred's Bar is one such place. It is described as having a "castle decor" and a polished oak dance floor. Recently I (here represented by my character or persona "ST") visited Dred's Bar with Tony, a persona I had met on another

From *The American Prospect* 24 (Winter 1996): 50–57. Adapted from *Life on the Screen* by Sherry Turkle. Reprinted with the permission of Simon & Schuster. Copyright © 1995 by Sherry Turkle.

MUD. After passing the bouncer, Tony and I encountered a man asking for a $5 cover charge, and once we paid it our hands were stamped.

The crowd opens up momentarily to reveal one corner of the club. A couple is there, making out madly. Friendly place ...
You sit down at the table. The waitress sees you and indicates that she will be there in a minute.
[The waitress here is a bot—short for robot—that is, a computer program that presents itself as a personality.]
The waitress comes up to the table, "Can I get anyone anything from the bar?" she says as she puts down a few cocktail napkins.
Tony says, "When the waitress comes up, type order name of drink."
Abigail [a character at the bar] dries off a spot where some drink spilled on her dress.
The waitress nods to Tony and writes on her notepad.
[I type "order margarita," following Tony's directions.]
You order a margarita.
The waitress nods to ST and writes on her notepad.
Tony sprinkles some salt on the back of his hand.
Tony remembers he ordered a margarita, not tequila, and brushes the salt off.
You say, "I like salt on my margarita too."
The DJ makes a smooth transition from The Cure into a song by 10,000 Maniacs.
The drinks arrive. You say, "L'chaim."
Tony says, "Excuse me?"
After some explanations, Tony says, "Ah, ..." smiles, and introduces me to several of his friends. Tony and I take briefly to the dance floor to try out some MUD features that allow us to waltz and tango, then we go to a private booth to continue our conversation.

Main Street, Mall, and Virtual Café

What changes when we move from Oldenberg's great good places to something like Dred's Bar on LambdaMOO? To answer this question, it helps to consider an intermediate step—moving from a sidewalk café to a food court in a suburban shopping mall. Shopping malls try to recreate the Main Streets of yesteryear, but critical elements change in the process. Main Street, though commercial, is also a public place; the shopping mall is entirely planned to maximize purchasing. On Main Street you are a citizen; in the shopping mall, you are customer as citizen. Main Street had a certain disarray: the town drunk, the traveling snake-oil salesman. The mall is a more controlled space; there may be street theater, but it is planned—the appearance of serendipity is part of the simulation. If Dred's Bar seems plausible, it is because the mall and so much else in our culture, especially television, have made simulations so real.

On any given evening, nearly eighty million people in the United States are watching television. The average American household has a television turned on more than six hours a day, reducing eye contact and conversation. Computers and the virtual worlds they provide are adding another dimension of mediated experience. Perhaps computers feel so natural because of their similarity to watching TV, our dominant social experience for the past forty years.

The bar featured for a decade in the television series *Cheers* no doubt figures so prominently in the American imagination at least partly because most of us don't have a neighborhood place where "everybody knows your name." Instead, we identify with the place on the screen. Bars designed to look like the one on *Cheers* have sprung up all over the country, most poignantly in airports, our most anonymous of locales. Here, no one will know your name, but you can always buy a drink or a souvenir sweatshirt.

In the postwar atomization of American social life, the rise of middle-class suburbs created communities of neighbors who often remained strangers. Meanwhile, as the industrial and economic base of urban life declined, downtown social spaces such as the neighborhood theater or diner were replaced by malls and cinema complexes in the outlying suburbs. In the recent past, we left our communities to commute to these distant entertainments; increasingly, we want entertainment that commutes right into our homes. In both cases, the neighborhood is bypassed. We seem to be in the process of retreating further into our homes, shopping for merchandise in catalogues or on television channels or for companionship in personals ads.

Technological optimists think that computers will reverse some of this social atomization; they tout virtual experience and virtual community as ways for people to widen their horizons. But is it really sensible to suggest that the way to revitalize community is to sit alone in our rooms, typing at our networked computers and filling our lives with virtual friends?

The Loss of the Real

Which would you rather see—a Disney crocodile robot or a real crocodile? The Disney version rolls its eyes, moves from side to side, and disappears beneath the surface and rises again. It is designed to command our attention at all times. None of these qualities is necessarily visible at a zoo where real crocodiles seem to spend most of their time sleeping. And you may have neither the means nor the inclination to observe a real crocodile in the Nile or the River Gambia.

Compare a rafting trip down the Colorado River to an adolescent girl's use of an interactive CD-ROM to explore the same territory. A real rafting trip raises the prospect of physical danger. One may need to strain one's resources to survive, and there may be a rite of passage. This is unlikely to be the experience of an adolescent girl who picks up an interactive CD-ROM called "Adventures on the Colorado." A touch-sensitive screen allows her to explore the virtual Colorado and its shoreline. Clicking a mouse brings up pictures and descriptions of local flora and fauna. She can have all the maps and literary references she wants. All this might be fun, perhaps useful. But in its uniformity and lack of risk, it is hard to imagine its marking a transition to adulthood.

But why not have both—the virtual Colorado and the real one? Not every exploration need be a rite of passage. The virtual and the real may provide different things. Why make them compete? The difficulty is that virtuality tends to skew our experience of the real in several ways. First, it makes denatured and artificial experiences seem real—let's call it the Disneyland effect. After a brunch on Disneyland's Royal Street, a cappuccino at a restaurant chain called Bonjour Café at an Anaheim shopping mall may seem real by comparison. After playing a video game in which your opponent is a computer program, the social world of MUDs may seem real as well. At least real people play most of the parts and the play space is relatively open. One player compares the roles he was able to play on video games and on MUDs. "Nintendo has a good [game] where you can play four characters. But even though they are very cool," he says, "they are written up for you." They seem artificial. In contrast, on the MUDs, he says, "There is nothing written up." He says he feels free. MUDs are "for real" because you make them up yourself.

Another effect of simulation, which might be thought of as the artificial crocodile effect, is that the fake seems more compelling than the real. In *The Future Does Not Compute: Warnings from the Internet*, Stephen L. Talbott quotes educators who say that years of exciting nature programming have compromised wildlife experiences for children. The animals in the woods are unlikely to perform as dramatically as those captured on the camera. I have a clear memory of a Brownie Scout field trip to the Brooklyn Botanical Gardens where I asked an attendant if she could make the flowers open fast. For a long while, no one understood what I was talking about. Then they figured it out: I was hoping that the attendant could make the flowers behave as they did in the time-lapse photography I had seen in Disney films.

Third, virtual experience may be so compelling that we believe that within it we've achieved more than we have. Many of the people I have interviewed claim that virtual gender-swapping (pretending to be the opposite sex on the Internet) enables them to understand what it's like to be a person of the other gender, and I have no doubt that this is true, at least in part. But as I have listened to this boast, my mind has often travelled to my own experiences of living in a woman's body. These include worry about physical vulnerability, fears of unwanted pregnancy and infertility, fine-tuned decisions about how much make-up to wear to a job interview, and the difficulty of giving a professional seminar while doubled over with monthly cramps. Some knowledge is inherently experiential, dependent on physical sensations.

Pavel Curtis, the founder of LambdaMOO, begins his paper on its social dimensions with a quote from E. M. Forster: "The Machine did not transmit nuances of expression. It only gave a general idea of people—an idea that was good enough for all practical purposes." But what are practical purposes? And what about impractical purposes? To the question, "Why must virtuality and real life compete—why can't we have both?" the answer is of course that we will have both. The more important question is "How can we get the best of both?"

The Politics of Virtuality

When I began exploring the world of MUDs in 1992, the Internet was open to a limited group, chiefly academics and researchers in affiliated commercial enterprises. The MUDders were mostly middle-class college students. They chiefly spoke of using MUDs as places to play and escape, though some used MUDs to address personal difficulties. By late 1993, network access could easily be purchased commercially, and the number and diversity of people on the Internet had expanded dramatically. Conversations with MUDders began to touch on new themes. To some young people, "RL" (real life) was a place of economic insecurity where they had trouble finding meaningful work and holding on to middle-class status. Socially speaking, there was nowhere to go but down in RL, whereas MUDs offered a kind of virtual social mobility.

Josh is a 23-year-old college graduate who lives in a small studio apartment in Chicago. After six months of looking for a job in marketing, the field in which he recently received his college degree, Josh has had to settle for a job working on the computer system that maintains inventory records at a large discount store. He considers this a dead end. When a friend told him about MUDs, he gave them a try and within a week stepped into a new life.

Now, eight months later, Josh spends as much time on MUDs as he can. He belongs to a class of players who sometimes call themselves Internet Hobos. They solicit time on computer accounts the way panhandlers go after spare change. In contrast to his life in RL, Josh's life inside MUDs seems rich and filled with promise. It has friends, safety, and space. "I live in a terrible part of town. I see a rat hole of an apartment, I see a dead-end job, I see AIDS. Down here [in the MUD] I see friends, I have something to offer, I see safe sex." His programming on MUDs is far more intellectually challenging than his day job. Josh has worked on three MUDs, building large, elaborate living quarters in each, and has become a specialist at building virtual cafés in which "bots" serve as waiters and bartenders. Within MUDs, Josh serves as a programming consultant to many less experienced players and has even become something of an entrepreneur. He "rents" ready-built rooms to people who are not as skilled in programming as he is. He has been granted wizard privileges on various MUDs in exchange for building food service software. He dreams that such virtual commerce will someday lead to more—that someday, if MUDs become commercial enterprises, he could build them for a living. MUDs offer Josh a sense of participating in the American Dream.

MUDs play a similar role for Thomas, 24, whom I met after giving a public lecture in Washington, D.C. After graduating from college, Thomas entered a training program at a large department store. When he discovered that he didn't like retailing, he quit the program, thinking that he would look for better opportunities. But things did not go well for him; he couldn't find a job that would give him the middle-class life he knew as a child. Finally, he took a job as a bellhop in the hotel where I had just spoken. "MUDs got me back into the middle class," Thomas tells me. He has a group of MUD friends who write well, program, and read science fiction. "I'm interested in MUD politics. Can there be democracy in cyberspace? Should MUDs be ruled by wizards or should they be democracies? I majored in political science in college. These are important questions for the future. I talk about these things with my friends. On MUDs."

Thomas moves on to what has become an obvious conclusion. He says, "MUDs make me more what I really am. Off the MUD, I am not as much me." Tanya, also 24, a college graduate working as a nanny in rural Connecticut, expresses similar aspirations. She says of the MUD on which she has built Japanese-style rooms and a bot to offer her guests a kimono, slippers, and tea, "I feel like I have more stuff on the MUD than I have off it."

Josh, Thomas, and Tanya belong to a generation whose college years were marked by economic recession and a deadly sexually transmitted disease. They scramble for work; finances force them to live in neighborhoods they don't consider safe; they may end up back home living with parents. These young people are looking for a way back into the middle class. MUDs provide them with the sense of a middle-class peer group. So it is really not that surprising that it is in this virtual social life that they feel most like themselves.

Is the real self always the naturally occurring one? If a patient on the antidepressant medication Prozac tells his therapist he feels more like himself with the drug than without it, what does this do to our standard notions of a real self? Where does a medication end and a person begin? Where does real life end and a game begin? Is the real self always the one in the physical world? As more and more real business gets done in cyberspace, could the real self be the one who functions in that realm? Is the real Tanya the frustrated nanny or the energetic programmer on the

MUD? The stories of these MUDders point to a whole set of issues about the political and social dimension of virtual community. These young people feel they have no political voice, and they look to cyberspace to help them find one.

Sex and Violence in Cyberspace

If real business increasingly gets done in cyberspace, what kinds of rules will govern it? And how will those rules be made, democratically or by fiat? The issue arises starkly in connection with sex and violence.

Consider the first moments of a consensual sexual encounter between the characters Backslash and Targa. The player behind Backslash, Ronald, a mathematics graduate student in Memphis, types "emote fondles Targa's breast" and "say You are beautiful Targa" and Elizabeth, Targa's player, sees on her screen:

Backslash fondles Targa's breast. Backslash says, "You are beautiful Targa."
Elizabeth responds with "say Touch me again, and harder. Please. Now. That's
how I like it." Ronald's screen shows:
Targa says, "Touch me again, and harder. Please. Now. That's how I like it."

But consensual relationships are only one facet of virtual sex. Virtual rape can occur within a MUD if one player finds a way to control the actions of another player's character and can thus "force" that character to have sex. The coercion depends on being able to direct the actions and reactions of characters independent of the desire of their players. So if Ronald were such a culprit, he would be the only one typing, having gained control of Targa's character. In this case 15-year-old Elizabeth, who plays Targa, would sit at her computer, shocked to find herself or rather her "self" begging Backslash for more urgent caresses and ultimately violent intercourse.

Some might say that such incidents hardly deserve our concern, as they involve "only words," nothing more. But can a community that exists entirely in the realm of communication ignore sexual aggression that takes the form of words?

In March 1992, a character calling himself Mr. Bungle, "an oleaginous, Bisquick-faced clown dressed in cum-stained harlequin garb and girdled with a mistletoe-and-hemlock belt whose buckle bore the inscription 'KISS ME UNDER THIS, BITCH!'" appeared in the Lambda-MOO living room. Creating a phantom that masquerades as another player's character is a MUD programming trick often referred to as creating a voodoo doll. The "doll" is said to possess the character, so that the character must do whatever the doll does. Bungle used such a voodoo doll to force one and then another of the room's occupants to perform sexual acts on him. Bungle's first victim was legba, a character described as "a Haitian trickster spirit of indeterminate gender, brown-skinned and wearing an expensive pearl gray suit, top hat, and dark glasses." Even when ejected from the room, Bungle was able to continue his sexual assaults. He forced various players to have sex with each other and then forced legba to swallow his (or her?) own pubic hair and made a character called Starsinger attack herself sexually with a knife. Finally, Bungle was immobilized by a MOO wizard who "toaded" the perpetrator (erased the character from the system).

The next day, legba took the matter up on a widely read mailing list within LambdaMOO called *social-issues. Legba called both for "civility" and "virtual castration." A journalist chronicling this event, Julian Dibbell, contrasts the cyberspace description of the event with what was going on in real life. The woman who played the character of legba told Dibbell that she cried as she wrote those words, but he points out that her mingling of "murderous rage and eyeball-rolling annoyance was a curious amalgam." According to the conventions of virtual reality, legba and Starsinger were brutally raped, but here was the victim legba scolding Mr. Bungle only for a breach of "civility." According to the conventions of real life, the incident was confined to the realm of the symbolic—no one suffered any physical harm—but here was the player legba calling for Mr. Bungle's dismemberment. Dibbell writes: "Ludicrously excessive by RL's lights, woefully understated by VR's, the tone of legba's response made sense only in the buzzing, dissonant gap between them."

Virtual rape—of which the incident on LambdaMOO was only one example—raises the question of accountability for the actions of virtual personae who have only words at their command. Similar issues of accountability arise in the case of virtual murder. If your MUD character erases the computer database on which I have over many months built up a richly described character and goes on to announce to the community that my character is deceased, what exactly have you, the you that exists in real life, done? What if my virtual apartment is destroyed along with all its furniture, VCR, kitchen equipment, and stereo system? What if you kidnap my virtual dog—my beloved bot Rover, which I have trained to perform tricks on demand? What if you destroy him and leave his dismembered body in the MUD?

The problem of civil order has come up sharply in the history of a MUD called Habitat, initially built to run on Commodore 64 personal computers in the early 1980s. It had a short run in the United States before it was bought and transferred to Japan. Its designers, Chip Morningstar and F. Randall Farmer, have written about how its players struggled to establish the rights and responsibilities of virtual selves. On Habitat, players were originally allowed to have guns and other weapons. Morningstar and Farmer say that they "included these because we felt that players should be able to 'materially' affect each other in ways that went beyond simply talking, ways that required real moral choices to be made by the participants." Death in Habitat, however, had little in common with the RL variety. "When an Avatar is killed, he or she is teleported back home, head in hands (literally), pockets empty, and any object in hand at the time dropped on the ground at the scene of the crime." This was more like a setback in a game of Chutes and Ladders than real mortality, and for some players thievery and murder became the highlights of the game. For others, these activities were a violent intrusion on their peaceful world. An intense debate ensued.

Some players argued that guns should be eliminated, for in a virtual world a few lines of code can translate into an absolute gun ban. Others argued that what was dangerous in virtual reality was not violence but its trivialization. These individuals maintained that guns should be allowed, but their consequences should be made more serious; when you are killed, your character should cease to exist and not simply be sent home. Still others believed that since Habitat was just a game and playing assassin was part of the fun, there could be no harm in a little virtual violence.

As the debate continued, a player who was a Greek Orthodox priest in real life founded the first Habitat church, the "Order of the Holy Walnut," whose members pledged not to carry guns, steal, or engage in virtual violence of any kind. In the end, the game's designers divided the world into two parts. In town, violence was prohibited; in the wilds outside town, it was allowed. Eventually a democratic voting process was installed and a sheriff elected. Participants then took up discussion on the nature of Habitat laws and the proper balance between law and order and individual freedom. It was a remarkable situation. Participants in Habitat were seeing themselves as citizens; they were spending their leisure time debating pacifism, the nature of good government, and the relationship between representations and reality. In the nineteenth century, utopians built communities in which political thought could be lived out in practice. On the cusp of the twenty-first century, we are creating utopian communities in cyberspace.

Some participants have devoted much energy to the political life of MUDs. LambdaMOO, like Habitat, has undergone a major change in its form of governance. Instead of the MUD wizards (or system administrators) making policy decisions, there is a complex system of grassroots petitions and collective voting. Thomas, the bellhop I met in Washington, goes on at length about the political factions with which he must contend to "do politics" on LambdaMOO. Our conversation is taking place in fall 1994. His home state has an upcoming race for the U.S. Senate, hotly contested, ideologically charged, but he hasn't registered to vote and doesn't plan to. I bring up the Senate race. He shrugs it off: "I'm not voting. Doesn't make a difference. Politicians are liars."

Resistance or Escape?

In *Reading the Romance*, the literary scholar Janice Radaway argues that when women read romance novels they are not escaping but building realities less limited than their own. Romance reading becomes a form of resistance, a challenge to the stultifying categories of everyday life. If we take Radaway's perspective, we can look at MUDs and other kinds of virtual communities as places of resistance to the many forms of alienation and to the silences they impose.

But what resistance do virtual communities really offer? Two decades ago, computer hobbyists saw personal computers as a path to a new populism. They imagined how networks would allow citizens to band together to run decentralized schools and governments. Personal computers would create a more participatory political system, the hobbyists believed, because "people will get used to understanding things, to being in control of things, and they will demand more." The hobbyists I interviewed then were excited, enthusiastic, and satisfied with what they were doing with their machines. But I worried about the limits of this enthusiasm, and in my earlier book about personal computers, *The Second Self*, I wrote: "People will not change unresponsive political systems or intellectually deadening work environments by building machines that are responsive, fun, and intellectually challenging."

My misgivings today are similar. Instead of solving real problems—both personal and social—many of us appear to be choosing to invest ourselves in unreal places. Women and men tell me that the rooms and mazes on MUDs are safer than city streets, virtual sex is safer than sex anywhere, MUD friendships are more intense than real ones, and when things don't work out you can always leave.

To be sure, MUDs afford an outlet for some people to work through personal issues in a productive way; virtual environments provide a moratorium from RL that can be turned to constructive purpose, and not only for adolescents. One can also respect the sense in which political activities in a MUD demonstrate resistance to what is unsatisfying about political life more generally. And yet, it is sobering that the personal computer revolution, once conceptualized as a tool to rebuild community, now tends to concentrate on building community inside a machine.

If the politics of virtuality means democracy on-line and apathy off-line, there is reason for concern. There is also reason for concern when access to the new technology breaks down along traditional class lines. Although some inner-city communities have used computer-mediated communication as a tool for real community building, the overall trend seems to be the creation of an information elite.

Virtual environments are valuable as places where we can acknowledge our inner diversity. But we still want an authentic experience of self. One's fear is, of course, that in the culture of simulation, a word like authenticity can no longer apply. So even as we try to make the most of virtual environments, a haunting question remains. For me, that question is raised every time I use the MUD command for taking an action. The command is "emote." If I type "emote waves" while at Dred's café on LambdaMOO, the screens of all players in the MUD room will flash "ST waves." If I type "emote feels a complicated mixture of desire and expectation," all screens will flash "ST feels a complicated mixture of desire and expectation." But what exactly do I feel? Or, what exactly do *I* feel? When we get our MUD persona to "emote" something and observe the effect, do we gain a better understanding of our real emotions, which can't be switched on and off so easily, and which we may not even be able to describe? Or is the emote command and all that it stands for a reflection of what Fredric Jameson has called the flattening of affect in postmodern life?

The overheated language that surrounds current discussion of computer-mediated communications falls within a long tradition of American technological optimism. The optimists today tend to represent urban decay and class polarization as out-of-date formulations of a problem that could be solved with the right technology—for example, technology that could enable every schoolchild to experience "being digital." Are our streets dangerous? Not to worry: The community will be "wired" so children can attend school without having to walk there! This way of thinking about cyberspace substitutes life on the screen for life in our bodies and physical communities.

But there is another way of thinking, one that stresses making the virtual and the real more permeable to each other. We don't have to reject life on the screen, but we don't have to treat it as an alternative life either. Virtual personae can be a resource for self-reflection and self-transformation. Having literally written our on-line worlds into existence, we can use the communities we build inside our machines to improve the ones outside of them. Like the anthropologist returning home from a foreign culture, the voyager in virtuality can return to the real world better able to understand what about it is arbitrary and can be changed.

IV

The Wired Homestead and Civic Life

We as individuals are linked to society through our relationships with other individuals and our membership in collectivities. Family and local community are among the primary contexts in which social relations form and grow. We learn to build trust and to engage in transactions of friendship, mutual support, and aid. These networks of trust and norms of reciprocity—what Robert Putnam and others refer to as the features of "social capital"—strengthen our capacity to work together effectively and to solve collective problems, whether at the household and community level or more globally. All aspects of social relations and civic life involve human communication, whether face-to-face or mediated by technology. The internet, like other networked communication tools such as the telephone, facilitates communication and information exchange. Does it also diminish the kinds of face-to-face interactions that may be essential to building social capital? How does internet use affect the link between families and their local communities?

The essays and articles in this section address the question whether family members' increasing reliance on home-based technology can help or hinder the development of neighborhood and community, as well as national civic life. To what extent and under what circumstances do people use household media predominantly to bypass their local community? Does household use of the internet facilitate involvement in non-local civic life? Are families less involved in their neighborhoods and local communities as a result of increased household internet use?

In the past 100 years, Americans have become less dependent on local leadership and fellow residents due to increases in industrialization, urbanization, literacy, mass media, political stability, and social mobility.

Jorge Reina Schement in his chapter on the relationship between home, community, and media argues that the lack of genuine interdependence erodes the essence of the feeling of community. In his review of patterns of household media adoption in the context of historical socioeconomic change, he sees two major trends affecting the evolution of American communities: increasingly thinner local social networks and a downward trend in household size. Concurrently, Americans have been using more information media in their homes. In the case of internet use, he argues, local reciprocity is replaced with feelings of belonging to online "virtual" communities.

How enduring is the feeling of belonging to a transient, invisible online community? Is attachment to local and non-local communities mutually exclusive? Studies of telephone diffusion show that people increased their interest and involvement in the world outside their immediate towns; at the same time they also used the telephone to expand their local activity. The telephone has always overwhelmingly been used to call people in the local exchange area.

But what happens when the cost of using technology is the same regardless of local or distant communication? This is a critical difference between household use of telephone and the internet. In Blacksburg, Virginia, where 90% of the town residents are connected to the internet, families use their connection to facilitate communication and information exchange with local and non-local friends and family and groups with which they are affiliated (church, soccer team, school teachers, national and local organizations) as described in Andrea Kavanaugh's chapter. The community network project known as the Blacksburg Electronic Village has helped to build social capital by facilitating communication among residents' local social networks and collectivities. Families have increased their awareness of and involvement in community issues and activities through convenient access to information that was previously difficult or time consuming to acquire: school board minutes, town maps and forms, real estate development propositions, and county budgets. More important, numerous controversial issues have been discussed and debated via e-mail and mailing lists that have provided interested residents with background information, historic detail, development trade-offs that have allowed participants to develop informed judgments and opinions on civic affairs. For most families in the poorer rural area just outside the university town, the value of the internet is not so much for increasing involvement in civic affairs, but rather for improving their children's skills and knowledge for a better job in the information economy. It also helps many of the parents learn new skills (usually from their kids) related to their work and to job promotion.

Working-class ethnic minority families in the urban environment of Austin, Texas, have experienced similar benefits, according to Lodis Rhodes. In his chapter on the community network program known as the Austin Learning Academy, he notes that internet resources must be meaningful to individual users to diffuse naturally through established social networks. Rhodes argues persuasively that whether and how well people learn to use information technology depends on how well suited the social context is to the learner. Is the location a place where the student already goes or feels comfortable going to? Are the fellow students similar to themselves? Are there supportive, helpful peers or teachers? The learning center not only provides a point of innovation diffusion for computing and related technical training but also provides a social network of fellow students, neighbors, coworkers, or parents who may be called upon for technical assistance and support.

Social capital that is engendered among participants in this process helps to overcome what Rhodes calls a "demand deficit" among working-class and low-income minority populations. These individuals do not typically use the internet at work or school as most other Americans do. Their learning the value of internet skills and resources, therefore, is a problem of introducing technologies and services into people's lives in ways and places that are meaningful and that enhance existing patterns of communication for information exchange and social relations.

Clearly, social relationships extend beyond the neighborhood and local community to the wider world. Keith Hampton and Barry Wellman in their chapter on neighborhood computer networking known as "Netville" underscore the importance of this point when considering the household use of networked communication tools. The internet is similar to the telephone in that it helps us stay in touch with and coordinate activities with members of our social networks and the collectivities with which we affiliate. The growth of markets and the increasingly public provision of social services have lightened people's dependence on neighbors for routine help, information, and emergency aid.

Rather than losing community, say Hampton and Wellman, we have gained greater choice in "customizing our community." The researchers show that the use of e-mail and listserv communication within the neighborhood of Netville clearly increased social contact and information exchange among residents. However, in Netville the majority of all active social relations were with people outside the users' immediate neighborhood. They were dispersed throughout the region and the wider world. Hampton and Wellman conclude that the internet, like the telephone, supports a variety of social ties: local and non-local, strong and weak, instrumental and emotional. It enhances and supports our household connectivity with both local and non-local social networks and activities. Among interested families, it also enhances engagement in both local and non-local civic life.

Hampton and Wellman's conclusion is an optimistic note on which to end a volume on the internet and the family. Theirs is, however, a limited optimism. The authors note the provisional nature of their conclusions. They would probably also be quick to admit that there are many issues covered in this book—for example, parental control, information privacy, and the digital divide—that their case study does not address. Clearly, the internet, like any other complex social phenomenon, has many facets with many implications. That is what makes it so important, and so fascinating, to think about and study.

18

Three for Society: Households and Media in the Creation of Twenty-First Century Communities

Jorge Reina Schement

I had three chairs in my house; one for solitude, two for friendship, three for society.

We are in great haste to construct a magnetic telegraph from Maine to Texas; but Maine and Texas, it may be, have nothing important to communicate.
—Henry David Thoreau[1]

I reread the great populist philosopher because he captures the essential meaning of home, community, and society as most Americans understand it. In the first quote, Thoreau uses stunning economy to describe the pith of society as an aggregation of individuals. In the second, the new-fangled electric telegraph arouses his skepticism; and, by responding to the new device in such a manner, he fails to appreciate the social import of the most radical technological invention of his day.[2] As the voice of what is most American in American culture, he dazzles me; but as the failed futurist, he gives me comfort.

One hundred and fifty years later, our skepticism seeks other targets; we can all point to the consequences of Mr. Morse's invention. In fact, much of Thoreau's doubt can be dispelled by a visit to any American household. Yet, though Thoreau's skepticism strikes us as preposterous, living as we do in the morning of the Information Age, we too struggle to understand the implications of technological change. And, just as in Thoreau's day, our focus continues to converge on home, community, and media.[3]

My purpose in this essay is to explore the relationship between home, community, and media in the age of information. The essay progresses

From *Center* 11 (1999): 75–86. Reprinted with permission.

from a discussion of the demographic characteristics of households, through a review of adoption patterns of household media, to an analysis of the functions Americans expect from their homes in the new electronic communities that are emerging.

Households

To write of the household as a simple concept belies the variety of the American experience.[4] There are 100 million households in the United States. Fifty-four million, or 54%, are traditional in the sense of a married couple constituting the core. Nearly 12.2 million (12%) are headed by women. Of all households, the census counts 11.6 million (11%) as African American, plus another 7.2 million (7.7%) as Latino. A further 25% contain solitary individuals, totaling 24 million single person households.[5] When considered along with the possible combinations of intermingling social variables one can see that few household characteristics are mutually exclusive and that America looks more like a quilt than a whole cloth.

Historically, two household-related tendencies bear directly on the continuing evolution of communities: the downward trend of household size, and increasingly thinner community networks. From 1780 to 1870, the average number of people per household remained close to five; but in the 20th century, household size begins to drop reaching approximately 2.5 individuals per household in 1990 (figure 18.1). The decline in household size has produced community networks of lower density because the household-as-node contains fewer members to connect to the rest of the households in the network. By contrast, though less than 4% of households were occupied by single individuals throughout the 19th century, the 20th century has witnessed a steady increase in single person households reaching 25% in 1990 and still climbing (figure 18.2). And, as with households of small size, single person households tend toward thinner, or even nonexistent, community networks.

Furthermore, both of these developments have occurred at a time when Americans have increased the numbers of information devices in their homes. Indeed, it seems likely that the connection between diminishing household size and information consumption goes beyond coinci-

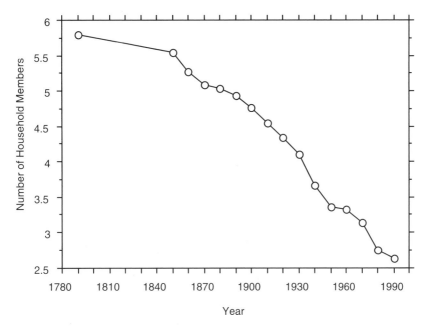

Figure 18.1
Average size of household, 1790–1990.
Sources: Table Series G 495-581, (1975). *Historical Statistics of the United States, Colonial Times to 1970* (Bicentennial ed.). Washington, D.C.: GPO. (1991). *Statistical Abstract of the United States: 1991.* Washington, D.C.: Bureau of the Census.

dence. The more people live alone, the more media serve as surrogates for interpersonal communications. The more media become available, the more living alone becomes attractive as an alternative life style. Individuals living alone tend to be high users of media; in fact, the largest numbers of media have entered homes since the meteoric rise of household individualization began in 1975.

Figure 18.3 offers a glimpse of the profound transformation taking place in the home as new media have become available. Beginning in the 1970s, Americans have gone on a shopping spree that has swollen to a crescendo in the '80s and '90s. In fact, the image of increasing abundance and diversity of media projected in figure 18.3 understates the inflow of media into American homes because it does not represent the growing tendency to own multiple devices. From the early decades of

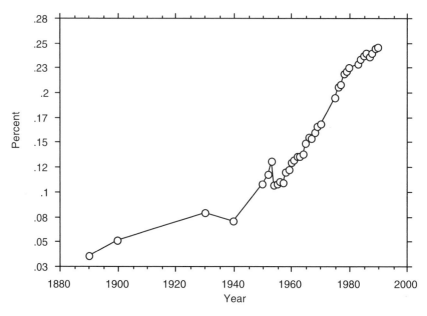

Figure 18.2
Single-person households as a percentage of total households, 1890–1990.
Sources: Series A 288-319, 335-349, (1975). *Historical Statistics of the United States, Colonial Times to 1970* (Bicentennial ed.). Washington, D.C.: GPO. Table 60, (1981). *Statistical Abstract of the United States: 1981.* Washington, D.C.: Bureaus of the Census. Table 56, (1988). *Statistical Abstract of the United States: 1988.* Washington, D.C.: Bureau of the Census. Table 55, (1990). *Statistical Abstract of the United States: 1990.* Washington, D.C.: U.S. Bureau of the Census. Table 2, (1991). *Statistical Abstract of the United States: 1991.* Washington, D.C.: Bureau of the Census.

the century when middle class householders dedicated telephone alcoves in the halls of their homes and set aside "radio rooms" for family entertainment, the national tendency has been to reserve domestic space for new media.[6] At century's end, nearly every room in a middle class home contains the ability to send and/or receive electronic information. At century's beginning, the description of the home as a node on a network rings more true than metaphorical.

The growing density of household media has also paralleled an increase in the amount of domestic time spent with media. Until the '90s, television viewing increased (see table 18.1). But with the introduction of

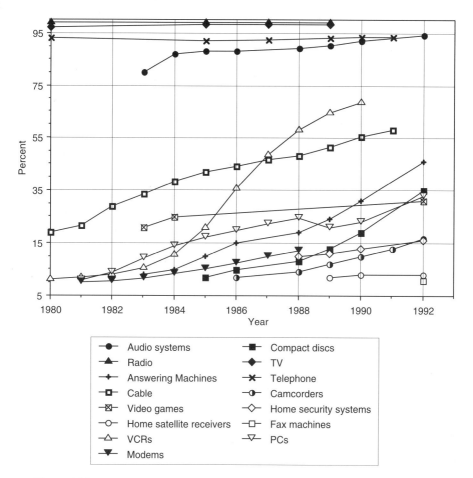

Figure 18.3
Household penetration of selected media, 1980–1993.
Sources: A. Belinfante. (1991). *Monitoring Report: Telephone Penetration and Household Family Characteristics.* (CC Docket No. 80-286). Federal Communications Commission. Electronic Industries Association. (1984–90, 1992). *The U.S. Consumer Electronics Industry Annual Review.* Washington, D.C.: Electronic Industries Association. (1992). *Electronic Market Data Book.* Washington, D.C.: Electronic Industries Association. Television Bureau of Advertising. Research Dept. (1991). *TV & Cable Factbook* (No. 60, 1992). U.S. Bureau of the Census. (1986, 1990, 1991, 1992). *Statistical Abstract.* Washington, D.C.: Bureau of the Census.

Table 18.1
Hours Watching TV (per TV home)

Year	TV Watching, Average Daily Hours per TV Household (I)	TV Watching, Average Daily Hours per TV Household (II)
1950	4:35	4.6
1955	4:51	4.9
1960	5:06	5.1
1965	5:29	5.5
1970	5:56	5.9
1975	6:07	6.1
1980	6:36	6.3
1985	7:10	7.1
1990	6:53	

Source: I. Television Bureau of Advertising. Research Dept. (1991). *Trends in Viewing.* New York: The Bureau. (Daily I and Weekly)
II. U.S. Bureau of the Census. (1981 & 1986). *Statistical Abstract: 1981, 1987.* Washington, D.C.: The Bureau. (Daily II)

new media into homes, some tradeoffs in behavior are taking place (see table 18.2). For example, while 28% percent of the adult population watches 3 or more hours of TV on an average day, only 20% do so if they own a computer, and that number drops to 16% of the computer user also owns a modem. By contrast, computer users with modems spend 60 minutes per day reading on average, while non computer users expend 47 minutes on reading. And, computer users tend to score higher on political knowledge.[7] Nor is time displacement the only approach to the use of more than one medium. Individuals consume several media at the same time. When my colleagues report that they work the *New York Times* crossword puzzle on Sunday mornings while listening to classical music and conversing with their spouses at the same time, and consider that pleasurable, they are engaging in a cluster of activities that most of us consider reasonable and commonplace.

The image of the household that emerges in the 1990s is one of a home increasingly dense with information devices, of a living space encroached upon by new information devices, and of occupants discard-

Table 18.2

Cross-over Use of Media among Computer Users/Non-users

Activity Yesterday	Computer User	Not a Computer User
Average minutes spent reading	58 min	47 min
Average minutes watching TV	2 hrs	2.5 hrs
Percent who read newspaper	65	56
Percent who watched 3 or more hours of entertainment television	20	28
Percent who read a book	38	29

Source: Technology in the American Home, Times Mirror Center for the People & the Press, May 1994, Washington, D.C.

ing previously acquired devices when they become outdated. It seems likely that nearly all time spent in households today is spent within quick reach of some kind of device for processing information; and, at least for a very large number of Americans, some device is turned on from the moment they get up until the moment they go to bed.

Media

The suggestion that information can be "consumed" will strike most Americans as an intuitive observation, yet it misrepresents the nature of information. After all, reading a newspaper produces no deterioration in the information itself, even though the value of the information may decrease as it loses its timeliness for the reader; and, though the paper itself degrades with use and time, this constitutes consumption of the medium or package, not of the information. Manipulation of the medium does not cause "exhaustion" or "depletion" of the information.[8] Still, the concept of "consumption" is an appropriate one because patterns of information use bear similarities to patterns for consuming material goods. Consumers master the evaluation, purchase, use, display, and replacement, of information exactly as they do for other goods. Plus, they purchase many information goods in the same markets in which they purchase material goods. And, just as it does for many classes of goods, the measure of value derives from the user not from the information. Over the course of the 20th century, the confluence of culture and capitalism has encouraged Americans to adapt information to the norms of market-centered consumption.

This confluence can best be observed in the home of the '90s; though, in a sense, the construction of domestic information environments is an old story. Americans have exhibited a tremendous appetite for media from the start of the century. In 1925, when radios were primitive crystal sets, fewer than 10% of all households owned radios (figure 18.4). However, five years later, household ownership stood at 46%. By 1940, having suffered through the privations of the Depression, Americans still managed to increase household ownership of radios to 82%. They bought radios at an astonishing rate, especially when one considers that the Depression forced personal expenditures on information goods and services to drop from 4.4% of all personal expenditures in 1930 to 3.5% in 1935, not recovering the 1930 level until 1945.[9] In addition, radio technology of the time meant that when Americans decided to purchase a radio many of them bought an expensive piece of furniture; yet, despite these obstacles, radio achieved virtual saturation by 1950, just in time for the arrival of the next wave—television.

Less than one household in ten owned TVs in 1950. However, fifteen years later, less than one household in ten remained without a TV. Television's embracement took less time than radio, in part driven by family and community expectations. This boyhood reminiscence of a family's decision to purchase their first TV is typical.

"The first time, I remember ... we ate dinner, and then went for a walk ... down to the corner to one of the main streets. There was an appliance store. And people gathered around the appliance store and watched the TV in the window. You didn't have any sound. People stood around. They enjoyed it. Then my uncle, who lived in L.A., got a TV. He had a twelve inch set, we used to drive all the way into L.A. to watch TV. We would go visit friends, friends of my parents. I mean they had some friends who lived way out in the San Fernando Valley, and we'd go to their house and have dinner, and then after dinner, they'd turn on the TV. You know, turn it on and watch.... These were adventures to me....

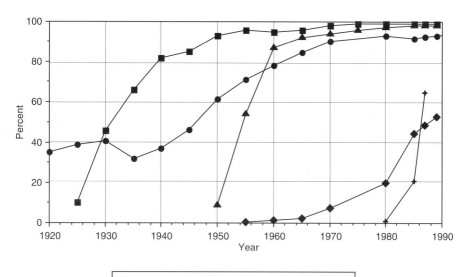

Figure 18.4
Diffusion of selected media: Household penetration of selected media, 1920–1990.

Sources: Series R 1-12 (1975). *Historical Statistics of the United States, Colonial Times to 1970* (Bicentennial ed.). Washington, D.C.: GPO. Table 956, (1981). *Statistical Abstract: 1981*. Washington, D.C.: Bureau of the Census. Table 884, (1992). *Statistical Abstract: 1992*. Washington, D.C.: Bureau of the Census. Tables 1.1, 1.3. A. Belinfante. (1991). *Monitoring Report: Telephone Penetration and Household Family Characteristics*. (CC Docket No. 80-286). Federal Communications Commission.

Well, one evening we went to these friends' house and somehow my dad just decided that it was time to buy a TV. So, we went down to Gold's, it was a store in South-Central L.A., and bought a Philco. I remember he wanted it delivered. He wanted it delivered as soon as they could, because there was some big boxing match. Joe Lewis was going to fight Kevin Shaw or Joe Walsh. It was one of his last fights. And he wanted to see the fight on TV. Except Gold's didn't make the delivery on time. We got the TV the day after the fight. Anyway, the delivery was a big event. And then we had a television, so we didn't have to go to my uncle's. We probably went to my uncle's less, then, because we didn't have to go there to watch TV all the time."[10]

Television arrived amidst family networks, neighborhood socializing, consumer expectations, and household interiors already adapted to radio. Those early expensive sets, with their implicit assumption of communal family watching, gave way to personal sets and cheaper models; so that, by the 1990s, Americans owned on the average 5 radios and 2 TV sets.[11]

By contrast, media that require people to go out in public, have fared enigmatically. Motion picture theater attendance generally rose from 1925 to 1945, the era we now think of as the golden age of Hollywood. American city culture had already established vaudeville as part of the rhythm of urban life so that city dwellers easily assimilated the movies into prevailing leisure culture.[12] During World War II, Americans with defense pay checks in their pockets, increased personal expenditures on movies to an all time high (figure 18.5). After the war, however, the combination of veterans' intent on starting families and the subsequent arrival of television knocked expenditures on movies into a 30 year decline. The curve in figure 5 indicates a turning away from public entertainment in favor of entertainment in the home; but more importantly, it reflects the decline of public life and the new dominance of the private sphere. Where once theaters and movies were synonymous, movies began to appear on TV; and, in the '80s, VCRs converted the home itself into a movie theater.

The picture that emerges is one of a home increasingly dense with information devices as new ones are added every year or so. Yet though popular, that image is misleading. Americans are transforming their

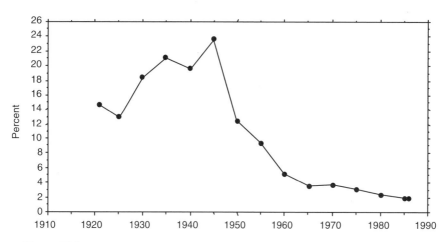

Figure 18.5
Admissions to motion picture theaters as a percentage of total personal consumption expenditures for recreation, 1921–1986.
Sources: Series H 878-893. (1975)*. Historical Statistics of the United States, Colonial Times to 1970.* (Bicentennial ed.). Washington, D.C.: GPO. Table 396 (1981). *Statistical Abstract of the United States: 1981.* Washington, D.C.: Bureau of the Census. Table 363 (1987). *Statistical Abstract of the United States: 1988.* Washington, D.C.: Bureau of the Census.

homes by doing more than adding new media; they are redefining the use value of old media. For example, as the number of radios, televisions, and VCRs has increased per household, newspapers have suffered a gradual decline. However, rather than drop the newspaper in favor of the television (or the Internet online news service), many Americans have shifted their reliance on the traditional newspaper to reframe it as a source of local information.

Nor are Americans moving toward a national homogeneity of media. For one thing, diffusion rates vary. CDs and answering machines have diffused quite rapidly, though they have not approached the diffusion rates for radio and television. By contrast, cable, security systems, and satellite receivers have diffused at a slower pace. Also, projected saturation rates for media differ. Video games and camcorders are associated with children and likely to reach saturation rates at a level close to the percentage of households with children (70%).[13] While all American households own some of the same media, and all are moving toward including more media with most devices owned in multiples, households are not all moving toward owning the same media at the same rate.

Seen as a whole, these tendencies alter the balance between the private and public spheres. Investment in home media for leisure purposes decreases disposable income; and, therefore, the motivation to seek amusement in public. Thus theater and the movies have been transformed from entertainment for general audiences to entertainment aimed at segmented audiences. A denser media environment in the home also leads to amplification of the home as a node that can carry more of the information load once borne by the public sphere. Needs, such as staying in touch with relatives, monitoring events in the neighborhood, coordinating school activities, shopping, and even conducting business, can be met from within the home. And, though differences in ownership of home media due to income insure that the possibilities for mediated access to the larger community will vary, the dominance of the private over the public sphere carries all regions, social classes, and ethnic groups. Thus, the potential for community is being influenced from within the home; and, as a result, setting the stage for a redefinition of community centered on communication.

Functions—Refuge, Window, Market, Workplace

The question often echoed in public discourse, "What's happened to our communities?" should begin by asking, "What's happened to our homes?" By embarking on a century-long buying binge, Americans have filled their homes with a long list of devices and systems for accessing and communicating information—with consequences for community. At the center of the rise of a household media environment is the shift in emphasis from public life to private life, a shift which has intensified demand for media in the home and the willingness to invest in it. Even so, however, private life will never displace public life entirely. Still, the tendency toward emphasizing home life will continue; and, therefore, encourage even more expenditures on electronic furnishings. Thus, the more potent the home becomes as an information crucible, the greater its impact on the evolution of community.

Americans expect the home to serve as a refuge—which explains the appeal of home-based information services that substitute for public transactions—but they also expect the home to serve as a window—which explains the continued appetite for media and information. The desire for refuge is perhaps the elemental human spatial need.[14] Within Americans' consciousness, it touches a deep nerve because Americans perceive themselves as living in a hostile environment. Fear of random crime and fear of one's neighbors incites the retreat into the private sphere; so that, for many, the boundary between public and private is not a friendly zone. Ironically, this same fear contributes to the drive to enhance domestic information environments. For if the home is the last refuge from a hostile society, then the environment created by domestic media functions as a watch tower of exceptional usefulness. Nevertheless, I don't want to make too much of fear as a causal agent. The desire to supplant public transactions probably ranks higher as a priority for most Americans. The use of the television, the phone, and the mails, for home shopping, medical service coordination, bill payment, and accessing governmental services, attests to the rising importance of the private sphere as the locus of important activities that were once firmly situated in public. Through the window, members of the household maintain connectedness with events in the larger world, coordinate (even conduct) their present and future jobs, and maintain relationships with significant others. The electronic home's capacity to focus the nation has astounded observers—from FDR's inaugural address, through the televised murder of Lee Harvey Oswald, to live coverage of the bombing of Baghdad.[15] In the '90s, the window is rapidly evolving into a node. The images of refuge and window may seem contradictory, yet they serve the purposes of a society with an expanding private sphere whose ideals of the home are realized within the possibilities of domestic media culture.[16]

When Americans embarked on the electronic conversion of the home, they further reinvented the home as a marketplace and as a workshop.

First, they brought consumer culture into the living room and then firmly established the home as a significant marketplace. To be sure, the home has long been a marketplace. Once Montgomery Ward and Sears pioneered the catalogue in the 19th century, rural families saw the kitchen table as a place for making numerous consumption decisions, and that expectation has continued to the present. However, beginning in the '80s, the convergence of new and old information technologies has brought increasing purchasing possibilities into the home. The simple magnitude tempts one to explain this tendency as stemming from the direct impact of technology; yet, the emergence of a consumer culture in the United States goes beyond technology. Its essence is bound up with the significance we attribute to material possessions, and the value we place on individualistic desires.[17] Retreat from public life has redirected the focus of consumer culture into the home; and, with that new alignment, there exists a danger to community. The home as market-window offers so many opportunities to avoid the shoving and nastiness associated with shopping in public, that home consumers may also avoid getting to know their fellow citizens. The siege mentality facilitated by taking the home window seriously may thus contribute to more rigidity on political positions and less empathy for the other groups that make up one's community.

Fifteen years ago an office worker relied on slow mail or voice-to-voice telephone, in order to send a message; whereas, now, by converting the home into a node, Americans fuse the workplace to the home as much as the marketplace. Of the 34% of Americans who work at home, 40% use a computer and constitute the core of a growing group of telecommuters.[18] Firms push employees to convert their homes into offices in order to cut down overhead costs by transferring those costs to their employees. When linked to part-time employment, telecommuting also becomes a tactic allowing firms to avoid paying for employee benefits. Even so, telecommuting also exerts a pull. Telecommuters who are busy converting their electronic cottages into electronic workshops can exploit a remarkable convergence taking place among information technologies; so much so, that the possibilities encroach on each other for attention. Certainly, many individuals are attracted by the ideal of independence, whereby they seek to exploit the refuge potential of the home to avoid the time and supervisory constraints of the office.[19] What's more, the communication possibilities of the home are just the tip of the iceberg; for them to function, the electronic workshop requires a computer-centered technological infrastructure of impressive proportions. Clearly, a rewiring of the home is underway that transcends the introduction of media to the home for purposes of domestic convenience. There can be no doubt that telecommuting made possible by the convergence of information technologies has already set a new standard for imagining the home. As tele-professionals and their individualistic work-home environments increase in numbers, values associated with their circumstances will influence American culture.

Window, refuge, market, and workplace—all four functions motivate the exploitation of media and can be conceived of as forces shaping the American conception of home. As a ferment of expectations, they intensify the potency of the home; and, when sustained by the infusion of electronic media, the balance between private and public swings away from a cohesive community network toward the home as a predominately isolated societal node capable of fulfilling functions once discharged in the public sphere.

The Third Chair

Americans are rushing to furnish their homes with a host of devices for sending, receiving, and processing huge quantities of information through diverse media across multitudes of channels (If we could lift the roof from the characteristic American home, we would see that it looks like a multiplex theater.). What once took place in the town square, in the neighborhood tavern, on market day, or in the library, now more often occurs in the study or in the bedroom. Perhaps irrevocably, the locus of communication and participation continues to shift from the public sphere to the private sphere.

Information enters the American home as a fragmented stream of unconnected messages stripped of their social context. This is the daily face of the public-private shift. Information arrives as separated bits without organic unity, so that individuals attempting to optimize their lives face a formidable challenge. To spend a day with one's TV and radio, wading through a pile of newspapers and magazines, and cruising the Internet, is to process an enormous number of messages: but not, necessarily, to be informed. Home information environments lack integration yet constitute an indispensable part of life in the information society.

Surely, then, the shift from public space to private space threatens older forms of community. In states like New Jersey, polls show that more Jerseyans know the names of the mayors of New York and Philadelphia than they know the names of the mayors in their own towns. And, though regions vary, this seems to be a characteristic of the American political landscape. The significance lies in the tension between media and community. Large media networks collect audiences by concentrating on stories that appeal to large blocks of viewers and readers.[20] Therefore, suburban and rural citizens are more likely to recognize the name of a city official for whom they can't vote. Individuals who commute to distant workplaces and whose personal networks are spread geographically are further disconnected. However, democracy in the United States began in local communities. That localness has become increasingly meaningless to so many Americans signals social and political change of a profound nature; for as long as community remained intact, libraries and churches and schools functioned to bring people together, to educate immigrants, and to reinforce the virtues of citizenship.

Americans experience persistent disconnection from local community networks. They increasingly conduct their every day lives among strangers or approximate strangers: the grocery clerk, the dry cleaning attendant, the security guard at the entrance to one's office building, most of one's fellow employees, and the telemarketers for the catalogs where many Americans purchase a vast array of goods. Americans live daily life amidst impersonal interactions; and many, if not most, are mediated through some form of communication technology. That is, though people maintain a small number of primary personal relationships, the number of secondary anonymous relationships has vastly increased as individuals seek to accomplish tasks by relying on mediated information received from strangers. The old cement of society has been replaced by a new glue. As Americans carve out home-centered, individualistic, information-heavy, approaches to their personal lives, they are bypassing traditional community and the public sphere.

What is at stake for community in the Information Age? As Americans replace a sense of local reciprocity with feelings of belonging brokered electronically across distance, interdependence—the essence of community—appears weakened. Secondly, with proximity no longer determined by immediate geographic, we may feel closer to a disembodied communicant on a chat line than we do to the grocery clerk, the gas station attendant, or the mail carrier. Thirdly, we continue to derive our identities from community, but we negotiate those identities less through embeddedness in relationships with people known as flesh and blood, and more through messages received from distant sources. Lastly, the communication networks that now define community vary from person to person each according to his or her media/information choices; whereas, geography, family, religion, and class, no longer serve as the common denominators that once led a person to equate community with "place." To be sure, I state these developments in the extreme, yet what passes for community in the Information Age is far thinner than the dense community networks of one or two generations ago which wove themselves out of interdependence, proximity, identity, and communication. Indeed, if communication creates community (and by extension society), then the choice of communication carries with it profound consequences.

I don't think much of Thoreau as a technological futurist, but I continue to heed Thoreau, the moral philosopher; especially, since now more than at any other time in this century, Americans look to the home, rather than the public arena, to live life as neighbors, workers, consumers, and citizens. So, I end with one more alarm from Thoreau that bears pondering for an age where community is mediated by technology.

But lo! Men have become the tools of their tools.[21]

Notes

The author wishes to acknowledge the valuable advice of Scott C. Forbes of Penn State University. The ideas presented herein are strictly those of the author.

1. Henry David Thoreau, *Walden; or Life in the Woods. On the Duty of Civil Disobedience*, Holt, Rinehart and Winston, 1854/1948, pp. 97, 40.

2. The magnetic telegraph preceeded the electric telegraph, the one invented by Morse and the focus of Thoreau's disdain. Thoreau's "confusion" probably reflects colloquial usage of the time. See, for example, Thompson, R. L. (1947). *Wiring a continent: The history of the telegraph industry in the United States 1832–1866*. Princeton, NJ: Princeton University Press.

3. Any natural element or technology capable of transmitting information from sender to receiver constitutes a medium. While most readers will be familiar with the use of "media" in conjunction with "mass," that combination of terms more properly refers to media that distribute messages from one source to a large mostly undifferentiated audience of receivers. Other information technologies, such as the telephone and the Internet, should also be considered media. Communications students meet these distinctions early in their studies; see, for example, Budd, R. W., & Ruben, B. D. (1988). *Beyond media: New approaches to mass communication* (2nd ed.). New Brunswick, NJ: Transaction. DeFleur, M. L., & Dennis, E. E. (1988). *Understanding mass communication.* Boston: Houghton Mifflin. McLuhan, M. (1964). *Understanding media: The extensions of man.* New York: New American Library. Schement, J. R., & Ruben, B. D. (Ed.). (1993). *The relationships between communication and information.* New Brunswick, NJ: Transaction Publications. Schramm, W. (1960). *Mass communications.* Urbana, IL: University of Illinois. Thus, the term "medium/media" more accurately describes the technologies that are discussed in this essay.

4. What is a household? According to the Bureau of the Census, "A household includes the related family members and all the unrelated persons, if any, such as lodgers, foster children, wards, or employees who share the housing unit. A person living alone in a housing unit, or a group of unrelated persons sharing a housing unit as partners, is also counted as a household." Over the years, census definitions have varied, with no consistent definition in the first hundred years of the survey. In the 20th century, the above definition has been relied on with fair consistency, although the boundary between a household with lodgers and a commercial hostelry has shifted from 5 or less lodgers to a household (1990) to as many as 11 (1930 and 1940). (1975). *Historical statistics of the United States, colonial times to 1970* (Bicentennial Ed. ed.). Washington DC: GPO, p. 6. Here, I use "household" to refer to the individuals living together in one housing unit; whereas, I use "home" to refer to the dwelling.

5. (1990). *Census of Population and Housing Summary.* U.S. Bureau of the Census: Washington DC. (1997). *Statistical abstract of the united states: 1996.* (Vol. 117th Ed.). Washington DC: Bureau of the Census.

6. For analyses of the early impact of the telephone on domestic space see, Fischer, C. S. (1992). *America calling: A social history of the telephone to 1940.* Berkeley, CA: University of California. and Pool, I. d. S. (Ed.). (1977). *The social impact of the telephone.* Cambridge, MA: MIT Press. For a glimpse into notions of domestic space at the inception of radio as discussed in the popular press, see (1923, August). Decorating the radio room: A new thought for the house in town or country where "listening in" is getting to be a serious pastime. *House & Garden, 49,* 50. and (1926, 27 February). How to be a lady at a loudspeaker party. *Literary Digest, 88,* 57–60.

7. Kohut, A. (1994). *Technology in the American household.* Times Mirror Center for the People and the Press, p. 5, 7.

8. Of course, information may be lost. One of the seminal documents of the information age, the original organization chart drawn up by Daniel C. McCallum for the New York and Erie Railroad has been lost to history. When a record no longer exists, and no human remembers, then information is irretrievable.

9. Series E 135–166, G 416–469 (1975). *Historical statistics of the united states, colonial times to 1970*. Washington DC: GPO. Table 708, 738 (1981). *Statistical abstract of the united states: 1981*. Washington DC: U.S. Bureau of the Census. Table 676 (1987). Statistical abstract of the united states: 1988. Washington DC: Bureau of the Census.

10. Interview with John Rodriguez, recorded in Oakland, CA, 19 March 1993, as part of 167 interviews for the *Wired Castle* Project, a study of household information environments in the 20th century.

11. U.S. Bureau of the Census. (1981). *Statistical abstract: 1981*. Washington, D.C.: The Bureau. U.S. Bureau of the Census. (1991). *Statistical abstract: 1991*. Washington, D.C.: The Bureau. *Trends in Media*, 1991. U.S. Bureau of Census. (1975). *Historical statistics of the United States: colonial times to 1970*. (Bicentennial ed.) Washington, D.C.: The Bureau. *TV & Cable Factbook*, no. 60 (1992).

12. For discussions of the importance of public entertainment in the first half of the century, see: Butsch, R. (1990). *For fun and profit: The transformation of leisure into consumption*. Philadelphia, PA: Temple University Press. Crane, D. (1993). *The production of culture: Media and the urban arts*. Newbury Park, CA: Sage. Nasaw, D. (1993). *Going out: The rise and fall of public amusements*. New York: Basic Books. Peiss, K. (1986). *Cheap amusements: Working women and leisure in turn-of-the-century new york*. Philadelphia, PA: Temple University Press. Strasser, S. (1989). *Satisfaction guaranteed: The making of the American mass market*. New York: Pantheon.

13. (1993). *Statistical abstract of the united states: 1993*. Washington DC: Bureau of the Census. Percentage is for 1992.

14. Refuge is a conflicted term at the end of the 20th century. For women who suffer abuse from their spouses, and for children who fear their parents, the home is a torture chamber rather than a refuge. My use of the term in this essay does not mean to diminish this pathology of our society. I use "refuge" here to elicit the expectations Americans bring to the ideal of the home. Regardless of what actually happens in domestic space, it is the ideal of the home that guides the motivation to create a media environment capable of seeing into the public sphere while keeping the public sphere at arms length.

15. It makes sense in a less obvious way to think of the power of the home to "focus," since *focus* is the Latin word for hearth.

16. The tension between window and refuge also implies a threat to privacy, although the question of privacy goes beyond the scope of this essay. The sale and resale of databases containing information on individuals has become a

central commodity in the information economy that adds a new dimension of social control to the marketplace. Often gathered passively without the subject's knowledge, the presence of this information may also constitute an assault on privacy. That Americans have converted their homes into windows suggests that they are willing to tolerate some intrusion. That they expect their homes to function as a refuge suggests that they seek to protect their privacy. As they pursue both ends of this contradiction, they deepen one of the fundamental tensions of the information age. Once thought of as the right to be left alone, privacy is now thought of as the control of information about oneself.

17. The implications of a culture of consumption go beyond the scope of this essay, but they have attracted commentary from some of the greatest thinkers of the century. Here is Erich Fromm. "In our culture ... consuming is essentially the satisfaction of artificially stimulated fantasies, a fantasy performance alienated from our concrete selves.... We are surrounded by things of whose nature and origin we know nothing. The telephone, radio, phonograph, and all other complicated machines are almost as mysterious to us as they would be to a man from a primitive culture; we know how to use them, that is, we know which button to turn, but we do not know on what principle they function.... We consume, as we produce, without any concrete relatedness to the objects with which we deal; we live in a world of things, and our only connection with them is that we know how to manipulate or to consume them." Fromm, E. (1955). *The sane society.* New York: Holt, Rinehart and Winston, p. 122. For a more recent view, see Fox, R. W., & Lears, T. J. J. (Ed.). (1983). *The culture of consumption: critical essays in american history, 1880–1980.* New York: Pantheon.

18. Kohut, p. 53.

19. The promise is not without perils. Telecommuters can avoid the office but not the office politics. For a fuller discussion of the counter-currents of telecommuting, see Kraut, R. E. (1987). *Technology and the Transformation of White-Collar Work.* Hillsdale, NJ: Lawrence Erlbaum Associates.

20. The first to recognize this seeming contradiction was Dallas Smythe. He understood that the exploitation of consumers occurred with their consent. See Smythe, D., W. (1977). Communications: Blindspot of western marxism. *Canadian Journal of Social and Political Theory* (Fall), 1–27. Smythe, D. (1981). *Dependency road: Communication, capitalism consciousness, and Canada.* Norwood, NJ: Ablex.

21. Henry David Thoreau, *Walden; or Life in the Woods. On the Duty of Civil Disobedience,* Holt, Rinehart and Winston, 1854/1948, p. 29.

19

When Everyone's Wired: Use of the Internet in Networked Communities

Andrea L. Kavanaugh

Why would families use the internet differently from other forms of communication and information exchange? Why would the effects of computer networks be different from other media? Connecting households and communities to local and worldwide resources has clearly affected the lives of both advantaged and disadvantaged families and children, economically and socially. Nonetheless, people are motivated by the same needs and incentives they had before they had access to the internet; they seek communication and information accordingly. Computer literacy and comfort levels are generally achieved when these incentives are in place and needs are gratified. Without them, potential users, including parents, remain skeptical or indifferent toward computer networking.

This chapter examines the diffusion of internet technology and services in the networked community of Blacksburg, Virginia, the "most wired town in America" (Reader's Digest 1996), and surrounding rural counties. The predictions and projections described in this chapter are based on six years of research and participant observation among households in a networked community. The general finding is that the internet does not change people's basic personalities. If you are predisposed to be asocial (unsocial, but not antisocial), access to the internet does not make you suddenly sociable. It simply provides you with tools and services that allow you to interact with people without the embarrassment or discomfort of a face-to-face setting (Ruberg 1994, Sproull and Kiesler 1991, among others). People use whatever tools are at hand to advance their goals: to do better in school, become more involved in the local community, or seek fellow hackers. Those in the small minority of the population that is predisposed to be to be *anti*social will have more powerful tools at their disposal in the internet suite, among others.

The Community Network Context

The community network known as the Blacksburg Electronic Village (BEV), established in 1993, is a virtual rendition of the geographic community (population 43,000) and surrounding rural Montgomery County, in the foothills of the Blue Ridge Mountains. The majority of the Blacksburg population (85%) is affiliated with Virginia Polytechnic Institute & State University (also known as Virginia Tech), a land grant university. The university established a partnership in the BEV project with the town government of Blacksburg and the regional Bell operating company (Bell Atlantic Telephone), although the bulk of project support (staff, equipment, overhead) came from Virginia Tech. Among the original purposes of the project was to build a critical mass of users through extensive internet access from residences, businesses, schools, local government, and other local groups and organizations.

When the developers of the community network project evaluated beta test users in 1993 (Patterson, Bishop, and Kavanaugh 1994), they were struck by respondents' strong interest in local as well as global services.[1] Project developers had imagined that the residents of this rural, isolated region of southwest Virginia would prefer contact with the world beyond Blacksburg. While residents did value contact with distant places and resources, they also sought local content and services online. Beta test researchers summarized the reflections of focus group participants on future uses of BEV as follows:

> The greatest excitement stemmed from the possibilities of developing local resources on BEV and attaining local ubiquity of the system; the desire to use BEV to enhance the town's sense of community was very strong. Some suggested future uses were based simply on access to local information, while others required interaction in the form of communication among people or the ability to actually perform transactions online that previously were conducted in person or over the phone. Participants want to see commercial and business applications and services added to BEV, which they saw as an important way to increase the convenience, flexibility, scope, and efficiency of conducting their day-to-day activities. People wanted to conduct commercial and personal business

transactions from their own homes, at the time of day or night that suited their lifestyles.[2]

The beta test focus group participants who are parents seemed to find many uses that would be helpful in managing and enriching the lives of their children. For example, they suggested that BEV could be used for checking children's homework assignments, parent-teacher communication, recreation department schedules, and providing a way for their children to develop an interest in global issues (Patterson, Bishop, and Kavanaugh 1994, p. 12). In the years following the launch of BEV, these applications, and many others, have been realized for parents in the county-wide school system. Parents with school age children were increasingly using e-mail with their child's teacher, and checking the World Wide Web for local school information. In 1996, three years after the launch of the BEV community network, only 9% of parents with school-age children reported using e-mail with their child's teacher. By 1999, this figure had more than quadrupled, to 37%. Use of the school web pages by parents of school age children nearly doubled (7% to 13% among those reporting they used school pages "frequently" and "sometimes"). Parents reporting they never used the school web pages fell from 74% to 50% between 1996 and 1999.

By 1999, an estimated 80 percent of the population in the town of Blacksburg was linked to the internet at home, work, or school. There were over a hundred community organizations with web sites and list-servs, and three-fourths of local businesses were online. The BEV community network web site links to information and web-based forms for local town and county government, social services, local schools, libraries, health care, and community organizations.

Early attempts to stimulate group discussion online, by establishing broad topic newsgroups (education, the environment, among others) were unsuccessful. The topics were too broad, and the users too diverse, to make communication meaningful or timely. Conversely, instrumental themes such as "For Sale" and "BEV News" (including technical support) are very active. Also, numerous small lists with focused discussion topics (parents of children with special needs, teachers of social studies, parents for gifted education, school board mailing list) or affiliated community groups are flourishing. Through their existing social networks, and organizational associations, people begin to use and come to understand computer technology in ways that have a basic utility in their daily lives. In addition to friends and family, they e-mail their child's teacher or Boy Scout leader, and coworkers; they access the high school band schedule, discuss church or school issues, or check out the proposed new sewer line on web-based zoning maps for their neighborhood.

Parents that have children in the local high school band report that having the band listserv has changed their lives. It has become so much easier for them than "telephone trees" to keep track of schedules, updates, or changes. The managers of the recreational and competitive soccer leagues in the New River Valley area (encompassing Blacksburg and environs) state that without electronic mail, they would not volunteer for the job as team manager. This sentiment among parent volunteers for a variety of community programs is expressed regularly. One community group changed volunteer directors when it was revealed that the original candidate did not have e-mail or experience with the web. To attract such volunteers, not only must the manager or director have e-mail, but at least most of the participants as well. In the process of reaching the team coach or a child's teacher, new users are motivated to persevere up the learning curve, and gain the skills that then help them protect their children from the relatively infrequent sources of potential harm online.

As with earlier media, we are seeing evidence of what Ithiel de Sola Pool (1977) identifies as "dual effects." As with the telephone, for example, we can expect the internet to increase or decrease communication among family members; improve or erode writing skills; enhance or invade privacy. Essentially, the multimedia channel of the internet amplifies what is already going on in the household and among family and community members. If family members are not inclined to spend time together, introducing a networked computer will not increase time shared among them, except in the short term, and until the novelty wears off.

There are people for whom internet tools and services will have significant effects. In fact, about a fifth of the population (22%) reports they are more involved in the local community since getting on the internet (Kavanaugh and Patterson 1998). The proportion of the population that seems to be drawn into community life more actively due to the internet is a group that scores significantly higher on measures of education, newspaper readership, and current community involvement levels. Thus, the internet does appear to facilitate increases in community involvement, but that growth occurs among people who are "predisposed to being active" in the community. Nonetheless, if the handful of people who are "actively involved" in the community increases because of the internet by even a small percentage, this helps to restore some of the social capital that has eroded over the past three decades, as Putnam (1993, 1995, 2000) and others have described.

In short, people are motivated to use the media to gratify existing communication and information needs. This is the message of media uses and gratification research. The social origins of needs generate expectations of the media, which leads to differential patterns of media use, resulting in need gratification (McQuail and Windahl 1981, among others). We can expect that families will begin to use online services if and when they decide the content is relevant to their needs.

It would seem more probable that parents living in areas where there are community networks would have lower anxiety about the internet than parents in other geographic areas. This is because the abundance of meaningful local content helps parents see benefits outweighing potential threats of predators and pornography. The parents' own experience, rather than mass media coverage of life online, informs their judgment and helps them see potential threats as minimal and manageable.

Families and Communication

Trust among members of a social network increases as people get to know each other, often through organized activities (e.g., the bowling league, the PTA, and other formal and informal groups). Williams (1988, p. 8) and Newton (1997, p. 578) distinguish between "thin" trust and "thick" trust in social networks. In small face-to-face communities (tribes, isolated islands, rural peripheries), "thick" trust is generated by intensive, daily contact between people. These tend to be socially homogeneous and exclusive communities, able to exercise social sanctions necessary to reinforce thick trust (Coleman 1988, pp. 105–108).

Traditional families tend to meet their communication and information needs face to face. The majority of traditional families, whether historically or in less-developed countries of the present day, live in close proximity with other family members, in rural areas or villages, where trust is "thick" and social networks are dense. Social networks of extended family and community members provide aid (health care, childcare, harvesting, and other basic needs); they also represent important sources of information on all subjects.

Thin trust is less personal, based on indirect, secondary social relations. It is the product of what Granovetter (1973) distinguishes as weak ties among members. Weak ties can link members of various social groups to help integrate them in a single social environment or geographic setting. Thin trust is also the basis for social integration in modern, large-scale society (Newton 1997, p. 579). Where people extend trust to others who are distant and unknown, but nonetheless share similar values or beliefs, trust is abstract. Abstract trust is increasingly engendered or undermined in modern society, through the institutions of the mass media and education (Wellman 1996).

The majority of modern families, including those in less developed countries, have pursued economic opportunity through education and employment. They have become dispersed from other family members and live in urban or suburban areas. Their social networks tend to be less dense than those of traditional families. Social networks no longer need to provide basic aid, insofar as it has been largely institutionalized through government (road building, education), and the market (housing construction, medical care). Trust is "thin" and abstract; bestowed upon "abstract" information sources that are dispersed and diverse (education and mass media, including books, newspapers, radio, television). The internet—a multimedia and increasingly broadband infrastructure— seems the logical progression toward dovetailing information and communication through any given channel.

There is evidence from research in Blacksburg (Kavanaugh 1999) that the internet routinely facilitates linkages between groups and social networks. Internet-based communication tools such as listservs and e-mail reinforce and supplement their face to face communication and information exchange.

Parents of school-age children are wisely cautious about the internet as a vehicle to invade privacy. When the telephone was first introduced into the household of the 1920s, it was met with skepticism and scorn, relegated to the mud room or garage, as it was considered an invasion of privacy. Not only did it disturb the household when it rang, but it also provided an opportunity—like the internet today—for household members to reveal information to the outside world in a manner less easily monitored and controllable than in face-to-face settings.

A panel of ten Blacksburg mothers with school-aged children were interviewed in three focus group rounds between 1996 and 1999 (Kavanaugh 1999, Wunderman, Cato, and Johnson 1996, 1997). These parents expressed their awareness of the dangers inherent in the medium before the mass media were covering such issues. The majority indicate that they tend to keep close observation of their children's internet use, with comments such as, "It's like TV; you have to monitor it" and "[You have to] keep the computer in a place that you walk by a lot." The majority recommended the good old-fashioned discipline of setting limits. This is not to say that there is not the category of "online worriers" among them. One mother when asked about pornography replied, "That's why I don't let them online."

The majority of the families that have serious concerns about the internet (what Turow [1999] calls "online worriers" and "offline worriers") have little or no experience with the internet. Their concern is a reasonable and appropriate response. As parents become more experienced with internet services and their benefits, they begin to see the risks as less worrisome. The declining worry with greater experience makes it especially important that public institutions such as libraries and schools offer internet training and support and provide local content. Local organizations, government, and community groups need to provide information and services, including social services and job databases, that are relevant and meaningful to citizens' daily lives. In the process of using e-mail with the school board chairman, checking online sports scores and the church newsletter, parents gain skills and knowledge to help protect their children from harmful aspects of the internet.

Turow raises the important question of why disenchanted parents (22% of online parents) continue accessing the internet from home. He suggests inertia may be one reason or that they see the technology as a kind of social leveler. I suspect they use their e-mail (and appreciate its more controlled communication), but they avoid the unpredictable world of the web.

Lessons from the Riner Study

For three years, a group of fifth grade students and their families in Riner (near Blacksburg) have been immersed in intensive computing at school and were granted a networked computer at home (Ehrich and McCreary 1999). Through the assistance of a special project with Virginia Tech, supported by the U.S. Department of Education, these young students have become agents of change and technology transfer to other family members.

One-on-one interview and focus group data collected by the author in collaboration with project researchers between 1997 and 1999 reveal that most family members teach each other everything they know about computers and networking and are usually more of a resource than formal lessons (Ehrich and McCreary 1999). This is consistent with research reported in diffusion of innovation literature. Innovation diffusion stresses the importance of social networks in understanding how an innovation diffuses and with what effects on a social system, including within a household (Fischer 1972, Rogers 1982). Some typical comments from parent interviews are these:

Interviewer: How about the parent [internet training] classes?

Parent: I liked them.

Interviewer: Did they help you?

Parent: No, [my daughter] helped me more.[3]

My kids really, as much as they know about computers, they could probably teach me everything I need to know really ... [my son] taught [my daughter] a lot and then [my daughter] has taught me.[4]

Family members also typically compete for access to the networked computer at home; for example:

It's hard to get [my daugher] off the phone. People are like, we were trying to call. We don't get no answer. Where have you been. Nobody is ever at home no more. And like, yeah, we are home. We are just on the computer. I mean I like it myself, I really do. But it is just really hard for me to get on it with them on it.[5]

The PCs for Families (PCF) project, initiated in 1996, ran for three years. Its purpose has been to determine the long-term educational and social changes that occur in children and within their families when they are given free and unlimited access to network-based computing both at home and at school (Ehrich et al. 1998). Prior to the PCF intervention, most of the families in the PCF group (67%, or 16 out of 24) and 58% of the control group already had a computer at home; a third of each group already had a network connection from home. Computers and internet connectivity were given to the roughly 24 families each year whose child joined an internet-intensive fifth-grade classroom by random selection. There were no financial commitments for these parents.

The Riner area is primarily a rural, farming community near Virginia Tech that has in recent years attracted faculty and staff to its rolling hills and peaceful countryside. Through random selection, the children and families in the PCF group represent a broad cross-section of backgrounds and economic and educational levels; networking and support was provided free of charge. Each child attended an after-school program for an hour a week, where teachers and project staff (from Virginia Tech) taught technology relevant to classroom work. Also, each parent had the option of attending an evening session for an hour a week for the same purpose. Upon graduation from fifth grade, each child moved on to a regular sixth-grade class (which was less internet-based); and the families retained their networked computer at home.

The fifth grade students in the 1998–99 school year kept records of their home computer use for the study (McCreary 2001). Complete data for 32 students in both the PCF group and the control group show some interesting use patterns. Over the school year, PCF students reported using their home computer an average of 58 minutes per day; the control group of students from the standard fifth-grade classroom in the same school reported an average of 85 minutes per day. Of this overall usage, PCF students reported playing computer games an average of 12 minutes per day, compared to 52 minutes for the control group. The PCF students reported a lower average of internet use from home (28 minutes), compared with 42 minutes per day for the control group. PCF students used the home computer for homework an average of 15 minutes per day, whereas the control group reported an average of 13 minutes per day. Overall, the PCF students spent less time on the home computer and less time playing games, although homework time was similar between the two groups. This may be because the PCF students had more computers (one per every two students) in the classroom and were therefore less interested in using them in the evening.

Most PCF families enjoyed e-mail, with many parents using it at work, or to communicate with family members.[6] But a second pattern that emerged was that some used it quite a bit, others hardly at all. Further investigation revealed that PCF families who do not have distant friends and relatives stopped using electronic mail after the initial learning phase. Households with distant friends and relatives continued and expanded their use (McCreary 2001).

Conclusions and Policy Implications

We need to separate what is new about "new media" from what is not new. There is no question that some of the specific technologies and services of the internet (hubs, routers, multimedia, discussion lists) are new. The scope of access to resources, such as information and individuals or organizations, is new. But the type of content and the need for guidelines and boundaries for young people exposed to that type of content are not new. Families and other nurturing groups (friends) and institutions (schools, government) need to set limits for children and young adults, as they always have. This role as guardian also imposes on them the onus of understanding the benefits and risks of new media (and particularly the internet). As a social policy, it is important that we maximize the opportunities for increasing citizens' literacy in network computing through public access and education. We know that computing diffuses predominantly from the workplace or school to home. The networked computer has become an increasingly common tool in the workplace, not only among white-collar workers, but blue-collar, as well. These days, most jobs, for example, a car mechanic or sales clerk, require some basic computing skills. In fact, car mechanics are under pressure to gain skills in computing as engines evolve from mechanical to electronic devices. Schools need to support teachers in learning to use internet resources and in teaching students where boundaries lie.

The Turow study (1999) finds that "gung ho online parents" have had a connection longer than other online parents (worriers and disenchanted parents)—they are more likely to go online at work and somewhat more likely to consider themselves advanced or expert users. This is consistent with findings in a 1999 study by Pew Charitable Trust (Kohut 1999) and the Annenberg Public Policy Center. The Pew/Annenberg study showed that later adopters of the internet are different from early adopters in terms of socio-economic status, personal attributes, interests, and comfort with the technology. For example, just 11% of those who came online within the last year turned to the internet for election news, compared to 19% of longtime users. Only 7% of new users e-mailed a group or official compared to 21% of experienced users; and 7% engaged in online discussions about politics, compared with 14% of the more experienced users (Kohut 1999, p. 18). The interests of later adopters tend to be more commercial (games, shopping) than earlier adopters. As a consequence, these services—from weather information to entertainment—are growing much faster than political information services or international news.

The differences in interests among segments of society mean that the private sector will seek to provide services to meet the greater demand by the bulk of society for online shopping and entertainment. Can the private sector mobilize a community to build local content and services? To date, private sector attempts, such as those of America Online to partner with a local newspaper and create, for example, Dallas Online, have not been successful (Cohill and Kavanaugh 2000). From a policy perspective, it is essential that local institutions (schools, libraries, civic organizations, local government, community groups) lead efforts to build content and train their members and constituencies. Community-based initiatives to scale services for local users and purposes will help to ensure local, nonprofit ownership of at least some online content. Moreover, in areas of the country where there is a well-established community network with a critical mass of users, we can expect parents to be less anxious about potential online threats.

At the same time that the internet is diffusing to a mass audience, the human computer interface is improving. It will continue to become easier to use a computer (in fact, appliances and tools will increasingly become computerized, such as the remote control for the TV). Software will increasingly accomplish daily small tasks (e.g., convert and store family photos and home video on CDs for editing and storage, help us select online music tracks and burn them onto our personal CD collection, or create an online jukebox of favorite hits). A generation has grown up using computers and is joining the workforce and establishing households. They are more comfortable with the internet and other information tools and services than their aging parents.

From a policy perspective, it is important for community network designers and managers to target inexpensive bundled services to local organizations and groups. Diffusion of internet services is more rapid, as a result, which also makes it possible for a greater proportion of interested individuals to become more involved in the local community and civic affairs. The listserv and related e-mail discussion tools clearly help members of organizations, groups, and social networks strengthen ties and exchange resources among members. When "weak" ties across different social networks are strengthened, communities mobilize resources more quickly and organize collective action more easily. In the process, members of organizations and social networks become familiar with the numerous benefits of internet resources and the extent to which these benefits outweigh risks. As parents, they gain the necessary skills and knowledge to mitigate against harmful effects of internet use.

Notes

1. The beta test lasted from January through October 1993, involving 183 participants. A subset of this group participated in focus group interviews and completed questionnaires.
2. S. Patterson, A. Bishop, and A. Kavanaugh. "Preliminary Evaluation of the Blacksburg Electronic Village." Final Report to the Council on Library Resources, p. 11.
3. Parent #22, 1999 Interview.
4. Parent #14, 1999 Interview.
5. Parent #6, 1999 Interview.

6. The author used NUDIST software to analyze three rounds of interviews with Riner parents and students (1997, 1998, 1999).

References

Bandura, A. 1977. "Self-efficacy: Toward a Unifying Theory of Behavioral Change." *Psychological Review* 84: 191–215.

Bandura, A. 1986. *Social Foundations of Thought and Action: A Social Cognitive Theory*. Englewood Cliffs, N.J.: Prentice-Hall.

Cohill, A., and A. Kavanaugh. 2000. *Community Networks: Lessons from Blacksburg, VA*. Norwood, MA: Artech House.

Coleman, J. 1988. "Social Capital in the Creation of Human Capital." *American Journal of Sociology* 94: 95–120.

Dutton, W. H., E. M. Rogers, and S. H. Jun. 1987b. "The Diffusion and Impacts of Information Technology in Households." *Oxford Surveys in Information Technology* 4: 133–193.

Ehrich, R., and A. Kavanaugh. 1997. "Managing the Evolution of a Virtual School." In A. Cohill and A. Kavanaugh (eds.), *Community Networks: Lessons from Blacksburg, Virginia* (1st ed.). Norwood, Mass.: Artech.

Ehrich, R., and F. McCreary. 1999. "Immersive Educational Technology: Changing Families and Learning." Paper presented at the American Education Research Association 1999, Montreal, April 19–23. Available online at ⟨http:// www.pixel.cs.vt.edu/edu/fix⟩.

Ehrich, R., F. McCreary, R. Reaux, K. Rowland, and A. Ramsey. 1998. "Home-School Networking to Support Constructivist Learning in a Rural Elementary School: Lessons from Families, Schools, and Researchers." Paper presented at the American Education Research Association, 1998, San Diego, April 13–17. Available online at ⟨http://pixel.cs.vt.edu/edu/fis⟩.

Granovetter, M. 1973. "The Strength of Weak Ties." *American Journal of Sociology* 78: 1360–1380.

Kasarda, J., and M. Janowitz. 1974. "Community Attachment in Mass Society." *American Sociological Review* 39: 328–339.

Kavanaugh, A. 1999. "The Impact of the Internet on Community Involvement: A Social Network Analysis Approach." Paper presented at the Telecommunications Policy Research Conference, Alexandria, VA, September 25–27, 1999.

Kavanaugh, A., and S. Patterson. 1998. "The Impact of the Internet on Social Capital: A Test Case." Paper presented at the National Communications Association, New York, November 1998.

Kohut, A. 1999. "The Internet News Audience Goes Ordinary." Report by the Pew Charitable Trust and the Annenberg Public Policy Center.

Marsden, P., and N. Lin, eds. 1982. *Social Structures and Network Analysis*. Beverly Hills, Calif.: Sage.

McQuail, D., and S. Windahl. 1981. *Communication Models for the Study of Mass Communication.* New York: Longman.

McCreary, F. 2001. "Empirical Evaluation of Technology-rich Learning Environment." Ph.D. dissertation, Department of Industrial and Systems Engineering, Virginia Polytechnic Institute & State University.

National Telecommunications and Information Administration. 1998. *Falling through the Net: Defining the Digital Divide.* Washington, D.C.: U.S. Department of Commerce.

Newton, K. 1997. "Social Capital and Democracy." *American Behavioral Scientist* 40(5): 575–586.

Patterson, S., A. Bishop, and A. Kavanaugh. 1994. "Preliminary Evaluation of the Blacksburg Electronic Village." Final Grant Report to the Council on Library Resources.

Patterson, S., and A. Kavanaugh. 1994. "Rural Users Expectations of the Information Superhighway." *Media Information Australia* 74 (November): 57–61.

Pool, I. 1977. *The Social Impact of the Telephone.* Cambridge, Mass.: MIT Press.

Putnam, R. 1993. "The Prosperous Community: Social Capital and Public Life." *The American Prospect* 4, no. 13 (Spring): Available online at ⟨http://www.prospect.org/v4/13/putnam-r.html⟩.

Putnam, R. 1995. "Bowling Alone: America's Declining Social Capital." *Journal of Democracy* 6: 67–78.

Putnam, R. 2000. *Bowling Alone: The Collapse and Revival of American Community.* New York: Simon & Schuster.

Reader's Digest. 1996. "The Most Wired Town in America: A Small Virginia Town Is Leading the Way to a Whole New Age." *Reader's Digest* (July), 54–58.

Rogers, E. 1982. *Diffusion of Innovation.* New York: Free Press.

Ruberg, L. 1994. "Computer Mediated Communication Environment." Ph.D. diss. Virginia Polytechnic Institute and State University, Department of Teaching and Learning, Blacksburg, Virginia.

Salancik, G. R., and J. Pfeffer. 1978. "A Social Information Approach to Job Attitudes and Task Design." *Administrative Science Quarterly* 23: 224–252.

Sproull, L., and S. Kiesler. 1991. *Connections: New Ways of Working in the Networked Organization.* Cambridge, Mass.: MIT Press.

Steinfield, C., W. Dutton, and P. Kovaric. 1989. "A Framework and Agenda for Research on Computing in the Home." In Jerry Salvaggio and Jennings Bryant (eds.), *Media Use in the Information Age: Emerging Patters of Adoption and Consumer Use.* Hillsdale, N.J.: Erlbaum.

Turow, J. 1999. *The Internet and the Family: The View from the Parents, the View from the Press.* Report No. 27, The Annenberg Public Policy Center of the University of Pennsylvania, Philadelphia.

Wellman, B. 1996. "Electronic Groups Are Social Networks." In Sara Kiesler (ed.), *The Culture of the Internet.* Hillsdale, N.J.: Erlbaum.

Wellman, B., and S. D. Berkowitz. 1988. *Social Structures: A Network Approach.* New York: Cambridge University Press.

Wellman, B., P. Carrington, and A. Hall. 1984. "Networks as Personal Communities." In S. D. Berkowitz and Barry Wellman (eds.), *Structural Sociology.* Cambridge: Cambridge University Press.

Wellman, B., and S. Wortley. 1988. *Brothers' Keepers: Situating Kinship Relations in Broader Networks of Social Support.* Research Paper No. 167. Centre for Urban and Community Studies, University of Toronto, Toronto, Canada.

Wellman, B., J. Salaff, D. Dimitrova, L. Garton, M. Gulia, and C. Hythornthwaite. 1996. "Computer Networks as Social Networks: Collaborative Work, Tele-work, and Virtual Community." *Annual Review of Sociology* 22: 213–239.

Williams, B. 1988. "Formal Structures and Social Reality." In D. Gambetta (ed.), *Trust: Making and Breaking Cooperative Relations.* Oxford: Basil Blackwell.

Wunderman, Cato, and Johnson. 1996. "Moms with Kids." Focus group transcription, May 20–24, Blacksburg, VA.

Wunderman, Cato, and Johnson. 1997. "Moms with Kids." Focus group transcription, June 10, Blacksburg, VA.

20

Families and the Web: Community Building at Work

Lodis Rhodes

Introduction

The Austin Learning Academy's annual literacy festival was about to begin. It was being held in the cafeteria at the neighborhood elementary school. The festival's theme was "Honoring Our Ancestors." The Austin Learning Academy (ALA) staff and the 100 families that participate in its education programs had been preparing for the festival for almost three months. Many of their children attended the elementary school. The festival itself would be a triumph of technical achievements. The achievers? They were a diverse group of ordinary families—families who had become part of ALA's extended family during the preceding year. More important, many of the parents were now also coming to the school campus four days a week to participate in their own learning programs, programs offered by the ALA.

A core group of twenty-five families, including the Mecha[1] family, had recently finished the ALA's FamilyCARE (Computer Assembly Refurbishment, and Enhancement) program. FamilyCARE, built on an ethic of community service, allowed families to "earn" new computers by learning to build them and then teaching other families how to do the same. In the center of the cafeteria, the Mechas eased into chairs around their new computer. Sylvia and her brother, Andy, had helped their parents, Daniel and Rosa, build it. Sylvia was nine years old. Her brother was twelve. Sylvia booted the machine. She and Andy quickly loaded the software the family used to create the web site of their family tree. They needed to print the banner of their family tree. Across the room other families were unpacking small quilted tapestries or pottery plates made of clay. The art and crafts depicted important events from the respective histories of each family.

ALA's Tech Teens, the heart and soul of the CARE program, were setting up a fully functional five-computer network in one corner of the cafeteria. The computers shared a phone line linked to the internet. The one-line network allowed people at each of the five computers to all use the internet at the same time. The teens had built the small network from new and reclaimed computer parts. They had also set up another computer, which was also fully functional. The collection of computer parts and cables had been taken from the case, reassembled on an anti-static mat, and powered up to drive a monitor and speakers. The teens would use this "naked" computer to play their favorite music CDs while they explained how the computer works. They had spent less than $1,000 of ALA money to assemble the six-computer exhibit. After the festival, the computers would be given to other non-profit community groups in the neighborhood.

In yet another corner of the room, members of the Dawson Neighborhood Association, which now included some ALA families, put the finishing touches on a scale model of their neighborhood. The association had developed the model, which was the key feature of the master plan that they presented to the Austin City Council, for their use in guiding changes in their neighborhood. The plan itself had also been posted to the association's new web site—a site that included an interactive, virtual tour of the neighborhood. In the months leading up to the festival, each family became a skilled user of computers and the internet and taught and learned from others.

The upcoming festival was the feature story on the front page of the local daily paper. The headline read, "Across the Great Divide." The story began, "... at first glance, an educational program that celebrates heritage and technology may appear to be looking backward and forward at the same time." The caption above the picture of the Mecha family was more significant, "celebrating meaningful connections."[2] The festival did represent meaningful connections. Wires, cables, and machines were connected; more important, however, the festival had been a catalyst to forge a civic network of new connections and working relationships among families and organizations.

If you would try to picture the buzz of activity that was the festival, add this image to it. Almost all the participants were working-class black and Latino families—ordinary, everyday folks who live on the "have-not" side of the digital divide. An irony in the festival was that it was not a showcase of computers and the internet. While technology had caught the attention of the media, the festival told a less obvious but more compelling story. The real story is how ordinary families, with proper guidance, support, and motivation had integrated internet technologies into their daily life.

The major theme of this less obvious story is the critical role small community-based organizations like ALA play in creating tech-friendly, family-oriented learning environments. A companion theme is how a few technology activists from the public, private, and non-profit sectors made free public access to the internet happen for moderate and low-income families. The story's central plot is the interplay of families, neighborhoods, and community-based organizations, as each grew more technically competent and self-reliant. There is also a moral to the story: Meaningful access to technology must be gauged in context, over time, and in multiple naturally connected learning environments.

Context

If we want to know more about how families use the internet, we must develop portraits as well as take snapshots. That is, we must assess behavior and attitudes in the natural organizations and neighborhoods— the important places—where families live, learn, work, and play. The key question, then, is to understand these places as teaching and learning environments. What makes some places more effective than others?

ALA is a small, community-based organization (CBO), which has provided learning and family-support programs[3] in Austin since 1988. It is a recognized leader in the field,[4] as well as a leader in a nationwide movement known as "community networks." Community networks (Nets) are shoestring operations, usually staffed with volunteers. The Nets rely on wit and ingenuity to survive on donated equipment, recycled PCs, and discounted rates for connectivity. ALA staff believes that effective use of internet technologies in low-income neighborhoods begins with carefully structured *public access* to them. It defines access at the neighborhood level and as a meaningful, effective use of technology. Neighborhood access has three distinguishing traits: (1) it is a network of multiple sites outside the home; (2) sites are easily accessible to neighborhood households, usually within walking distance; and (3) the sites are engaged in complementary teaching and learning activities. Structured access is purposive activity in the right places. If the place is right, families will find relevant uses for the technology when they are in those places.

Austin has an extensive network of public access sites. ALA, along with two other small organizations, the Austin Free-Net (AFN) and MAIN (Metropolitan Austin Interactive Network), pushed their development. ALA came up with innovative ways to introduce new users to the technology and engage them in using it. AFN provided connectivity, server computers, and a network administrator for ALA and other public access sites. MAIN used its server to host web sites and found volunteers to help neighborhood organizations build their own. A small, local for-profit ISP discounted rates for AFN. A media firm helped raise money and donated design services to MAIN and community groups. Large public and private institutions, the University of Texas, the City of Austin, Southwestern Bell, and Time-Warner, played critical but secondary roles. The university provided researchers, student volunteers, and a participatory approach to doing research that included neighborhood residents and organizations as being something more than research subjects. The phone and cable companies helped with several demonstration projects. These large and small organizations launched the experiment in public access in Austin.

ALA and its partners built a network of public access sites on the strong sense of neighborhood and place that already existed in Austin. They started with two neighborhoods where ALA already had a presence and positive identity. The partners knew they faced a dynamic problem: the challenge of providing access changed daily with the changing character of the internet technology and its competing industries. Their first step was to tie access to the places that were already important destination points for families in the target neighborhoods. The next step was helping those places develop the creative learning environments it would take for each organization and neighborhood to become more self-reliant problem solvers. While this was a simple idea, it was not an easy one to implement. The partners used technology and the internet as the catalyst to make things happen in neglected areas of Austin.

Place exists in real space. ALA is careful in deciding when and where to locate its programs. While the partners heard a lot about cyberspace being a new place, ALA considered it a qualitatively different and secondary learning environment. ALA, however, would make it part of the real places of families. They would introduce cyberspace as an extension of already familiar places. For ALA families, this meant the learning centers where family members could learn new and interesting things and activities like the festival.

The first general lesson then of the festival is that people learn to use technology in specific places—the where. Place influences how the technology is used. The places in this case are ALA's family learning centers; ALA became part of the neighborhood rather than merely providing services in the neighborhood. Each ALA learning center has its own look and feel. ALA families quickly become attached to their own neighborhood center even though they regularly visit other ALA centers and its main tech lab in other neighborhoods. The ALA staff develops ownership through participatory techniques like advisory and problem solving groups of program participants. In a real sense, participants become extended family and the centers become family activity rooms.

A second lesson of the festival is the tech talent in low-income neighborhoods. It is usually found at its vibrant, creative best in adolescents and teens.[5] For example, the Tech Teens, as shown with their one-line network and the naked computer, learned to think critically and change situations that had proven to be problems for them. Their projects got them more for their money and more individual time on the internet. From the standpoint of innovation, the teens had been encouraged to tinker with ideas and things at the center. The teens quickly came to see the centers as places where their tech talent and curiosity met opportunity.

The ALA staff faced another obstacle in successfully introducing families to computers and the internet. It had to counter mistaken images shaped by media and markets of a digital divide as metaphor for "haves" and "have-nots." The imagery is a biased, impoverished view of both the capacity and potential of technologies. The bias views private control, commercial applications, and entertainment as the only solutions to access. It further frames differences in access mostly in terms of race, ethnicity, and gender. Whites have more access than ethnic minorities. Boys have more access than girls. The exhibitions at the festival offer different images and lessons.

Use of the internet is not simply a matter of cost, "killer" applications, or access to a high-speed connection to the internet. Novak and Hoffman (1998) provide insight into a deeper complexity. They found that while income levels affect internet access and computer use for blacks and whites, there are significant differences, especially for children. Seventy-three percent of white children have computers at home, while only 32.9 percent of black children have PCs at home. Level of income does not explain all the differences. Equally significant, white children who do not have PCs at home are more likely to have alternative places to find and use them. That is, a white child's social network (friends, relatives, parent's workplace) is more likely to produce a PC and access to the internet than the social network of a black child.

A disturbing feature of the digital divide is the gap between "haves" and "have-nots" is widening. A 1999 NTIA study documents the trend.[6] Access from home is increasing for all groups, faster for whites than ethnic minorities at all income levels. The trend is significant for two reasons. It suggests that a healthy economy and falling computer prices do not bridge the divide. It also suggests that by defining access as home access, we severely limit how we think about accessibility. We overlook the significance of social networks in where and how people actually use PCs and the internet. An analogy is phone use. As Rhodes and Hadden (1995) showed in their research on phone use, individuals who do not have phones at home nonetheless value communicating by phone. They seek out and use the phones of friends, relatives, and neighbors. They also use public pay phones. In this case, understanding patterns of phone use requires understanding behavior, attitudes, and demand in context.

In effect, Novak and Hoffman (1998) hint at what Chapman and Rhodes (1997) described as a "demand deficit" in low-income communities.[7] That is, most people—up to 70 percent of users, according to some surveys—access the internet primarily at work or at school. In turn, they use it for purposes defined by those places. When we learn to use the internet at work or school, we develop habits of use to fit the tasks defined by those places, even when we are using the internet at home. People in low-income communities, however, typically do not have meaningful access to the internet either at school, work, or public buildings. Therefore, they must discover their own reasons to use the technology, as well as a place to use it. While they may not have as many choices of where they use the internet, their habits of use are usually not shaped by school or the work place. They have neither the advantages nor disadvantages of computer habits learned in such places. Ironically, limited access in highly regulated environments may be an advantage when the goal is experimentation. Since marketers have ignored low-income communities as places to invest in physical infrastructure, the communities may have more time and freedom to experiment if the technology that does come their way gets to the right places. In short, we should not mistake limited demand as a lack of money, talent, skill, or effort.

Unpacking the "Demand Deficit" Idea

Several ideas are packed into the concept *demand deficit*. Probably the most important one is the unasked question of purpose—"access for what?" As with access to phones, research shows that when people need to use a phone, they find and use one. Families are resourceful. The point holds for computers and the internet in low-income neighborhoods.

Demand deficit involves another idea—social capital. Social capital boils down to who you call when you need help in solving a problem. The phone, in this case, is a tool of social engagement. It enables people to interact. Who we call depends on the names in our personal phone book. How we actually use the phone depends on our relationship with the person at the other end of the line. In the end, what is relevant to us is not the technology but if we solve our problem. This same logic should lead us to want to know about the existing networks of social relationships. Access then becomes a problem of introducing technologies into neighborhoods in ways and places that enhance existing patterns of communications—the social glue—and extend to new relationships—the social bridges.

The current approaches most often used to define and study the digital divide produce snapshots, not portraits. We plot and track trends. We also need assessment approaches that allow us to listen more carefully to families and for longer periods of time. To listen, we must find the community places where people talk to each other and stay there long enough to actually hear what they say and mean. Oldenberg (1991) describes such a place as a "third place" away from home (the "first place") and work or school (the "second place"). These are the low-profile, easily accessible places in the community where conversation among regulars is the main activity.

Finally, the idea of "demand deficit" implies a process of learning. Learning is a social activity. Children illustrate it when they play with video games. They exhibit technical knowledge and skill. Where and how did they learn to use the technology? They did not take a class. They did not learn at school or work. They did learn from a friend. And, most likely, they learned at that friend's home or with that friend at an arcade—a kids' version of Oldenberg's third place. Another significant point is that learning is enhanced by how video game equipment is designed. The engineering in the design presupposes social interaction. It accommodates multiple players. The software is interactive. The games are most interesting and challenging when players cooperate with each other. Good design, then, quickly and efficiently gets children way up on the technical learning curve.

Children quickly acquire the technical competence to play video games for two reasons. First, their learning is not detached from their use of the equipment. They are motivated to learn because they can immediately use what they are learning. Second, their learning is a secondary feature of other social activity. Learning is not the objective, having fun with friends is. The video game and learning has a relevant context for children. The context is having fun with a buddy in ways that get organized and controlled by the buddies.

The process children use to teach and learn from each other is almost the direct opposite of what we impose on adults and on children when they are in school. For example, we tell adults they must be trained, as is the case in workforce technology programs. We tell children the internet and computers are for homework. In neither case is the new learner allowed to discover his own interests and reasons for learning the technology. The challenge is not only to find the right places to listen, but to figure out how to reconnect learning the internet to the practical, everyday needs and interest of the prospective user.

If children are the most creative users of interactive technologies, we might wonder when and how they shift from learning basic skills to creative use of the newly acquired skills. That is, what is the learning curve for individuals and communities to go from learning basic skills to using technologies for their own purposes? Does an environment that fosters cooperative work affect movement along the curve? If it does, then we should be looking for the places that emphasize cooperative work and trusting social relationships. Unfortunately, school, work, and government buildings are not the places we think of as steeped in the ethic of trust and cooperation. Then why do we take our snapshots in such places?

A Different Way: The Austin Access Model

In the same way that there is a different way to think about access, there is a different way to think about helping low-income communities and families become more technically competent and self-reliant. Rather than focusing only on *economic* development, as is typically the case, one might focus on the precursors of development that sustain it over time: learning networks, critical thinking, and innovation. The Austin Access Model for public access is a way to build and sustain the physical infrastructure, social infrastructure, and a collective technical competence in target neighborhoods. The activists who lead the effort for public access needed several elements that were already in place.

Austin, Texas, is one of the nation's leading high-tech cities. It is similar to other high-tech cities such as Seattle, Portland, and San Jose. Austin has the University of Texas. Universities are usually the largest gateways to the internet in the communities where they are located. They provided dial-up connectivity in their respective communities and large-scale exposure to the internet before the emergence of commercial ISPs.

The University of Texas, with its over 75,000 students, faculty, and staff, accounted for much of the city's early connectivity. In this sense, UT was for Austin and public access what Virginia Tech was for Blacksburg, Virginia, and the WELL.[8]

Very early in Austin's high-tech surge, Austin's city government adopted an entrepreneurial approach to information technology. Public officials developed a plan to make Austin the "wired" city it has become. The city's plan called for developing broadband communications capability for businesses, homes, and public institutions. It also included distribution of broadband technologies within city government to improve delivery of city services. Finally, it required promoting access to information technologies for Austin's low-income neighborhoods.

The city plan, ambitious and thwarted by the state legislature,[9] did create the opportunity for ALA and its community partners to bring high-speed access to Austin's low-income neighborhoods and families. Their plan had three prominent features: (1) it was project oriented and emphasized education and building social capital; (2) it valued experimentation especially in finding cost-effective ways to get more equipment and connectivity into neighborhoods; and (3) it embraced quiet advocacy, activism, and innovative successes like the Heritage and Literacy Festival. Each feature is empowering for families.

While it is too early to declare a long-term success, the strategy has brought meaningful, effective access to families in Austin who would otherwise be without it. For example, ALA's work with its partners and the University of Texas's LBJ School has put more than 100 internet-ready PCs in fifteen community sites in two Austin neighborhoods, all of the city's public libraries, and fifteen households. The partnership includes an impressive list of business firms.[10] The Dell Foundation provided the initial support for ALA's highly successful FamilyCARE project. FamilyCARE is a community service project wherein families learn to build PCs for their own use and for other community non-profit agencies. Families participating in the CARE program assembled and distributed more than thirty-five PCs last year. Some neighborhood residents learned to build a web site. The process and festival showed other neighborhood residents how they could use the internet to tell their own story about their neighborhoods. This is why the Dawson Neighborhood Association created its neighborhood web site.

The Austin Access Model is unusual in part because of Austin's uniqueness. Austin is a big and small city. It is big enough to have sufficient resources to divert some of them to building an infrastructure in low-income neighborhoods. It is small enough so that key people in key institutions know each other. The depth and reach of the social network—Austin's social capital—is not only focused on the digital divide but also consciously experimenting with ways to bridge it.

Wit at Work and Lessons Learned

The fugitive group of schoolteachers who started ALA in 1988 wanted to escape the straitjacket of the local school district. They implemented a problem-centered approach to teaching. They believed learning must emphasize choice, control, and content. Learners needed the control to choose content that interested them and which they could use immediately. The schoolteachers reasoned that new knowledge and skills are useful only to the degree they help solve the everyday problems that confront families and communities—practical problems like limited access to computers and the internet. They made sure that ALA's goal was and is "access to literacy." Access to literacy is broader and better idea than access to technology.

ALA's embrace of the access to literacy concept, and its view of the digital divide, borrows from several intellectual traditions. One is the community-of-inquiry concept of Jane Addams and John Dewey's Hull House.[11] Another is the model of applied research as embodied in the extension service of the land grant university. Finally, there are Amartya Sen's thoughts on economic development. In the very accessible *Development as Freedom*, Sen (1999) argues that most forms of development follow from expanded individual human freedoms. That is, civic and political participation, economic development, and social progress follow from expanding opportunities to learn and committing to good health. These traditions share themes. Each stresses inclusive, cooperative working relationships. Each is strongly empirical. Finally, each assumes that communities have assets that can and should be developed. The themes, in turn, are guides to help decide how to design learning activities that foster creative use of the internet and decide on the places to offer them in low-income neighborhoods.

While small, community-based organizations like ALA face substantial obstacles, they have turned their wit and ingenuity to the content side of the access equation. ALA's schoolteachers are doing it by combining their commitment to teaching with the tactics of community organizing. They have developed a highly collaborative process, the Austin Access Model, which can be adapted and used in other communities with a similar situation.

ALA's Heritage and Literacy Festival was a capstone to the first stage of Austin's effort to achieve equitable access. ALA reshaped its philosophy of access to literacy to capitalize on the attention being focused on the internet and the so-called digital divide. In the process, ALA helped forge what has become known nationally as the Austin Access Model. ALA's founding group of schoolteachers has learned some surprising lessons. The group has been actively experimenting for four years on ways to introduce interactive technologies to low-income communities and engage families in using them. During that period, it has developed a nationally recognized strategy of community service to get more equipment into the homes and community places in neighborhoods. The community service program incorporates activities that permit neighborhood residents to quickly learn the basic skills needed to use the neighborhood computer network. They learn to use the network not as a stand-alone resource. Rather, individuals and families become information assets in the neighborhood's newly developing knowledge network. Increased use of the internet occurs as a family activity both at home and in other places, especially the third places in neighborhoods where residents were introduced to and learned to use the internet. The knowledge network and the community competence it represents come about because of the emphasis on social capital. The increasing level of collective competence is a byproduct of this social dynamic.

Use Follows Relevance

The silence we think we hear coming from low-income neighborhoods about their interest in interactive technology is not the absence of demand. The silence is the voice of "exit." It says clearly, "we do not see and hear ourselves in cyberspace." The families participating in the festival should remind us to trust the judgment and skills of citizens. Give ordinary folks, even poor ones, adequate information and the proper support, and they will figure out things for themselves. They will discover their own uses for the internet. By taking a closer look at the old-fashioned kind of community network, we might come to appreciate the ability and strength of civic associations to regulate the behavior of their members.

The Learning Curve

The personal computer, the PC, is a metaphor for a particular approach to both engineering design and learning. The approach is almost diametrically opposed to the tenets of democratic participation.[12] It presupposes highly individualized definition of technical competence and uses of the competence that favor private rather than public interests. Is there little wonder that the commercial internet has transformed the acquisition of competence into a commodity to be packaged and sold? This as contrasted with viewing technical competence as a resource to be developed and shared. In assuming that technical competence is something to share rather than hoard, ALA's schoolteachers note that the learning curve for families has a distinct three-stage arc:

1. "I can do this,"
2. "Look at this," and
3. the creative stage, "There ought to be a way."

In the first stage new users gain confidence mastering basic skills. They realize they will not break the machine and that it is relatively easy to work the keyboard and mouse to surf the web. In the process, they succeed in using the technology in ways most people do. They retrieve information, send and receive e-mail, and write letters, resumes, and journals. The quickly move to stage two. They begin sharing items of personal interest with someone else. This stage also marks a shift in thinking about the internet. New users realize that PCs and the internet are more than entertainment and work. They begin using it to help think, share ideas, and solve problems. This is when talent meets opportunity as it did for the Tech Teens.

You Can't Do It Alone

The success of the Austin Access Model is testament the digital divide is a complex problem. There is no single solution. Large organizations must learn to work with small one in ways that do not crush the smaller partners. Small organizations must be clear about their own mission and purpose so as not to divert their already scarce resources. Those in the government and business sectors must realize that the *public* interest is not the same as government and that *private* interest is not the same as business.

Conclusion

You hear many voices and conversations about computers and the internet in Austin. The conversations ALA families are having sound nothing like what we usually read and hear about in the media. The families seldom talk obviously about technology. However, given the chance in the right places, they quickly learn to integrate it into their daily routines. They are eager to learn to use technology. Parents are not unduly anxious about their children's use of the internet, probably because parents and children have played together as they learned to use the technology. The "play" was a learning process whereby parents and children were immediately able to use their technical savvy in community-service projects important to them.

The ALA experience in bridging the digital divide also tells us that the major casualty of limited access is creativity. Moreover, the best response to irresponsible content on the internet is to crowd it out with more responsible content. Responsible use of the internet is not necessarily just a matter of policy and regulation. It is also an issue of content and capacity. Policy must encourage experimentation. The experimentation will lead to innovative ways to increase access in low-income neighborhoods. Trust the good judgment of citizens. Give them the right tools, support, and learning environments, and they will find their own reasons to use computers and the internet.

Notes

1. Family names and the names of program participants have been changed.

2. The story appeared in the April 18, 1999, edition of the *Austin American Statesman*, p. B1.

3. The Austin Learning Academy programs and services include parenting and family literacy programs; GED, ESL and ABE education programs for adults; Even Start early childhood program; academic enrichment; citizenship; and environmental and conservation programs.

4. In 1995 the Harvard University Family Research Project identified the Austin Learning Academy's Family Learning Center model as one of eight exemplary comprehensive family support programs nationwide.

5. See Horrigan (1999) for a discussion universal service policy and how it might be shaped to encourage innovative approaches to equitable access.

6. National Telecommunications and Information Administration (1999), *Falling through the Net*. Washington, D.C.: U.S. Department of Commerce.

7. Gary Chapman and Lodis Rhodes (1997) develop the concept "demand deficit" in an article. See "Nurturing Neighborhood Nets," *Technology Review* 100, no. 7 (October): 48–54.

8. See Servon (2000) for a detailed case study of Austin emergence as a high tech city and the evolution of local community technology programs.

9. The Texas Legislature passed a bill to prevent a political jurisdiction from owning an equity interest in a telecommunications network.

10. The list includes the Dell Foundation, Time-Warner, Southwestern Bell, and KLRU, the public television affiliate. Each has contributed money and/or services.

11. The early pragmatists Charles Sanders Peirce, John Dewey, and Jane Addams developed the community-of-inquiry concept. Time or space does not define the "community" in "community of inquiry." A common question, problem, or interest helps forge the connection. See Shields (1999) for a discussion of the concept as it applies to social activism and public administration.

12. The early concept and application of the PC was "distributed computing"— a way to computing power directly in the hands of the end-user engineers and scientists. While this might be considered a democratizing impulse, it was also not thought of as extending to ordinary citizens.

References

Chapman, G., and L. Rhodes. 1997. "Nurturing Neighborhood Nets." *Technology Review* 100, no. 7 (October): 48–54.

Horrigan, J. B. 1999. Universal Service Policy and Community. Unpublished paper. Presented at 27th Telecommunications Policy Research Conference. September 27, 1999. Washington, D.C.

Lassen, M. M. 1995. *Community-Based Family Support in Public Housing.* Harvard Family Research Project, Harvard University, Cambridge, Mass.

National Telecommunications and Information Administration. 1999. *Falling through the Net*. Washington, D.C.: U.S. Department of Commerce.

Novak, T. P., and D. L. Hoffman. 1998. Bridging the Digital Divide: The Impact of Race on Computer Access and Internet Use. Available at ⟨http://ecommerce. vanderbilt.edu/papers/race/science.html⟩, Retrieved on August 9, 1999.

Oldenberg, R. 1991. *The Great Good Places: Cafes, Coffee Shops, Community Centers, Beauty Parlors, General Stores, Bars, Hangouts, and How They Get You through the Day.* New York: Paragon House.

Rhodes, L. 1998. "I Can Do It!". *Discovery: Research and Scholarship at the University of Texas at Austin.* 15, no. 2: 14–17. Available online at ⟨www.utexas.edu/admin/opa/discovery/disc1998v/5n2/disc_empower.html.⟩

Rhodes, L., and S. Hadden. 1995. *The Evolution of Universal Service Policy in Texas.* Policy Research Project Report No. 116. Lyndon B. Johnson School of Public Affairs, University of Texas, Austin.

Sen, A. 1999. *Development as Freedom.* New York: Knopf.

Servon, L. (2000). *Bridging the Digital Divide: Technology, Community and Public Policy.* Oxford, U.K.: Blackwell. Available online at: ⟨http://policy. rutgers.edu/cupr/aspen/.⟩

Shields, P. M. 1999. The Community of Inquiry: Insights for Public Administration from Jane Addams, John Dewey, and Charles S. Peirce. Unpublished paper presented at the Public Administration Theory Network Conference, March 1999. Portland State University, Portland, Oreg.

21

Examining Community in the Digital Neighborhood: Early Results from Canada's Wired Suburb

Keith N. Hampton and Barry Wellman

21.1 Introduction

A connected society is more than a populace joined through wires and computers. It's a society whose people are connected to each other. For the past two years we have been looking for community online and offline, locally and globally, in the wired suburban neighborhood of "Netville." We want to find out how living in a residential community equipped with no cost, very high speed access to the Internet affects the kinds of interpersonal relations people have with coworkers, friends, relatives, and neighbors.

Advances in personal computer technology, and the rise of computer mediated communication (CMC), have ignited a debate into the nature of community and the effects of cyberspace on social relations. Despite the breathless "presentism" of the current discourse [33], scholarly debate on the nature of community did not originate with the introduction of new computer technologies, but arose out of earlier concerns about the transition from agrarian to urban industrial societies [3] [23]. The discourse surrounding this debate has argued community to be *lost,* *saved,* and even *liberated* in the industrial city [26] [35]. The effect of new communication and information technologies on community and society is the latest chapter in this ongoing debate.

From *Digital Cities: Technologies, Experiences, and Future Perspectives*, ed. Toru Ishida and Katherine Isbister (Heidelberg, Germany: Springer-Verlag, 2000), pp. 194–208. Reprinted with permission from Springer-Verlag GmbH & Co.

Early urban theorists[1] worried about the effects of urbanization on community just as modern dystopians suggest that the lure of new communication technologies will withdraw people from face-to-face contact and further disconnect them from their families and communities [7] [20]. Yet, several scenarios are possible, indeed each scenario may happen to different people or to the same person at different times. In an "information society" where work, leisure, and social ties are all maintained from within the "smart home," people could completely reject the need for social relationships based on physical location. They might find community online, or not at all, rather than on street corners or while visiting friends and relatives. New communication technologies may advance the home as a center for services that encourage a shift towards greater home-centeredness and privatization. At the same time the location of the technology in the home facilitates access to local relationships, suggesting that domestic relations may flourish, possibly at the expense of ties outside the household.

Whatever happens, new communication technologies are driving out the traditional belief that community can only be found locally. Cyberspace has enabled people to find each other through electronic mail (e-mail), group distribution lists, role-playing games, and Web chat rooms (the list is incomplete and obviously evolving). For more than one hundred years, researchers have confronted fears that community is falling apart by searching for it in localities: rural and urban villages. For the most part, their investigations have adhered to the traditional model of community as little groups of neighbors intensively socializing, supporting and controlling one another [31]. Since the 1970s, some of us have argued that community does not have to be local. It is the sociable, supportive, and identity-giving interactions that define community, and not the local space in which they might take place [22] [25].

We are not members of "little-box" societies who deal only with fellow members of the few groups to which we belong: at home, in our neighborhoods, workplaces, or in cyberspace [34]. Social ties vary in intensity, are multistranded, crosscutting, and diverse. They extend across our environment to kinship and friendship relations that traverse a variety of social settings and are maintained through a multiplicity of means that include direct physical contact, telephone, postal mail, and more recently fax, email, and online environments.

Our research has been guided by a desire to study community offline as well as online. We are interested in the totality of relationships in community ties and not just in behavior in one communication medium or locale. In this we differ from studies of "virtual community" that only look at relationships online[2] and from traditional sociological studies of in-person, neighborhood-based communities [10] [15] [37]. The former overemphasizes the prevalence of computer-only ties while the latter ignores the importance of transportation and communication in connecting community members over a distance. Unlike many studies of CMC that observe undergraduates in laboratory experiments,[3] we are keenly interested in studying people in real settings. We are taking into account their social characteristics (gender, socioeconomic status and the like), their social positions (prominence, power), and the broad nature of their participation in social networks. We wonder how the tie between A and B is affected by the presence of absence of their tie with C [28], and how their community involvement intersects with their institutional involvements (work, unions, church, bowling leagues, etc.) and their attitudes toward society (social trust, alienation, etc.) [19].

This chapter looks at the research goals and methods of the Netville project and explores preliminary results on a subsection of the total social relations maintained by the residents of Netville, those within their local neighborhood.

21.2   Research Goals

The Netville project addresses the following questions:

1. Can supportive, sociable and meaningful relations be maintained online as they heretofore have in public (such as cafes, street corners) and private (such as homes, clubs).

2. How do online relationships articulate with offline relationships? Will life online replace, complement, or supplant life in the flesh? How do ties with the same persons incorporate online and offline relationships?

3. What will be the fate of community? Will it atrophy as people stay home to work, learn, and entertain themselves online? Will it foster new solidarities as people get drawn into compelling virtual communities? Will it encourage limited involvement in specialized, partial communities as people surf between interest groups?

4. Will the Internet amplify "glocalization": on the one hand, intensely local—indeed, domestic—involvement; on the other hand, wider ranging social ties maintained in part through computer-mediated communication?

5. Will the Internet encourage social integration and civic involvement? Will it foster social networks and transitive relationships ("friends of friends") that cut across group boundaries, build online institutions, and articulate pressing concerns?

21.3   Netville: The Research Setting

Netville is a good place to investigate these questions. It is a newly-built development of approximately 120 homes, most with three or four bedrooms plus a study.[4] These are detached, closely-spaced, single-family homes in the outer suburbs of Toronto.[5] The typical Netville house, 2,000 square feet on a 40 foot lot, costs about CDN$228,000 in 1997 (US$171,000). The price is 7 percent less than the average price in 1997 for a new home in the same area,[6] or 13 percent less than the fourth-quarter median for the Metropolitan Toronto new-home market [2]. Netville is similar to other developments in the area and is in an area of rapid population growth and home construction.

Netville looks like many other developments except that as you enter you pass a chuckwagon[7] with the saying "Canada's First Interactive New Home Community, *Welcome Pioneers*" written across its canvas. It is one of the few developments in North America where all of its homes were equipped from the start with a series of advanced communication technologies supplied across a high-bandwidth local network. For two years the local network provided residents with high speed Internet access (including electronic mail and Web surfing), computer-desktop videophone (but only within Netville), an online jukebox, a number of entertainment applications, online health services, and local discussion forums, all provided free of charge.[8] In return for all of this free, very high-speed access to the information highway, the residents agreed to be studied by the corporate and nonprofit members of the "Magenta" consortium. This agreement was only lightly enforced and often forgotten by the residents. No resident was ever denied service for refusing to participate, and no data were ever collected without the residents' knowledge.

Netville's local network is a dual hybrid fiber coax technology with an ATM (asynchronous transfer mode) backbone. A coaxial cable drop wire from a coax node was brought into the home where it connects to a PCCU (Personal Computer Connection Unit) located in the basement. The PCCU connected a minimum of five computer ports within each home to the local network. Unfortunately the PCCUs installed in homes were limited in that they only allowed one household port to connect to the local network at a time. A substantial number of households installed independent software, or rigged up internal networks, to circumvent this limitation. Users could reliably expect a bit rate of 16.96 Mbps upstream and 13.57 Mbps downstream across the network. The Magenta consortium provided computer and software support and the major telecommunications member of the consortium staffed 24-hour help lines to support the network.

As technology developed and fashions changed, the telecommunications company responsible for the network decided that the hybrid fiber coax technology used in the development was not the future of residential Internet services. As the telco viewed Netville as a site for technical rather than social research[9] they terminated the field trial early in 1999 to the dismay of the residents who had grown to love the system and assumed it would be there indefinitely [13].

The people living in Netville are largely lower-middle class, English-speaking, and married. About half have completed a university degree [11]. Some are first-time home owners, others were looking for a convenient suburban home, while some were attracted by life in a wired suburb. Those with older children often moved to Netville from a nearby suburb and plan to remain there for the foreseeable future. Those in the early stages of raising a family have less settled plans. More than half of all couples had children living at home when they moved into the community, but as with most newly occupied suburbs a baby boom has since ensued. Most are white, but an appreciable number are racial and ethnic minorities. However, race and ethnicity is less an organizing factor in Netville than lifestyle, stage in the life-cycle, and to a lesser extent socioeconomic status. Residents work at such jobs as technician, teacher, police officer, and small business person. Their median household income in 1997 was CDN$75,000 (US$50,000).

Only a minority of Netville residents were experienced with technology when they moved in. Yet these families are somewhat more involved with home technology than most Canadians. Seventy-eight percent had a personal computer in their homes prior to moving to Netville, as compared to 57 percent of Canadians in 1997 [4]. The great majority of Netville homes have more than one television, own a videocassette recorder, and own a compact disc player: these rates are higher than the Canadian average [11].

Approximately 65 percent of Netville homes participated in the high bandwidth trial and had access to the network for up to two years. To our surprise, the other 35 percent of households were either unable, or unwilling, to participate in the trial despite the no-cost, low-fuss manner in which equipment and service were provided. These households provide a convenient comparison group for studying the effects of computer-mediated communication.

21.4 Research Design

Our research objectives led us to gather information about the residents' community ties online and offline, globally and locally. We have concentrated on learning about residents' interactions within Netville, personal networks (which extend well beyond Netville), civic involvement, Internet use, and individual attitudes. We have relied on a variety of research methods to increase the validity and reliability of our research including ethnographic observation, surveys, monitoring an online community forum, and focus groups.

21.4.1   Ethnographic Observation

Netville's small and compact area made it feasible and desirable to live in the research setting. In April 1997, one of us, Keith Hampton, began participating in local activities (community barbecues, meetings, etc.). Hampton moved into Netville in October 1997 (living in a resident's basement apartment) for a stay that extended until August 1999. He identified himself to all residents he encountered informally and in groups as a student and researcher interested in Netville. Given the widespread public interest in Netville, residents were not surprised about his activity. They treated him kindly and respected his decision to live in Netville as a full participant.

Hampton worked from home, participated in online activities, attended all possible local meetings (formal and informal), walked the neighborhood chatting, and completed a community ethnography similar to that of Gans (1967) in the New Jersey suburb of Levittown [now known as Willingboro]. Observations of the day-to-day experiences of the community provided details about how residents used the available technology, information about local social networks, information about domestic and neighborhood relations, and details of the residents' use of time and local space.

Survey data is useful in tapping information on individual behavior, preferences, and opinions. Yet, the ethnographic observations tell much of Netville's story. The ethnography serves as a record of the group perspective, not in the aggregate reporting of statistics, but in a contextual historical account of the day-to-day events and activities of local residents. The ability to have a participant observer physically present in Netville provided first hand access to information that would have been difficult to collect through surveys, or it would have gone unreported, unobserved and unquestioned during surveys or through the online forums.

For example, residents frequently talked online about burglaries in the community: who was robbed, who witnessed what on the night of the burglary, and future plans for prevention. When a suspicious fire burned down a house one week before its new occupants were scheduled to take possession, nothing related to the fire was ever discussed online. Over the following days, when residents were approached by Hampton on the street, they each recounted a similar story surrounding the house fire, revealing a network of community information that existed externally to the online forum. Residents also wondered why the fire was never discussed online: We believe that it would have crossed an invisible line between the provision of support and aid and community gossip. The online forum was almost exclusively used for the search and provision of various types of support. Since the owners of the burnt-out home were not yet community residents they were not members of the local email list and could not benefit from online offers of support. This suggests that Netville's email list goes a long way in meeting expectations for increasing local support and interaction, but may avoid the sometimes repressive nature of local gossip.

Netville was damaged by a major storm in June 1998 that caused power outages and the shutdown of the local network. Residents mobilized offline, when in the past similar activity had largely been achieved online, to check on the safety of their neighbors and their property, as a series of car prowlings and attempted burglaries were discovered from the same night. Community cliques and organizers were identified. These were based on geography and not on the friendship and interest groups observed online. The observation of, and participation in, mutual support and cooperative strategies in face of what was a relatively small scale disaster revealed the seeds and context to how residents would react to future problems.

The opportunity to conduct a detailed ethnography provided a unique source of information and played a key role in developing rapport with participants. The insights gained through observation and daily interaction were instrumental in developing the kinds of questions asked in our surveys. Moreover, Hampton's visibility and credibility in Netville were vital to convincing many residents to take time from their busy lives to respond to our survey.

Hampton's relationship to community participants became particularly important when the field trial ended. Although most residents were angry at the telco partner and Magenta, because Hampton was a Netville resident—and subject to the same loss of high-speed service—our research was able to continue. Residents continued to be interviewed, and our research goals took on an additional dimension as we studied how residents responded to the threat, and subsequent fact, of the loss of their high-speed service.

21.4.2 Surveys

Our survey obtained information on geographic perception, personal and neighborhood networks, neighboring, community alienation, social trust, work, experience with technology, time-use, and basic demographics. Learning about the residents' social networks—in Netville and outside of it—is a central concern. It is the nature of these networks that will show if personal communities are abundant, strong, solidary-fragmented, and local-nonlocal. Hence the survey used modified versions of social network protocols used by Wellman in earlier research [27].

To obtain information about network ties within Netville, we presented residents with a list of up to 271 adult residents of Netville, asking them "do you recognize this person?" [5]. In addition to asking whom they recognized we were able to collect more detailed information on each name selected, such as: if they socialized, how often they socialized, and how they kept in touch. Reaction to this question type was very positive, almost all seemed to enjoy the exercise, and many reported how interesting they found the question type [12].

To elicit information about socially close members of the residents' personal networks, wherever they live, residents were presented with thirteen "name-generator questions" [6] [27] [1]. For each question, respondents were asked to provide a list of names, using only first names and last initials to create a sense of anonymity and reduce any fear that we would attempt to contact those people listed. There was no limit on the total number of names that a respondent could provide. Once respondents listed names, the survey software created a master list of all the people listed and asked for more detailed information on each member of the personal network: demographics, where and how they met, how often they communicated, and through what means.[10]

The survey was launched in April, 1998 with intentions to administer the survey to all household members 18 years of age or older during both a pre-move and post-move interview. The pre-move survey was to be administered approximately three months prior to moving into

Netville, and the post-move survey approximately one year after living in the community. An adapted version of the pre-move survey was to be administered to all residents who had moved into Netville before they could be contacted for a pre-move survey. Unfortunately, we were forced to move from a pretest-posttest survey design to a single cross-sectional survey of people already living in Netville. There were a series of construction problems, and the telco partner unexpectedly announced plans to withdraw from the field trial and discontinue supplying Netville with access to the high-speed local network. The discovery that a sizeable minority of homes were not connected to the network made comparative analysis possible and the loss of longitudinal information more palatable. We modified the survey for use with people already living in Netville and continued interviewing.

When the Magenta consortium and the telco partner publicly announced the end of the experiment, Netville residents quickly mobilized and used their networked connectivity in an unsuccessful attempt to obtain the continuation of the field trial. Netville residents did not become complete technological have-nots when the trial ended. They are using 56Kb dial-up service (provided free for six months by the telco partner), waiting and hoping for ADSL service, or they have signed up with the high-speed "@Home" cable modem service. This means that a few interviews undertaken in 1999 are more retrospective than is usual in survey research, reporting about past experiences with the local network as well as their continued experience with high-speed Internet access via the @Home network.

As all of our surveying has been computer assisted, data preparation for statistical analysis largely avoids the data entry phase. *SAS* and *SPSS* are being used for statistical analysis, including special procedures developed by our group for personal network analysis [29] [17].

In an ideal situation it would be appropriate to collect survey data at least twice, pre and post-move. Given the potential complications of doing research in a setting with many factors beyond the immediate control of the research team it may only be possible, and indeed prudent, to complete one wave of surveys over as short period of time as possible. In the end, we were able to interview a cross-section of residents, including a small number of people who "intended" to move into Netville but never did, in addition to those who had lived in the community for up to two years and had access to the high-speed network for none to two years.

21.4.3   Focus Groups and Monitoring of the Online Community Forum

As ethnographic observation and surveying have taken the bulk of our time and attention, here we briefly review two other data gathering techniques.

Online Community Forum   The community email list has been one of the more detailed and revealing sources of information. All Netville residents participating in the field trial were automatically subscribed to it. The list provided information on community activities, social networks, the provision of local support and aid, and proved to be a forum for community issues. The list was publicly available to Netville residents and messages were easily recorded without interfering with residents' activities. Since the list was publicly available, and participating residents agreed to have their online activities monitored in exchange for access to the local network, there are few privacy issues beyond protecting the identity of participants in publications. The content of these forums has been completely saved and will be analyzed using *Nud.ist* textual analysis software.[11]

Focus Groups   Focus groups were held by Magenta every six months starting in June, 1997. These groups discussed the challenges of living in a wired suburb, experiences with available technologies and services, and expectations for future technologies and services. Although aimed primarily at future planning for members of the Magenta consortium, the focus groups gave us opportunities to meet small numbers of residents, build rapport, and clarify information obtained through surveys and ethnographic observation. In March 1999 we interviewed key members of the Magenta consortium including the developer, the head of the consortium, and various trial managers.

21.5   Preliminary Results

Despite the availability of local ties, the majority of all active social relations are with those outside of the local area. In North America neighborhood relations typically represent less than one quarter of all active social ties [6] [32]. North Americans typically know about a dozen of their neighbors well enough to speak with them (usually on the street), but few know more than one neighbor well enough to consider them among their closest social ties [26] [30] [32]. The reasons for this lack of social contact at the local level are not directly associated with a loss of civic society or a decrease in community involvement. Rather, propinquity is a limited factor in determining friendship formation. People are much more likely to associate with those that are more like themselves in terms of lifestyle, stage in the lifecycle, beliefs, and participation in common activities, than what can be easily found through physical availability.

The car, telephone, and airplane are indispensable in the maintenance of contemporary social relations and in the provision of most companionship and emotional aid. Yet, despite the extent to which contemporary relationships have overcome the limitations of space, physical proximity still plays some role in the formation of social ties. Physical access promotes the sharing of small and large services, such as household items, aid in dealing with organizations, and help with housework and repairs [36]. Neighborhood relations are particularly important during the early stages of settling into a new housing development [6] [8] [9] [16].

When residents first move into a new residential development, the only thing that they knowingly share is that they have all chosen to settle in the same neighborhood. As a result physical closeness becomes the easiest and most available method for the formation of social contacts. Since all residents share the experience of being both strangers and new home owners, they are likely to develop social contact with everyone who is easily accessible [9]. It is at this time that the location of front doors, kitchen windows, and porches help determine who is most accessible and with whom people are likely to develop early social contact. As relationships develop, the extent to which neighbors share common characteristics becomes more apparent and people are able to choose the degree of social closeness they wish to maintain in each relationship. As time progresses, children start new schools, people join organizations, and through a variety of different social settings people find others more like themselves to form lasting social relations outside of the local area. Gans (1968) suggests that the process of selecting neighbors for stronger social relations, from those with whom one will eventually only become "neighborly" (i.e., say or wave "hello" on the street), is typically completed within three months of social contact. Regardless, as time progresses, local spatial patterns become less important for friendship formation [16].

Figure 21.1 is an example of how the formation of social relationships in Netville differs from relationships formed in traditional non-wired housing developments. Figure 21.1a depicts a hypothetical example of how early social relations might form in a newly settled non-wired residential development. Social contact is with those who are most easily available and the strength of the social relation is relatively weak, based on the recency of tie formation. Figure 21.1b depicts social relations in the same non-wired setting at a time period greater than three months from that depicted in Figure 21.1a. At this time social relations in the immediate area vary in strength, extending to no more than the twelve houses in the immediate proximity to the home, and almost never extend around corners, or to the other side of the block [8] [9] [16]. Figure 21.1b also introduces a new type of social relationship, the "knowing tie." Knowing ties can be described as those people with whom you have never experienced any direct social contact, but yet you have some specific knowledge of their personal characteristics. Possible examples include knowledge, through information provided by another neighbor or through observation, of a neighbor's occupation or hobbies.

Figure 21.1c and figure 21.1d are examples of the pattern of social relations found in Netville based on ethnographic observation, analysis of the community email list, and preliminary analysis of the network of neighborhood social ties. Figure 21.1c is identical to the initial stage of social contact found in the non-wired development. However, there are significant differences between what has been observed in Netville (figure 21.1d) and what is typically observed in non-wired developments (figure

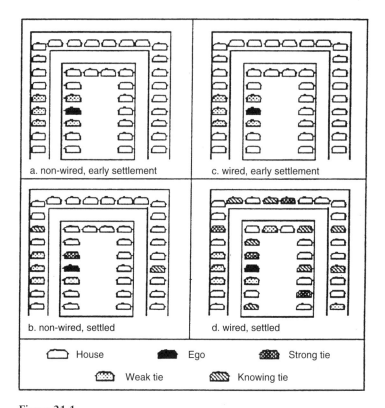

Figure 21.1
Comparison of social tie formation in a newly built non-wired housing development to social tie formation in a newly built "wired" development.

21.1b). There are a greater number of strong ties, weak ties, and knowing ties within Netville. Social contact is no longer limited through accessibility, but extends around corners and to the other side of the block.

Table 21.1 summarizes the difference between Netville residents who were connected to the high-speed network and those who were not, in terms of the number of Netville residents that they recognize and socialize with.[12] Wired residents recognize almost three times as many neighbors, talk with nearly twice as many, and have been invited, and have invited, one and a half times as many neighbors into their home in comparison to their non-wired counterparts. These results suggest that there

Table 21.1
Number of Netville Residents Recognised by Name and Socialized with Depending on Whether the Respondent Was Connected to the High-speed Network

	Mean	S.D.	Min.	Max.
Number of people residents recognized by name in Netville:				
Wired	26.7	19.1	4	91
Non-wired	9.4	4.9	3	19
Number of Netville residents people talk to on a regular bases:				
Wired	6.8	7.3	0	38
Non-wired	3.7	3.3	0	11
Number of residents who have invited other Netville residents into their home in the past six months:				
Wired	4.1	4.3	0	16
Non-wired	2.9	3.0	0	10
Number of residents who have been invited into the home of another Netville resident in the past six months:				
Wired	4.1	3.7	0	18
Non-wired	2.7	2.9	0	10

is something significantly different about wired Netville residents that makes them more likely to have a greater number of local social contacts, of various strengths, that are more widely spread across the local area. These results are consistent with the following comments from Netville's community e-mail list:

I have walked around the neighborhood a lot lately and I have noticed a few things. I have noticed neighbors talking to each other like they have been friends for a long time. I have noticed a closeness that you don't see in many communities.

I would love to see us have a continuation of the closeness that many of us have with each other, even on a very superficial level. Do not lose it, we know each other on a first name basis.

If this had been a regular subdivision no doubt I would know my neighbors but I would not know those of you around the corner and down the road

One possible explanation for the higher levels of social interaction among Netville residents connected to the high-speed network is that they were somehow friendlier, or more community orientated, when they moved into Netville than those who were never connected to the network. However, this seems unlikely as everyone who moved into Netville had the same expectation of being connected to the network. There was no preset method in selecting who would, and would not, be connected to the network. Failure to connect all residents to the network was a result of organizational problems internal to the Magenta consortium. A more likely explanation is that there was something about being connected to the network that contributed to greater social contact. One possibility is the use of the community email list.

The community email list served a number of purposes in the community including early introductions, invitations to social events, the sharing of information on local services and organizations, and providing a forum for mobilization against the developer and eventually the Magenta consortium [13]. Preliminary analysis of the first ten months of email messages sent over the community list revealed that 80 percent of all messages dealt either with local activities or local support, 21 percent were requests for some type of aid or support, 21 percent involved selling items or services from the home, 19 percent were messages believed to contain information of a common local concern, 10 percent were offers of aid or support, and 7 percent were aimed at forming local activities [11].[13] In addition a number of smaller personal distribution lists were created allowing clusters within the community to maintain discussions about specific interests. The email list increased levels of communication, improved knowledge of each other (for example, occupations, hobbies, and individual backgrounds), and increased the speed at which residents could mobilize to counter perceived threats.

The success of the community network and the local discussion list in encouraging social contact within Netville does not necessarily mean that the introduction of a similar technology in other neighborhoods will always increase social contact.[14] Netville is a unique situation in that it was a trial of a new high bandwidth technology, it was provided free of charge, and it was part of a new housing development. Existing neighborhoods have existing communication patterns and consist of individuals with established social networks. People have a limited amount of time to spend in social contact with others in a given day. If established social networks and existing means of communication provide much of the companionship, aid, and support individuals need, there is little incentive to divert time and energy towards new and less certain means of maintaining and forming these ties. The same can be said about any "virtual community," that unless it fills some missing need in the lives of the intended user group, it is unlikely that it will meet with expectations for high levels of social interaction.

21.6 Conclusion

This paper has focused on an introduction to the methodologies used in the Netville project and briefly explores some preliminary results. Key to the methodology behind this project has been the use of multiple data collection methods to increase the reliability and validity of our results. The use of surveys, an ethnography, online records and focus groups enabled us to clarify and refine our data continuously, as well as to collect the best information possible, given the evolving nature of our field site.

In studying community, on or offline, it is imperative to recognize that community does not have to be local, but that it is the sociable and supportive aspect of interaction that defines community and not the local space in which interaction may take place. It must be recognized that relationships extend beyond the neighborhood and include a personal network of friends, relatives, and coworkers that can extend across the city or around the world. Similarly, the study of virtual communities should not be limited to interactions that take place in that setting, but should look at how these interactions fit into the entire set of social ties that make up the multiple communities in which most of us are involved. That said, it is important to realize in assessing our early results that we have yet to analyze the social networks of Netville residents that extend beyond the local setting or into the very local setting of the household. How does the maintenance of a greater number of local social contacts affect relations with other network members? How does the availability of free, very high-speed, Internet access affect how people maintain ties with social network members?

Preliminary analysis suggests that the Internet supports a variety of social ties, strong and weak, instrumental, emotional, social and affiliative.

Relationships are rarely maintained through computer-mediated communication alone, but are sustained through a combination of online and offline interactions. Despite the ability of the Internet to serve as a global communication technology, much online activity is between people who live (or work) near each other, often in Netville itself. In Netville, the local network brought neighbors together to socialize, helped them to arrange in-person get-togethers—both as couples and as larger groups (barbecues, etc.)—facilitated the provision of aid, and enabled the easy exchange of information about dealing with the developer. The high rate of online activity led to increased local awareness, high rates of in-person activity, and to rapid political mobilization at the end of the field trial. The extent to which the use of no cost, very high-speed access to the Internet influenced the personal networks of Netville residents remains to be explored in more detail.

Notes

Portions of this work are reprinted with permission from "Netville On-Line and Off-Line: Observing and Surveying a Wired Suburb," American Behavioral Scientist, Vol. 43 No. 3., (November/December 1999) 475–492, copyright 1999 Sage Publications, Inc. This research was supported by the Social Science and Humanities Research Council of Canada, Bell Canada University Laboratories, and Communication and Information Technologies Ontario. At the University of Toronto, we have received support from the Centre for Urban and Community Studies, the Department of Sociology, and the Knowledge Media Design Institute. We thank a host of people for their comments, assistance, and support. At the University of Toronto: Ronald Baecker, Dean Behrens, Nadia Bello, Bonnie Erickson, Nancy Howell, Todd Irvine, Emmanuel Koku, Alexandra Marin, Antonia Maughn, Dolly Mehra, William Michelson, Nancy Nazer, Christien Perez, Janet Salaff, Anne Shipley, Richard Stren, and Carlton Thorne. Others: Ross Barclay, Donald Berkowitz, Damien DeShane, Jerome Durlak, Herbert Gans, Paul Hoffert, Timothy Hollett, Thomas Jurenka, Robert Kraut, Marc Smith, Liane Sullivan, and Richard Valentine. Our greatest debt is to the many residents of Netville who have given us their time and patience, allowing us into their homes, and answering many, many, questions.

1. For example, see Park (1925) and Wirth (1938).

2. See some of the chapters in Smith & Kollock, 1999.

3. See the review in Walther, et al., 1994.

4. To protect privacy, "Netville" is a pseudonym as is the "Magenta" consortium. The final number of homes is in flux as new ones continue to be built.

5. Quite "outer": It takes an hour to drive to downtown Toronto without traffic; two hours during rush hour. This may have increased the attractiveness of using computer-mediated communication with friends, relatives and coworkers living in the main centers of Toronto.

6. Based on unpublished data provided by the Canadian Mortgage and Housing Corporation, 1999.

7. The chuckwagon was a covered wagon used on long journeys as a frontier kitchen on wheels by early homesteaders of the Canadian and American West.

8. In addition to the free services, approximately 20 percent of residents purchased additional in-home computer-based technologies, such as: within-household networks, advanced home security systems, and "smart home" technologies.

9. To our dismay, and surprise, we could never interest the engineering-driven arm of the telco responsible for this experiment to see this as a window into how people would use technology of the future.

10. For a complete discussion on social network questions and the use of computer assisted interviewing (CAI) in the Netville project see Hampton, 1999.

11. Although technically feasible, because of ethical concerns and because we feared it would upset the residents, we did not monitor private email messages within Netville or from Netville residents to members of their personal communities living outside of the neighborhood.

12. Note: Numbers reported in table 21.1 represent preliminary findings and should be considered approximate until more detailed analysis can be performed.

13. The discussion list was created in July 1997 and continues to be used as of this chapter.

14. Netville received much publicity. The publicity and the intrinsic sense of being involved in an innovative use of technology may have made some residents susceptible to the "Hawthorne effect": people self-consciously modifying their behavior on account of their being studied. Fieldwork suggests that only a small number of residents may have been affected in this way.

References

1. Campbell, K., Lee, B. (1991) Name Generators in Surveys of Personal Networks. *Social Networks*, Vol. 13: 203–221.

2. Canadian Mortgage and Housing Corporation. (1997) Ontario Housing and Market Report: Fourth Quarter. Canadian Mortgage and Housing Corporation, Ottawa.

3. Durkheim, E. (1964) *The Division of Labor in Society*. Free Press, New York. (Original work published 1893.)

4. Ekos Research Associates. (1998) Information Highway and the Canadian Communications Household: Overview of Findings.

5. Erickson, B., Nosanchuk, T. A. (1983) Applied Network Sampling. *Social Networks*, Vol. 5: 367–382.

6. Fischer, C. (1982) *To Dwell among Friends: Personal Networks in Town and City*. University of Chicago Press, Chicago.

7. Fox, R. (1995) Newstrack. *Communications of the ACM*, Vol. 38, No. 8: 11–12.

8. Gans, H. (1967) *The Levittowners*. Vintage Books, New York.

9. Gans, H. (1968) *People and Plans: Essays on Urban Problems and Solutions*. Basic Books, New York.

10. Gans, H. (1982) *The Urban Villagers: Group and Class in the Life of Italian-Americans*. Free Press, New York.

11. Hampton, K. (1998) The Wired Suburb: Glocalization On and Offline. Paper presented at the annual meeting of the American Sociology Association, San Francisco, California.

12. Hampton, K. (1999) Computer-assisted Interviewing: The Design and Application of Survey Software to the Wired Suburb Project. *Bulletin de Methode Sociologique*, No. 62.

13. Hampton, K. (2003) Grieving for a Lost Network: Collective Action in a Wired Suburb. *The Information Society*, Vol. 19, No. 5.

14. Hampton, K., Wellman, B. (1999) Netville On-line and Off-line: Observing and Surveying a Wired Suburb. *American Behavioral Scientist*, Vol. 43, No. 3: 475–492.

15. Liebow, E. (1967) *Tally's Corner*. Little, Brown, Boston.

16. Michelson, W. (1976) *Man and His Urban Environment: A Sociological Approach* (revised). Addison-Wesley, Reading, Mass.

17. Muller, C., Wellman, B., Marin, A. (1999) How to Use SPSS to Study Egocentric Networks. *Bulletin de Methode Sociologique*, No. 64.

18. Park, R. (1925) The Urban Community as a Spatial Pattern and a Moral Order. In Turner, R. H. (ed.), *Robert E. Park on Social Control and Collective Behavior*. University of Chicago Press, Chicago.

19. Putnam, R. (1995) Bowling Alone: America's Declining Social Capital. *Journal of Democracy*, Vol. 6, No. 1: 65–78.

20. Slouka, M. (1995) War of the Worlds: Cyberspace and the High-Tech Assault on Reality. Basic Books, New York.

21. Smith, M., Kollock, P. (eds.) (1999) *Communities in Cyberspace*. Routledge, London.

22. Tilly, C. (1974) Introduction. In Tilly C. (ed.), *An Urban World*, pp. 1–35. Little Brown, Boston.

23. Tonnies, F. (1955) *Community and Organization*. Routledge, London. (Original work published 1887.)

24. Walther, J. B., Anderson, J. F., Park, D. W. (1994) Interpersonal Effects in Computer-Mediated Interaction: A Meta-Analysis of Social and Antisocial Communication. *Communication Research*, Vol. 21, No. 4: 460–487.

25. Wellman, B. (1972) Who Needs Neighbourhoods? In Powell, A. (ed.), *The City: Attacking Modern Myths*, pp. 94–113. McClelland and Stewart, Toronto.

26. Wellman, B. (1979) The Community Question: The Intimate Networks of East Yorkers. *American Journal of Sociology*, Vol. 84, No. 5: 1201–1231.

27. Wellman, B. (1982) Studying Personal Communities. In Marsden, P., Lin, N. (eds.), *Social Structure and Network Analysis*, pp. 61–80. Sage, Beverly Hills, Calif.

28. Wellman, B. (1988) Structural Analysis: From Method and Metaphor to Theory and Substance. In Wellman, B., Berkowitz, S. D. (eds.), *Social Structures: A Network Approach*, pp. 19–61. Cambridge University Press, Cambridge.

29. Wellman, B. (1992) How to Use SAS to Study Egocentric Networks. *Cultural Anthropology Methods Bulletin*, Vol. 4: 6–12.

30. Wellman, B. (1992) Which Types of Ties and Networks Provide What Kinds of Social Support? *Advances in Group Processes*, Vol. 9: 207–235.

31. Wellman, B., ed. (1999) *Networks in the Global Village*. Westview, Boulder, Colo.

32. Wellman, B., Carrington, P., Hall, A. (1999) Networks as Personal Communities. In Wellman, B., Berkowitz, S. D. (eds.), *Social Structures: A Network Approach*. Cambridge University Press, Cambridge.

33. Wellman, B., Gulia, M. (1999) Net-Surfers Don't Ride Alone: Virtual Communities as Communities. In Wellman, B. (ed.), *Networks in the Global Village*, pp. 331–366. Westview, Boulder, Colo.

34. Wellman, B., Hampton, K. (1999) Living Networked in a Wired World. *Contemporary Sociology*, Vol. 28, No. 6: 648–654.

35. Wellman, B., Leighton, B. (1979) Networks, Neighborhoods and Communities. *Urban Affairs Quarterly*, Vol. 14: 363–390.

36. Wellman, B., Wortley, S. (1990) Different Strokes from Different Folks: Community Ties and Social Support. *American Journal of Sociology*, Vol. 96: 558–588.

37. Whyte, W. (1981) *Street Corner Society: The Social Structure of an Italian Slum*. 3rd ed. University of Chicago Press, Chicago.

38. Wirth, L. (1938) Urbanism as a Way of Life. *American Journal of Sociology*, Vol. 44: 3–24.

Contributors

Daniel R. Anderson is Professor, Department of Psychology, University of Massachusetts at Amherst.

Bonka Boneva is Post-Doctoral Fellow, Human Computer Interaction Institute, Carnegie Mellon University.

Catherine Burke is Lecturer, Child and Family Studies, School of Education, University of Leeds.

Anne Crawford is Post-Doctoral Fellow, Human Computer Interaction Institute, Carnegie Mellon University.

Jonathon Cummings is Post-Doctoral Fellow, Human Computer Interaction Institute, Carnegie Mellon University.

Susan Dray is President of the Consulting Firm Dray and Associates, Incorporated.

Marie K. Evans is a Ph.D. candidate, Department of Psychology, University of Massachusetts at Amherst.

David Frohlich is Senior Research Scientist, Hewlett-Packard Labs in Bristol, England.

Mark Griffiths is Professor, Psychology Division, Nottingham Trent University, United Kingdom.

Keith Hampton is Assistant Professor, Department of Urban Planning,

Massachusetts Institute of Technology.

Vicki Helgeson is Professor, Department of Psychology, Carnegie Mellon University.

Steven Izenour, who died in 2001, was a Principal in the architectural firm Venturi, Scott Brown & Associates.

Amy B. Jordan is Senior Research Investigator, Annenberg School for Communication, University of Pennsylvania

Elihu Katz is Distinguished Trustee Professor of Communication, Annenberg School for Communication, University of Pennsylvania.

Andrea L. Kavanaugh is Senior Research Scientist and Assistant Director, Human Computer Interaction Center, Department of Computer Science, Virginia Polytechnic Institute & State University.

Sara Kiesler is Professor, College of Computer Science, Carnegie Mellon University.

Robert Kraut is Herbert A. Simon Professor in the School of Computer Science and Graduate School of

Industrial Administration, Carnegie Mellon University.

Sonia Livingstone is Professor, Department of Social Psychology, London School of Economics and Political Science.

Lisa-Jane McGerty is a Ph.D. candidate, Department of Applied Social Sciences, University of Bradford, United Kingdom.

Lilach Nir is a Ph.D. candidate, Annenberg School for Communication, University of Pennsylvania.

Maria Papadakis is Associate Professor, Department of Urban Affairs and Planning, Virginia Polytechnic Institute & State University.

Byron Reeves is Paul C. Edwards Professor, Department of Communication, Stanford University.

Lodis Rhodes is Professor at the LBJ School of Public Affairs, University of Texas at Austin.

Jorge Reina Schement is Professor of Communications and Information Policy and Co-Director, Institute for Information Policy, Penn State University.

Ellen Seiter is Professor, Department of Communication, University of California, San Diego.

Amy Silverman is Customer Insight Consultant, Hewlett-Packard Vancouver Division, Vancouver, Washington.

Gitte Stald is Assistant Professor, Film and Media Studies, University of Copenhagen.

Sherry Turkle is Abby Rockefeller Mauze Professor of the Sociology of Science in the Program in Science, Technology, and Society at the Massachusetts Institute of Technology, and Director of the MIT Initiative on Technology and Self.

Joseph Turow is Robert Lewis Shayon Professor of Communication, Annenberg School for Communication, University of Pennsylvania.

Ellen Wartella is Dean of the College of Communication, Walter Cronkite Regents Chair in Communication, and Mrs. Mary Gibbs Jones Centennial Chair in Communication at the University of Texas at Austin.

Barry Wellman is Professor of Sociology and Director of NetLab, Center for Urban & Community Studies, University of Toronto.

Name Index

Subject Index

Regulation sections circled